Undergraduate Topics in Computer Science

'Undergraduate Topics in Computer Science' (UTiCS) delivers high-quality instructional content for undergraduates studying in all areas of computing and information science. From core foundational and theoretical material to final-year topics and applications, UTiCS books take a fresh, concise, and modern approach and are ideal for self-study or for a one- or two-semester course. The texts are all authored by established experts in their fields, reviewed by an international advisory board, and contain numerous examples and problems, many of which include fully worked solutions.

The UTiCS concept relies on high-quality, concise books in softback format, and generally a maximum of 275–300 pages. For undergraduate textbooks that are likely to be longer, more expository, Springer continues to offer the highly regarded Texts in Computer Science series, to which we refer potential authors.

More information about this series at http://www.springer.com/series/7592

Konstantinos Domdouzis •
Peter Lake • Paul Crowther

Concise Guide to Databases

A Practical Introduction

Second Edition

 Springer

Konstantinos Domdouzis
Sheffield Hallam University
Sheffield, UK

Peter Lake
Sheffield Hallam University
Sheffield, UK

Paul Crowther
Sheffield Hallam University
Sheffield, UK

ISSN 1863-7310   ISSN 2197-1781   (electronic)
Undergraduate Topics in Computer Science
ISBN 978-3-030-42223-3   ISBN 978-3-030-42224-0   (eBook)
https://doi.org/10.1007/978-3-030-42224-0

This Springer imprint is published by the registered company Springer Nature Switzerland AG
The registered company address is: Gewerbestrasse 11, 6330 Cham, Switzerland

Dedicated to our mate Andy McEwan
Paul and Peter

Dedicated to my wife Lucy
Konstantinos

Preface

Overview and Goals

Databases are not new and there are many textbooks available which cover various database types, especially relational. What is changing, however, is that Relational Database Management Systems (RDBMS) are no longer the only database solution. In an era where Big Data is the current buzzword and Data Scientists are tomorrow's big earners, it is important to take a wider view of database technology.

Key objectives for this book include:

- Present an understanding of the key technologies involved in Database Systems in general and place those technologies in an historic context
- Explore the potential use of a variety of database types in a business environment
- Point out areas for further research in a fast-moving domain
- Equip readers with an understanding of the important aspects of a database professional's job
- Provide some hands-on experience to further assist in the understanding of the technologies involved

Organisation and Features

This book is organised into four parts:

- Part I introduces database concepts and places them in both a historic and business context;

- Part II provides insights into some of the major database types around today and also provides some hands-on tutorials in the areas concerned;
- Part III is devoted to issues and challenges which face Database Professionals;
- Part IV is focused specific advanced applications of databases.

Target Audiences

This book has been written specifically to support the following audiences:

Advanced undergraduate students and postgraduate students should find the combination of theoretical and practical examples database usage of interest. We imagine this text would be of particular relevance for modern Computer Science, Software Engineering, and Information Technology courses. However, any course that makes reference to databases, and in particular to the latest developments in computing will find this textbook of use. As such, University Instructors may adopt the book as a core text.

Especially in Part II, this book adopts a learning-by-doing approach, with the extensive worked examples explaining how to use the variety of databases available to address today's business needs. Practising Database Professionals, and Application Developers will also be able to use this book to review the current state of the database domain.

Suggested Uses

A Concise Guide to Databases can be used as a solid introduction to the concept of databases. The book is suitable as both a comprehensive introduction to databases, as well as a reference text as the reader develops their skills and abilities through practical application of the ideas. For University Instructors, we suggest the following programme of study for a twelve-week semester format:

- Weeks 1–3: Part I
- Weeks 4–8: Part II
- Weeks 9–11: Part III
- Week 11-12: Part IV
- Week 12: Assessment

Review Questions

Each chapter concludes with a set of review questions that make specific reference to the content presented in the chapter, plus an additional set of further questions that will require further research. The review questions are designed in such a way that the reader will be able to tackle them based on the chapter contents. They are followed by discussion questions, that often require research, extended reading of other material or discussion and collaboration. These can be used as classroom discussion topics by tutors or used as the basis of summative assignments.

Hands-on Exercises

The technology chapters include extended hands-on exercises. Readers will then progressively engage in more complex activities, building skills and knowledge along the way. Such an approach ensures that a solid foundation is built before more advanced topics are undertaken. Some of the material here is Open Source, whilst some examples are Oracle specific, but even these latter can be applied to other SQL databases.

Chapter Summary

A brief summary of each of the nineteen chapters is as follows:

Chapter 1: Data is the lifeblood of all business systems and we place the use of data in its historical context and review some of the key concepts in handling data.

Chapter 2: Provides an examination of the way that data has been handled throughout history, using databases of a variety of types.

Chapter 3: Considers how we actually store data. Turning information into a series of 1s and 0s is at the heart of every current database system and so an understanding of issues like physical storage and distribution are important concepts to understand.

Chapter 4: The de facto standard database solution is, without doubt, the relational database. In this chapter we look at how RDBMS works and provide worked examples.

Chapter 5: The NoSQL movement is still relatively new. Databases which store data without schemas and which do not necessarily provide transactional security may seem like a bad idea to experienced relational database practitioners, but these tools do certainly have their place in today's data rich society. We review the area in general and then look at specific examples of a Column-based and a Document-based database, with hands-on tutorials for each.

Chapter 6: Look at many leading database vendors' web sites and you will see that we are in the Big Data era. We explore what this actually means and, using a tutorial, review one of the key concepts in this era—that of MapReduce.

Chapter 7: Object databases were once thought of as the next important design for databases. When used by developers using Object programming they can seem very appealing still. There are half-way house solutions also available—Oracle, for example, has an Object-Relational option. We explore this area with more tutorial material.

Chapter 8: Reading data from disk is far slower than reading from RAM. Computing technologies now exist that can allow databases to run entirely in memory, making for very rapid data processing. These databases may well become the norm as RAM becomes cheaper and hard disk technology becomes less able to improve in performance.

Chapter 9: The chapter is focused on the way data are organised in a hierarchical database and the way data are processed in such a database. It also provides different examples of how these databases are used.

Chapter 10: Distributed databases find great applicability in a range of different fields. Characteristics such as distributed data storage and distributed query processing makes them ideal for applications in the banking and in the transportation industry. The importance of distributed databases lies on the fact that many modern applications use data that are distributed by nature where there is great need between the different structures of an organisation to communicate with each other and share data and resources. This chapter focuses on specific characteristics of distributed databases as well as their applications.

Chapter 11: A graph database is a database that uses graph structures in order to execute queries with nodes and edges. The graph is used for the development of relationships amongst data based on nodes and edges. Specifically, the edges represent the relationships between the nodes. Graph databases are part of NoSQL and they have been developed in order to face the challenges that cannot be faces by relational databases. The chapter also provides descriptions of applications of graph databases, such as those met in social networking, enterprise management and the modelling of chemical data connections.

Chapter 12: Once you have designed your database, especially when supporting a web- or cloud-based solution, you need to be sure that it can grow if the business that the application supports is successful. Scalability is about ensuring that you can cope with many concurrent users, or huge amounts of data, or both.

Chapter 13: Once your system is built, you need to be able to have it available for use permanently (or as close to permanently as can be achieved within the financial resources at your disposal). We review key concepts such as back-up, recovery, and disaster recovery.

Chapter 14: For a DBA the dreaded phone call is "my report is running very slowly". For a start, what is mean by slowly? What is the user used to? Then there is the problem of how you establish where the problem is—is it hardware related? Or Network related? At the Server or Client end? The solution may be indexes, or partitions: we review a variety of performance related techniques. We include some tutorial material which explores some performance management tools.

Chapter 15: Data is one of an organisation's most important assets. It needs to be protected from people wanting to either take it or bring the system down. We look at physical and software-related weaknesses and review approaches to making our databases secure.

Chapter 16: Database adaptiveness is a significant capability of databases. It allows a database to adjust to the continuous dynamic changes of the requirements of the problem to which the database is applied to. Furthermore, in order for adaptiveness to be realised, a number of changes that that affect the structure and the operation of the database need to happen. Databases are also characterised by the capability to be integrated to other technologies. This is a capability that allows databases to be used to a range of different applications such as social media and real-time sensing applications.

Chapter 17: Blockchain is an increasing list of records that are linked together through the use of cryptography. A blockchain is also a distributed ledger which records transactions between two blocks. Blockchain offers a number of benefits such as less transaction time, less cost, protection from fraud and transparency. Security is also a major advantage offered by blockchain technology as blockchain and especially for the handling of a large amount of distributed data, this advantage is invaluable. The chapter focuses on the applications of blockchain in banking, in education, in healthcare management, in the transportation industry and in human resources.

Chapter 18: Biological databases are databases that include information from areas such as genomics, metabolomics, proteomics and microarray gene expression. These databases contribute significantly in Bioinformatics. Biological databases can be classified as sequence and structure databases. Structure databases are for protein structures whilst sequence databases are used for nucleic and protein sequences. Biological databases are used in the comprehension of a number of biological phenomena such as the structure of biomolecules and how they integrate to each other, the metabolism of organisms and the comprehension of the evolution of species.

Chapter 19: A Geographic Information System (GIS) is a framework for the acquisition, management and analysis of data. GIS analyse spatial location and they develop visualisations based on the organisation of different layers of data. GIS can be used in the identification of patterns and relationships amongst data, thus enabling better decision making. GIS process different types of data, such as cartographic, photographic and digital data. Geographical Information Systems are implemented in a range of different situations and problems. Examples of such situations and problems are found in urban planning, in environmental impact analysis, in disaster management, in agricultural applications and in the tracking and planning of energy usage.

Sheffield, UK   Konstantinos Domdouzis
                                                                                       Peter Lake
                                                                                       Paul Crowther

Contents

Part IV   Advanced Applications of Specialised Databases

Part I
Databases in Context

Data, An Organisational Asset

1

What the reader will learn:

- The rise of the organisation
- The evolution of data usage and processing in organisations
- Technological change and its impact on data
- Data storage, retrieval and analysis—the road to competitive advantage
- Data exploitation and privacy.

1.1 Introduction

Today an organisation depends on data for its very survival. Data is used to make strategic decisions about the future direction an organisation will take and for that the data must be both current and accurate. Because data is an asset to a company it can be given a value and it can be traded. This chapter will look at data as an organisational asset tracing its importance in recording, analysing and planning as organisations grew and became more sophisticated. The impact of industrialisation on data requirements will be examined and finally with the advent of electronic data storage and processing, the emergence of data as an important component of a company's assets. Finally there will be a discussion of big data the current issues surrounding privacy when everything that can be recorded is recorded.

There are many examples of data being an organisational asset, but we will start with a specific well known example. Amazon, is an on-line retailer which originally sold books. It has now become an organisation dealing with a large variety of goods and services both as the primary seller and as a facilitator for other retailers. Any web user can search for items using key words and can restrict their search in various ways. Once you buy an item from Amazon you can create an account. Amazon uses the information about what you bought (and searched for) to suggest other items you might like to buy. It also cross references this with what other

© Springer Nature Switzerland AG 2021
K. Domdouzis et al., *Concise Guide to Databases*, Undergraduate Topics
in Computer Science, https://doi.org/10.1007/978-3-030-42224-0_1

people bought. So if you bought a wireless networking card for your desktop computer, you would also get a list of what other people bought with it. Google is exploiting data in your transaction in real time to influence your shopping decisions.

This is an example of how an organisation uses data in an on-line transaction in a real time way. It is the current stage of an evolutionary process of storing, processing and exploiting data which began with the first record keeping.

1.2   In the Beginning

Religious orders and governments were the first large organisations to gather and actively exploit data to raise revenue. Recorded data has been known to exist since at least 2800 BC in ancient Egypt. These included records of the earliest known forms of taxation. Records were held on limestone flakes and papyrus. The Rosetta Stone, famous for holding the key to translating hieroglyphics (the same information was written in three languages on the stone, one of which could be understood and was used to translate the other two) was created to show a temples exemption from taxes.

1.3   The Rise of Organisations

Before considering electronic data and its use in modern commercial organisations we need to consider how non-government organisations developed and how their data needs grew more and more sophisticated. In any government or business organisation, there are always records. At its most basic you need to know who owes you money and who you owe money to. More sophisticated records would include the value of infrastructure such as buildings and machinery as well as its depreciation—loss of value—due to wear and tear plus the costs of maintenance. Where the organisation consists of more than a single trader records of employees need to be kept.

In Britain pre-dissolution monasteries maintained excellent records and accounts of the estates they controlled (something that was also of value to Henry VIII and which Thomas Cromwell exploited from 1534 as part of the Dissolution). Lands and money were donated to the monasteries with many of them becoming large landowners. Income from these estates made many of them extremely wealthy. This growth in wealth along with numbers of lay brothers who filled ancillary roles and provided labour created a complexity that could only be managed by keeping records. The monk in charge of these records and the finances of the monastery was the bursar who oversaw the maintenance of detailed records of both income and expenditure of the estate. In many cases this was structured within specific categories, for example capital expenditure (on buildings). In today's terminology the bursar would be called the database administrator.

1.4   The Challenges of Multi-site Operation

The monasteries in sixteenth century England were independent organisations loosely federated by their allegiance to the Roman Catholic Church based in Rome. As mentioned, they often owned vast estates with many farms or granges which could be considerable distances (for the day) from the monastery. These granges needed to keep local records, but also needed to submit accounts to the monastery. This could be regarded as a form of distributed data where there was a need for day to day local account keeping along with a centralised master account system. A problem was maintaining data integrity. Once accounts from the granges had been submitted to the monastery counting house, records could be updated but there was always a time delay. At the time this was not regarded as important because at the time there was no competitive advantage in very rapid processing of records.

1.5   Internationalisation

Despite the previous example most early organisational data was held centrally because the reach of the organisation tended to be geographically small. This changed with exploration and colonisation. There needed to be data kept in multiple locations. With European colonisation of other parts of the world, trading companies had to start keeping data locally as well as at head office. Some of these companies were huge, for example the East India Company came into being in 1600 and by the eighteenth century effectively controlled large parts of India and had its own army and navy. Its base was London, but it had multiple trading centres in India and China. The London base was called East India House and it housed the company records. These and the people needed to maintain them kept growing with the result that the building was continually being expanded. The demand for more space and the poor condition of the original building lead was the justification for a new building. This was completed in 1729. Even this was not enough and as the company continued to grow adjoining properties were acquired.

What the company developed was effectively a distributed database. Day to day operations in the colony were handled locally with records being transported back to head office where the ever expanding central records were updated and processed. Since long distance data transmission was by ship and there was a risk of the ship not making it home, there was always going to be a problem with data currency and integrity. This could be solved by a certain level of data redundancy. For example, rather than relying on one ship for your records, you replicated everything and sent it by two or more ships. You also distributed valuable cargo between your ships. If one sank, all the records, including about what was on the missing ship survived. This was an example of backup and security. It was also a form of insurance.

The East India Company was wound up in 1858 primarily due to public and government concern about its activities. It had been blamed in part for triggering American war of Independence (the tea in the Boston tea Party was company stock) and laying the foundations for the First Opium War where Indian opium was used to trade for tea. However, the British government took over many of the operations of the Company in the building became the India Office.

The East India Company has been used to illustrate the development of an organisation with international reach, but it was by no means an isolated example. Around the time the company was wound up technological advances including the development of the telegraph and faster and more reliable transport improved the efficiency of national and international organisations. With more data which was increasingly more current better planning and control could be implemented. The following sections look at the new technologies and their impact on data and the organisation.

1.6 Industrialisation

Between the late eighteenth and early nineteenth there was a change from small scale hand manufacturing to large scale mass manufacturing. This is usually referred to as the industrial revolution although there were several phases covering not just manufacturing but also the supporting infrastructure. In this period, manufacturing progressively moved from a cottage industry to a factory-based enterprise. This required detailed records to effectively manage a large scale operation.

Materials required for the industrial process were much larger than previously required in cottage industries. Although the term was not really used until the 1950's in business this was supply chain logistics. Consumables had to be bought and transported. It is costly to have stock in a warehouse; therefore you want to have as little raw material on hand as possible but no so little as to affect production. Likewise finished goods need to be shipped as soon as possible. Labour needed to be hired and managed. All of this required record keeping to plan and manage operations, in other words data. It also led to a transport revolution, first with canals and then with railways to move primarily goods and later in the case of the railways, people. Both of these had their own data requirements.

The sophistication of the industrialisation process kept increasing through the nineteenth and twentieth century. The introduction of the assembly line further increased efficiency but it was dependent on the line being supplied. This is a supply process known as logistics (although the term was not used for business until the mid-1950's) and requires: "having the right item in the right quantity at the right time at the right place for the right price in the right condition…" (Mallik 2010). This required processing of data to make sure the right decisions on where and when to buy materials was made. Even today, a break in supply of components can shut down an entire operation. In Australia, BorgWarner supplied gearboxes to most of the country's vehicle manufacturers. Only two days' supply of these components were held at the assembly factories, so a strike at BorgWarner effectively shut down the rest of automotive manufacturing centre.

1.7 Mass Transport

Another impact of the industrial revolution was on transport. Up until the nineteenth century transport had been either by horse or ship. Neither was particularly fast and most people rarely travelled far outside their local community. Mass movement of goods inland tended to be by boat but was restricted to navigable rivers. Although canals for navigation were not new, it was the Bridgewater Canal opened in 1761 for the transport of coal that proved the efficiency of this form of transport. The success of Bridgewater Canal lead to many more being developed and resulted in dramatic falls in the transport costs of bulky materials. The dominance of canals was relatively short. The rapid development of the Railway network from 1840, initially for freight but also for passengers meant that meant material goods and people could be moved great distances quickly and cheaply. The railway system was however dependent on data for its successful (and safe) operation. Trains had to be scheduled which meant timetables had to be developed. There were several forms of these. One was for passengers who wanted to know when a train was leaving. There was also a roster for engines, carriages and their crews—basically another timetable but one which had to be updated more often because of availability. To make sure you had a place on the train (particularly if you were a first class passenger) meant seat reservations had to be implemented. This is a description of just a small part of the records and data processing needed for running railways in the Victorian era.

Things didn't really change until the advent of mass air travel. Consider an airline booking systems. Today you can book a seat with an airline specifying the date and time of your flights and even your seat on the plane by accessing a website. Before networked computers, the system was paper based. At head office there would be a record of each flight scheduled for a specific period in the future. Based on experience, travel agents would be assigned a number of seats on each plane which they could sell over the counter. If they ran out of seats or they had not been allocated seats on a particular flight they would have to phone the flight centre to request a seat. If there were some in reserve, once again they could book it directly, otherwise, the customer had to be logged and told they would be contacted once a check of available seats had been made. The booking centre would then have to call around other agents who had been assigned seats and see if any were still left. Depending on the outcome, the customer would be contacted. This was a cumbersome system and with the growth in air travel it became increasingly sophisticated. Introduction of computerised booking meant the number of staff needed to run it declined dramatically.

There was also another effect of the computerisation of data. Once you had booked on a plane, you had a record of who the customer was and where they were going which was easily retrievable. If they were a frequent traveller you could start building a profile of where they tended to go and how often. That meant you could be sent targeted marketing material. Initially this was by post, but now is most likely to be via e-mail.

1.8 Communication

Before the advent of technology to transmit information electrically (and it was electrical rather than electronic) transmission of data was by hand. Faster technologies, such as the semaphore system and other line of sight communication systems did exist. In Tasmania (then Van Diemen's Land) a semaphore system built in 1811 could be used to report an escape from the penal settlement at Port Arthur within seven minutes. Port Arthur is approximately 100 kilometres (60 miles) from Hobart by road meaning such a message could take a day or more to get through by hand. The big disadvantage of the system was it was only useable in daylight in clear conditions. The semaphore system in Tasmania was discontinued in 1880 with the installation of a telegraph system (Fig. 1.1).

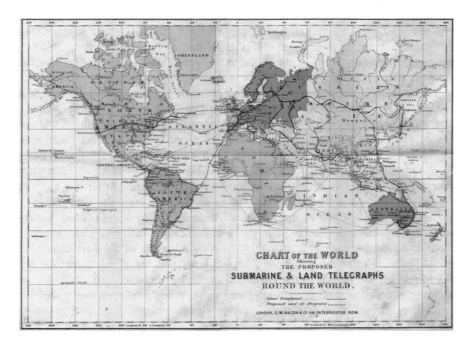

Fig. 1.1 1865 map showing proposed submarine and land telegraphs around the world. (Bill Burns: Altlantic-Cable.com Website)

The electric telegraph which was developed in the early nineteenth century meant data could be transmitted much more quickly and reliably using a standardised code—Morse code. This was a series of dots and dashes which represented numbers and letters. More commonly used letters had shorter codes then longer ones, for example T was a single dash while J was a dot and three dashes. Accuracy could still be a problem, however. A solution to this was to send important information twice and then investigate any discrepancies. Another solution was to introduce a check number where the final digit was a function of the preceding digits. This meant a calculation had to be done at both the sending and receiving end slowing down transmission. This issue was solved in computers using a similar process—the main difference being it was automated and quicker.

Although the electric telegraph was superseded by telephone and radio technology, Morse code continues to be used because it is less sensitive to poor signal conditions. Aeronautical systems such as VHF omnidirectional radio range (VOR) constantly send identification signals in the code.

1.9 Stocks and Shares

An important invention using telegraph technology was invented in 1870. The ticker tape machine was a device that allowed information about stocks and shares to be transmitted via the telegraph system. Unlike the telegraph Morse code tapper key, the sending device had a keyboard (which originally looked like a piano keyboard) to send plain language text. At the receiving end the information was printed in readable text on a thin strip of paper. Speeds were typically one character per second so abbreviations for company names were used. This was the first example of dedicated electrical commercial information transmission and it survived into the 1960's.

The next two communication technologies which had a major impact on data transmission were the telephone and the radio (although the latter still relied more on the Morse code than voice). Major systems were built around the use of telephones as already illustrated by the airline booking system example. Direct recording of the majority of data sent this way was rare however. It was almost always transcribed by an operator which always resulted in a certain level of transcription errors.

Direct data transmission between remote users, computers and other computers started in the late 1950's and was originally devised because of cold war concerns. However, as early as 1964 SABRE (Semi-automated Business Research Environment) was used by the airline industry to keep bookings correct in real time and was accessible to travel agents around the world. The amount of transcription and hence errors was also reduced by this system as the user was entering data directly into the system and automated checks could be applied.

Up to this point the discussion has been about organisations that either produce things or supply the infrastructure to enable production along with the supporting role of records and data processing. However one of the biggest users and producers of data has always been financial sector. This sector makes money by buying and selling holdings in other companies, in other words shares, lending and storing money for individuals and organisations (banks) and indemnifying individuals and organisations against loss (insurance).

Stock Exchange The London Stock Exchange was set up in 1801 although trade in stocks and shares had been going on for a much longer time. For example John Castaing, operating out of a coffee house in London's Exchange Alley published the prices of a few commodities (including salt and coal) several times a week in 1698. The new exchange was different in that it was regulated and only licensed traders dealing in listed stocks could operate. The new exchange kept records of trades and the price they could be traded at. This could be used along with information on supply and demand to make decisions on whether to buy or sell stock—what we now call market intelligence.

Banking Modern banking had its origins in the city states of Renaissance Italy such as Venice, Genoa and Florence. In the United Kingdom lack of trust in the government (for example the appropriation of £200,000 of private money in 1640 by Charles I) led merchants to deposit gold and silver with the Worshipful Company of Goldsmiths. Originally the goldsmiths were an artisan company but over time incorporated silversmiths and jewellers.

Goldsmiths discovered they now had an asset (money) they could lend at an interest. This turned out to be quite profitable. The next logical step was to actively solicit deposits on which they paid interest, but which could be loaned out at a higher interest. A side effect of this was deposit receipts started being used in lieu of payment by coin. This in turn meant Goldsmiths didn't have to have to lend real money—a deposit receipt would be treated in the same way. You could therefore lend more than you actually had. This system is still in place today but is regulated. The basis of banking is records and data. Originally these were kept at your physical bank branch and arrangements had to be made if you wished to make a transaction (particularly a withdrawal) at another branch. Banks opened their doors quite late and closed quite early in comparison to other institutions because of the need to keep complex accounts including applying interest calculations. The speed of manual data processing was limiting the availability of the banking system to users.

Insurance This was a way of spreading risks against loss, especially of ships and cargo. The concept is not a new one with Chinese merchants distributing cargo between several ships so that the loss of one would not mean total loss. Modern insurance had roots in the Great Fire of London of 1666 in that in 1680 an office opened to insure brick and timber framed buildings against loss by fire. The concept was you paid a premium (which was invested) based on the risk of your house. It assumed lots of people would do that so if a house burned down, the cost of the loss would be covered out of the pool of money received in insurance premiums. A side effect was insurance companies setting up their own fire brigades to fight fires in buildings insured by them.

Once again this required a lot of record keeping including who was insured, what their premiums were and what the risk of them making a claim was. Like today some areas and some individuals were more risky than others. Another aspect was keeping control of how the premiums were invested. Insurance companies had to store large amounts of money, and just like the banks, were able to invest it to make more money. Insurance companies therefore became important players in both the stock exchange and banking. It is also no surprise that the first commercial organisation to buy a computer was an insurance company.

1.10   Corporate Takeovers

Companies are often the target of takeover bids, or attempt takeovers of other companies. The part that usually reaches the headlines is the amount the company is bought or sold for and only rarely the issues of assimilating the takeover target.

One reason company will become a takeover target is because their shares are seen as undervalued. However, a company may become a target because the buyer wants to either expand their range of goods and services, gain access to more customers, enter into a new regional market or a combination of all three. After a takeover, issues with corporate data rarely make the headlines but there are almost always issues with assimilating an organisation's systems.

The data stored by one company will have one or more of the following incompatibilities:

- different vendor supplied system(s)
- different data formats
- different database design
- duplication of key data (for example customer numbers)
- and that is only part of the of a potential list. Given these issues, a number of options are available:
  - run more than one system (Channel 4 took this approach).
  - load the data from one system into another. This may require programming to automate the system, but data verification will be necessary.

1.11   The Challenges of Multinational Operations

Many of the world's big companies are multinational, or transnational. This is a step on from the idea of internationalisation previously mentioned. It is possible that the location of the company head office is dictated by tax issues and very little actual data processing takes place there. Amazon is one example of this.

"Amazon.co.uk is thought to have classified itself as a service provider to its Luxembourg business, Amazon EU Sarl, in order to reduce its tax bill. Its UK business employed 4,200 people at the end of 2012, compared with 380 in Luxembourg." (BBC News https://www.bbc.co.uk/news/business-22549434).

Further the product being bought may have been manufactured in Taiwan, purchased by a customer in Australia using the Amazon UK website referencing data stored on a server in the United States. The single purchase may therefore involve multiple subsidiary companies operating under a multitude of different national legislation.

What appears on the surface to be a single organisation is, therefore, often a federation of companies with a complex ownership and management structure. Data in the Amazon example has to be distributed both geographically and organisationally. You buy a book from Amazon UK which is where the transaction is recorded. The local warehouse were the product is located may run its own segment of the corporate database to locate stock and generate packing lists. Actually payment is then routed through Luxembourg company which would also have a local database segment of the corporate database. The data therefore becomes distributed amongst a number of businesses. Distributed database systems and transaction processing will be discussed in more detail in the next chapter.

1.12   The Data Asset

As already mentioned, corporate account data was initially held in paper ledgers and journals. This was often supplemented by indexed files—small cards arranged in some order containing information. For example, each customer would have an index card recording their name and address and possibly other comments.

Index cards appeared in the eighteenth century. The first recorded use of them was by the botanist Carl Linnaeus who needed a system to record species he was studying. He wanted something that was easy to insert new data into and easy to retrieve existing data. The zenith of the card system was its use in libraries. Here there were a number of card indexes which indexed the physical book collection. Usually there were indexes for author, title and subject. Details of the book along with its physical shelf location were recorded. From the late nineteenth century shelf locations were organised by the Dewey decimal classification which was founded on subject.

Variations of card indexes, for example recipe cards are still in use today although electronic databases applications are making inroads and library catalogues are almost all now electronic.

Index cards were usually only organised in one way. Personal data would normally be sorted on surname for example. This was not a problem when only one record was wanted and the data happened to be sorted in a way compatible with the search. Once you wanted to search on more than field, then you had a problem. This was partially overcome by the use of edge-notched cards. These consisted of a border with small holes punched in it, then a body where information could be written. The cards could be classified by clipping the holes so they extended to the edge of the card. By using one or more needles inserted through the holes, cards could be lifted out—those that remained were the search results. This system meant the cards need not be in any fixed order although they all had to be oriented the same way. The orientation was achieved by bevelling one corner, a system also used on Hollerith punch cards). Any card not in the correct order would then be immediately obvious. This system had one major drawback—it only worked on relatively small numbers of cards and it was impossible to do instant data analysis.

These examples were all for manual data storage and retrieval. It worked but it was slow and unsuitable for handling large amounts of data that had to be processed on a regular basis. Census data was a particular problem and in 1890 Herman Hollerith came up with a proposal for storing census data on punched cards which could be read by a machine.

The idea of using punched cards was not new in 1890. They had first appeared in the early eighteenth century for controlling textile looms—the pattern to be woven was stored on the card which automatically 'programmed' the machine. The most often quoted examples are the punched cards of the Jacquard loom of 1801.

The Hollerith card was at the centre of a technology that created, sorted and tabulated data. Hollerith created the Tabulating Machine Company which joined with three other companies to become the Computing Tabulating Recording Company in 1901. This company was eventually renamed International Business Machines (IBM) in 1924 and went on to become a dominant player in the mainframe and early personal computer industry.

The original Hollerith card had 12 rows and 24 columns but in 1928 the number of columns was increased to 80. Initially these were only used for numeric data, with the bottom ten holes representing the digits 0 through to 9. The top two rows were used for indicating positive and negative. Alphabetic data was stored by using a combination of holes, so a hole in row 1 and row 4 represented the letter 'A' (Fig. 1.2).

The 80 column card became an industry standard and also influenced other early computing technology. For example early monitors tended to have 80 column displays and the coding forms for the COBOL programming language was also organised in 80 columns because early programs were also entered via punched cards.

This paper technology had a number of significant issues:

- It was bulky.
- Individual cards could not be updated—they had to be re-punched which slowed down turnaround. There are stories of operators sticking chats back into the holes.
- Order (particularly of program code stored on cards) was important—the authors boss once came off his motorbike while carrying two boxes of punch cards on the back. It was quicker to reproduce the cards than to try sorting them.

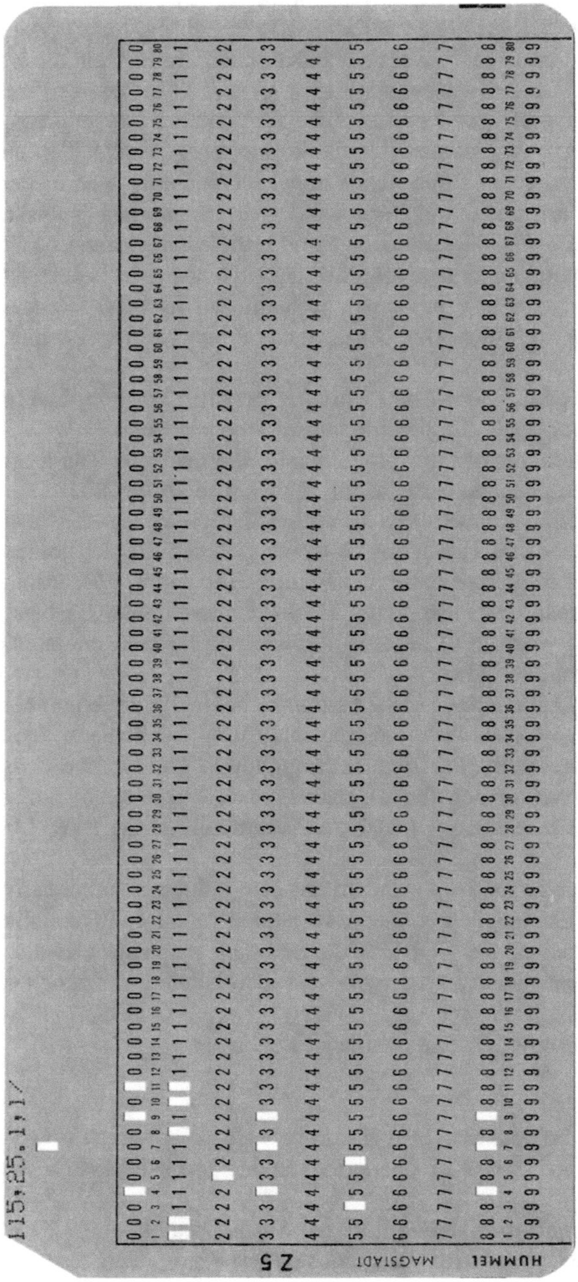

Fig. 1.2 80 column punch card. Note: in this example the meaning of holes is printed above each column, so this array of holes represents 115.25.1.1/(original image by Harke available at http://commons.wikimedia.org/wiki/File:Punch_card_80_columns_(2).j

- It was sensitive to environmental conditions. High humidity caused the cards to swell and jam the processing machines.
- Care had to be taken to avoid rodent attacks.
- They were a fire hazard.

Card processing reached its peak with the popular IBM 360 series of computers.

During the 1970's card technology became less and less common and had all but disappeared by the 1980's replaced by tape and disk technology.

1.13   Electronic Storage

Punched card technology had an initial advantage over electronic technology—it was very cheap. However tape and disk technology were available at the same time. These technologies became progressively cheaper, faster and able to store more and more data in a compact form.

Magnetic tape was used on the first commercial computer, UNIVAC 1, however it was IBM's tape technology that became the industry standard during the 1950's. Initially this was a half inch wide seven track tape which gave way to nine track tape with the introduction of the IBM 360 series of computers. Depending on the recording density between 5 MB and 140 MB data could be stored on a single tape. Data is written to the tape in blocks which contain a number of records. Between each block was an inter-block gap. This was needed because the memory buffer on the tape drive had a limited size and once full had to be transferred to the central processing unit. The tape had to be stopped while this was happening, then accelerated back to read speed for the next block. This resulted in the characteristic jerky movement of early tape drives.

Magnetic tape stores data sequentially, so in that regard it is very similar to cards. It is also a relatively cheap technology which makes it very convenient for making backups of systems. It does however have a number of problems.

1. The tape and the recording heads are in contact with each other which means over time both wear with increasing read/write errors as they get older. It also means tape heads have to be cleaned on a regular basis.
2. Although less bulky than cards, they are still bulky and prone to damage.
3. Sequential access limits the applications it can be used for.

The final type of magnetic technology is disk based. This was also introduced in the 1950's by IBM and is a random access device. When first introduced they were the most expensive storage device and had relatively low capacities beginning at 3.7 Mb. However, right from the beginning storage capacities went up while price came down. Data could now be accessed directly on the disk—a big advantage over tape technology where to find an individual record you had to read, on average half the records on a tape, something you would never do. Storage on disk meant the data had to be organised and this lead to the development of theoretical, then practical frameworks which became databases. The evolution of database technology will be discussed in the next chapter.

Although disk technology was the last new technology, it too is being superseded for new data storage and retrieval applications by main memory. As mentioned in the previous paragraph, the cost of disk storage has come down, but so has the cost of computer memory. Early core memory—so called because it was made up of magnetic rings or cores was very expensive and bulky. The introduction of semi- conductor memory resulted in massive reductions in size and price and increase in speed. Initially a major problem semiconductor memory was that it was volatile—if the power went off you lost all the data stored in memory. Today that is no longer an issue. Chapter 3 will talk in detail about physical aspects of data retrieval.

It is now feasible to store a database in a computer's memory—in-memory databases which will be discussed in Chap. 8. This gives the advantages of very fast processing not limited by the input/output speed restrictions of disk drives. Disk backup is still required for backup and recovery operations.

1.14 Big Data

Whenever you use a loyalty card, for example a Nectar card in Britain or a Wal-Mart card in the USA to gain points which can be used to purchase goods and services you also 'give' the card owner a lot of information about your buying habits. What you bought, where you bought it, when you bought it and how you bought it are all captured at the point of sale. Because you will have given them other information such as your age, address and gender, this can also be cross-referenced and other information generated, for example, how far from home your purchase was made and was it likely to have been made on your way to or from work. Now think of how many people go through all Tesco supermarkets a day using their loyalty cards and you get an idea of how much data is generated. The new term for this is big data—recognition of the fact that it is difficult to process using traditional database management tools.

The concept is not new however and grew out of the field of data warehousing. A data warehouse is a repository for organisational data uploaded from its operational system. Point of sale transactions as described in the Tesco example above are linked to other systems such as inventory to generate restocking orders but copies of all transactions are place in the data warehouse. The warehouse is not a database because its organisation is different and data is added, retrieved and analysed, but not modified. It is therefore a write once, read many system which continually grows. Processing data like this can yield unexpected patterns. For example it was discovered that male shoppers under 30 had a tendency to buy nappies (or diapers) and beer in single shopping run. It turned out fathers were being sent to stock up on nappies and took the opportunity to buy beer at the same time. The supermarket chain involved used this information to reconfigure isles so nappies and beer were close together increasing the chance of male customers' impulse buying beer.

Big data technologies are also of interest to government, particularly intelligence agencies. The National Security Agency (NSA) has built what is arguably the largest data storage facility in the world, the Utah Data Centre. We explore Big Data in more detail in Chap. 6.

1.15 Assets in the Cloud

In 2006 Amazon announced the release of Amazon Elastic Compute Cloud (EC2). This was one of the first commercial Cloud applications where, rather than storing data on your own server, you stored it somewhere else. That 'somewhere else' was something you didn't need to worry about (although many organisations did), you just bought space and time from the cloud provider who provided the resource you wanted on a server who's physical location could be anywhere in the world. The advantage of cloud computing was that you didn't have to worry about capacity or even backup and recover y. There are numerous examples of cloud computing being used for operational systems. For example, G-Cloud (http://gcloud. civilservice.gov.uk/) is a system used by the United Kingdom civil service to make services widely available and to distribute a range of material through its CloudStore.

With Cloud computing an organisation no longer has to store its data asset itself, it can be left with a trusted provider in much the same way an organisation deposits money (an asset) with a bank. It does raise issues of security and privacy, some of which are addressed in the next section.

1.16 Data, Data Everywhere

An issue which has emerged in the last few years is the question: Is technology and more specifically databases destroying privacy? This claim has gained momentum with revelations about the use the data at the Utah Data Centre will be put to. Claims of assaults on privacy are not new. In 1890 in the United States of America William Brandeis and Samuel Warren writing in the Harvard Law Review claimed there was an unprecedented assault on privacy. The media they were referring to was the tabloid press and cheap photography. Up until that point the issue of privacy had not been a major issue—publicity was the exception rather than the norm. Privacy could be ensured by physical walls and the distance from neigh-bours. That is not to say spying did not occur.

The introduction of a national postal service brought the first real concerns about data privacy. Once you posted a letter it was almost impossible to ensure no one tampered with it, even if it was sealed. That ultimately resulted in laws outlawing tampering and establishing a legal right to privacy in correspondence. The thing about this kind of written data was that although it could be copied, that was time consuming. Also letters (and telegraphs) that were not intercepted could be destroyed after they were read which also ensured their confidentiality.

Today we exist in a world where everything that can be recorded is recorded and correcting or deleting all copies of data is difficult if not impossible. Aaron Bady writing in the MIT Technology Review in 2011 states:

> We shouldn't worry about particular technologies of broadcasting or snooping—for instance the way Facebook trumpets our personal information or deep packet inspection allows government to trawl through oceans of internet data. The most important change is not the particular technology but, rather, the increase in the number of pathways through which information flows

(Bady 2011, 'World Without Walls', MIT Technology Review, Vol. 114(6) p. 68).

Bady says that the baseline of our information environment has become a tendency towards total availability and recall—indefinitely storing and circulating everything. We often add to the circulation ourselves by agreeing to allow the sharing of our details. This is often in the 'fine print' of the terms and conditions of loyalty card application forms or when you set up an account with an on-line retailer. All this means that collecting standardizing, processing and selling vast pools of data has become big business—data as a true, tradable international organisational asset. It is not just legitimately acquired data that is being sold. Cases of files of personal information that could be used for a variety of fraudulent activities being traded have been reported. In an example from the BBC in 2009 it was reported: 'Staff at mobile phone company T-Mobile passed on millions of records from thousands of customers to third party brokers, the firm has confirmed.' (17/11/2009, http://news.bbc.co.uk/1/hi/8364421.stm accessed 22/06/2013). In actual fact this case was illegal rather fraudulent with the information being used for direct marketing. The case resulted in prosecutions.

It should be noted, that data is not just an asset for private organisations, Government intelligence agencies increasingly see data as an intelligence asset. Using data mining techniques, automated systems can monitor data, tracking and analysing anomalies. It is another question as to who decides what an anomaly is. In the United States a lot of the impetus for this type of analysis was the 9/11 2001 terrorist attacks where the investigating commission blamed a 'failure to connect the dots' as part of the failure to predict the attacks.

Governments can gain access not only to their citizen's data, but often to the data of citizens in other countries, particularly given the growing popularity of cloud storage where the physical servers may be located anywhere, but come under the laws of the country where they are located. This has caused international tensions. In June 2013 The European commission's vice-president, Viviane Reding *said "Direct access of US law enforcement to the data of EU citizens on servers of US companies should be excluded unless in clearly defined, exceptional and judicially review- able situations"* (http://www.guardian.co.uk/world/2013/jun/11/europe-us-privacy last accessed 22/06/2013). This was in response to revelations from a whistle-blower in the American National Security Agency (NSA) that the organisation was conducting widespread surveillance of United States citizens and possibly citizens of other countries using data stored on servers in America.

1.17 Summary

In this chapter we have concentrated on data and its value to organisations. Evidence of commercial data has been found in ancient organisations, but much of this chapter has been devoted to the rise of the modern organisation. In parallel to the increasing sophistication of organisations and their need for data we looked at the technologies which helped facilitate its storage and transport noting the rapid changes which started in the nineteenth century and which are still continuing.

We concluded with looking at the vast amount of data which both governments and commercial organisations are amassing and how they are using it. We also looked at the increasing public concerns about privacy.

In the following chapters we will look first at how electronic data is stored and processed. This will show the evolution of database management systems. After that various aspects of database technology will be looked at in more depth.

1.18 Exercises

1.18.1 Review Questions

The answers to these questions can be found in the text of this chapter.

1. When were the first financial records kept and in what format
2. What is a ticker tape machine and what was its importance in data communications?
3. Why were punched cards a popular technology and why did their use decline?
4. List the data issues that can occur when one company takes over another
5. Why is privacy more a concern now than 200 years ago?

1.18.2 Group Work Research Activities

These activities require you to research beyond the contents of the book and can be tackled individually or as a discussion group.

Activity 1 Make a list of the loyalty cards you have. Go the web site associated with each of them (they almost certainly will have a web site) and for each find:

- terms and conditions.
- are they allowed to share your data with other organisations?
- have you (can you) opted out of that sharing?
- do they state what they are going to do with any data stored on you?
- what are their privacy policies?

Activity 2 There have been a number of articles about 'going off grid' where you do not leave a digital footprint of your activities or movement. John Platt in his 2012 article 'Going off the grid: Why more people are choosing to live life unplugged' (available at https://www.treehugger.com/going-off-the-grid-why-more-people-are-choosing-to-live-life-un-4863633 last accessed 2/7/2013) says there are lots of grids: car grid, supermarket grid and the bank grid are among those mentioned.

- How difficult is it to go completely off grid?
- Is it desirable to go completely off grid?
- How many grids could you opt out of?—make a list with advantages and disadvantages for each you choose to opt out of.

References

Bady A (2011) World without walls. MIT. Technol Rev 114(6):66–71

Mallik S (2010) In: Bidgoil H (ed) The handbook of technology management: supply chain management, marketing and advertising, and global management, vol 2. Wiley, Hoboken, p 104

Further Reading

Anderson KB, Erik D, Salinger MA (2008) Identity theft. J Econ Perspect 22(2):171–192

Bocij P, Greasley A, Hickie S (2008) Business information systems: technology, development and management, 4th edn. Prentice Hall, Harrow, Chap, p 3

Brandeis W, Samuel Warren S (1890) The right to privacy. Harvard Law Rev 4(5). Available at http://groups.csail.mit.edu/mac/classes/6.805/articles/privacy/Privacy_brand_warr2.html, last accessed 12/06/2013

Lawson P (1993) The East India Company: a history. Longman, London

London Stock Exchange (2013) Our history. https://www.londonstockexchange.com/, last accessed 22/06/2013

McKinsey and Company (2011) Big data: the next frontier for innovation, competition, and productivity. https://www.mckinsey.com/business-functions/mckinsey-digital/our-insights/big-data-the-next-frontier-for-innovation, last accessed 22/06/2013

National Archives (2013) Dissolution of the monasteries 1536–1540. https://www.nationalarchives.gov.uk/help-with-your-research/research-guides/dissolution-monasteries-1536–1540/, last accessed 22/06/2013. This site gives links to monastic records of the time

A History of Databases

2

What the reader will learn:

- The Origins of databases
- Databases of the 1960s and 1970s
- Current mainstream database technologies—relational versus object orientation
- The need for speed in database systems
- Distributed databases and the challenges of transaction processing with distributed data.

2.1 Introduction

In Chap. 1 we discussed data as an organisational asset. We saw data, usually in the form of records has been with us since at least ancient Egyptian times. We also so that the big drivers of the need to keep detailed records were trade and taxation. Basically, you needed to keep track of who owed you how much for what. This meant you not only needed a way of recording it, you also needed a way of retrieving it and updating it. Ultimately this led to the development of double entry bookkeeping which emerged in the 13th and 14th centuries. Retrieving data was another issue and in paper-based systems indexes were developed to ease and speed this process. Producing reports from data was manual, time consuming and error prone although various types of mechanical calculators were becoming common by the mid nineteenth century to aid the process. Because of the time taken to produce them, major reports were usually published once a month coinciding reconciliation of accounts. An end of year financial position was also produced. On demand reports were unheard of. As a result the end of the month and the end of the year were always extremely busy times in the accounts section of an organisation.

© Springer Nature Switzerland AG 2021
K. Domdouzis et al., *Concise Guide to Databases*, Undergraduate Topics
in Computer Science, https://doi.org/10.1007/978-3-030-42224-0_2

2.2   The Digital Age

The first commercial computer UNIVAC 1 was delivered in 1951 to the US Census Bureau (Fig. 2.1). In 1954 Metropolitan Life became the first financial company to purchase one of the machines. This was a significant step forward giving Metropolitan Life a first mover advantage over other insurance companies. The UNIVAC was followed by IBM's 701 in 1953 and 650 in 1954. At the time it was envisaged by IBM that only 50 machines would be built and installed. By the end of production of the IBM 650 in 1962 nearly 2,000 had been installed. Data could now be processed much faster and with fewer errors compared with manual systems and a greater range of reports which were more up to date could be produced. One unfortunate side effect was regarding things as 'must be right, it came from the computer' and conversely 'I can't do anything about it, it is on the computer'. Fortunately, both attitudes are no longer as prevalent.

2.3   Sequential Systems

Initial computer systems processing data were based on the pre-existing manual systems. These were sequential systems, where individual files were composed of records organised in some predetermined order. Although not a database because there was no one integrated data source, electronic file processing was the first step towards an electronic data-based information system. Processing required you to start at the first record and continue to the end. This was quite good for producing payroll and monthly accounts, but much less useful when trying to recall an

Fig. 2.1 UNIVAC 1
(original https://www.
computer-history.info/Page4.
dir/pages/Univac.dir/, last
accessed 07/08/2013)

individual record. As a result, it was not uncommon to have the latest printout of the file which could be manually searched if required kept on hand until a new version was produced. Printing was relatively slow by today's standards, so usually only one copy was produced although multi part paper using interleaved carbon paper was used sometimes when multiple copies could be justified. Sequential file processing also meant there had to be cut offs—times when no new updates could be accepted before the programs were run.

Although disk storage was available it was expensive, so early systems tended to be based on 80 column punched cards, punched paper tape or magnetic tape storage, which meant input, update and output had to be done in very specific ways. IBM used card input which was copied onto magnetic tape. This data had to be sorted. Once that was done it could be merged with and used to update existing data (Fig. 2.2). This was usually held on the 'old' master tape, the tape containing the processed master records from the previous run of the system (when it was designated the 'new' master). Once updated a new master tape was produced which would become the old master in the next run. Processing had to be scheduled. In our example, the first run would be sorting, the second processing. Since only one program could be loaded and run at a time with these systems demand for computer time grew rapidly. As well as data processing time was needed to develop, compile and test new computer programmes. Ultimately many computer systems were being scheduled for up to 24 h a day, 7 days a week.

There were also very strict rules on tape storage so if a master tape were corrupted it could be recreated by using archived old masters and the transaction tapes. If there were any issues with one of the transactions, it would not be processed, but would be copied to an exception file on another tape. This would be later examined to find out what had gone wrong. Normally the problem would rectified by adding a new transaction to be processed at the next run of the program.

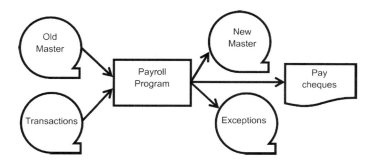

Fig. 2.2 A tape-based system

2.4   Random Access

IBM introduced hard disk drives which allowed direct access to data in 1956, but these were relatively low capacity and expensive compared to tape system. By 1961 the systems had become cheaper and it was possible to add extra drives to your system. The advantage of a disk drive was you could go directly to a record in the file which meant you could do real time transaction processing. That is now the basis of processing for nearly all commercial computer systems. At the same time operating systems were developed to allow multiple users and multiple programs to active at the same time removing some of the restrictions imposed by tight scheduling needed on single process machines.

2.5   Origins of Modern Databases

It was inevitable that data would be organised in some way to make storage and retrieval more efficient. However, while they were developing these systems there was also a move by the manufacturers to lock customers into their proprietary products. Many failed forcing early adopters of the 'wrong' systems to migrate to other widely adopted systems, usually at great expense. For example, Honeywell developed a language called FACT (Fully Automated Compiler Technique) which was designed for implementing corporate systems with associated file structures. The last major user was the Australian Department of Defence in the 1960's and 70's. They took several years and a large budget to convert to UNIVAC's DMS 1100 system which will be described below.

UNIVAC and IBM competed to develop the first database where records were linked in a way that was not sequential. UNIVAC had decided to adopt the COBOL (Common Business Oriented Language) programming language and therefore also adopted the CODASYL (COnference on DAta SYstems Languages) conventions for developing their database. CODASYL was a consortium formed in 1959 to develop a common programming language which became the basis for COBOL. Interestingly despite Honeywell being a member of the CODASYL group, they tried to put forward their FACT language as tried and functioning alternative to the untried COBOL. As shown this strategy was not successful. In 1967 CODASYL renamed itself the Database Task Group (DBTG) and developed a series of extensions to COBOL to handle databases. Honeywell, Univac and Digital Equipment Corporation (DEC) were among those who adopted this standard for their database implementations.

IBM on the other hand had developed its own programming language PL/1 (Programming Language 1) and a database implementation known as IMS (Information Management System) for the extremely popular IBM Series 360 computer family. The UNIVAC system was a network database and the IBM a strictly hierarchical one. Both were navigational systems where you accessed the system at one point then navigated down a hierarchy before conducting a sequential search to find the record you wanted. Both systems relied on pointers.

The following sections will look at transaction processing which underlies many database systems, then different database technologies will be briefly examined in roughly the order they appeared. Many of these will be dealt with in more detail in later chapters.

2.6   Transaction Processing and ACID

Many database applications deal with transaction processing; therefore we need to look at what a transaction is. Basically, a transaction is one or more operations that make up a single task. Operations fall into one of four categories; Create, Read, Update or Delete (so called CRUDing). As an example, you decide to make a withdrawal at a cash machine. There are several transactions involved here, first you need to be authenticated by the system. We will concentrate on the actual withdrawal. The system checks you have enough money in your account (Read); it then reduces the amount in your account by the amount requested (Update) and issues the money and a receipt. It also logs the operation recording your details, the time, location and amount of the withdrawal (Create). Several things can happen that cause the transaction to abort. You may not have enough money in the account, or the machine may not have the right denomination of notes to satisfy your request. In these cases, the operations are undone or rolled back so your account (in other words the database) is returned to the state it was in before you started.

ACID stands for atomicity, consistency, isolation and durability and is fundamental to database transaction processing. Earlier in this chapter we saw how transactions were processed in sequential file systems, but with multiuser systems which rely on a single database, transaction processing becomes a critical part of processing. Elements of this discussion will be expanded on in the chapters on availability and security.

Atomicity refers to transactions being applied in an 'all or nothing' manner. This means if any part of a transaction fails, the entire transaction is deemed to have failed and the database is returned to the state it was in before the transaction started. This returning to the original state is known as rollback. On the other hand, if the transaction completes successfully the database is permanently updated—a process known as commit.

Consistency means data written to a database must be valid according to defined rules. In a relational database this includes constraints which determine the validity of data entered. For example, if an attempt was made to create an invoice and a unassigned customer id was used the transaction would fail (you can't have an invoice which does not have an associated customer). This would also trigger the atomicity feature rolling back the transaction.

Isolation ensures that transactions being executed in parallel would result in a final state identical to that which would be arrived at if the transactions were executed serially. This is important for on line systems. For example, consider two users simultaneously attempting to buy the last seat on an airline flight. Both would initially see that a seat was available, but only one can buy it. The first to commit to buying by pressing the purchase button and having the purchase approved would cause the other users' transaction to stop and any entered data (like name and address) to be rolled back.

Durability is the property by which once a transaction has been committed, it will stay committed. From the previous example, if our buyer of the last seat on the aeroplane has finished their transaction, received a success message but the system crashes for whatever reason before the final update is applied, the user would reasonably think their purchase was a success. Details of the transaction would have to be stored in a non-volatile area to allow them to be processed when the system was restored.

2.7   Two-Phase Commit

Two-phase commit is a way of dealing with transactions where the database is held on more than one server. This is called a distributed database and these will be discussed in more detail below. However, a discussion on the transaction processing implications belongs here. In a distributed database processing a transaction has implications in terms of the A (atomicity) and C (consistency) of ACID since the database management system must coordinate the committing or rolling back of transactions as a self-contained unit on all database components no matter where they are physically located. The two phases are the request phase and the commit phase. In the request phase a coordinating process sends a query to commit message to all other processes. The expected response is 'YES' otherwise the transaction aborts. In the commit phase the coordinator sends a message to the other processes which attempt to complete the commit (make changes permanent). If anyone process fails, all processes will execute a rollback.

Oracle, although calling it a two-phase commit has defined three phases: prepare, commit and forget which we will look at in more detail. In the prepare phase all nodes referenced in a distributed transaction are told to prepare to commit by the initiating node which becomes the global coordinator.

Each node then records information in the redo logs so it can commit or rollback. It also places a distributed lock on tables to be modified so no reads can take place. The node reports back to the global coordinator that it is prepared to commit, is read-only or abort. Read-only means no data on the node can be modified by the request so no preparation is necessary and will not participate in the commit phase. If the response is abort it means the node cannot successfully prepare. That node then does a rollback of its local part of the transaction. Once one node has issued an abort, the action propagates among the rest of the nodes which also rollback the transaction guaranteeing the A and C of ACID.

If all nodes involved in the transaction respond with prepared, the process moves into the commit phase. The step in this phase is for the global coordinator node to commit. If that is successful, the global coordinator instructs all the other nodes to commit the transaction. Each node then does a commit and updates the local redo log before sending a message that they have committed. In the case of a failure to commit, a message is sent and all sites rollback.

The forget phase is a clean-up stage. Once all participating nodes notify the global coordinator they have committed, a message is sent to erase status information about the transaction.

SQLServer has a similar two-phase commit strategy but includes the third (forget) phase at the end of the second phase.

2.8   Hierarchical Databases

Although hierarchical databases are no longer common, it is worth spending some time on a discussion of them because IMS, a hierarchical database system is still one of IBM's highest revenue products and is still being actively developed. It is however a mainframe software product and may owe some of its longevity to organisations being locked into the product from the early days of mainstream computing. The host language for IMS is usually IBM's PL/1 but COBOL is also common.

Like a networked databases, the structure of a hierarchical database relies on pointers. A major difference is that it must be navigated from the top of the tree (Fig. 2.3).

Fig. 2.3 Hierarchical database

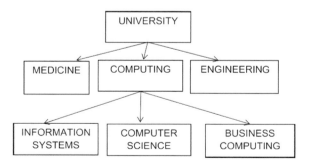

2.9   Network Databases

In a network database such as UNIVAC's DMS 1100, you have one record which is the parent record. In the example in Fig. 2.4 this is a customer record. This is defined with a number of attributes (for example Customer ID, Name, Address). Linked to this are a number of child records, in this case orders which would also have a number of attributes. It is up to the database design to decide how they are linked. The default was often to 'next' pointers where the parent pointed to the first child, the first child had a pointer to the second child and so on. The final child would have a pointer back to the parent. If faster access was required, 'prior' pointers could be defined allowing navigation in a forward and backward direction. Finally, if even more flexibility was required 'direct' pointers could be defined which pointed directly from a child record back to the parent. The trade-off was between speed of access and speed of updates, particularly when inserting new child records and deleting records. In these cases, pointers had to be updated.

The whole of the definition of the database and the manipulation of it was hosted by the COBOL programming language which was extended to deal with DMS 1100 database applications. It is the main reason why the COBOL language is still in use today. It is worth noting that deficiencies in the language led to fears there would be major computer (which actually meant database) failure at midnight on 31st December 1999. This was referred to as the Y2K or millennium bug and related to the way dates were stored (it was feared some systems would think the year was 1900 as only the last two digits of the year were stored). The fact that the feared failures never happened has been put down to the maintenance effort that went into systems in the preceding few years.

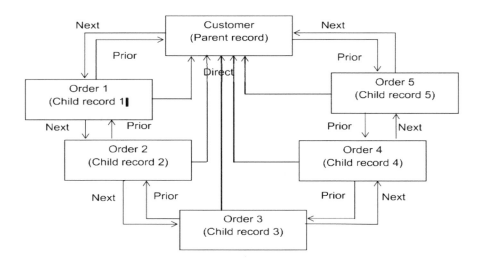

Fig. 2.4 Network database

2.10   Relational Databases

These will be discussed in detail in Chap. 4. They arose out of Edgar Codd's 1970 paper "A Relational Model of Data for Large Shared Data Banks" (Codd 1970). What became Oracle Corporation used this as the basis of what became the biggest corporate relational database management system. It was also designed to be platform independent, so it didn't matter what hardware you were using.

The basis of a relational system is a series of tables of records each with specific attributes linked by a series of joins. These joins are created using foreign keys which are attribute(s) containing the same data as another tables primary key. A primary key is a unique identifier of a record in a table. This approach to data storage was very efficient in terms of the disk space used and the speed of access to records.

In Fig. 2.5 we have a simple database consisting of 2 tables. One contains employee records, the other contains records relating to departments. The Department ID can be seen as the link (join) between the two tables being a primary key in the department table and a foreign key in the Employee table. There is also a one to many relationship illustrated which means for every record in the Department table there are many records in the Employee table. The converse is also true in that for every record in the Employee table there is one and only one record in the Department table.

The data in a relational database is manipulated by the structured query language (SQL). This was formalised by ANSI (American National Standards Institute) in 1986. The have been seven revisions of SQL86, the most recent revision being SQL2011 or ISO/IEC 9075:2011 (International Organization for Standardization/International Electrotechnical Commission). SQL has a direct relationship to relational algebra. This describes tables (in relational algebra terms—relations), records (tuples) and the relationship between them. For example:

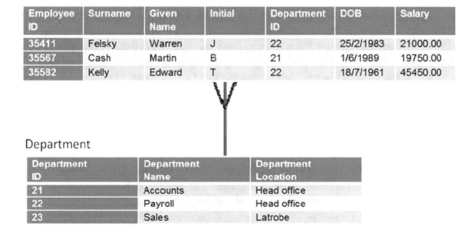

Employee ID	Surname	Given Name	Initial	Department ID	DOB	Salary
35411	Felsky	Warren	J	22	25/2/1983	21000.00
35567	Cash	Martin	B	21	1/6/1989	19750.00
35582	Kelly	Edward	T	22	18/7/1961	45450.00

Department

Department ID	Department Name	Department Location
21	Accounts	Head office
22	Payroll	Head office
23	Sales	Latrobe

Fig. 2.5 Relational database consisting of two tables or relations

$$P1 = \bullet type\_property = {}'\,House'(Property\_for\_Rent)$$

would be interpreted as find all the records in the property for rent table where the type of rental property is a house and would be written in SQL as:

SELECT $*$ FROM property_for_rent WHERE type_property $= {}'\,House'$;

Oracle and Microsoft SQL server are examples of relational database systems. Microsoft Access has many of the features of a relational database system including the ability to manipulate data using SQL, but is not strictly regarded as a relational database management system.

2.11   Object Oriented Databases

Most programming today is done in an object-oriented language such as Java or C++. These introduce a rich environment where data and the procedures and functions need to manipulate it are stored together. Often a relational database is seen by object-oriented programmers as a single persistent object on which a number of operations can be performed. However, there are more and more reasons why this is becoming a narrow view.

One of the first issues confronting databases is the rise of non-character (alphanumeric) data. Increasingly images, sound files, maps and video need to be stored, manipulated and retrieved. Even traditional data is being looked at in other ways than by traditional table joins. Object oriented structures such as hierarchies, aggregation and pointers are being introduced. This has led to a number of innovations, but also to fragmentation of standards.

From the mid 1980's a number of object-oriented database management systems (OODBMS) were developed but never gained traction in the wider business environment. They did become popular in niche markets such as the geographic and engineering sectors where there was a need for graphical data to be stored and manipulated. One of the big issues with object-oriented databases is, as mentioned creating a standard. This was attempted by the Object Data Management Group (ODMG) which published five revisions to its standard. This group was wound up in 2001. The function of ODMG has, been taken over by the Object Management Group (OMG). Although there is talk of development of a 4th generation standard for object databases, this has not yet happened

An issue with developing object-oriented systems was that a lot of expertise and systems had been developed around relational databases and SQL had become, for better or worse, the universal query language. The second approach to object orientation therefore was to extend relational databases to incorporate object-oriented features. These are known as object relational databases. They are manipulated by SQL commands which have been extended to deal with object structures.

Chapter 7 will look in detail at both Object and Object Relational Databases.

2.12   Data Warehouse

A problem with an operational database is that individual records within it are continually being updated, therefore it is difficult to do an analysis based on historical data unless you actively store it. The concept behind a data warehouse is that it can store data generated by different systems in the organisation, not just transactions form the database. This data can then be analysed and the results of the analysis used to make decisions and inform the strategic direction of an organisation. Data warehouses have already been mentioned in Chap. 1 where they were discussed in their role of an organisational asset. Here we look briefly at some of their technical details.

A data warehouse is a central repository of data in an organisation storing historical data and being constantly added to by current transactions. The data can be analysed to produce trend reports. It can also be analysed using data mining techniques for generating strategic information. Unlike data in a relational database, data in a data warehouse is organised in a de-normalised format. There are three main formats:

- Star schema: tables are either fact tables which record data about specific events such as a sales transaction and dimension tables which information relating to
- the attributes in the fact table (Fig. 2.6)
- Snowflake schemas are also based around a fact table which has dimension tables linked to it. However, these dimension tables may also have further tables linked to them giving the appearance of a snowflake (Fig. 2.7)
- Starflake schema which is a snowflake schema where only some of the dimension tables have been de-normalised.

Data mining is a process of extracting information from a data warehouse and transforming it into an understandable structure. The term data analytics is starting to be used in preference to data mining. There are a number of steps in the process:

- Data cleansing were erroneous and duplicate data is removed. It is not uncommon in raw data to have duplicate data where there is only a minor difference, for example two customer records may be identical, but one contains a suburb name as part of the address and one does not. One needs removing.
- Initial Analysis where the quality and distribution of the data is determined. This is done to determine if there is any bias or other problems in the data distribution
- Main analysis where statistical models are applied to answer some question, usually asked management.

Data mining is just one method in a group collectively known as Business Intelligence that transform data into useful business information. Others included business process management and business analytics. A further use for data in a data warehouse is to generate a decision system based on patterns in the data. This

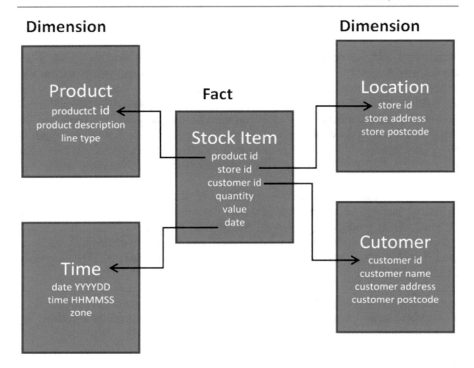

Fig. 2.6 Star schema

process is known as machine learning. There are two main branches: neural net-works which use data to train a computer program simulating neural connections in the brain for pattern recognition and rule-based systems where a decision tree is generated.

2.13   The Gartner Hype Cycle

Gartner began publishing its annual hype cycle report for emerging technologies in 2007. Technologies such as Big Data and Cloud Computing both feature so we will have a brief look at the hype cycle before continuing. The hype cycle is based on media 'hype' about new technologies and classifies them as being in one of five zones.

- **The Technology Trigger** which occurs when a technological innovation or product generates significant press interest
- **The Peak of Inflated Expectations** where often unrealistic expectations are raised

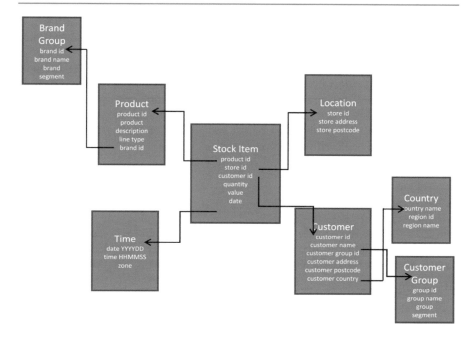

Fig. 2.7 Snowflake schema

- **The Trough of Disillusionment** where, because of failing to meet expectations there is a loss of interest
- **The Slope of Enlightenment** where organisations which have persisted with the technology despite setbacks begin to see benefits and practical applications
- **The Plateau of Productivity** where the benefits of the technology have been demonstrated and it becomes widely accepted

In practice it is not really a cycle but a continuum. Gartner has produced many different hype cycles covering many different topics from advertising through to wireless network infrastructure (see Gartner Inc. 2013).

One of the exercises at the end of this chapter involves examining hype cycles. By completing this you will see what they look like and how technologies move across the cycle on a year-by-year basis.

2.14 Big Data

As mentioned in Chap. 1, the amount of data available that an organisation can collect and analyse has been growing rapidly. The first reference to big data on Gartner's Hype Cycle of emerging technologies was in 2011 when it was referred to as 'Big Data and Extreme Information Processing and Management'. As a term it grew out of data warehousing recognising the growth of storage needed to handle massive datasets some organisations were generating.

The definition of "Big data" is often left intentionally vague, for example McKinsey's 2011 report defines it as referring '… to datasets whose size is beyond the ability of typical database software tools to capture, store, manage, and analyze.' (Manyika et al. 2011, p. 1). This is because different organisations have different abilities to store and capture data. Context and application are therefore important. Big Data will be explored in depth in Chap. 6.

2.15   Data in the Cloud

The 2012 Gartner Hype Cycle also identifies database platform as a service (as part of cloud computing) and like in-memory databases it has been identified as over-hyped. However, like in-memory databases it is also thought to be within five years of maturity.

Cloud computing is distributed computing where the application and data a user may be working with is located somewhere on the internet. Amazon Elastic Compute Cloud (Amazon EC2) was one of the first commercial cloud vendors supplying resizable computing and data capacity in the cloud. The Amazon cloud is actually a large number of servers located around the world although three of the biggest data centres are located in the United States, each with thousands of servers in multiple buildings. An estimate in 2012 suggested Amazon had over 500,000 servers in total. As a user you can buy both processing and data storage when you need it. Many other vendors including British Telecom (BT) are now offering cloud services.

The impact on database systems is you no longer have to worry about local storage issues because you can purchase a data platform as a service in the cloud. It also means whatever an organisations definition of big data is, there is a cost-effective way of storing and analysing that data. Although concerns have been raised about security including backup and recovery of cloud services, they are probably better than policies and practice in place at most small to medium sized businesses.

2.16   The Need for Speed

One of the technologies facilitating databases was hard disk drives. These provided fast direct access to data. As already stated, the cost of this technology has been falling and speed increasing. Despite this the biggest bottleneck in data processing is the time it takes to access data on a disk. The time taken has three components: seek time which is how long it takes the read/write head to move over the disk and rotational latency, basically the average time it takes the disk to rotate so the record you want is actually under the read/write head. Data then has to be moved from the disk to the processor—the data transfer rate.

For many applications this is not a problem, but for others performance is an issue. For example, stockbrokers use systems called High Frequency Trading or micro-trading where decisions are made in real time based on transaction data. This is automated and based on trading algorithms which use input from market quotes and transactions to identify trends. Requirements for speed like this are beyond disk-based systems but there are ways to get around the problem. The first is to move the entire database into memory; the second is to use a different access strategy to that provided by the database management system; finally, there is a combination of the two.

The 2012 Gartner Hype cycle for emerging technologies identifies in-memory database management systems and in-memory analysis as part of its analysis. However, both of these are sliding into what Gartner term the 'trough of disillusionment' meaning they have probably been overhyped. On the other hand, they are also predicted to be within 5 years of maturity which Gartner calls the 'plateau of productivity'

2.17   In-Memory Database

Early computer systems tried to optimise the use of main memory because it was both small and expensive. This has now changed with continued development of semi-conductor memory, specifically non-volatile memory. This was a major development as it meant data stored in memory was not lost if there was a power failure. It is now possible to hold a complete database in a computer's memory. There is no one dominant technology at the moment. Oracle, for example has taken the approach of loading a relational database in its TimesTen system. The problem with this approach is a relational database is designed for data stored on disk and helps optimise the time taken to transfer data to memory. This is no longer an issue as the data is already in memory meaning other ways of organising and accessing data can be implemented. In-memory databases will be looked at in detail in Chap. 8.

2.18   NoSQL

One problem with the relational database model was that it was designed for character-based data which could be modelled in terms of attributes and records translated to columns and rows in a table. It has also been suggested it does not scale well which is a problem in a world where everyone is talking about big data. NoSQL (some say Not Only SQL) is an umbrella term for a number of approaches which do not use traditional query languages such as SQL and OQL (Object Query Language). There are a number of reasons for the rise in interest on No SQL. The first is speed and the poor fit of traditional query languages to technologies such as in-memory databases mentioned above. Secondly there is the form of the data which people want to store, analyse and retrieve. Tweets from Twitter are data that do not easily fit a relational or object-oriented structure. Instead column-based approaches were a column is the smallest unit of storage or a document based approach where data is denormalised can be applied. NoSQL will be discussed in Chap. 5.

2.19 Spatial Databases

Spatial databases form the basis of Geographic Information Systems (GIS). Most databases have some geographic information stored in them. At the very least this will be addresses. However, there is much more information available and combining it in many ways can provide important planning information. This process is called overlaying. For example, you may have a topographic map of an area which gives height above sea level at specific points. This can then have a soil, climate and vegetation map overlaid on it to.

An issue with spatial databases is that as well as storing 'traditional' data you also have to store positional and shape data. As an example, let's take a road. This can be stored as all the pixels making up the road (known as a raster representation) or it could be stored as a series of points (minimum two if it is a straight road) which can be used to plot its location (vector representation). Along with a representation of its shape and location you may also want to store information such as its name and even information about its construction and condition. As well as plotting this object you may want to know its location in relation to service infrastructure such as sewer lines, for example where the road crosses a major sewer or where access points to it are.

Despite expecting GISs' to be object oriented, for the most part they are relational. For example, the biggest vendor in this field is ESRI which uses a proprietary relational database called ArcSDE. Oracle Spatial is a rapidly emerging player and has the advantage of offering this product as an option to its mainstream database management system (currently 11 g). As Oracle Spatial is part of the wider group of Oracle products, it means there are associated object-oriented features and a development environment available.

2.20 Databases on Personal Computers

Before 1980 most database systems were found on mainframe computers, but the advent of personal computers and the recognition that they were viable business productivity tools lead to the development of programs designed to run on desktop machines. The first widely used electronic spreadsheet to be developed was Visi-Calc in 1979 which spelled a rather rapid end to the paper versions. Word processors and databases followed soon after.

In the early days of personal computers there was a proliferation of manufacturers many of whom had their own proprietary operating systems and software. The introduction of IBM's personal computer in 1980 using Microsoft's operating system resulted in a shake out of the industry. Most manufacturers who remained in the market started producing machines based on the IBM PC's architecture (PC clones) and running Microsoft software. In 1991 the LINUX operating system was released as an alternative to Microsoft's operating system. The largest of the other companies was Apple which vigorously opposed the development of clones of its machines.

There are several databases systems which run on personal computers. One of the earliest was DBase developed by Ashton Tate in 1980. Versions of this ran on most of the personal computers available at the time. The ownership of the product has changed several times. The product itself has developed into and object-oriented database whose usage is not common among business users, but is still quite popular among niche users.

Microsoft Access was a much later product being released in 1992. It was bundled with the Microsoft Office suite in 1995 and has become one of the most common desktop databases in use today. One of its attractions is that its tables and relationships can be viewed graphically but it can also be manipulated by most SQL statements. It is however not a true relational database management system because of the way table joins are managed. It is compatible with Microsoft's relational database system SQL Server. One of its major disadvantages is that it does not scale well.

An open source personal computer databases is MySQL released in 1995. This is a relational database and is very popular. However, although the current open source market leader NoSQL and NewSQL based products are gaining on it according to Matt Asya's in his 2011 article 'MySQL's growing NoSQL problem'. (Available at http://www.theregister.co.uk/2012/05/25/nosql_vs_mysql/ last accessed 04/07/2013.)

2.21 Distributed Databases

In Chap. 1 we saw the evolution of organisations often lead to them being located on multiple sites and sometimes consisting of multiple federated but independent components. Therefore, rather than all the data in an organisation being held on a single centralised database, data is sometimes distributed so operational data is held on the site where it is being used. In the case of a relational database this requires tables or parts of tables to be fragmented and in some case replicated. Early versions of distribution was happening in the mid 1970's, for example the Australian Department of Defence had a centralised database system but bases around Australia replicated segments based on their local needs on mini computers. This was not a real time system, rather the central systems and the distributed machines synchronised several times a day.

Today it is possible to have components or fragments of a database on a network of servers whose operation is transparent to users. There are four main reasons to fragment or distribute databases across multiple sites or nodes. The first is efficiency where data is stored where it is most frequently used. This cuts the overhead of data transmission. Obviously, you don't store data that is not used by any local application. This also leads to the second reason—security, since data not required at local nodes is not stored there it makes local unauthorised access more difficult. The third reason is usage. Most applications work with views rather than entire tables, therefore the data required by the view is stored locally rather than the whole table. The final reason is parallelism where similar transactions can be processed in parallel at different sites. Where multiple sites are involved in a transaction a two-phase commit process is required and is described in the following section.

There are some disadvantages, however. The database management system has to be extended to deal with distributed data. Poor fragmentation can result in badly degraded performance due to constant data transfer between nodes (servers). This may also lead to integrity problems if part of the network goes down. There needs to be a more complex transaction processing regime to make sure data integrity is maintained.

2.22   XML

XML stands for eXtensible Markup Language and is used for encoding a document in a form that is both human and machine readable. It is not intended to give a full description of XML here. What is important from a database point of view is that you can define a database in terms of XML which is important for document databases. There are two forms of XML schema which constrains what information can be stored in a database and constrain the data types of the stored information. It must be noted an XML document can be created without an associated schema, but those will not be considered here.

Document Type Definition (DTD) This is an optional part of a XML document and performs the task of constraining and typing the information in the document. This constraining is not like the basic types of integer and characters (VARCHAR) we have already seen. Instead it constrains the appearance of sub-elements and attributes within an element. An example DTD may look like:

```
<!DOCTYPE account [

    <!ELEMENT invoice (invoice-number total)>

    (!ATTLIST invoice

        account-number ID #REQUIRED

        owner IDREF #REQUIRED>

    <!ELEMENT customer (customer-name customer street customer-city)>

    (!ATTLIST customer

        customer-id ID #REQUIRED

        accounts IDREF #REQUIRED

    .

]>
```

where an attribute of type ID must be unique and a IDREF is a reference to an element and must contain a value that appears in an ID element. This effectively gives a one-to-many relationship.

DTD have limitations, however. They cannot specify data types and are written in their own language, not XML. Also they do not support newer XML features such as namespaces. Namespaces are used to contain definitions of identifiers. Once a namespace is set up a developer will be confident of identifiers definitions. The same identifier in a different namespace could have different definitions.

XML Schema This is a more sophisticated schema language designed to overcome the deficiencies of DTD at the same time providing backwards (and forwards) compatibility. It also allows user defined types to be created and text that appears in elements to be constrained to more familiar types such as numeric including specific format definitions. Most importantly it is specified by XML syntax.

Once a database is set up using XML it can be queried using a number of languages:

- XPath is designed for path expressions and is the basis for the following two languages.
- XSLT is a transformation language. It was originally designed to control formatting of XML to HTML but it can be used to generate queries.
- XQuery is the current proposed standard for querying XML data.

It should be noted that many database management systems including Oracle are compatible with XML and can format output and receive input as XML. As mentioned in Chap. 1, there is a tendency to store anything that can be stored. Much of this data is in the form of complete documents. XML databases are an ideal way to store these therefore they are likely to become more and more common.

2.23   Temporal Databases

A temporal database is a database with built-in support for handling data involving time. A lot of data has a time element to it just as we have seen data often has a geographic element to it. Unlike the geographic element however, the time attributes are less often stored. The exception is transaction logs were temporal data is critical.

Two aspects of time are valid time—the time during which a fact is true in the real world and transactional time where it is true in a database. For example, when an electricity meter reading is taken, at the instance it is taken it is true in real time. It is then entered into the supplier's database along with the time the reading was taken. This is the beginning of when it is true in transactional time. It remains true until the time the next reading is entered. It means the reading has start and an end point (the time of the next reading) during which it is true.

2.24   Summary

In this chapter we have looked at the origins of organisational data processing beginning with systems based around sequential file processing. We then looked at the origins and development of database technology as random-access devices became cheaper, faster and more reliable. The impact of Edgar Codd's influential work and the rise to dominance of relational database systems was examined in detail and will be the subject of further parts of this book. Competing with the relational database model is the object-oriented model which is gaining traction because the amount of non-structured and non-character based data is increasing.

We looked at developing requirements for databases. New applications demand faster processing of data held in a database. Cheaper, stable computer memory is facilitating this so a database can be held in-memory. As well as a need for speed there is a need for volume as typified by Big Data and the tools need to analyse it. Lastly we looked at distributed databases placing data where it is needed.

2.25   Exercises

2.25.1   Review Questions

The answers to these questions can be found in the text of this chapter.

- What is the difference between a Hierarchical and a Network database?
- Define the following relational database terms: relation, tuple, attribute, relationship.
- What is ACID and why is it important?
- Describe the stages in the two-phase commit process.
- Why have object-oriented databases not become the standard commercial database management systems?

2.25.2 Group Work Research Activities

These activities require you to research beyond the contents of the book and can be tackled individually or as a discussion group.

Activity 1 Search for the yearly Gartner Hype Cycle on-line. The earliest of these is from 2009. Look for database related technologies. When did they start to appear? From 2011 Gartner also produced Hype for the Cloud. Look at this as well and identify relevant technologies. Are the technologies you identified moving along the hype cycle year on year? When did they first appear on the hype cycle?

The most recent version of the hype cycle is likely to be a document you have to pay for, but earlier versions are freely available.

Activity 2 Retrieve M. Asya's (2011) 'MySQL's growing NoSQL problem' article. (Available at http://www.theregister.co.uk/2012/05/25/nosql_vs_mysql/ last accessed 04/07/2013.) This makes predictions on the growth of MySQL, NoSQL and NewSQL. Research whether Asya's predictions are on track and if there are significant variations what is causing them?

References

Codd EF (1970) A relational model of data for large shared data banks. Republished in Commun ACM 26(1):64–69 (1983). Available on-line at http://dl.acm.org/citation.cfm?id= 358007, accessed 21/06/2013

Gartner Inc (2013) Research methodologies: hype cycles. Available online https://www.gartner. com/en/documents/3887767/understanding-gartner-s-hype-cycles, accessed 21/06/2013

Manyika J, Chui M, Brown B, Bughin J, Dobbs R, Roxburgh C, Hung Byers A (2011) Big data: the next frontier for innovation, competition, and productivity. McKinsey Global Institute. https://www.mckinsey.com/business-functions/mckinsey-digital/our-insights/big-data-the-next-frontier-for-innovation, accessed 23/06/2013

Further Reading

ODBMS.ORG (2006) 4th generation standard for object databases on its way. http://www.odbms. org/2006/02/4th-generation-standard-for-object-databases-on-its-way/, accessed 23/06/2013

Özsu MT, Valduriez P (2010) Principles of distributed database systems, 3rd edn. Springer, Berlin. Available at https://www.springer.com/gp/book/9781493941742, accessed 25/06/2013

Physical Storage and Distribution

3

What the reader will learn:

- That databases need to be able to make the information they store permanent.
- That the biggest factor upon the way a database functions is the physical environment it runs in.
- That whilst there are alternative approaches to database architecture design, storage on a disk is likely to be at the core of the physical system.
- That hardware failure is a fact of life in computing and database architecture is about minimising the impact of any such failure.
- That processing and data can be distributed in response to availability or performance requirements.

3.1 The Fundamental Building Block

At the time of writing this book Researchers at Google claim their quantum computer has solved a problem that would take even the very best conventional machine thousands of years to crack. As reported in the New Scientist this computer is likely to have cost more than $10 million and works not with the *bits* we have become so used to in our digital era, but *quibits* which can be in different states simultaneously, rather than just the on and off we have become used to. If, like the author, your brain can't cope with quantum theory, don't worry—we will here be concentrating on more everyday computing. However, as always, database professionals do need to keep their eyes on what is happening in the field of computer science if they are to continue to provide the best service possible to their organisation. Perhaps in a few years' time this chapter will be out of date as we all become used to quantum computing!

© Springer Nature Switzerland AG 2021

K. Domdouzis et al., *Concise Guide to Databases*, Undergraduate Topics in Computer Science, https://doi.org/10.1007/978-3-030-42224-0_3

However, in the meantime, we can safely make the assertion that a modern computer-based database system's primary purpose is to store and retrieve binary digits (bits). All the data in even the most highly encrypted critical systems, resolves itself into a series of 1 s and 0 s, or Ons and Offs.

Since only simple, Boolean data such as true/false or Yes/No can be stored in a bit, eight bits are connected together to form a unit called a byte which can store an unsigned integer of between 0 and 255. If the first bit is used to sign the subsequent value (+ or −), then the byte can store 0–127.

Various encoding systems have been used to allow the numbers in a byte to represent characters. Perhaps the most famous, and still in use, with western character sets, is ASCII. Text datatypes are relative simple, but even objects like audio or images can be stored in a database. Oracle, for example, has the Blob (Binary Large Object) which is a variable-length string of bits up to 2,147,483,647 characters long.

3.2 Overall Database Architecture

As we see by reviewing the chapters in this book, there are many different approaches to storing ons and offs in the form of a database management system. Without doubt the most commonly used approach is variations around the relational model.

Whilst the NoSQL databases may approach data storage differently to RDBMSs, two key elements exist in all common databases: the permanent storage of data, usually on disks, and the processing of data, usually carried on in the RAM of machine running the database. We will look at some of these structures and processes in detail below. The examples given will be from the Oracle environment, but most of what follows will also be true in other RDBMSs. The final section of the chapter will review how these may differ with NoSQL databases, and distributed databases.

> **Information**
> Most databases will need to carry out the four processes that make up the acronym CRUD which is used by many database professionals:
> - Create
> - Read
> - Update
> - Delete

3.2.1 In-Memory Structures

One important factor in the design of database systems is that Hard Disk Drives (HDD) are the slowest aspect of any system. It can be hundreds of times slower for a RDBMS to read a row from a HDD than from RAM. This is largely to do with the fact that there are mechanical moving parts involved in HDD technology, but no such hindrance exists in RAM.

Because of this databases will typically attempt to keep as much data as they can in memory, using a variety of caching techniques to make data more readily accessible to users. In RDBMS systems data is often stored in RAM once it has been read from disk for as long as is possible (that is, whilst the RAM has available space for the data), just in case another user wants to access the same data.

As was hinted in the last paragraph, data placed in RAM will be automatically timed-out and removed if it isn't used. Oracle manages this with a LRU list (Least Recently Used). You can force data to be permanently pinned in memory if you never want it to be removed. This can be used, for example, to keep code for stored procedures in memory for speedy access by users. The Oracle procedure for this is called: DBMS_SHARED_POOL.KEEP

Oracle's in-memory structure which holds copies of data read from disk is called the Database Buffer Cache. It resides within an overall structure called the System Global Area, referred to as the SGA. Users who are connected to the system, and have appropriate privileges, can share access to the database buffer cache. The reason for this is that some data requests are frequently repeated by many users. The request to populate a drop-down list of Region_Codes on a form, for example, may be in constant use, and after the first user makes the request, no subsequent user will need to wait for a disk read to get the data returned.

3.2.2 Walking Through a Straightforward Read

Before we go any further, let us see how a request for some information might be treated in the RDBMS. In the process we will come across other structures which we will review in detail afterwards, but, for now, let's concentrate on the overall operation.

Our user, called User_A, needs to know the address of one of their customers. They may well write something like:

```
Select Surname, Firstname, address1, address2, address3, city, county, nation,
telephone
From Customers
Where Customer ID = 2314;
```

Of course, this query may not have been explicitly written by User_A. They may have just made some selections on a page in an application, and the application could have fashioned the SQL itself on their behalf.

However the SQL is formed, there will be a connection between the user and the database sitting on a server. The SQL request is sent down to the server where it is parsed. This process checks not only that the query syntax is valid, but also that User_A has sufficient privileges to actually access this data.

Now we know User_A is allowed to ask this question and that the query is valid, the next question is: has anyone else asked the same question recently and, more importantly, is the answer to the query in memory, in the SGA? If the answer is yes then the process can skip the following operations and go straight to returning the dataset—which is why, when you see what has to happen (below) if the data isn't in the shared area, keeping data in memory is a good strategy.

In this example, this data is not in memory as no-one else has recently asked for the data. Next the parsed query is passed on to an optimiser. There are likely to be many access paths (routes to the data) available to the database. Perhaps it would be quicker for the database to use an index to discover the exact physical location of the required row, or maybe it would be quicker to just read the whole table at one go and discard what isn't required (see the chapter on Performance). It is the optimiser's job to decide which will be the fastest route.

Having decided, the optimiser creates an execution plan, listing the tasks that need to be carried out and in what order. This query is relatively simple, but queries with multiple joins, for example, will have quite complex plans.

As we said, the required data is not in memory, so we will have to read the row from the disk. Actually, what the disk is storing is 1 s and 0 s that can be made to describe the data. The start of those 1 s and 0 s for our data will be at a physical location on the HDD described by its Hex Address, and that information, in Oracle, is stored in a Rowid. A Rowid is a pseudocolumn which contains a pointer to the row and which provides a unique identifier of that row.

The disk will be spun-up and the head reader moved to the location indicated by the Rowid, and then it will read as many data-blocks as is needed to fulfil the data requirement and place the information into the Database Buffer Cache. It will stay there until such time as, if it is not reused, it falls to the bottom of the LRU list and is lost. A copy is parcelled together as the response dataset and sent over the connection back to the user. The process is illustrated in Fig. 3.1.

> **Information**
> The term Data Dictionary is used to describe the place where the database stores reference information about the database, such as about its users schemas and objects.

The database buffer cache is by no means the only memory structure. Caches will exist for things like SQL statements and Data Dictionary information that is being used at any point in time. There are several other specialist pools in an Oracle environment, but we only need worry about them if we are going be an Oracle DBA!

3.2.3 Server Processes

There are a number of independent processes that make up the overall database server system. Some are to do with the management of the RDBMS, and others are to do with the handling of the data. Again, the examples here are Oracle specific, but the principles will be present in other RDBMS.

> **Information**
> The term Instance is used to describe the processes and structure that exist in an Oracle server. In Oracle terminology, the Server is the Instance plus the disks-based information, which it calls the database.

As its name suggests, the **System Monitor**'s major task is to make sure the instance is running OK. If need be it can perform a recovery when the instance starts up.

Process Monitor looks after the instance's processes, including user processes. If, for example, a session is idle for too long, Process Monitor will kill the session to free up resources.

The Database Writer's task, as you can probably guess, is to make data changes and inserts permanent by writing them down to the disks. Changes to data are actually made in the Database Buffer. Thus changed, but not yet written to disk, the buffer is described as a "dirty" buffer. Because of the bottleneck that disk operations can create, dirty buffers are not written to disk the second that a commit is issued. Rather they remain, flagged as dirty, until the time to write is judged by Oracle to be right.

This can come as quite a shock, especially to people coming from an Access-like environment where the database IS what is on the disk. Here, the current content of the server is described as "what is on the disk" plus dirty database buffers.

Database writer will flush dirty buffers to disk when there is insufficient clean reusable buffer space left, or prior to a Checkpoint (see below).

The Redo Log Writer manages the redo logs. Redo is discussed in more detail later in this chapter but suffice it here to say that Redo Logs are used to protect against instance failure by storing information (known as change vectors) about what changes have been made to the database. Using Redo logs it is possible to reconstruct all the changes that have been made to the database since a backup by replaying the changes onto the recovered database from the logs.

Archiver is connected in a way to the Redo Logs process, in that it copies the redo log files to a designated storage device before they get overwritten.

The **Checkpoint process** is about regularly ensuring that the database is consistent. It forces Database Writer to flush dirty buffers to disk so that the current contents of the database are all in disks. At that point the System Change Number (SCN) is incremented and that number is stored in the datafiles and the control files (see below). This is used if Oracle needs to discover when the database was last consistent and to discover inconsistent datafiles (perhaps because of disk corruption) since any datafile which does not have the current SCN in its header is not consistent. This event is triggered when the redo log buffer is switched and when a hot back-up is taken.

The other process which is of vital importance is the User Process. When a user attempts to log on to an instance they negotiate with a **Listener service** on the server. The listener's job is to receive incoming requests to talk to the server. If the user meets log-in requirements, then the listener will create a **connection**. This means that the user is connected to the server. On the server itself a process runs on behalf of that client and runs jobs on their behalf.

3.2.4 Permanent Structures

The most obvious permanent structures in an Oracle Server are the datafiles that store the database data on disks.

The connection between the physical aspects of a database and its logical design are these datafiles since they support tablespaces. And tablespaces are logical structures that store logical objects such as tables, indexes, functions and even the data dictionary itself.

An Oracle database will always create at least two tablespaces for itself: The **System** tablespace contains the data dictionary; the **Sysaux**, which is used as an auxiliary for the System tablespace. DBAs then can create tablespaces as they think fit. An example of the SQL structured Query.

Language (SQL) command to create a tablespace called FRED is:

```
CREATE TABLESPACE FRED DATAFILE '/u02/oracle/data/FRED01.dbf' SIZE 50M EXTENT
MANAGEMENT LOCAL AUTOALLOCATE;
```

Here we provide a 50 Mb file called FRED01.DBF to support a tablespace called FRED. The autoallocate parameter tells Oracle it can keep adding diskspace to this tablespace as it grows.

To have users create objects stored in that tablespace you would issue an SQL statement like this:

```
CREATE USER peter IDENTIFIED BY p2P2p2 DEFAULT TABLESPACE FRED;
```

The important thing to note is that the 1 s and 0 s that describe the rows in a table created by peter will all be found in the physical operating system file called FRED01.DBF.

All the elements mentioned above work together to create an Oracle Instance (see Fig. 3.2).

Now we have an overview of how the key physical elements of a server (RAM structures, Processes and HDD) work together to create an instance of a database management system, we will now review some of the architecture in more detail.

3.3   Data Storage

Remembering that the way that information is actually stored in a database is in 1 s and 0 s, we should examine how these bits are managed by the database management system. We will do this by building up from the bottom the storage of a row of data. The example is from a very simple Customer database in which we store the customer's birthday.

The table structure looks like this:

Column Name	Data Type
CUSTOMERNO	NUMBER
CUSTOMERFIRST	VARCHAR2(30)
CUSTOMERLAST	VARCHAR2(30)
BIRTHDAY	DATE

The table create script looks like this:

```
CREATE TABLE "CUSTOMERBIRTHDAYS"
  ( "CUSTOMERNO" NUMBER (*,0),
    "CUSTOMERFIRST" VARCHAR(30),
    "CUSTOMERLAST" VARCHAR(30),
    "BIRTHDAY" DATE,
    CONSTRAINT "CUSTOMERBIRTHDAYS_PK" PRIMARY KEY
      ("CUSTOMERNO") ENABLE
  )
/

CREATE INDEX "CUSTOMERBIRTHDAYS_IDX1" ON
  "CUSTOMERBIRTHDAYS" ("BIRTHDAY")
/
```

And this is a sample of the data:

CUSTOMERNO	CUSTOMERFIRST	CUSTOMERLAST	BIRTHDAY
1	John	Smith	10/MAY/1963
2	Joanne	Smith	11/JUN/1967
3	Fred	Delus	29/JAN/1862
4	Cliff	Spock	11/AUG/1977
14	Eddie	Greig	12/DEC/1980

The first thing we observe is that the columns are of different data types, except the two text columns. The size of each column, in terms of bytes used to store it, will therefore differ. Oracle uses 21 bytes to store numbers, so the CustomerNo column will be 21 bytes long.

The VARCHAR2 data type is a variable-length string of characters, the length of which is set by the parameter passed in the brackets, but which can be, at most, 4000 bytes long. In our table the two name fields are 30 bytes long.

The date column is 7 bytes long. Each of the bytes is used to store an element of any date such that:

Bytes 1 and 2 store the century and the year

Bytes 3–7 store Month, Day, Hour, Minute, Second

Every row also has a pseudocolumn created by Oracle called the ROWID which contains the unique identifier for the row, and its physical address on the file system using Hexadecimal notation. On the author's system this is what is output from the SQL statement:

Select Rowid from CustomerBirthdays;

ROWID
AABBQFAAHAAAD/TAAA
AABBQFAAHAAAD/TAAB
AABBQFAAHAAAD/TAAC
AABBQFAAHAAAD/TAAD
AABBQFAAHAAAD/TAAE

Thankfully we mere mortals do not to understand this! But we need to be aware that this is how Oracle maps a logical row to a physical position on a disk. However, this information is not stored with the row data; rather it is used by the DBMS to locate a row on a disk when required.

When the data in a row is stored the row has a header which indicates the number of columns in the row, and also points to other data blocks if there is chaining involved (see below). Our row might look something like Fig. 3.3.

This row is then stored in a **data-block**. The data block is a logical concept. It is basically a pot which stores rows, or other objects—a collection of 1 s and 0 s. The link with the physical disk is that a data block size will be a multiple of the physical OS block size. In other words, if the OS block size was 4 k, and the data block was 8 k, when the disk head is sent to read some data from the disk, it will read two consecutive OS blocks before it has read an Oracle data block. Data-block size is set during database creation using the DB_BLOCK_SIZE parameter, and once set it has to remain that size.

Rows are inserted into a data block from the bottom, as in Fig. 3.4.

It is important to note that any deleted row will remain in the data-block, and just be marked as deleted so that it does not appear in any queries. The space will only be reused when new rows are inserted and can be fitted into the space left by the deletion.

Each block has a header which describes the contents and which Oracle uses when locking rows as part of a write. The rest of the block is then either "freespace" or data. Leaving free space in a data block is deliberate. Imagine our Birthday example above. We could decide to populate the table with a series of inserts, like this:

```
Insert into CustomerBirthdays(CustomerNo, CustomerFirst, CustomerLast) Values (125, 'Trevor', 'Jones' );
Insert into CustomerBirthdays(CustomerNo, CustomerFirst, CustomerLast) Values (127, 'William', 'Jones' );
```

Note that there is no Birthday recorded, but this is still a valid row and would be stored in a data block, one row straight after the other. If we did this enough times we would fill the data block and subsequent rows would need to be in another data block. The problem with that is that we can't guarantee that the next data block will be physically located next to the first one, and that might mean the OS might need to do multiple reads, slowing up any queries.

So, we have a block full of rows like this, when we suddenly get to find out what the customers' birthdays are. We do an SQL update statement, but because the row resides in a full data-block Oracle will have to place this extra information in another data-block. Again, this could result in needless extra reads, slowing down any queries.

So the free space is kept in a data-block so that rows can expand if need-be. Of course, too much free space means you are wasting HDD space. Too little means you are more likely to need to extend a row to another data-block.

Once a data-block has insufficient free space to store an update, the row just has to be split across two data-blocks. This is called chaining.

3.3.1   Row Chaining and Migration

Sometimes, such as when the contents of a row are bigger than the data-block size, Oracle just has to use more than one data-block to store the data. This also happens when an update is bigger than the free space left in the original data-block. The early part of the row will be stored in the first data-block; there will then be a pointer to another data-block where more of the row is stored. This is known as chaining. If this isn't big enough, the chain can continue growing until the data is stored.

If a row grows too big to fit in a data-block, but can fit into another data-block Oracle may migrate the row to a new data-block to eliminate the chaining cause by the update.

3.3.2   Non-relational Databases

As we will see in later chapters not all databases are relational, and they may well store data in a different way. As an extreme example, MongoDB has no schema, and you can write data of any size however you wish. Data is not stored in tables. But for now, let us just concentrate on RDBMSs.

3.4   How Logical Data Structures Map to Physical

When we design our relational databases we tend to think in terms of rows, columns and tables. As we have seen above, these are all logical structure, not physical. But there does have to be a mapping between those structures and the permanent storage. Again, different RDBMSs use different terms, but have similar approaches. In
   Oracle terms the key elements in a logical hierarchy are:
   Data blocks store the actual data, or indexes, or other objects.
   The many data-blocks that represent the table, index, or other object, reside in a logical container called a **Segment**. If segments need to grow, then physical disk space needs to be acquired. This is managed at the **tablespace** level, since the tablespace is supported by one or more data (OS) files.
   Several tablespaces make up a database. This can be represented as in Fig. 3.5.

3.5   Control, Redo and Undo

We now move from the actual data to some of the supporting aspects of the RDBMS's processes.
   Databases are designed with the realisation that things do go wrong with technology. The chapter on Availability explores this in more detail, but dealing with failures is so central to making a database robust that there are elements of the systems that are in place only as fall-backs, just in case something goes wrong.
   Remembering that the "current" status of the database will include a mix of data on a HDD and in dirty buffers, the first thing the database will want is some way of knowing when a database was last consistent; that is when all the data changes were written to disk. Put another way, it is the point just before the oldest dirty buffer in memory. This information is very important at shut-down so that all data is saved before exit, and during any recovery situation after a database failure.
   To manage this process Oracle uses a System Change Number (SCN). This gets incremented by every transaction that changes the state of the database after a commit. It is managed within the SGA and just keeps incrementing for ever. In this way Oracle can discover what order events took place in. This is important during a restore and recovery of a failed database, for example. The Checkpoint process we

discussed earlier writes information about the SCN into a binary file called the Control File. This is so important to Oracle that it is suggested you have more than two duplicates, preferably each on a different HDD in case of disk failure.

In order to ensure that no committed data is ever lost, Oracle keeps a log of every change made to any data-block. These are called the Redo Logs. They contain change vectors to enable any changes made to be replayed should the need occur, for example in a recovery scenario. The change vector is written BEFORE the commit is actioned. This means that if the user gets confirmation that their commit has been processed, the data post-commit can be replaced even if it was not written to disk before the instance failed.

Redo logs are clearly an important part of ensuring robustness. Again, Oracle allows these files to be multiplexed, that is two or more identical copies of log are automatically updated in separate locations to guard against a disk failure on the disk containing the Redo Log.

The default operation for Redo Logs is that they are circular, in other words, data is written until the log is full, and then it keeps on writing over the previous data. The length of time data is stored for will clearly depend upon how big the Redo Log file is, and how many transactions happen in any given period.

When an instance fails the process is that you go to the last back-up and restore from it. You then "replay" the changes as stored in the Redo Log. If those changes are not recorded for any period between the back-up and now, you will only be able to run with the database as it was backed-up—potentially forcing irate users to replicate the work they did over the missing days. If this is likely to be a problem, then you need to save the data in the Redo Log before it gets overwritten. This is called archiving, and a back-up plus a fully archived Redo Log means you can restore a database to any point in time you require.

Oracle also maintains UNDO information, not to be confused with Redo. Undo is the mechanism for allowing the user to issue the Rollback command—in other words, to undo the changes they have made, and it does so by storing the old data values. The other important task for Undo is to allow for multiple users to be able to read the database in a read-consistent way. This means that, by using the Undo data, snapshots of data as at a point in time can be created, meaning that users are not blocked from accessing the data by other users who are making changes.

3.6 Log and Trace Files

As Oracle completes tasks or encounters error it writes out information to an Alert Log. This is a text file which is constantly being written to (and so can grow quite large). Being a text file, it can be read even if the database is down. Oracle will put the file in the directory specified by the BACKGROUND_DUMP_DEST parameter.

Figure 3.6 contains some Alert Log content. As well as being readable in a text editor, you can also access it through the GUI management tool, Enterprise Manager.

3.7   Stages of Start-up and Shutdown

With so many structures and processes to manage, it is perhaps not surprising that starting an instance is not as simple as hitting an on/off switch. Not only do a lot of things have to be in place for an instance to be usable, but there may be circumstances when a DBA wants the database to be available for maintenance, but not for users to access.

The start-up stages can be transparent to the DBA if they simply type the STARTUP command. The output at the terminal simply describes a successful start- up:

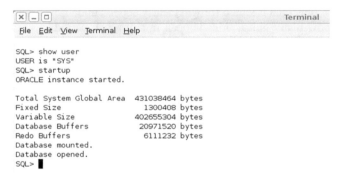

The stages shown above are:

1. The instance has started—in other words, the program is running.
2. The required memory structures have been acquired by the instance.
3. Then, remembering that in Oracle terms the database is what is stored on disk, we are told that the disks have been mounted—in other words the instance can talk to the disks.
4. Finally, the database is made available to users.

Although it is not obvious from these messages, the first thing Oracle tries to do is read the initialisation parameters from an initialisation file which is stored in a platform-specific location. This file contains the default settings for Oracle's start-up parameters, including the locations of important files and the database name. If you want to see what the parameters have been set to, whilst at the SQL> prompt in SQLPLUS, logged in as SYS, type; SHOW PARAMETERS.

   Instead of issuing the STARTUP command, a DBA can issue the STARTUP
NOMOUNT command. This starts the instance and creates the memory structures
but does not mount the disks or open the database for users. More likely, however,
is the STARTUP MOUNT command. This means the DBA has an instance talking
to disks, but no users are able to attach, so that maintenance can be carried out.
After the work is completed the database can be opened by issuing the
ALTER DATABASE OPEN command.
   Closing the database is also a staged affair, but there are extra complications
which are around what happens to anyone using the database when the SHUT-
DOWN command is issued. The steps are the reverse of a start-up, and the reassurance messages tell us exactly what is happening:

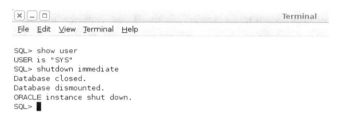

   In the example above the DBA issued the SHUTDOWN IMMEDIATE command. This will close all open sessions and rolls back all uncommitted transactions.
There are several other SHUTDOWN options. SHUTDOWN NORMAL waits for
transactions to finish and users to log off. This can take hours and despite being
called NORMAL, is therefore not used that often.
   If you want to be kinder to the user, but not wait for hours, you can issue the
SHUTDOWN TRANSACTIONAL which waits for transactions to complete and
then logs users off.

3.8   Locking

Whilst the database is open users will be accessing the rows from a variety of
tables. Whilst each of them is reading the rows we do not have a problem. If the row
data is in the shared memory, we can simply send a copy of it off to the user.
   Problems start to occur in multi-user databases when more than one person tries
to write data to the same physical part of a disk. Let us look at a few examples for
the sample CUSTOMERBIRTHDAYS table we described earlier.
   Example A Two separate users want to add new rows to this table. This is not a
problem for Oracle since it operates Row level locking rather than table level
locking. Multiple rows can therefore be added at any time. This assumes that the
primary key used by both is indeed a unique identifier.

Example B One user is writing data to the table whilst a separate user wants to read some rows from that table. Again, not a problem for Oracle since it always ensures that Writers can't block Readers. To make sure the data the reader sees is always as it was at the moment, they issue the SELECT, Oracle will use the Undo data to provide read consistency if another user changes row data at the same time.

Example C Both users are wanting to update the same row at about the same time. This is where the problems start. At the moment that the first UPDATE statement is seen by Oracle, issued by User_1, it places a lock on the data contained in the row. No other user can now access that row to update it, at least until a commit is issued, at which point the lock is released. User_2 then obtains ownership of the lock on the row, and no-one else can gain access to that row until the User_2 commits.

The potential problem in Example C is that User_2 might have to wait hours if User_1 doesn't issue a commit. This situation might well end up with the DBA being called by USER_2, and then User_1 would need to be contacted and asked to commit or rollback, or their session could be killed by the dba to release the lock, causing them to lose their changes.

The worst case variation on Example C is called a deadlock. This happens when both User_1 and User_2 have an unresolvable need for a lock to be released. Take the CUSTOMERBIRTHDAYS example and the input of the two users:

User_1	User_2	Time
Update CUSTOMERBIRTHDAYS SET CustomerFirst = 'John' WHERE CustomerNo = 5 ;	Update CUSTOMERBIRTHDAYS SET CustomerLast = 'Villa' WHERE CustomerNo = 7 ;	12:00:00
Update CUSTOMERBIRTHDAYS SET CustomerFirst = 'Ricardo' WHERE CustomerNo = 7 ;	Update CUSTOMERBIRTHDAYS SET CustomerLast = 'Smyth' WHERE CustomerNo = 5 ;	12:05:00

Since both users are waiting for access to a row that will never be granted, this conflict can't be resolved in any way other than for one of the transactions to be rolled-back. The way to make deadlocks less likely is to commit often, and have all users commit often.

3.9 Moving Data

The need to move data around is not new and will be with us while ever there are different DBMSs. We need to move data internally, between systems for example: when exchanging data between disparate information systems; moving from an OLTP system to a Data Warehouse or upgrading legacy systems.

Externally too, data needs to be moved between organisations: to and from suppliers; to and from customers; to and from a variety of government agencies.

Often this movement is enabled by dumping data from the source database, storing it in a file of some description, and then sending that file to the server running the target database, which then reads the file and inserts the data into one or more of its tables.

Traditionally the file used was a Comma Separated Variable (CSV) file. Occasionally there would be a TSV (Tab Separated Variable). In both of these the record runs from column one until the end-of-line marker, and each field in that record is separated from the previous one by a comma (or tab) character. Here is an example of three rows from the CUSTOMERBIRTHDAYS table stored in a file called Newcustomers.csv:

```
14, Raj, Patel
17, Maurice, Ravel
19, Boris, Jackson
```

At the target end a program with a couple of loops in it iterates through the file looking for the end-of-line marker, and then breaking that line up by looking for the next comma. This sort of programming is bread and butter for most DBAs and this simplicity meant that CSVs became the de facto standard way of passing data between databases.

In more recent times XML has become a common means for moving data between systems. It has the additional benefit of being readable by a browser, and so more understandable to the human reader, but because of the repeated data description tags these files can become very large. If this becomes an issue, there is also a compacted version known as Binary XML.

Database vendors recognised a need and produced tools to help. In Oracle there is an exceedingly powerful tool called SQLLoader, which can bring data in from a variety of formats and map the fields being read in directly to columns in the target table on the fly by automatically creating a series of SQL insert commands. The user no longer has to write any code but does have to create a control file which tells Oracle how to do the reading and mapping. An example of such a file, which reads the above CSV and inserts the data into the appropriate table would be:

```
OPTIONS (ERRORS=999)
LOAD DATA
INFILE "f:\tutorials\moving\Newcustomers.csv"
BADFILE "f:\tutorials\moving\Newcustomers.bad"
INSERT
INTO TABLE CUSTOMERBIRTHDAYS
FIELDS TERMINATED BY ',' OPTIONALLY ENCLOSED BY ' " '
(
CUSTOMERNO, CUSTOMERFIRST, CUSTOMERLAST
)
```

The INFILE is the location of the incoming CSV file, the BADFILE is where Oracle puts any records that error. Then Oracle is told to INSERT records into the table mapping the first field to CustomerNo, second to CustomerFirst, and so on.

The options at the top tells Oracle to keep processing even when it encounters errors, and only stop if it encounters more than 999. You would save this into a file called something like Newcustomers.con and then pass that filename as a parameter when calling the SQLLoader executable from the command line:

```
$sqlldr userid=peter/pword control=Newcustomer.con
```

Whilst this may seem a little messy, it is certainly easier than writing code from scratch. And the beauty of SQLLoader is that it can accept data in lots of different formats. Another common medium, for example, is the Fixed Length file, where the fields within the record are always at a certain position in a file.

3.10   Import and Export

There are sometimes occasions when we need to take a subset of the database and move it to another database. This is often referred to as Exporting and Importing the data. We need to be cautious with the terms Import and Export, however, since different vendors use the words slightly differently. In Oracle parlance and Export of data is a collection of objects, like Tables and Procedures, saved to an external file. The file is not human-readable and is in such a format that only an Oracle Import would be able to deal with it.

As an example, let us Export the CUSTOMERBIRTHDAYS table to a file which we will call BDAY.DMP, which then could be imported to another Oracle database elsewhere.

As with SQLLoader this process involves calling an executable from the command line and passing a parameter which points to a control file, here known as a parameter file (PARFILE):

```
$EXP peter/pword PARFILE=expparams.par
```

The contents of the parameter file expparams.par might look something like this:

```
FILE="f:\mydata\bday.dmp"
TABLES=(CUSTOMERBIRTHDAYS)
GRANTS=y
INDEXES=y
ROWS=y
TRIGGERS=y
```

This reads the table CUSTOMERBIRTHDAYS and also permissions granted against that table; and indexes connected with that table; all the data (ROWS = n would give you just the table definition); and any triggers associated with the table.

At the target database all the DBA would need to type would be:

```
$imp peter/pword FILE=bday.dmp
```

Ms Access on the other hand allows you to pick a format to export to, including. CSV format. It also allows you to Import from a variety of formats.

3.10.1 Data Is Important

When dealing with actual data it is all too easy to forget that each row is potentially as important as the others. Our task has to be not only to move the data, but to move it accurately.

Think of a situation where you transfer a row from one system to another using any of the methods alluded to above. Perhaps the count of inserted rows does not exactly equal the count of rows exported. And perhaps a particularly slovenly DBA doesn't notice and declares the data safely transferred. But what if the missing row was in the Allergies table of a medical database and it holds the information that Patient X is allergic to penicillin? Now imagine that Patient X is administered penicillin and then dies after a severe allergic reaction. How would you feel if you were that DBA?

Data can be a matter of life and death, but even in less severe circumstances it is likely to be important and we have a duty to look after it appropriately.

In some circumstances the data we are provided with is itself unclean. We therefore need to ensure we understand the data we are dealing with and that when it completes its journey it is a valid and exact representation of the information being stored. However, it is not a DBA's job to guess what unclean data should be. Data cleansing should be carried out cautiously and with the approval of the owner of the data.

3.11 Distributed Databases

Up until this point we have been thinking in terms of our data being stored in one place. As we have seen it is entirely probable that a large enterprise database will use many individual HDDs to make a permanent record of the data. For availability reasons (see Chap. 10) there may be some identical data stored on another system, maybe in a geographically distant location, but those individual HDDs are really just parts of a single, central database accessed by all users.

Imagine, however, that we work in an organisation with three offices: one in Chennai (India), one in Perth (Australia), and one in Reykjavik (Iceland). Each collects data about its customers in their part of the world. The company happens to be Icelandic, so the head office is in Reykjavik.

One solution in this case would be to have a single Server running in Reykjavik and for the other offices to connect into that server in the normal client/server fashion. But what if the people in Chennai want to collect slightly different information about their customers to people in the other offices? In that case, with a single server system the schema would have to be made flexible enough to cope with the differences. And what if the office in Perth wants to add a column to one of the tables? Changing schemas can cause problems, but the people in Perth may think it worth the risk, whereas the others may not.

Distributed databases can get around these problems of data ownership by allowing each local office to maintain its own database using a local version of the DBMS, whilst also running a Distributed DBMS (DDBMS) which, at a meta level, allows some users to see the database as the sum of all three.

For clarity, we will here define a distributed database as:

More than one logically interrelated database elements which are connected by a computer network, and are typically in different geographic locations.

What this means is that the SQL statement:

```
select customer_name from customers;
```

will return all the customer names from all offices for the user of the DDBMS, but for the local DBMS user, they would see only a list of customer from their region.

And the benefits are not just about allowing local flexibility. Bandwidth and network communications can be more problematic across great distances. In the centralised solution, if the Perth office loses access to the internet it loses access to the system, whereas if they are connecting to the local version, they may well be able to carry on working.

As we see in the chapter about Scalability, relational databases can begin to slow when storing large numbers of rows. A distributed database like the one we are discussing here could greatly help performance by spreading the storage load around the individual sites. Moreover, when the DDBMS is asked to gather rows from all the local systems, the fact that the select statement is being run on three different servers means that we automatically get a degree of parallel processing which could speed up the return of the data.

There are, naturally, downsides to opting for a distributed solution, not least of which is the added complexity of such a system. A central resource looked after by a single team of experts may be seen as easier and less expensive than having three teams, especially as there also needs to be some effort put into the gluing together of the various elements of the overall database. You could also argue that, because there are more remote access points, a distributed database is more vulnerable to security problems.

Distributed is not the same as replicated. As we see in the Availability chapter having data on different servers replicated can help with Disaster Recovery and can allow parallel processing of queries to enhance performance. The downside is the extra overhead involved in keeping the different systems in step, with each having the same consistent data. Waiting for consistency can occur because of networking problems and the user will see this as poor performance or a lack of robustness.

The distributed model has come to the fore in recent years with the advent of the Internet first, and then of Cloud computing. These days data can be spread over thousands of servers all around the globe, and the need to query that amount of information caused lots of headaches using traditional technology. The problems became very apparent to Google when they were trying to search for and retrieve information from across the Web.

In the end they went back to basics and created their own file handling system to be able to cope with the particular needs of their search engine which has to work in a highly distributed environment (data is stored all over the world) and with extremely large volumes of data. They called their system GFS (Google File System), and it remains proprietary, but, as we see in the Big Data chapter, Hadoop is an open source equivalent and it has become the de facto solution to this sort of problem in the last couple of years.

One of the important drivers in this change was the realisation that it takes up less computing resource to move the data processing than it does to move the data itself, especially when we are talking about such large volumes.

In the Hadoop version of distributed databases, the data is chunked up and distributed to a number of nodes (which will be commodity servers). The Hadoop equivalent to GFS is called HDFS and it looks after the distribution of these chunks of data across the nodes. As well as managing this sharing out of the data, the Master node also decides how to replicate the chunks on other nodes to assist with availability by building in redundancy.

HDFS is designed to cope with large blocks of data, usually of at least 64 Mb in size. The downside to this is that it is not good at handling many small files. On top of this it is optimised for write-once read-many type applications. In short, whilst it does answer the problem of querying large collections of distributed data, it is not suitable for other types of application.

When the user makes a request for data the Hadoop master node will establish which nodes contain the data and instruct the Hadoop slaves on those nodes to process the request and return the data. In this way the data is not moved at all before retrieval and processing is carried out in the most efficient way possible.

Many database vendors, such as Oracle and SAP now include Hadoop in their portfolios, and there is little doubt that there will continue to be a strong demand for this solution as we see digital data continue to expand exponentially in the next few years.

Figure 3.6 contains some Alert Log content. As well as being readable in a text editor, you can also access it through the GUI management tool, Enterprise Manager.

Fig. 3.1 The SQL query
process

3.12 Summary

This chapter has discussed the key physical building blocks of memory, processors and disks in database systems. We explored how the limitations of those fallible components have led to the development of performance and availability focused additions to database management systems. We looked at the mechanisms involved in starting and stopping a modern client/server database, and the processing steps required to respond to a user's request for data.

We have also seen that there are different approaches available in terms of the ways data is stored and in the ways we choose to move data about between systems. We looked at the differences between client/server and distributed databases and explored their relative strengths and weaknesses.

3.13 Review Questions

The answers to these questions can be found in the text of this chapter.

- Why does Oracle prefer to return data to a user from the Shared Pool rather than read it from disk?
- What is the purpose of the Redo Logs?
- What does row chaining mean and what causes it?
- When does a deadlock occur and what is a good way of reducing the risk of one occurring?
- What types of application are not suited to running on Hadoop?

Column Name	Data Type
CUSTOMERNO	NUMBER
CUSTOMERFIRST	VARCHAR2(30)
CUSTOMERLAST	VARCHAR2(30)
BIRTHDAY	DATE

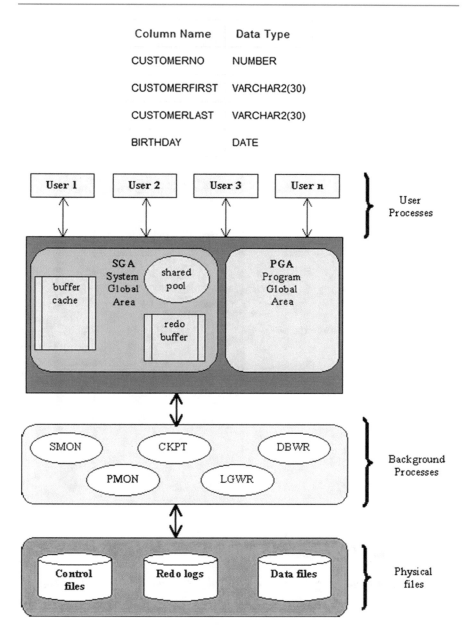

Fig. 3.2 Oracle Instance

Fig. 3.3 Row structure

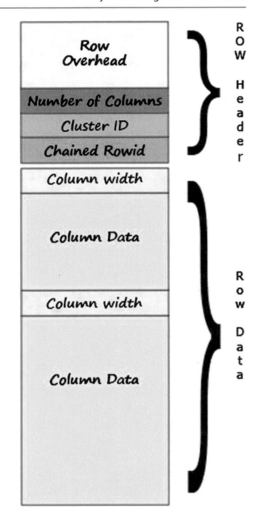

3.14   Group Work Research Activities

These activities require you to research beyond the contents of the book and can be tackled individually or as a discussion group.

Discussion Topic 1 The company you work for has just acquired another company. You are asked to look at ways to quickly retrieve data from the acquired company's Oracle based systems. Discuss the alternative approaches you might take, listing the potential benefits and weaknesses of each approach, and clearly state any assumptions you make.

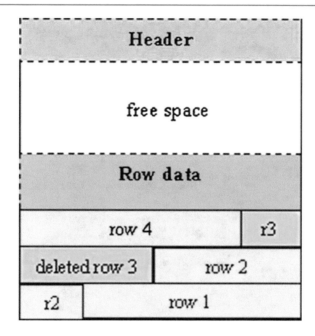

Fig. 3.4 Data block architecture

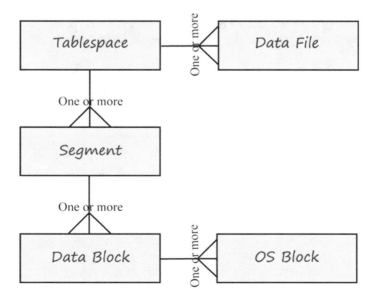

Fig. 3.5 Logical to physical mapping

```
[ alert_orcl.log  ✕ ]
Wed Apr 03 14:11:18 2013
Stopping background process VKTM: |
Wed Apr 03 14:11:21 2013
Instance shutdown complete
Sat Jun 15 17:20:22 2013
Starting ORACLE instance (normal)
LICENSE_MAX_SESSION = 0
LICENSE_SESSIONS_WARNING = 0
Picked latch-free SCN scheme 2
Using LOG_ARCHIVE_DEST_1 parameter default value as /u01/app/oracle/product/11.1.0/orcl/dbs/arch
Using LOG_ARCHIVE_DEST_10 parameter default value as USE_DB_RECOVERY_FILE_DEST
Autotune of undo retention is turned on.
IMODE=BR
ILAT =18
LICENSE_MAX_USERS = 0
SYS auditing is disabled
Starting up ORACLE RDBMS Version: 11.1.0.6.0.
Using parameter settings in server-side spfile /u01/app/oracle/product/11.1.0/orcl/dbs/spfileorcl.ora
System parameters with non-default values:
  processes              = 150
  memory_target          = 412M
  control_files          = "/u01/app/oracle/oradata/orcl/control01.ctl"
  control_files          = "/u01/app/oracle/oradata/orcl/control02.ctl"
  control_files          = "/u01/app/oracle/oradata/orcl/control03.ctl"
  db_block_size          = 8192
  compatible             = "11.1.0.0.0"
  db_recovery_file_dest  = "/u01/app/oracle/flash_recovery_area"
  db_recovery_file_dest_size= 2G
  fast_start_mttr_target = 25
  undo_tablespace        = "UNDOTBS1"
  remote_login_passwordfile= "EXCLUSIVE"
  db_domain              = "localdomain"
```

Fig. 3.6   Alert Log contents

Discussion Topic 2 Five years have passed since the other company was acquired
and still key systems are not working well together. Some of the problems are
around networking issues and the wide geographic divide between the two head
offices.

You are asked to propose a new database design from scratch. Discuss the
comparative benefits and problems of adopting a distributed approach with
adopting a single, central client/server system.

Reference

New Scientist Quantum World Topic Guide. https://www.newscientist.com/article/2220968-its-
    official-google-has-achieved-quantum-supremacy/#ixzz6iJPIzmc5

Part II
Database Types

Relational Databases

4

What the reader will learn:

- The Origins and terminology of relational databases
- Database design—normalisation
- Database design—entity modelling
- Moving from design to implementation
- The basics of Structured Query Language

4.1 Origins

No discussion of relational databases would be complete without a reference to Edgar Codd's 1970 paper "A Relational Model of Data for Large Shared Data Banks". This was a mathematical description of what we now call Relational databases and operations to manipulate them. This is called relational algebra. Codd considered data could be organised into relations consisting of tuples, each with consistent attributes. A tuple containing 6 attributes would be called a 6-tuple. Most database professionals would translate this as meaning data can be organised into tables consisting of records (or rows), each with consistent attributes (see Fig. 4.1).

It is not intended to give a description of relational algebra here, but for those who want more information see Date (2005), Chap. 5.

Each record (or tuple) in a table is uniquely identified by a primary key which is stored as an attribute or combination of attributes. For example a key could consist of name, street, house number and postcode that could be put together to uniquely identify a person (assuming two people with the same name do not live at the same address). However, the key is more commonly an attribute created specifically for the purpose of uniquely identifying a record, its name often ending in -ID. A quick glance of my own data reveals I have many unique identifiers—my National Insurance Number, my employee ID number, my library ID, my driving licence

© Springer Nature Switzerland AG 2021
K. Domdouzis et al., *Concise Guide to Databases*, Undergraduate Topics in Computer Science, https://doi.org/10.1007/978-3-030-42224-0_4

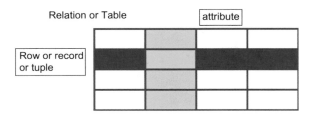

Fig. 4.1 Relational nomenclature

number and my bank account number are but a small selection of all the unique identifiers associated with me.

As well as describing the structure of the data, Codd also described a number of operations which could be performed on it. These included selection, projection and joins between tables. Selection and joins are common terminology in databases, but projection defines conditions on the data you want to retrieve, for example people with an age greater than 18.

Ultimately these operations were formalised into a structured query language or SQL. This was released in 1979 by what was to become Oracle Corporation.

4.2   Normalisation

Normalisation is a bottom-up approach to database design concentrating on attributes and dependencies. Edgar Codd introduced the concept of normalisation. The primary aim of normalisation is to remove data redundancy, specifically repeating data in a single record. This reduced storage space and increased performance as duplicated data was kept to a minimum and only used to connect tables together.

A good example of why this is important can be seen by looking at the invoice in Fig. 4.2. At first glance this could be regarded as a single record and in paper filing systems it was often treated that way. However, retrieving information from it was difficult and a series of indexing systems were developed. For example, there was often a card index with customer details record in it. This information changed very rarely but was a quick method of finding customers details.

The problem with documents like delivery notes, invoices and purchase orders is they consist of data which is from three or more separate tables. For example, there is the customer information. This appears on every invoice for that customer. Secondly there is what the customer ordered—this repeats—just look at your supermarket bill. You don't want to store all this information every time you create a new delivery note, so you store it separately and develop relationships between it. Once repeating data is removed, you have your records in first normal form.

So, if we look in detail at Fig. 4.2 we see that although it is a single physical record it contains information about:

BETTER BOOKS AND BARGAINS
PO Box 2314
London SW3 5JK

Invoice for	**Billing Address**	**Shipping Address**
Your order of 11/12/12	Paul Crowther	Paul Crowther
Invoice ID 2134-5454398	8 Mien Pl	C/- Loxley University
Customer ID 5417- 678U	Sheffield S6 9JH	Loxley LO1 5XC
Invoice date 11/12/12		

Qty	Code	Item Description	Price	Vat	Total
1	9781906040130	Memory of Flames Armond Cabasson	£7.50	20%	£9.00
1	9781906040376	Strangled in Paris Claude Izner	£7.50	20%	£9.00
		Pack and post	£3.00		£3.00
		Total			£21.00

Fig. 4.2 A typical delivery note included with goods in an on-line purchase

- Invoice
- Customer
- Stock item (often called a line item).

Because this is a company system there is no need to store information about the company (there would only be a single record!)

Although you can divide the data into these separate tables you need a means of linking them together. So, to tell which customer an invoice belongs to you need to store something that identified them. These days that tends to be an identification number or ID whereas in the past it was more likely to be name and address. Earlier I mentioned how many different ID's were associated with me. How any ID numbers do you think you have associated with you? Each one of these will be specific to some system and you may be generating new ones every day when you are shopping on-line. Try making a list.

4.2.1 First Normal Form (1NF)

Normalisation requires you to go through a series of well-defined steps. First, remove repeating groups and create a new table to store these attributes. Include a link to the table you have removed it from in the form of the key item. This will be the foreign key. The main reason for removing repeating groups is to make sure you don't end up with variable length records.

It is necessary to identify a primary key to uniquely identify records in the repeating group you have removed. Sometimes you may have to invent one, either for uniquely identifying a record, or because the combination of other attributes is cumbersome. For example, if an invoice number did not exist, you could use a combination of the invoice date and billing name to uniquely identify an invoice (although this only works if a customer has a maximum of one invoice a day).

There may be more than one unique identifier—in this case you have candidate keys and you need to choose the most appropriate one. Sometimes it is a combination of attributes. In the example, the Invoice ID is a unique identifier for the invoice. The repeating group is the attributes of the items which were ordered on the invoice—often called line items. In this case the unique identifier is the code (which just happens to be the International Standard Book Number—ISBN). So you know which invoice the line item belongs to, you need to include that as part of the primary key. You then end up with a compound key consisting of Invoice ID and Code. Invoice ID is also a foreign key giving a link back to the invoice the line item relates to. The 2 new tables are therefore:

Invoice

- Order date
- Invoice ID (PK)
- Invoice Date
- Customer ID
- Billing Name
- Billing address
- Shipping Name
- Shipping Address

Line Item

- Invoice ID (PK, FK)
- Code (PK)
- Qty
- Item Description Price
- VAT
- Total

4.3   Second Normal Form (2NF)

Remove data that is only dependent on part of primary key (if there is no compound key, it is probably already in 2NF) and create a new table. What you want is for every non-key attribute to be dependent on the whole key.

In this case much of the Line item is only dependent on the code, so Line item gets decomposed into Line Item and Stock Item: If you didn't do this you would have to store the item description, price and VAT multiple times—once every time it was included on an invoice—a very bad use of storage. The Line Item table therefore becomes 2 tables with the code giving the link (foreign key) to the new Stock Item table:

Line Item

- Invoice ID (PK, FK)
- Code (PK, FK)
- Qty
- Total

Stock Item

- Code (PK)
- Item
- Description Price
- VAT

4.4   Third Normal Form (3NF)

Remove any data that is dependent on a non-key field and create a new table. This happens when there is more than one candidate key and it would be unique. Create a new table with this as the primary key. What you are trying to do here is separate two entities which have become combined. They only appear once on the invoice in this example, but only some of the information contained in the invoice changes with every new invoice.

In the example Name and Address are dependent on the Customer ID, so this can be removed into a new table. The customers details are not going to change very often, so there is no point re-entering and storing them every time a new invoice is created. The Invoice would still need to contain the Customer ID so you would know which customer the invoice related to:

Invoice

- Order date
- Invoice ID (PK)
- Invoice Date
- Customer ID (FK)

Customer

- Customer ID (PK)
- Billing Name
- Billing address
- Shipping Name
- Shipping Address

To achieve third normal form you also remove calculated field. In this case Total can be calculated so you don't need to store it. There are occasions where you might want to store data that can be calculated because of the overhead of doing the calculation is higher than that of storing the calculated value.

In Line item 'Total' can be calculated as you know the quantity, price and VAT, so it can be removed.

Line Item

- Invoice ID (PK, FK)
- Code (PK, FK)
- Qty

It is not unusual to find that once a table is in first normal form, it is also in third normal form. Despite this it is still worth going through the steps.

The end result is there are 4 tables (see Fig. 4.3).

In all of them the tables in Fig. 4.3 all the attributes are fully dependent on the primary key and cannot be decomposed further.

Often this is drawn in as an ER (entity relationship) diagram. It should be noted there are a number of packages available to draw these diagrams. In this chapter they are drawn using Microsoft Visio (Fig. 4.4).

A number of concepts have been introduced in this example. The main one is the idea of a key. There are a number of different types of key. The first is Candidate Key. This is something that uniquely identifies a record. In some cases, there may be more than one, for example in our exercise we had ISBN which uniquely identified an item, but it is possible there could have been a locally used stock code as well. It would be up to the developer to decide which was best to use as the main

Invoice	Customer	Line Item	Stock Item
Order date	Customer ID (PK)	Invoice ID (PK, FK)	Code (PK) Invoice ID (PK)
	Billing Name	Code (PK, FK)	Item Description Invoice Date
	Billing address	Qty	Price
Customer ID (FK)	Shipping Name		VAT
	Shipping Address		

Fig. 4.3 The final tables

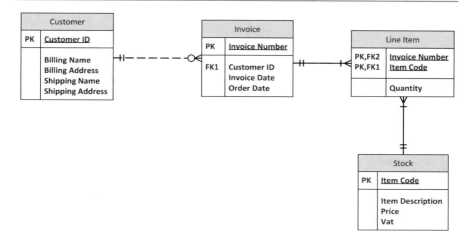

Fig. 4.4 Entity Relationship diagram using crows foot notation to show one to many relationships

identifier of the record. That would become the Primary Key. The second type of Key is the Foreign Key. This provides a link to another table and often has the same name as a primary key in another table. Both primary and foreign keys can be composed of more than attribute. The criteria is they are the minimum needed to uniquely identify a record in the table.

4.5   Beyond Third Normal Form

Most developers stop at third normal form as this resolves most of the issues associated with making data storage and retrieval efficient. However, it can be taken further to reduce other anomalies which can arise around keys, updates and temporal issues.

Bryce-Codd Normal Form (BCNF) deals with multiple overlapping candidate keys. In these a combination of attributes may create a candidate key. A different combination may form another. BCNF is not always achievable because it would mean losing the dependencies determined at third normal form.

Fourth Normal Form (4NF) is concerned with multivalued dependency. This can occur in a table with three or more attributes when all the attributes in a table are part of the composite key. It may in this case be necessary to decompose the table into 2 or more tables.

Consider the following example:

Garage	Speciality	Suburb Served
Speedy Motors	Ford	Nether Edge
Speedy Motors	Ford	Abbeydale
Speedy Motors	Ford	Hunters Bar
Speedy Motors	Volvo	Nether Edge
Speedy Motors	Volvo	Abbeydale
Speedy Motors	Volvo	Hunters Bar
A1 Service Centre	Peugeot	City
A1 Service Centre	Volvo	City
Sid's Super Service Station	Volvo	Nether Edge
Sid's Super Service Station	Volvo	Abbeydale
Sid's Super Service Station	Peugeot	Abbeydale

Each of the attributes of Garage, Speciality and Suburb Served are key values and form a composite key in third normal form, however the garage's speciality is not affected by the suburb served, so this table should be split into two as the speciality is dependent on the garage and the suburb served is dependent on the garage. As a result we end up with two tables:

Garage_Speciality

Garage	Speciality
Speedy Motors	Ford
Speedy Motors	Volvo
A1 Service Centre	Peugeot
A1 Service Centre	Volvo
Sid's Super Service Station	Volvo
Sid's Super Service Station	Peugeot

Garage_Region

Garage	Suburb Served
Speedy Motors	Nether Edge
Speedy Motors	Abbeydale
Speedy Motors	Hunters Bar
A1 Service Centre	City
Sid's Super Service Station	Nether Edge
Sid's Super Service Station	Abbeydale

Fifth Normal Form (5NF) is again related to multivalued dependency. A table is said to be in the 5NF if and only if every join dependency in it is implied by the candidate keys. Rarely does a 4NF table not be in 5NF.

Sixth Normal Form (6NF) relates to temporal databases and is intended to reduce database components into irreducible components. In the example database there is a problem with stock item. If the price of the item changes, the resulting change would be applied to all historical invoices which is clearly incorrect. Likewise, VAT can vary, and this will be independent of price. There therefore needs to be extra tables containing historical price data with the item code and the date they were effective. This would also create a join to the invoice table.

A disadvantage of normalisation, particularly among novice database designers is that it provides a cookbook approach which can be followed without any understanding of the individual attributes and their relationships to one another. Another issue is that of the performance hit caused by joins. In the current era where memory and disk space is relatively cheap denormalised forms such as those found in NoSQL (Chap. 5) and in-memory databases (Chap. 8) may be preferred for speed.

4.6   Entity Modelling

An alternative approach to developing a logical design of a database is to identify entities in the system and then map the relationships between them. This raises a number of issues, the first of which is how do we identify entities and secondly which ones are within the domain of the system.

4.7   Use Case Modelling

Use Cases are one part of the Unified Modelling Language (UML) which, although designed for object oriented systems (see Chap. 7), can be used to develop a relational database design. Use Case diagrams are essentially a view of what an external entity (either a user or an interfacing system) want to do with the data.

This allows the designer to work out both what the requirements of the user are and what entities are required in the system.

- **A Use Case** is a statement of functionality required of the software, expressed in the format
- **Actor** Action Subject
- An **Actor** represents a stimulus to the software system. The stimulus can be internal or external.
- An **Action** represents a capability of the software system.
- A **Subject** represents the item acted upon by an Action of the software system.

Fig. 4.5 Use case diagram

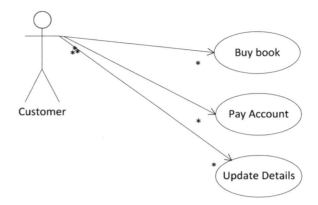

In the following example we may want to have a customer as an on-line user (Fig. 4.5).

From this we can identify a number of entities: Customer, Book (which could be generalised to stock' and account. Investigation of 'Details' would identify a number of attributes of the customer.

What we are identifying here are regular entities which will be transformed into tables. Once these have been established, attributes can be investigated. Many will be simple attributes, but others will be composite attributes, For example Name, and address are both composite attributes. Name consists of Surname and given name (there is a decision to be made as to how many given names are to be stored—anything above 1 may be blank or null).

Occasionally a multivalued attribute may be identified, for example in an employee table you might want to store qualifications. In this case a new table should be created using Employee-ID and Qualification as a composite key. Other attributes may include year obtained and institution.

The example above is also an example of a weak entity. That means it does not have an independent existence. If the employee gets deleted, then the associated records in the qualification table also get deleted. Without the employee, to which there is a one to many relationship, they have no meaning.

You also need to be aware of 'heavy' entities. These are entities where there are many null attributes. This may come about because data in one attribute may mean that another attribute must be null. This often happens where the entity is actually a hierarchy of entities. A decision needs to be made as to whether to keep the heavy entity or map it so it reflects the hierarchy. An example of this comes later in this chapter (Fig. 4.6).

Once entities and their attributes have been identified binary relationships should be identified. Initially map one-to-many relationships. In this the item at the 'many' end will include the primary key of the entity at the 'one' end as a foreign key. For example, a customer may have many orders (although an order can only be associated with one customer). In this case the order contains the customer-id as a foreign key.

works #	name	start date	leave date	car reg
w123	sam	1/1/1991	1/1/2008	a123xjz
w456	jill	1/7/2012		
w789	hal	1/1/2013		v21abc

Fig. 4.6 Heavy entity

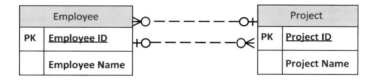

Fig. 4.7 Many-to-many relationship

The more complex part is unravelling many-to-many relationships. For example, an order may contain many stock items, but a stock item may occur on many orders. Many-to-many relationships should not be part of a database design. They are usually resolved by creating an associative entity.

Consider the following situation. An employee may be assigned to several projects and a project may have one or more employees assigned to it (Fig. 4.7).

In this case a new entity called an associative entity needs to be created. The name of this entity will depend on what the database is used for. It may be as simple as 'Employee Assignment', or more complex, like 'Employee Time Tracking' where time spent and the activity could be stored as entities (Fig. 4.8).

In both cases the new entity would have a composite key of Employee_ID and Project-ID (although in rare cases a unique key may be created).

Occasionally you may find you have a three (or more) way many-to-many relationship. For example, many suppliers may supply many parts to many customers.

Also, any supplier can supply any part to any customer. This can be resolved in much the same way as a many-to-many relationship by adding an associative entity. This will have a composite key composed of the primary keys of the customer, supplier and part tables (Fig. 4.9).

Generally this will solve most of the design issues, however there may be times when a number of other issues arise. One of these are unary relationships. The most often quoted example of this (and the one used in standard Oracle exercises) is where one employee is the manager of another employee. In this case a manager

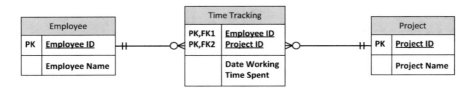

Fig. 4.8 Resolved many-to-many relationship

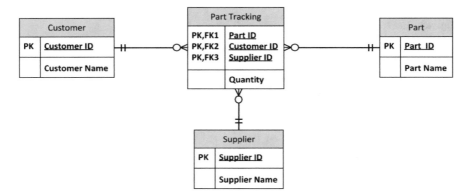

Fig. 4.9 Resolved three-way relationship

Fig. 4.10 Unary relationship
—self join

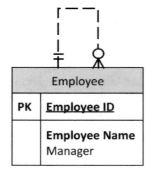

manages many employees, but an employee has only one manager. In practice this means a employee entity has an attribute, probably called 'manager' which is a foreign key pointing back to the same table. Ultimately one or more employees have a null value in this field because they have no manager (they are the top of the organisations hierarchy) (Fig. 4.10).

Rarely, there may be a unary many-to-many relationship. For example, in manufacturing a product may be composed of many parts. Those parts may be used in many products which themselves be a part of another product (Fig. 4.11).

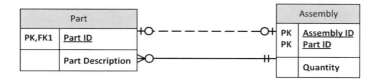

Fig. 4.11 Resolved unary many-to-many relationship

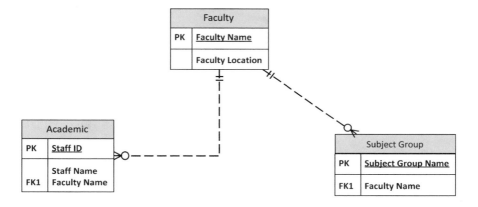

Fig. 4.12 Fan trap

To make this work both the components of the primary key of assembly reference the primary key of part. That way the assembly has a one-to-one relationship with part so the assembly can have a name, but at the same time there is another relationship between assembly and part showing the assembly is made up of many parts.

There are two potential problems when modelling entities, the fan trap and the chasm trap. These situations usually arise because of missing relationships. They can often be identified by going back to the original use case diagrams and testing the relationships to see if the required processes can be achieved (Fig. 4.12).

In the above ER diagram it is not possible for an academic staff member to work out which subject group they are in.

This could be redrawn as Fig. 4.13, but this now gives us a chasm trap as not all staff are in subject groups, but all staff belong to a faculty. The way to resolve the problem is to add the missing relationship (Fig. 4.14).

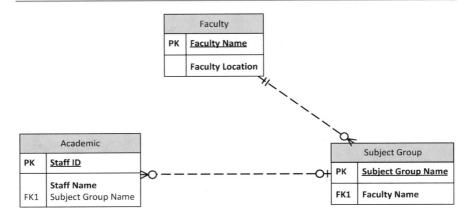

Fig. 4.13 Chasm trap

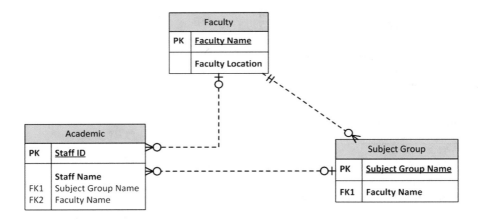

Fig. 4.14 Resolving the traps

The steps in entity modelling are therefore as follows:

(1) Conduct a use case analysis to identify regular entities

   (a) Identify composite attributes
   (b) Identify multivalued attributes
   (c) Map weak entities
   (d) Identity 'heavy' entities and decide on a mapping resolution

(2) Map Binary relationships

  (a) Identify one to many relationships
  (b) Identify Many-to-many relationships
  (c) Map associative entities

(3) Map unary relationships
(4) Check for fan and chasm traps.

4.8   Further Modelling Techniques

With the advent of object oriented modelling, particularly where modellers are using UML toolkits, hierarchy models are sometimes constructed. This makes logical sense, but they can't be directly implemented in a relational model. An object relational database system is the usual way this kind of model is implemented, and this will be discussed in depth in Chap. 7. However, in the current context consider the following simple hierarchy (Fig. 4.15).

There are three ways this could be translated into relational tables:

1. Collapse all the sub types into the super type—the heavy entity approach (Fig. 4.16).

   This has the advantage of creating a very simple structure—a single table. It has the disadvantage that for every record there will be four null fields, in other words we have created a heavy entity. For example if we had a record for a car, the data for a van and a motor bike could be null.

Fig. 4.15 Hierarchy diagram showing superclass (motor vehicle) and three subclasses

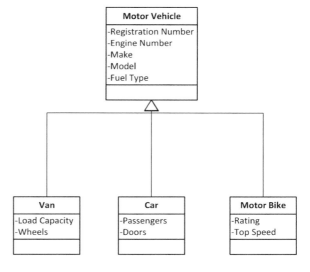

Motor Vehicle	
PK	**Registration Number**
	Engine Number Make Model Fuel Ytpe Year of Manufacture Load Capacity Wheels Passengers Doors Rating Top Speed

Fig. 4.16 Heavy entity approach

Van			Car			Motor Bike	
PK	**Registration Number**		**PK**	**Registration Number**		**PK**	**Registration Number**
	Engine Number Make Model Fuel Ytpe Year of Manufacture Load Capacity Wheels			Engine Number Make Model Fuel Ytpe Year of Manufacture Passengers Doors			Engine Number Make Model Fuel Type Year of Manufacture Rating Top Speed

Fig. 4.17 Attributes moved down into subtypes

This approach is best used where there are more attributes in the super type than in the subtypes.

2. Combine the attributes of the super type with the subtypes (Fig. 4.17).

This has the advantage that every distinct entity is now modelled separately and there are no null fields. The main disadvantage is that relationships start to become complex. For example if we had an entity called owner, each of the above entities would need a foreign key attribute to join to the owner attribute. This approach is best used where the majority of the attributes are in the sub type.

3. Implement the structure by making each of the types an entity in its own right and adding appropriate keys (Fig. 4.18).

This has the advantage of retaining most of the original hierarchy structure with the main disadvantage being the introduction of an extra attribute to allow joining of the tables.

This approach is best used where the number of attributes in all the types is about equal and the structure if the hierarchy wants to be maintained.

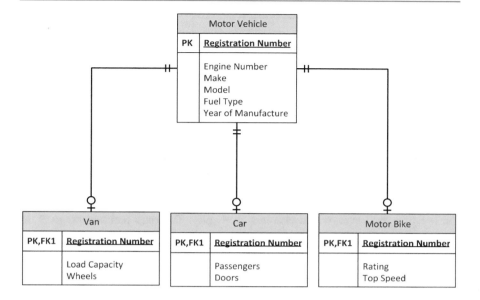

Fig. 4.18 All types mapped as entities

4.9   Notation

In this chapter we have been using the 'crows foot' notation of describing relationships. However many designers (and the packages they use) adopt the UML convention with the cardinality of the relationship expressed at each end. The diagram below shows the equivalences (Fig. 4.19).

A further notation form by Chen (1976) shows entities and relationships using the symbols, shown in Fig. 4.20.

Fig. 4.19 Crows foot
compared to UML notation

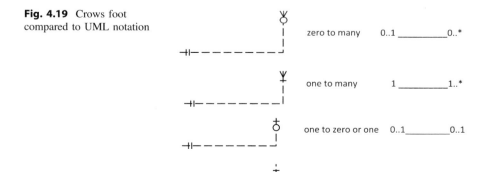

Fig. 4.20 Chen's notation

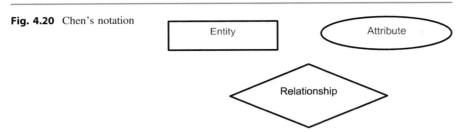

The bookshop example therefore can be redrawn in Chen's notation (Fig. 4.21). This can be compared with the modified entity-relationship diagram shown in Fig. 4.22.

Which the author finds particularly messy and complicated when compared to the notation used everywhere else in this chapter. The only real advantage is the diagram forces you to name relationships.

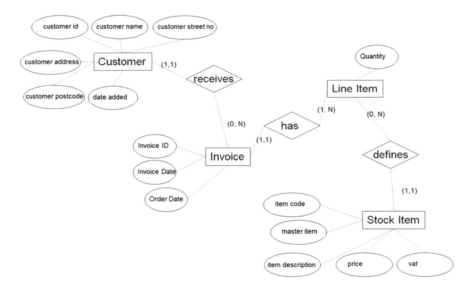

Fig. 4.21 The example using Chen's notation

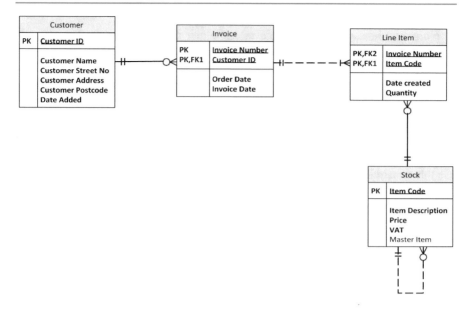

Fig. 4.22 Modified ER diagram

4.10 Converting a Design into a Relational Database

Once you have created your database design using either of the methods mentioned above, you then need to convert it into a physical database. To do this there are some other questions to be answered.

Does any of the design need denormalising? You should look at any 1:1, 1:0 or 1:n relationships, particularly where n is 3 or less. This will reduce the number of tables and hence the complexity of the design. The overhead may mean some attributes with null values.

What are the datatypes that will be used for each of the attributes? This may be a decision influenced by the vendor package. For example, not all RDMS support boolean datatypes. Oracle supports:

CHAR: This is a fixed length datatype which is backfilled if the data stored is less than the field size, or returns and error is the data is longer than the field size.

VARCHAR2: is a variable length data type which is more efficient than CHAR. However, you still need to specify a maximum length and an error will be returned if this is exceeded.

NUMBER: There may be issues with very large and very small numbers. Oracle stores numbers up to 38 significant digits (both positive and negative). This is more than adequate for most applications, but may be an issue if the database is storing scientific data.

Other types include: **DATE, CLOB, BLOB**.

No matter how you develop your tables, either through normalisation or entity modelling, you also need to identify constraints. These will help maintain data integrity.

Primary Key constraint: This is basically identifying the primary key. It means values must be unique and they must not be blank (null).

Foreign Key constraint: Identifies the table the foreign key references.

Not Null constraint: The entity must contain data, in other words it cannot be blank.

Unique constraint: but that does not mean it is a primary key. You don't have to use this constraint on the primary key because that and NOT NULL are part of the primary key constraint.

Check constraints: These give rules as to what is valid data. They include mathematical constraints where data must be in a specific range and alphanumeric conditions where data must come from a specified list or contain (or not contain) specific characters. There will be a more in depth discussion of this in the Security chapter.

It is not uncommon for a particular entity to have several constraints.

Most database management system will allow you to name the constraints you create however if you do not name them, they will still be created and assigned a system name which will be almost impossible to retrieve. It is therefore recommended you name your constraints and use a systematic naming convention (for example foreign keys are prefixed with FK_). The name and the constraint type are held in the systems data dictionary.

4.11   Worked Example

The following exercise uses Oracles SQL Plus, but as few of Oracle specific operators will be used as possible and the syntax works in Microsoft's SQL Server except where stated. The customer details have been slightly altered to include a postcode and a date when the customer was added to the system. In practice the address and name attributes would probably be broken down further, for example, surname, given name and initial for name and street number, street, city for address.

4.12   Create the Tables

In this example we are going to create the database seen in Fig. 4.22. This has been modified from the original example in order to illustrate some features of SQL. Tables can be created in any order; however it is more efficient if you create tables which have no other tables dependent on them first. They can usually be identified by not having the foot of the crows foot notation attached to them, alternatively they are the 1 end of a 1:many relationship. Using this rule the first tables to be created are **Customer** and **Stock Item**. The next is **Invoice** because it is only dependent on **Customer** and finally **Line Item** because it is dependent on both **Invoice** and **Stock Item**

CREATE TABLE customer
  (customer_id VARCHAR(6),
  customer_name VARCHAR (24),
  customer_Street_no NUMBER(3),
  customer_address VARCHAR (36),
  customer_postcode VARCHAR(6),
  date_entered (DATE));

This syntax would create the table, but does not identify any constraints. Customer ID should be identified as the primary key, the rest of the fields should have data in them, that is should be NOT NULL.

Therefore the CREATE statement becomes:

CREATE TABLE customer (customer_id VARCHAR(6)
  customer_name VARCHAR (24) NOT NULL,
  customer_Street_no NUMBER (3),
  customer_address   VARCHAR   (36)   NOT   NULL,   customer_postcode
VARCHAR(6),
  date_entered (DATE),
  CONSTRAINT customer _pk PRIMARY KEY (customer_id));

Constraints can be added and modified after the tables are created, but wherever possible it is best to include them here. It is also important to name constraints so that can be easily found in the data dictionary. If they are not named, they will still be stored, but will be assigned a system name making them difficult to retrieve. In this exercise a postscript convention to indicate the type of constraint is adopted:
  _pk primary key constraint
  _fk foreign key constraint
  _uk unique constraint
  _ck check constraint
The Stock item table is created in a similar way

CREATE TABLE stock_item
  (code VARCHAR(13),
  item_description VARCHAR (24) NOT NULL,
  price NUMBER (7,2) NOT NULL,
  vat NUMBER (2) NOT NULL,
  master_item VARCHAR(15),
  CONSTRAINT stock_item_pk PRIAMRY KEY (code),

CONSTRAINT stock_item_fk FOREIGN KEY master_item REFER-ENCES stock_item(code),
CONSTRAINT item_description_uk UNIQUE (item));

This create statement illustrates how numbers are handled. **price NUMBER (7,2)** defines price as being able to store numbers up to 9999.99. The 7 gives the size of the field including the decimal point, and the 2 gives the number of places after the decimal point. The VAT definition means two digits can be stored. Since this is normally a percentage, it could have been defined as **vat NUMBER (3,2).**

As well as a primary key constraint, this definition also contains a unique constraint which means no two descriptions can be the same. In theory this could have been used as the primary key, but from a labelling and scanning perspective which is how most items are handled today, the code (which happens to store the data on a bar code) is the better candidate.

The new master_item attribute is to be used where there may be several individual items making up another item. For example, three books may be sold as a box set. The books can be purchased individually or as a box set. Since not all items are grouped, the new master_item attribute must not have the 'NOT NULL' clause associated with it. If they are a box set they will have a unique code. There is also a new foreign key constraint linking the table with itself.

The invoice table is created in a similar way, but in this case there is a foreign key constraint which allows a join between this table and the customer table:

CREATE TABLE invoice
(invoice_id NUMBER (8),
invoice date DATE NOT NULL,
order_date DATE NOT NULL,
customer_id VARCHAR(6)
CONSTRAINT invoice_id_pk PRIMARY KEY (invoice_id),
CONSTRAINT customer_id_fk FOREIGN KEY (customer_id)
REFERENCES customer (customer_id));

The foreign key constraint creates a link between customer and the invoice table. It also means you can't have an invoice unless there is an associated customer record in the customer table. Another impact of this constraint is you can't delete a customer record if there are still any associated invoices.

The final table to create is the line item table:

CREATE TABLE line_item
(invoice_id NUMBER (8),
code VARCHAR(13),
qty NUMBER (4),
CONSTRAINT line_item_pk PRIMARY KEY (invoice_id, code),
CONSTRAINT invoice_id_fk FOREIGN KEY (invoice_id) REFERENCES invoice (invoice_id),

CONSTRAINT code_fk FOREIGN KEY (code) REFERENCES stock_item (code));

In this case there is a combined primary key and two foreign key clauses. This is common where a many-to-many relationship is being resolved. If any of the constraint clauses is violated, an error will be returned. If more data than the field you have defined is entered, an error will be returned. There are two ways of handling these errors. One is by displaying the error directly to the user. A better way is to have some programming code which handles the error in a more friendly way. This aspect is beyond the scope of this discussion.

4.13   CRUDing

When working with a database you normally want to do four things: Create, Retrieve, Update and Delete data. Update and Delete operations are usually done in conjunction with a Retrieve operation. It is always a good idea to show a user what they are about to either change or delete before they do it and give them the option of aborting the operation if they discover they have the wrong record. The rest of this section will take you through a selection of structured query language statements. It is not meant to be a complete set of examples, is provided to introduce SQL. Further details of SQL for Oracle and SQL Server can be found in the further reading section at the end of this chapter.

4.14   Populate the Tables

Once a table is created, it needs to be loaded with data. What will be demonstrated below is how an initial load could be done. From a user point of view, the normal day to day entry of data would be done via web forms created using a package such as Oracles Developer or via web forms.

To insert a new record into the customer table you would use the syntax:

INSERT INTO customer VALUES ('OS3457', 'Warren Felsky', 8, 'Mien Place, Sheffield', 'S7 4GH', '20-APR-13');

It should be noted that different database management systems have different ways of handling time information. In the case of Oracle rather than '**20-APR-13**', **TO_DATE ('APR 20 2013', 'MON DD, YYYY')** could be used where TO_DATE is an Oracle built in function.

Remember, you would not be able to insert records into the invoice table until you had records with customer ID's in the customer table. If you tried you get a foreign key constraint error.

4.15 Retrieve Data

The power of a relational database lies in the ability to easily search for data which meets a particular condition. This condition may require data to be retrieved from one or more tables. In the next section we will work from simple retrieval statements to more complex ones which show the power of SQL.

Perhaps the simplest statement is one where you want to retrieve all the records in a table. In this case we will use the customer table

SELECT ∗ FROM customer;

This is not a particularly useful statement as in a production system it could retrieve hundreds of records.

SELECT ∗ FROM customer
WHERE billing_name = 'Warren Felsky';

Would return all customer records for the name Warren Felsky. You can add multiple conditions, for example:

SELECT ∗
FROM customer
WHERE billing_name = 'Warren Felsky' AND date_entered >
'01-JAN-2010';

The ∗ in **SELECT** ∗ means all columns are retrieved. It may be that you only want data from certain columns to be to returned. To do this replace the ∗ by the column names required. Some systems like Oracle will automatically label the output with these column names.

SELECT billing_name, billing_address, billing_postcode, date entered
FROM customer
WHERE billing_name = 'Warren Felsky' AND date_entered >
'01-JAN-2010';

4.16 Joins

Retrieving data from one table is seldom enough. For example, we might want to retrieve the invoice date and order date of a customer. Unless the customers id number is know, this would require retrieving data from two tables. This is known as a table join. There are a number of types of joins:

SELECT billing_name, invoice_id, invoice_date
    FROM customer, invoice
    WHERE customer.customer_id = invoice.customer_id
    billing_name = 'Warren Felsky' AND
    date_entered > '01-JAN-2010';

The first part of the **WHERE** clause defines how the tables are going to be joined by linking the primary key in one table (in this case the customer table) with its equivalent foreign key in the invoice table. Because customer_id is common to both tables it must be prefixed by the table name to avoid ambiguity.

The above example is called an Equijoin. This means that only records which have matching values in both tables will be returned.

Inner Join (Also known as a simple join) returns those rows that satisfy the join condition

SELECT customer_name, invoice_id, invoice_date
    FROM customer
    INNER JOIN invoice
    ON customer.customer_id = invoice.customer_id;

This syntax would retrieve those customers who have invoices. Any customers without an invoice would not be shown. Note that 'INNER' is an optional statement and does not need to be included.

In Oracle an **Equijoin** and an **Inner Join** are equivalent.

Outer Join extends the idea of an inner join by including some or all records from the other table in the join which do not meet the join condition. There are three types of outer joins:

Left Outer Join This will return all records from the table on the 'left' (literally to the left of the LEFT clause) which have no matching records in the table on the right. A null will be displayed instead. In the following example customers including any which don't have any invoices associated with them will be returned. This will have spaces (null) in the invoice_id and invoice_date output column.

SELECT customer_name, invoice_id, invoice_date
    FROM customer
    LEFT OUTER JOIN invoice
    ON customer.customer_id = invoice.customer_id;

The word 'OUTER' is optional in the syntax so LEFT JOIN would give the same result.

Right Outer Join This will return all records from the table on the 'right' (literally to the left of the RIGHT clause) which have no matching records in the table on the right. A null will be displayed instead. In the following example all stock items and their codes will be displayed regardless of whether they have appeared on an invoice. Those which have no associated invoice will have a null displayed instead of the invoice_id.

SELECT invoice_id, stock_item.code, item
  FROM line_item
  RIGHT JOIN stock_item
  ON line_item.code = stock_item.code;

Full Outer Join This will return all records from both the 'left' and the 'right' tables whether there is a matching record in the other table or not. The syntax uses **FULL JOIN**. Like the **LEFT** and **RIGHT** joins, any unmatched record will have nulls displayed.

Self Join Self joins are, as the name suggests a join that links a table to itself. Let's consider the definition of the **stock_item** table again where we set up the conditions for a self join:

CREATE TABLE stock_item (code VARCHAR(13),
  item VARCHAR (24) NOT NULL,
  master_item VARCHAR (24),
  price NUMBER (7,2) NOT NULL,
  CONSTRAINT stock_item_pk PRIMARY KEY (code),
  CONSTRAINT stock_item_fk FOREIGN KEY master_item REFER-
  ENCES stock_item(code),
  CONSTRAINT item_description_uk UNIQUE (item));

There is no specific self join syntax, but a LEFT JOIN can be used.

SELECT m.item, i.item,
  FROM stock_item AS m LEFT JOIN stock_item AS i
  ON m.master_item = i.item;

In the example the syntax AS m and AS i is used to establish aliases to distinguish between instances of the table, in other words are we looking at the 'master item' or 'ordinary' item? Remember the master_item field may be NULL because not all items are bundled into box sets. In this example only unmatched records on the left will be displayed. Since these are box sets, it is unlikely there will be any.

Cartesian Join A final type of join is the. In this case every record in one table is matched with every record in the joined table. So if you had two tables each of 10 records, you would end up with 100 records returned. This is obviously an error and usually happens where matching join records are not specified. About the only time this is likely to happen is if an equijoin is being used and the WHERE clause linking the associated primary and foreign keys is left out

Now we know how to retrieve data from tables and how to join tables together we can start looking at more complex data manipulation. This includes more complex WHERE clauses and grouping of data, for example, how could we find the total value of an invoice, particularly as we dropped that attribute as part of the normalisation process because it was a calculated field.

4.17 More Complex Data Retrieval

It is not unusual to know part of what we are looking for in our data base. For example, we know that there is the word 'Paris' in the title of the book we are looking for. Most databases allow the use of wildcard searches. A wildcard is a character that takes the place of one or many other characters. It may be an *, or in the case Oracle it is % for many characters and _ for a single character. So to search for Paris in our stock_item table we can use:

SELECT code, item, price
  FROM stock_item
  WHERE item LIKE '%Paris%';

If you wanted to see the cheapest book with Paris in the title you could add the ORDER clause:

SELECT code, item, price
  FROM stock_item
  WHERE item LIKE '%Paris%'
  ORDER BY price DESC;

Omitting the DESC clause would make the order most expensive first. You can have several levels of ordering, for example, if you wanted to sort first by price, then by title the ORDER clause would become:

  . . . ORDER BY price DESC, item;

A further requirement in most systems is to be able to calculate data. This is done on a group of records that are returned. For example, how many invoices do customers have?

SELECT COUNT(invoice_id)
  FROM invoice
  GROUP BY customer_id;

This can get quite complicated when a number of tables are involved, for example, what is the total value of an invoice. This requires at least three of the tables in our database and there is an argument for all four if the customers' names is required as well. The joins here are all INNER joins because we are only concerned equal matches.

```
SELECT invoice_id, COUNT (code), SUM (price)
  FROM invoice JOIN line_item
  ON invoice.invoice_id = line_item.invoice_id,
  line_item JOIN stock_item
  ON line_item.code = stock_item.code
  GROUP BY invoice_id;
```

4.18   UPDATE and DELETE

The final two classes of operations in a relational database are UPDATE and DELETE where you want to make changes to the data. Let's say we want to update a customer's address. First it is a good idea to make sure you have the correct customer so we could use:

```
SELECT * FROM customer
  WHERE billing_name = 'Warren Felsky';
```

which we have seen before to retrieve all the customers with the name Warren Felsky. We see from the data returned that one customer, OS3457 is the one we want. We can then issue the UPDATE command to change the customers' address:

```
UPDATE customer
  SET customer_Street_no = 6,
  customer_address = 'McGregor St, Sheffield'
  customer_postcode = 'S11 1OD'
  WHERE cutomer_id = 'OS3457';
```

The WHERE clause can contain any of the conditions you have seen so far. It may have the effect of updating more than one row so it is essential you retrieve and verify records before you update them. It is also possible to get an integrity constraint error if you try and update a record with a constraint, for example if you try and update an attribute defined as a foreign key.

Removing data from a table is both very simple and very dangerous. Like with UPDATE you need to be sure that the record you are deleting is the one you want to delete. Let's say we want to remove Warren Felskys record

```
DELETE FROM customer
  WHERE customer_name = 'Warren Felsky';
```

Two things could go wrong here. If there is more than one warren Felsky, both will be deleted. It would have been better to use the customer_id. Secondly, if Warren Felsky still had any live invoices in the system there would be an integrity constraint error. In other words, all invoices associated with Felsky would have to be deleted before the customer record could be removed.

The database is not permanently changed until a COMMIT command is issued and up to that point a ROLLBACK command could be issued to return the database to its original state. Most systems do a COMMIT when a user logs off.

This is related to ACID which was covered in Chap. 2 where we looked at transaction processing.

4.19   Review Questions

The answers to these questions can be found in the text of this chapter.

- What is a tuple?
- What is the difference between a primary key, candidate key and foreign key?
- What is CRUDing?
- What is a heavy entity?
- What is a weak entity?

4.20   Group Work Research Activity

This activity requires you to research beyond the contents of the book and can be tackled individually or as a discussion group.

The Agency currently rents out various types of domestic accommodation (flats and houses) to clients. The clients (e.g. students or groups of students) may require 1 year leases or (e.g. families) longer term lets.

Details are kept on each property and in particular:

- Address (this must be searchable by postcode or partial post code or by district)
- Owner details
- Lead tenant details
- Tenancy start
- Tenancy end
- Rent
- Type of property (flat, detached house, terrace house etc.)
- Furnished/Unfurnished (for Furnished, further details of the furnishings may be kept)
- Number of bedrooms
- Number of bathrooms
- Number of reception rooms
- Optionally also:
- A textual description Photographs.
- A history of occupancy needs to be kept including periods were the property is unoccupied.

In order to make searching for appropriate properties easier it has been decided that details of individual rooms within a property will also be stored. This will include:

- room type (bedroom/bathroom/kitchen etc.)
- room dimensions (in feet and meters)
- heating (e.g. radiator/fire)
- for kitchens: appliances
- for bathrooms: fittings
- any special features e.g. patio windows.

The tourist business has started to boom in the area and the Agency wishes to move into the business of holiday lettings. This will involve much shorter lets and a much greater requirement for up-to-date availability information.

1. Using normalisation, create an entity relationship diagram for the scenario. Was it possible to go beyond third normal form?
2. Repeat the exercise but this time use entity modelling. Were the results the same?
3. Write the create statements necessary for the scenario. What constraints are necessary?

References

Chen P (1976) The entity-relationship model—towards a unified view of data. ACM Trans Database Syst 1(1):9–36

Codd EF (1970) A relational model of data for large shared data banks. Commun ACM 13 (6):377–387

Date CJ (2005) Database in depth: relational theory for practitioners. O'Reilly, Sebastopol

Further Reading

Chen P (2006) Suggested research directions for a new frontier: active conceptual modeling. In: Conceptual modeling—ER 2006. Lecture notes in computer science, vol 4215. Springer, Berlin/Heidelberg, pp 1–4

Microsoft (2013) Microsoft SQL server library. Available online at https://docs.microsoft.com/en-us/sql/sql-server/?view=sql-server-ver15. Accessed 22/04/2013

Oracle® (2010) Database SQL language reference 11 g release 1 (11.1). Available online at http://docs.oracle.com/cd/B28359_01/server.111/b28286/toc.htm#BEGIN. Accessed 22/04/2013

NoSQL Databases

5

What the reader will learn:

- that Web 2.0 and Cloud Computing brought new challenges to the database arena
- that a number of data-centric solutions that are not relational have come to the fore
- how these new data storage mechanisms work by exploring three in detail
- that each new data storage type addresses a particular business need
- some of the strengths and weaknesses of these new approaches, together with an appreciation of why Relational may be with us for many years to come

5.1 Databases and the Web

From the very earliest days of web development programmers have been using databases to provide permanency, and a single source of truth, for their web-based systems. In the beginning this would typically mean connecting to a Relational database (RDBMS) back-end. This is particularly true for the many online trading systems that were developed, as the transactional nature of their raison d'e⁻tre demanded the robustness provided by leading RDBMS to ensure reliable financial dealings.

To a degree, of course, the database itself will not care whether its clients are connecting using a two- three- or n-tier architecture. And the functionality they provided also quickly found a place in the far more interactive type of application that came about as a result of Web 2.0, and Cloud computing.

For many designers the choice usually was seen as one of Open Source (such as MySQL) or vendor supplied (such as Oracle). The debate often revolved around cost of purchase, cost of ownership, and trustworthiness. What it seldom revolved around was whether the database should be relational or not. Universities running

© Springer Nature Switzerland AG 2021
K. Domdouzis et al., *Concise Guide to Databases*, Undergraduate Topics in Computer Science, https://doi.org/10.1007/978-3-030-42224-0_5

computing courses would typically have a module called "Database Systems", which examined almost exclusively, the relational model. Naturally, therefore, as the students left and began to develop exciting new applications for the commercial world, there was little doubt in their mind that a database problem was to be solved with a relational solution.

However, as web driven systems began to expand, particularly when mass-usage systems such as Facebook and Twitter began to take off, it became clear that the relational model is not good at everything. It is said in some quarters, for example, that Relational does not scale well. And the fact that these new mass-usage systems are global and data is typically spread across many nodes in many countries, is seen by some as something that relational does not cope with well.

As well as pointing up some potential weaknesses in the relational approach, these new applications were often not actually transactional in nature. As we saw in Chap. 4, the ACID test is at the heart of providing the transactional robustness. However, it is a big processing overhead for a RDBMS to maintain the robustness required in an ACID compliant database. And that overhead becomes extremely difficult to manage if the data is spread over many servers all over the world. This usually manifests itself in very poor performance.

In addition to problems with the actual data storage aspect of systems, the retrieval of data from many nodes across the globe was also becoming problematic. Google, for example, have built a world leading brand on their ability to search and retrieve data quickly, and they recognised the weakness in the relational approach.

In the end organisations eventually took the decision to write their own database systems to meet these new demands. Google, famously, designed their own database to suit their needs, called BigTable. This is a proprietary database and you cannot buy a copy to use in your own environment, but the story is well documented, especially by Chang et al. (2006). It is NOT relational. Instead it is a distributed hash mechanism built on their own file handling system, GFS. Although it is Google's own product, and not openly available, other such databases do exist. HBase is an open source database that claims to have a similar data model to that of BigTable, for example. We review what Hbase and similar products allow us to do in the era of "Big Data" in the next chapter.

5.2 The NoSQL Movement

We must not lose sight of the tremendous leaps forward in data management and manipulation techniques that have occurred because of the powerful relational model. This chapter will go on to review some current alternative approaches, but readers should recognise that many corporations have invested many $millions in their RDBMS architecture and will not, especially in a period of comparative recession, rush to spend money on new database technology. Moreover, for many organisations, the current RDBMS does exactly what is required of it.

To quote from the Guide to Cloud Computing (Hill et al. 2013):

> [in the 1980s]… middle managers who needed information to help them to make business decisions would think nothing of having to wait days for the data they needed. The request would need to be coded, probably into Cobol, then perhaps handed to a punch-card operator who would punch the programme, and then on to await an allotted, and very valuable, processing slot. Output from this request would probably be on a continuous run of sprocket-holed paper, along with many other outputs. A further wait might ensue whilst awaiting the specialist paper decollator or burster.

> With the advent of personal computing in the 1980s managers were able to collect and manipulate data without waiting for the still very powerful mainframe. The Relational Database, with its English-like SQL language also helped empower decision makers. Critical information could be delivered in a few seconds and organisations could gain competitive advantage by accessing information swiftly. Moreover, new information might be uncovered by using Data Mining techniques.

But Relational databases have been with us for over 30 years. In that period we have seen, for example, the birth and rise to predominance of the Windows Operating System at the cost of command-line interfaces. We are seeing now a move away from traditional client-server applications towards available anywhere, browser or App driven applications. When you consider the technological change underpinning these advances, it is hardly surprising that database technologies, too, should be reviewed and improved.

As we will see in later chapters, three areas of great import for any database administrator (DBA) are Scalability, Availability and Performance.

For many of the RDBMS vendors availability has always been a key selling point. The traditional measure for assessing how available a database has been is Uptime, often expressed as a percentage of total elapsed time. An uptime of 50% would mean that the database was available for only half of the elapsed time (probably ensuring the host company went bust if it relied on the database for online trading!). The dream target for a DBA is what is called "Five Nines" availability, which is 99.999% available.

It is true, however, that we are now in an era when differences between availability statistics for different vendor databases are slim. As a way of differentiating between vendor products, therefore, except for applications which are most sensitive to outages however small—one would hope that the system looking out for incoming nuclear warheads is offline for as short a time as possible, for example—this measure becomes less useful.

Today's sales battlegrounds are therefore more often based around Scalability and Performance. And it is precisely these two aspects that tend to be pushed by NoSQL tool providers as they claim their products outperform and out-scale traditional RDBMS. Naturally the traditional vendors are fighting back and making counter claims. Equally naturally the real position is somewhere between the two, with most answers starting with "It depends".

When examining the context in which database professionals work these days, we can perhaps get a better understanding of why the new tools might excel; in short, the task often now before them is to quickly find relevant data from terabytes of unstructured web content which may be stored across many widely dispersed nodes. Relational databases, with their large processing overhead in terms of maintaining the ACID attributes of the data they store, and their reliance on potentially processor hungry joins, are not the right tool for these needs.

Relational databases can, and do, store and manipulate very large datasets. In practice these are often vertically scaled systems; that is, they may have access to multiple CPUs to distribute the processing burden, but they share RAM and disks.

NoSQL databases tend to be horizontally scaled; that is the data is stored on one of many individual stand-alone systems which run relatively simple processes, such as key look-ups, or read/write against a few records, against their own data. The individual system onto which the data itself will be stored will be managed according to a key. This is known as "sharding".

Cattell (2010) provides a nice clear definition of horizontal scaling:

> The term "horizontal scalability" means the ability to distribute both the data and the load of […] simple operations over many servers, with no RAM or disk shared among the servers.

5.2.1 What Is Meant by NoSQL?

Unfortunately the answer to this also begins with "It depends…". This is a new term and is therefore going through a common phase in the process of new word definition wherein different people treat the meaning differently.

One frequent usage is merely "any database which doesn't use SQL". The problem with that is that it seems to start from the premise that SQL is the only existing database query tool. Object Query Language (OQL), for example has been with us for many years but is not normally thought of as NoSQL.

To add to the complexity, SQL is a well-known, even well loved, query language. So much so that NoSQL databases are beginning to provide SQL-type support to help the poor old relational expert find data in the mysterious world of non-related data stores. Cassandra, for example, after starting with just a command-line, java- like query tool, now (since version 0.8) provides CQL.

Another definition is that NoSQL is N.O.SQL and that the N.O. stands for Not Only. Cassandra after this release might be seen as an example of this.

In this book, whilst not particularly favouring one or other definition, for clarity we will use NoSQL to mean:

> A database which does not store data using the precepts of the relational model and which allows access to the data using query languages which do not follow the ISO 9075 standard definition of SQL.

Perhaps the best way to get an understanding of what NoSQL actually means is to look at examples. Further on in the chapter we will be using a Column- based database and a Document-based database. These are two types of approach to storing data that are generally accepted to be "NoSQL". A good single source for most of the approaches available, and examples thereof, can be found at: https://en.wikipedia.org/wiki/NoSQL.

5.3 Differences in Philosophy

Data processing tasks today can involve vast volumes of data which may be duplicated across many nodes in the Web. This can be when RDBMS start to struggle.

Traditionally a DBA would consider indexing as an approach to speeding up the location of particular data items. However, the index process is itself burdensome for the RDBMS, especially if the data is volatile. An index is, after all, just a pointer to the physical location of some data, so there has to be a secondary read process involved in any retrieval based on indexes. In addition, traditional RDBMS databases will have data in a number of tables which often need to be joined to respond to a user query. This too is process intensive for the management system.

When trying to impose ACID rules on data, ensuring that all data items on all nodes are identical before the user can access them is a vital, but time consuming step. The issue is that rows can become locked whilst they wait for network issues to be resolved. (More information on locking and indexes is to be found in the Performance chapter of this book.

In recent years, however, some interesting papers have been published which argue that ACID is not the only legitimate set of rules for a database to abide to. CAP theorem, for example (Brewer 2012), makes the point that there is always a balance between competing desires to be found when designing distributed systems in general, and for the Web in particular. The three competing needs are said to be:

- Consistency
- Availability
- Partition Tolerance (coping with breaks in physical network connections)

Before we go any further, we need to establish just what is meant by these terms, especially since the "Consistent" used here does not use the same definition as the one in the ACID approach.

The **consistent** as used in the ACID test means that the data that is stored in the database has all rules or constraints applied to it. In other words, the data complies with all the business rules designed into the database.

The **consistent** as used in the CAP theorem means that all the data accessible by clients, across all nodes, is the same. As we will see below, this is not always the case in NoSQL databases. Often these databases do not have schemas and whatever data validation rules there are have to be implemented at the client end.

The other two terms in CAP Theorem are more straight-forward:

Availability refers to the ability of the database to serve data to clients. In general, the more redundant nodes a database has, the more available it will be since anyone trying to gather data from a node which is "down" can get the data from other nodes. The downside is that performance can suffer.

Partition Tolerance refers to the ability of the database to find alternate routes through the network to get at data from various nodes should there be breaks in communications. As Gilbert and Lynch (2002) suggest tolerance means:

> No set of failures less than total network failure is allowed to cause the system to respond incorrectly.

As these rules can seem a little strange to users of stand-alone RDBMS, it is worth looking at an example scenario and seeing how CAP plays out. Most readers will be used to online shopping applications. Let us take an example of a simple system that maintains data about the number of candles a hardware supplier has in stock. It is a distributed system in that identical data is stored on two geographically separate networks, Network 1 and Network 2.

We should recognise that the importance of the repressions of what CAP Theorem predicts is dependent upon the sort of application we are dealing with. Any transactional system requires Atomicity—that is, a candle is either purchased or it is not, a bank account is either updated or it is not.

However, as we have seen, this sort of atomicity comes at a cost in terms of resource usage and performance. There may be circumstances where the transactional security needed by banks, or shops, is not needed. Take for example, an online Discussion Board application. Just to keep the example simple we look at a two node system.

Julia goes on to the discussion board and asks a question, Question J. She is logged on through Network 1 (though of course she isn't aware of that). Question J gets replicated to Network 2. Users K, L, M write answers to network 1 over the next few minutes. But only K and L get replicated since the connection between the two networks breaks at the time that M is writing a response.

Now hundreds of other users of the Discussion Board log on, some through Network 1 and some through Network 2. Those using the latter will not see Answer M. But does it really matter? When you first think about this you might well say "of course it matters!". But just think about the users who logged on to Network 1 the second before M sent their answer. They were seeing exactly what users of Network 2 are seeing now. And it could well be that Answer K was the most helpful one, so they are not really any worse off because of it.

If you are still not convinced, ask yourself another question—if you want to know every user will be guaranteed access to exactly the same data, are you willing to pay for the service? Naturally such a consistent database is achievable, but it may well mean that you need to purchase an ACID compliant RDBMS, as opposed to using an open source NoSQL solution. And even if that is your preferred solution, you will then need to be prepared to see a fall in performance since no-one will be able to see Answer M until the partition is removed.

As we see in the next section there are various consistency approaches available, depending upon the application's requirements. Many of the mechanisms used in a RDBMS to ensure there is only ever one valid value stored involve preventing users seeing data by locking rows whilst transactions are under way. For the locked-out user this seems like the database is performing poorly, or worse, is not functioning properly. That user might prefer to see stale data, rather than have to wait, potentially hours, for "actual" data.

For the reader interested in proof, Brewer's CAP theorem is proved in the Gilbert and Lynch (2002) paper; *Brewer's Conjecture and the Feasibility of Consistent, Available, Partition-Tolerant Web Services.*

5.4 Basically Available, Soft State, Eventually Consistent (BASE)

BASE is, in effect, the operating premise for most NoSQL databases, in the same way RDBMS databases apply the ACID rules. Hill et al. (2013) note:

> that we move from a world of certainty in terms of data consistency, to a world where all we are promised is that all copies of the data will, at some point, be the same.

However, even this less certain consistency can be managed in different ways. The eventual consistency can be brought about, for example, by:

Read Repair: When a read operation happens and discovers that some data on a node is stale (that is, it has an earlier time-stamp than that on the other nodes), the outdated data is refreshed.

Delayed Repair: The application will return the value it finds, even though it may be stale, but marks it as needing updating. The timing of that update is in the hands of the controlling, or master database. This is known as weak consistency. It is a performance-oriented approach.

What we have seen is that we now have more control over whether we want an absolutely consistent collection of nodes, which a traditional ACID-focused DBMS would automatically provide us, or varying degrees of consistency, with the upside to the loss of consistency being in typically better performance.

Many of the NoSQL databases available today use the BASE design philosophy. Many also allow you to manage the degree of consistency required by any application. We will now move on to look at how this different design philosophy is actually implemented by reviewing some NoSQL tools. They all have different approaches to data storage because they aim to meet different needs, but they share the notion that traditional RDBMS rules and practices are not necessarily always the most appropriate.

5.5 Column-Based Approach

Tables of data stored in rows are such a common part of today's ICT systems that even non-database people recognise the concept. This common understanding is probably also helped by the omnipresence of spreadsheets, also made of rows.

Many readers will already be aware of design and implementation techniques, including normalisation and indexing, which can assist in optimising storage and speeding the return of data. Often, this row-oriented tabular storage is taken for granted. If there are specialist requirements to get data out of a database, for example, looking for values from a particular column, the storage approach remains relational, but tools like views, cubes, and star schema are used to speed the search and retrieval process and assist the user in navigating a complex series of joins.

For many Decision Support applications, examining a column, looking for trends, averages and other statistical analysis is a frequent event. And yet the data is stored so that rows can be read as efficiently as possible, not columns. We must always remember that the seek and read from disk is one of the slowest aspects of any database system. At the heart of the problem is that the DBMS has to read every row, discarding unwanted information (or at least moving the read position so that it skips unwanted data) to get to the data in the desired column.

There are many relational databases which have optimisation techniques that make this problem seem trivial. And yet, the question remains; if we are retrieving data from columns more frequently than looking at several attributes from a row of data, why don't we store the data in columns instead of rows?

And that is exactly what the column-based approach provides us. The data items for each attribute are stored one after another. The read process is thus made very simple and there are only start-toread and end-reading pointers to worry about and no jumping around to different disk segments to jump over unwanted data (see diagram in Fig. 5.2 showing the same data as in Fig. 5.1).

In the type of system we are discussing the column oriented approach improves read efficiency because there is no need for a row identifier, and packing similar data together allows compression algorithms to reduce the volume of disk storage required. Whilst this does allow for more rapid analysis of those column values, it

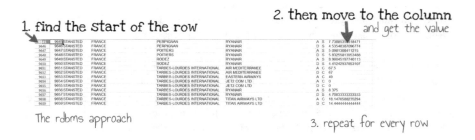

Fig. 5.1 The Row approach

The column approach

9645, 9646, 9647, 9648
etc
PERPIGNAN , PERPIGNAN, POITIERS, POITIERS
etc
7.73885350318471 , 4.5354838709677, 5.0981308411215, 5.83255813953488

Just read the column data sequentially

Fig. 5.2 The Column approach

does mean that the reverse problem is true—if there is a need to create a record (or row of data), it would have to be recreated by using positional information to look up the other data items from columns. This would clearly be very inefficient.

A second slight issue is that best performance, in terms of compression, will happen when similar values are adjacent to each other. If the data being recorded is volatile and many inserts and updates occur, this efficiency will eventually be lost. One insert could result in many rewrites as the data is shuffled to ensure similar values are adjacent to each other.

So when would you choose to use a column-based approach? Hill et al. (2013) suggest:

> Column based databases allow for rapid location and return of data from one particular attribute. They are potentially very slow with writing however, since data may need to be shuffled around to allow a new data item to be inserted. As a rough guide then, traditional transactionally orientated databases will probably fair better in a RDBMS. Column based will probably thrive in areas where speed of access to non-volatile data is important, for example in some Decision Support Applications. You only need to review marketing material from commercial vendors to see that business analytics is seen as the key market, and speed of data access the main product differentiator.

To get a feel for the potential of the column-based approach we now go on to use Cassandra. This is only one of the Column-based databases available. You should look at review the web to seek information about others.

5.6   Examples of Column-Based Using Cassandra

The Cassandra data model is very different to RDBMS. Some of the concepts seem alien if you have become very familiar with the relational model. It may help to start by simply thinking of this as a mechanism for storing a key, and a value. This key-value pair storage mechanism is extended by allowing the pairs to be nested. There is a section in this chapter about Key-Value stores, so you might want to review that if this is a new concept to you.

5.6.1 Cassandra's Basic Building Blocks

A **keyspace** in Cassandra is roughly equivalent to a database schema in a Relational DBMS and it is a group of related column families (see below). Remembering that we are dealing with a database that allows for horizontal scaling, there is an attribute called placement strategy which allows the user to define how to distribute replicas around the nodes they will be using.

A **Column Family** is roughly equivalent to a table in a RDBMS. Each such Family is stored in a separate physical file which is sorted into key order. To help reduce disk reads, and therefore improving performance, columns which are regularly accessed together should be kept together, within the same column family.

A **Column** is the smallest unit of storage in Cassandra. A standard column is composed of a unique name (key), value and a timestamp. The key identifies a row in a Column Family.

The **timestamp** is used to ensure distributed conflict resolution. It is usually defined as the difference between the current time and 00:00:00 UTC on 1 January 1970, also known as Unix epoch. The level of granularity is usually in milliseconds, or microseconds. The timestamp is provided by the client. This can be a problem in cases where the data is volatile and the accuracy of the client timestamp is uncertain. An external time server service can be a solution to this, but it does have performance implications.

A **SuperColumn** is a list of columns. Although we have to remember that Cassandra is schema-less, you can think of this as a pot into which to put a variety of columns, rather like a view in a RDBMS. It is a mechanism for containing multiple columns with common look-up values. Again, thinking in relational terms, you might have a transaction with several attributes (Price, date, salesperson, for example). You could have a SuperColumn called TransationID which contains those attributes, each stored as columns.

A SuperColumn does not have a timestamp.

5.6.1.1 Getting Hands-On with Cassandra

The tutorial material in this chapter demonstrates the use of Cassandra on Ubuntu Linux. Cassandra will also run on other Linux servers, and can be installed on Windows. These notes were created using Ubuntu Linux 11.10 with release 1.1.6 of Cassandra.

We start with the expectation that the reader has basic Unix skills, and has a version of Linux with Cassandra installed on it.

5.6.2 Data Sources

The data in the following tutorial material is from the UK Civil aviation Authority, made publicly available as Open Data. Many other data sources are available from: http://data.gov.uk/.

5.6.3   Getting Started

Assuming you have followed the default installation of Cassandra, as set out in the appendix, you should open a terminal session and, from you home location, list what is on your file system (Fig. 5.3).

You may see different files and folders, but the one we need to concentrate on here is the apachecassandra-1.1.6 folder, which contains the Cassandra software.

Next, issue the CD command to move to the apache-cassandra-1.1.6\bin folder and see the executable files installed (Fig. 5.4).

In this tutorial we will be using the **cassandra** executable, which provides the database functionality and needs to be started, and kept running whilst we work with Cassandra. We will then interact with this programme through the client programme; **cassandra-cli**. And then we will begin to use the query language; **cqlsh**.

As we will be regularly using these programmes it may be an idea to create scripts to launch them for us, and place them on the home folder.

Start the text editor and insert the following lines. Once inserted, save to your home folder as something like **startCass**:

```
#!/bin/bash
cd apache-cassandra-1.1.6
cd bin
./cassandra
```

We will also want to start the client often. Using the text editor, create startCass-Cli with the following content:

```
#!/bin/bash
cd apache-cassandra-1.1.6 cd bin
./cassandra-cli
```

Both of these files need to be turned into executable files. From the $ prompt you will need to type:

```
  ⊗ ⊖ ⊕   peter@ubuntu: ~
peter@ubuntu:~$ ls -l
total 60
drwxrwxr-x  9 peter peter 4096 2012-11-27 09:23 apache-cassandra-1.1.6
drwxr-xr-x 14 peter peter 4096 2012-04-24 13:28 data-integration
drwxr-xr-x  2 peter peter 4096 2012-11-27 09:23 Desktop
drwxr-xr-x  2 peter peter 4096 2012-06-20 10:13 Documents
drwxr-xr-x  2 peter peter 4096 2012-11-24 09:09 Downloads
```

Fig. 5.3 Listing files in the home directory

```
⊗⊖⊡   peter@ubuntu: ~/apache-cassandra-1.1.6/bin
peter@ubuntu:~$ cd apache-cassandra-1.1.6/bin
peter@ubuntu:~/apache-cassandra-1.1.6/bin$ ls -l
total 176
-rwxr-xr-x 1 peter peter   6453 2012-10-12 06:28 cassandra
-rwxr-xr-x 1 peter peter   3952 2012-10-12 06:28 cassandra.bat
-rwxr-xr-x 1 peter peter   1667 2012-10-12 06:28 cassandra-cli
-rwxr-xr-x 1 peter peter   1807 2012-10-12 06:28 cassandra-cli.bat
-rw-r--r-- 1 peter peter   1575 2012-10-12 06:28 cassandra.in.sh
-rwxr-xr-x 1 peter peter 104628 2012-10-12 06:28 cqlsh
-rwxr-xr-x 1 peter peter    995 2012-10-12 06:28 cqlshrc.sample
-rwxr-xr-x 1 peter peter   1696 2012-10-12 06:28 json2sstable
-rwxr-xr-x 1 peter peter   2291 2012-10-12 06:28 json2sstable.bat
-rwxr-xr-x 1 peter peter   2165 2012-10-12 06:28 nodetool
-rwxr-xr-x 1 peter peter   1859 2012-10-12 06:28 nodetool.bat
-rwxr-xr-x 1 peter peter   1697 2012-10-12 06:28 sstable2json
-rwxr-xr-x 1 peter peter   2291 2012-10-12 06:28 sstable2json.bat
-rwxr-xr-x 1 peter peter   1780 2012-10-12 06:28 sstablekeys
-rwxr-xr-x 1 peter peter   2163 2012-10-12 06:28 sstablekeys.bat
-rwxr-xr-x 1 peter peter   1672 2012-10-12 06:28 sstableloader
-rwxr-xr-x 1 peter peter   1680 2012-10-12 06:28 sstablescrub
-rwxr-xr-x 1 peter peter   1175 2012-10-12 06:28 stop-server
peter@ubuntu:~/apache-cassandra-1.1.6/bin$ ▮
```

Fig. 5.4 Listing Cassandra related files

```
$chmod 777 startCass
$chmod 777 startCassCli
```

The first thing we need to do to use Cassandra is run the server. We start it, and then leave it running, probably minimising so the terminal session is out of the way. And then we start the client application.

From the $ prompt in your home folder, run the script we just created above:

```
$./startCass
```

Once the server is started, open a second terminal session. In that one, start the client session:

```
$./startCassCli
```

Your desktop should look something similar to the one in Fig. 5.5.

Minimise the terminal window with the server process running. It looks like it has hung as there is no input prompt on it, but do not worry, it is working as it should!

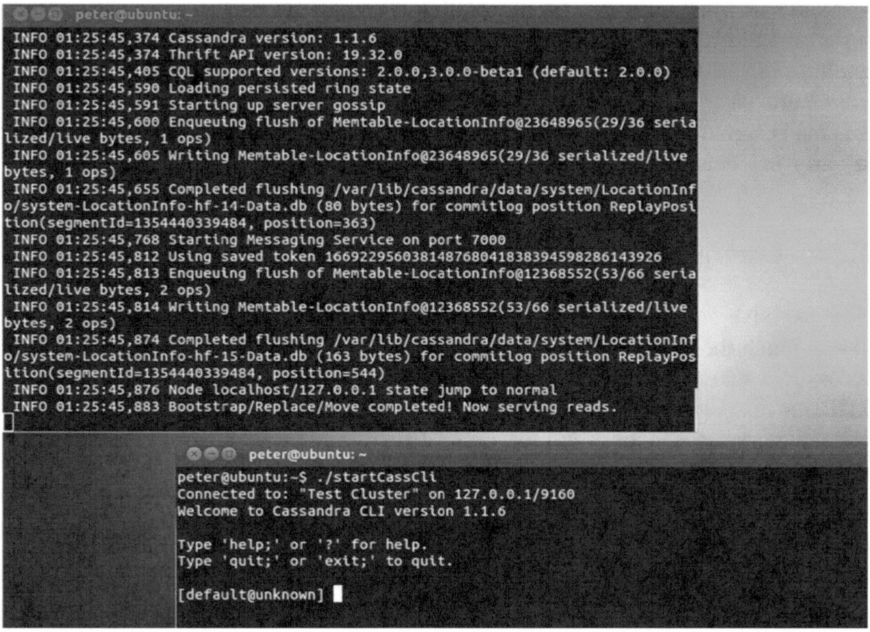

INFO 01:25:45,374 Cassandra version: 1.1.6
INFO 01:25:45,374 Thrift API version: 19.32.0
INFO 01:25:45,405 CQL supported versions: 2.0.0,3.0.0-beta1 (default: 2.0.0)
INFO 01:25:45,590 Loading persisted ring state
INFO 01:25:45,591 Starting up server gossip
INFO 01:25:45,600 Enqueuing flush of Memtable-LocationInfo@23648965(29/36 seria
lized/live bytes, 1 ops)
INFO 01:25:45,605 Writing Memtable-LocationInfo@23648965(29/36 serialized/live
bytes, 1 ops)
INFO 01:25:45,655 Completed flushing /var/lib/cassandra/data/system/LocationInf
o/system-LocationInfo-hf-14-Data.db (80 bytes) for commitlog position ReplayPosi
tion(segmentId=1354440339484, position=363)
INFO 01:25:45,768 Starting Messaging Service on port 7000
INFO 01:25:45,812 Using saved token 166922956038148768041838394598286143926
INFO 01:25:45,813 Enqueuing flush of Memtable-LocationInfo@12368552(53/66 seria
lized/live bytes, 2 ops)
INFO 01:25:45,814 Writing Memtable-LocationInfo@12368552(53/66 serialized/live
bytes, 2 ops)
INFO 01:25:45,874 Completed flushing /var/lib/cassandra/data/system/LocationInf
o/system-LocationInfo-hf-15-Data.db (163 bytes) for commitlog position ReplayPos
ition(segmentId=1354440339484, position=544)
INFO 01:25:45,876 Node localhost/127.0.0.1 state jump to normal
INFO 01:25:45,883 Bootstrap/Replace/Move completed! Now serving reads.

peter@ubuntu:~
peter@ubuntu:~$ ./startCassCli
Connected to: "Test Cluster" on 127.0.0.1/9160
Welcome to Cassandra CLI version 1.1.6

Type 'help;' or '?' for help.
Type 'quit;' or 'exit;' to quit.

[default@unknown]

Fig. 5.5 Cassandra running and waiting for input

The input prompt in client terminal session is telling us that we have no user
(default) or keyspace defined. We can use the default user for now, but we do need
to create a keyspace for us to work in (Fig. 5.6).

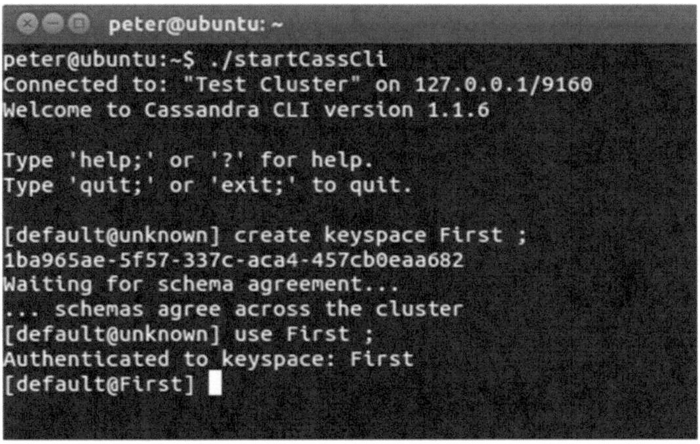

peter@ubuntu:~
peter@ubuntu:~$ ./startCassCli
Connected to: "Test Cluster" on 127.0.0.1/9160
Welcome to Cassandra CLI version 1.1.6

Type 'help;' or '?' for help.
Type 'quit;' or 'exit;' to quit.

[default@unknown] create keyspace First ;
1ba965ae-5f57-337c-aca4-457cb0eaa682
Waiting for schema agreement...
... schemas agree across the cluster
[default@unknown] use First ;
Authenticated to keyspace: First
[default@First]

Fig. 5.6 Creating a keyspace

Note that when creating new objects Cassandra needs to ensure that all instances across the cluster of servers now have this definition in place. As we are currently working in standalone mode, this may seem unhelpful, but we must remember that Cassandra was always designed to work in a distributed environment. After the schema is signalled to be agreed by the cluster we can use the keyspace called First to carry out our work in.

5.6.4 Creating the Column Family

Now we have an area to work in we can begin building structures to store our data in—in much the same way that you can start creating tables in SQL once you have access to a schema. Indeed, a **Column Family** is roughly equivalent to a table in a RDBMS and a **Column** is the smallest unit of storage in Cassandra. A standard column is composed of a unique name (key), value and a timestamp. The key identifies a row in a Column Family.

The first Column Family we are going to work with is a simple list of UK airlines and their domestic flights. The downloaded.csv is bigger than this, but we have edited it down so that it only contains columns we will be using:

Airline Name, Km Flown (x1000), Number of Flights, Number of Hours flown, and the Number of Passengers handled

The data is shown in Fig. 5.7. There aren't many rows but we are just cutting our teeth at the minute!

We will need a Column Family called DomesticFlights with columns to take this data. We will also need a KEY to uniquely identify each row. Later we will load data straight from a.csv file, but here we are just getting used to the client tool.

	A	B	C	D	
1	AURIGNY AIR SERVICES	▸ 193	1388	887	26585
2	BA CITYFLYER LTD	▸ 300	545	686.1	30031
3	BLUE ISLANDS LIMITED	▸ 168	991	520.8	15308
4	BMI GROUP	▸ 1067	2435	2922.7	142804
5	BRITISH AIRWAYS PLC	▸ 1510	3327	4116.6	307849
6	BRITISH INTERNATIONAL HELICOPTER SERVICES LTD	▸ 10	162	57.9	2169
7	EASTERN AIRWAYS	▸ 496	1406	1353	23074
8	EASYJET AIRLINE COMPANY LTD	▸ 1826	3922	4297.2	399308
9	FLYBE LTD	▸ 2505	6755	5635.4	297435
10	ISLES OF SCILLY SKYBUS	▸ 12	176	55.3	1200
11	JET2.COM LTD	▸ 22	71	65	4059
12	LOGANAIR	▸ 504	2440	1958.7	32994
13					

Fig. 5.7 Domestic Flights data

With the follow examples you can either type in directly to the $prompt, or cut and paste from this tutorial onto the $prompt.

```
Create Column Family DomesticFlights WITH comparator =
UTF8Type AND key_validation_class = UTF8Type AND
column_metadata =
[
    {column_name: airline, validation_class: UTF8Type, index_type: KEYS},
    {column_name: Kms, validation_class: IntegerType},
    {column_name: Flights, validation_class: IntegerType},
    {column_name: Hrs, validation_class: FloatType},
    {column_name: Pass, validation_class: IntegerType}
];
```

Things to note from the above Column Family creation are that:

The **comparator** is required by Cassandra because it is needs to know the order in which to store columns.

Key_validation_class tells Cassandra what datatype the key is going to be. We will be using Airline so we have chosen UTF8, which is a string of characters and may have been described as a varchar in a RDBMS.

The **validation** class is similar to the definition of a datatype in a relational database schema and provides, as its name suggests, the opportunity to validate data on input, only allowing data of the appropriate datatype to be written.

5.6.5   Inserting Data

To insert data we can use the SET command. Here are two examples:

```
set DomesticFlights['Aurigny Air Services']['Kms'] = 193;
set DomesticFlights['Aurigny Air Services']['Flights'] = 1388;
set DomesticFlights['Aurigny Air Services']['Hrs'] = 887;
set DomesticFlights['Aurigny Air Services']['Pass'] = 26585;
set DomesticFlights['BA CityFlyer']['Kms'] = 300;
set DomesticFlights['BA CityFlyer']['Flights'] = 545;
set DomesticFlights['BA CityFlyer']['Hrs'] = 686;
set DomesticFlights['BA CityFlyer']['Pass'] = 30031;
```

After you have carried this out your terminal should look something like Fig. 5.8.

5.6.6   Retrieving Data

To retrieve information we can use LIST or GET depending upon if we know the Airline we want to return data for. Try these two queries:

```
[×][—][□]   peter@ubuntu: ~
Type 'quit;' or 'exit;' to quit.

[default@unknown] use First ;
Authenticated to keyspace: First
[default@First] Create Column Family DomesticFlights
...       WITH comparator = UTF8Type AND
...       key_validation_class=UTF8Type AND
...       column_metadata =
...       [
...          {column_name: airline, validation_class: UTF8Type, index_type: KEYS}
,
...          {column_name: Kms, validation_class: IntegerType},
...          {column_name: Flights, validation_class: IntegerType},
...          {column_name: Hrs, validation_class: FloatType},
...          {column_name: Pass, validation_class: IntegerType}
...       ];
694d7497-d45e-3032-9b3d-5d2b39107022
Waiting for schema agreement...
... schemas agree across the cluster
[default@First]
[default@First] set DomesticFlights['Aurigny Air Services']['Kms'] = 193 ;
Value inserted.
Elapsed time: 27 msec(s).
[default@First] set DomesticFlights['Aurigny Air Services']['Flights'] = 1388 ;
Value inserted.
Elapsed time: 1.19 msec(s).
[default@First] set DomesticFlights['Aurigny Air Services']['Hrs'] = 887 ;
Value inserted.
Elapsed time: 1.94 msec(s).
[default@First] set DomesticFlights['Aurigny Air Services']['Pass'] = 26585 ;
Value inserted.
Elapsed time: 3.12 msec(s).
[default@First]
[default@First] set DomesticFlights['BA CityFlyer']['Kms'] = 300 ;
Value inserted.
Elapsed time: 1.54 msec(s).
[default@First] set DomesticFlights['BA CityFlyer']['Flights'] = 545 ;
Value inserted.
Elapsed time: 1.03 msec(s).
[default@First] set DomesticFlights['BA CityFlyer']['Hrs'] = 686 ;
Value inserted.
Elapsed time: 1.34 msec(s).
[default@First] set DomesticFlights['BA CityFlyer']['Pass'] = 30031 ;
Value inserted.
Elapsed time: 2.44 msec(s).
```

Fig. 5.8 Inserting data to Cassandra

```
LIST DomesticFlights;
```

```
GET DomesticFlights['BA CityFlyer'];
```

LIST Output is shown in Fig. 5.9.

However, unlike data in a RDBMS column, where you would just use the WHERE clause on any column, you can't retrieve data by searching for specific data value in Cassandra unless the data is indexed.

Try this:

```
GET DomesticFlights where Kms = 193;
```

You will get an error message back telling you that there are No indexed columns present. We can make this query work by adding a secondary index. This also demonstrates the use of the UPDATE command to change Column Family metadata.

```
[default@First] LIST DomesticFlights ;
Using default limit of 100
Using default column limit of 100
-------------------
RowKey: BA CityFlyer
=> (column=Flights, value=545, timestamp=1354875194019000)
=> (column=Hrs, value=686.0, timestamp=1354875194033000)
=> (column=Kms, value=300, timestamp=1354875194010000)
=> (column=Pass, value=30031, timestamp=1354875201897000)
-------------------
RowKey: Aurigny Air Services
=> (column=Flights, value=1388, timestamp=1354875193983000)
=> (column=Hrs, value=887.0, timestamp=1354875193991000)
=> (column=Kms, value=193, timestamp=1354875193958000)
=> (column=Pass, value=26585, timestamp=1354875194001000)

2 Rows Returned.
Elapsed time: 26 msec(s).
[default@First] GET DomesticFlights['BA CityFlyer'] ;
=> (column=Flights, value=545, timestamp=1354875194019000)
=> (column=Hrs, value=686.0, timestamp=1354875194033000)
=> (column=Kms, value=300, timestamp=1354875194010000)
=> (column=Pass, value=30031, timestamp=1354875201897000)
Returned 4 results.
Elapsed time: 59 msec(s).
[default@First]
```

Fig. 5.9 Sample LIST output

```
UPDATE COLUMN FAMILY DomesticFlights WITH comparator =
UTF8Type AND key_validation_class = UTF8Type AND column_metadata
=
  [
     {column_name: airline, validation_class: UTF8Type, index_type: KEYS},
     {column_name: Kms, validation_class: IntegerType, index_type: KEYS},
     {column_name: Flights, validation_class: IntegerType},
     {column_name: Hrs, validation_class: FloatType},
     {column_name: Pass, validation_class: IntegerType}
  ];
```

Now try the same GET command and you should get an answer back this time.

5.6.7   Deleting Data and Removing Structures

To remove a particular column from one row we use the **DEL** command. So, to remove the Hrs column from the BA CityFlyer row we type:

```
del DomesticFlights['BA CityFlyer']['Hrs'];
```

To remove the entire row we type:

```
del DomesticFlights['BA CityFlyer']['Hrs'];
```

If we want to remove the entire Column Family, or Keyspace, we use the **Drop** command:

```
drop column family DomesticFlights;
```

Try each of the above, followed by **LIST** to see the effects.

5.6.8   Command Line Script

Just as Oracle allows you to run SQL and PL/SQL scripts from the operating system, so does Cassandra. This allows database administrators to automate, replicate and schedule particular tasks.

Here we will create a script that will drop our DomesticFlights Family and create another one called DomFlights, inserting some rows, and then querying the data.

Save to the Cassandra directory the following, using your editor, naming it egscript.txt:

```
Use First; Drop Column Family DomesticFlights; Create Column
Family DomFlights
WITH comparator = UTF8Type AND
key_validation_class = UTF8Type AND
column_metadata =
  [
      {column_name: airline, validation_class: UTF8Type, index_type: KEYS},
      {column_name: Kms, validation_class: IntegerType},
      {column_name: Flights, validation_class: IntegerType},
      {column_name: Hrs, validation_class: FloatType},
      {column_name: Pass, validation_class: IntegerType}
  ];
      set DomFlights['Aurigny Air Services']['Kms'] = 193;
      set DomFlights['Aurigny Air Services']['Flights'] = 1388;
      set DomFlights['Aurigny Air Services']['Hrs'] = 887;
      set DomFlights['Aurigny Air Services']['Pass'] = 26585;
      set DomFlights['BA CityFlyer']['Kms'] = 300;
      set DomFlights['BA CityFlyer']['Flights'] = 545;
      set DomFlights['BA CityFlyer']['Hrs'] = 686;
      set DomFlights['BA CityFlyer']['Pass'] = 30031;
      LIST DomFlights;
```

Once you have saved that file, from the Linux $prompt type this command to run it:

```
./bin/cassandra-cli -host localhost -port 9160 -f egscript.txt
```

You should now have the same data that we had before, but in a different Column Family.

5.6.9   Shutdown

At the end of our busy day we may need to bring down the Cassandra Client. To do this we simply use the quit; or exit; command from the client terminal session.

If we want to shutdown the Cassandra server we use the CTRL + C keys. BUT do not do this unless you have finished your session since restarting can need a system reboot.

5.7   CQL

In earlier versions of Cassandra the client interface we have just been using was the only way to interact with the database without writing code, for example Java, to call the APIs. Many users wanting to experiment with the new NoSQL databases found this a problem. Most database professionals know SQL well and an SQL-like language was needed to remove the hurdle of forcing potential users to learn a new language.

In Cassandra 0.8 we saw the birth of Cassandra Query Language (CQL). It was deliberately modelled on standard SQL, but naturally the commands are mapped back to the column orientated storage model.

An example of this is that you can actually use the SQL command CREATE TABLE test…, despite the fact that there is no such structure as a table in Cassandra. The above code generates a Column Family, and the two names can be used interchangeably.

Before we use the CQL environment interactively, as promised earlier, let us use the enhanced script facility available using CQL. In the following example we are going to create a Keyspace, Column Family and then insert data from a CSV file called domDataOnly.csv. It contains the data displayed in the spreadsheet at the start of these notes.

Create a script file using your editor and save it as cqlcommands in the Cassandra directory. It should have the following content, which you should make sure you understand before copying it:

```
CREATE KEYSPACE Flights WITH strategy_class = SimpleStrategy
AND strategy_options:replication_factor = 1;

use Flights;

create ColumnFamily FlightDetails
(airline varchar PRIMARY KEY, Kms int, Noflights int, Hrs float, Pass int);

copy FlightDetails (airline, Kms, Noflights, Hrs, Pass) from 'domDataOnly.csv';

select * from FlightDetails;
```

Note that the syntax is very SQL-like, even down to the commands ending in a semicolon. However, it also maintains its connection with the traditional Cassandra Cli interface commands. Some details are slightly different. The datatypes for the columns, for example are different. They are also case sensitive in CQL. Int will not be allowed, for example, but int would.

Another thing to point out is that, unlike the Cassandra Cli environment, you do have to define the Replication Strategy. Cassandra was built from the start as a multiple node database. Copying data to different nodes, known as replication, helps to improve availability and fault tolerance.

The advice in the online guide is that the replication factor (the number of times each row is replicated) should be less than or equal to the number of nodes being used to hold the replicated data. As this worked example expects the user to be on a standalone, single node version, we have set the strategy to SimpleStrategy and the replication factor to 1—in other words, only one copy will exist on the single node. The line that saves us manually inserting the data is the copy command. We are telling CQL which Column Family is receiving the data, and then into which Columns the data should go. These columns need to be in the same order that they appear in the CSV file.

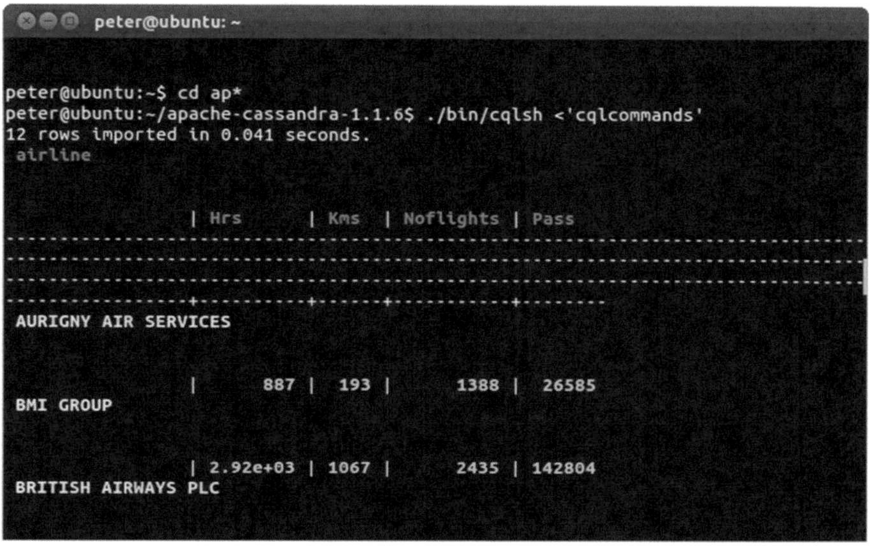

Fig. 5.10 Sample CQL output

To run the script file from the Cassandra directory type this at the $prompt:

```
./bin/cqlsh < 'cqlcommands'
```

You don't get reassurance messages about the creates, but the select shows that the data exists. Your terminal should look like in Fig. 5.10.

5.7.1 Interactive CQL

Just as with the older CassandraCli, you could launch CQL by creating a script like this:

```
#!/bin/bash
cd apache-cassandra-1.1.6
cd bin
./cqlsh
```

(Don't forget to do a Chmod 777.)

Once you have issued the USE command you can begin querying the data we have just input. In this example we see a SELECT using the WHERE clause, and the use of COUNT(*). These will all be straight forward to anyone who has some SQL experience (Fig. 5.11).

```
peter@ubuntu: ~
peter@ubuntu:~$ ./startCQL
Connected to Test Cluster at localhost:9160.
[cqlsh 2.2.0 | Cassandra 1.1.6 | CQL spec 2.0.0 | Thrift protocol 19.32.0]
Use HELP for help.
cqlsh> use Flights ;
cqlsh:Flights> select * from FlightDetails where airline = 'LOGANAIR' ;
 airline  | Hrs      | Kms | Noflights | Pass
----------+----------+-----+-----------+-------
 LOGANAIR | 1.96e+03 | 504 |      2440 | 32994

cqlsh:Flights> select count(*) from FlightDetails ;
 count
-------
    12
```

Fig. 5.11 Interactive CQL output

We still need to apply the same rules that we discovered using CassandraCli when retrieving data—there needs to be an index on a column to search on that column. The example above worked because we defined airline as the KEY and there is therefore an index created for it. Let's try to access data by the Kms column. You will note that the addition of a secondary index allows this to happen (Fig. 5.12).

By accessing the material available on the web, you could experiment further with this data.

```
peter@ubuntu: ~
peter@ubuntu:~$ ./startCQL
Connected to Test Cluster at localhost:9160.
[cqlsh 2.2.0 | Cassandra 1.1.6 | CQL spec 2.0.0 | Thrift protocol 19.32.0]
Use HELP for help.
cqlsh> use Flights ;
cqlsh:Flights> select * from FlightDetails where Kms = 504 ;
Bad Request: No indexed columns present in by-columns clause with "equals" operator
cqlsh:Flights> create index K_ind on FlightDetails(Kms) ;
cqlsh:Flights> select * from FlightDetails where Kms = 504 ;
 airline  | Hrs      | Kms | Noflights | Pass
----------+----------+-----+-----------+-------
 LOGANAIR | 1.96e+03 | 504 |      2440 | 32994

cqlsh:Flights> █
```

Fig. 5.12 Using indexes in CQL

5.7.2 IF You Want to Check How Well You Now Know Cassandra

Using a freely available dataset showing airport locations and Cassandra, answer the question:

How many airports are there in Great Britain north of Heathrow?

You can do this with what we have just learned. You need to know that the country code is GB and that Heathrow's code is LHR.

You should also be aware that CQL does not allow subqueries in the way that SQL does so this process will have to be a two stage one.

If you get the answer without looking for help, award yourself a pat on the back! If you need a pointer or two, have a look at the end of the chapter!

5.7.3 Timings

Now we have enough information to be able to begin comparing Cassandra to other databases. You could, for example normalise the AirportLocations data and load it into two related tables (Airport and Country) using MySQL. Using the Linux TIME command, you could do some comparisons of load time, and retrieval time.

Figure 5.13 shows an example of TIME being used with a CQL command called timetest which contains this code

```
use Flights;
select count(*) from Airports where CountryCode = 'GB' and Lat > 51;
```

You could now try to answer the same question in MySQL, or any other environment you choose.

```
    peter@ubuntu: ~/apache-cassandra-1.1.6
peter@ubuntu:~/apache-cassandra-1.1.6$ time ./bin/cqlsh <'timetest'
 count
-------
   129

real    0m0.334s
user    0m0.140s
sys     0m0.140s
peter@ubuntu:~/apache-cassandra-1.1.6$
```

Fig. 5.13 Using the "time" command

5.8 Document-Based Approach

Many of us are taught that well-structured, normalised data is the only form of good database design when we first encounter large scale database systems. Indeed, this is true for many systems. However, even in RDBMS design there is sometimes a case for denormalising the data for performance.

The document approach takes this even further. It is schemaless, meaning there can be no "correct" design. The application developer using MongoDB, for example, is therefore responsible for data quality issues, rather than relying on the centralised constraints typical of RDBMS.

Why remove these seemingly sacrosanct rules? Well, performance and flexibility are probably two of the main reasons. A large part of a RDBMS's processing time is spent ensuring that the data entered is correct and so not having to check will, it is suggested, speed up write operations. On top of that, adding fields to MongoDB is a relatively trivial task—something which often isn't the case in an RDBMS system. When you have ill-structured data to store this flexibility can be a great advantage.

As Hill et al. (2013) put it:

Many of the document-centric databases don't allow data to be locked in the way that is required for atomic transactions in RDBMS systems. Since locking is a significant performance overhead this enables them to claim performance advantages over traditional databases. The downside, of course, is that some applications absolutely require secure transactional locking mechanisms. Document-oriented is probably not the right vehicle for highly structured data in a transaction dependant environment, as occurs in many OLTP systems.

The performance advantages that accrue from document-centric implementations mean that they are often used when there are large volumes of semi-structured data, such as webpage content, comment storage, or event logging. They may well also support sharding (spreading a table's rows) of data across multiple nodes, again as a performance device.

There is a growing number of Document Databases. Besides MongoDB, for example, there is CouchDB, which, like MongoDB, is open source. Both databases provide APIs for many programming languages, although they have their own inbuilt client environments as well.

They are both written with distributed data handling at their core. They both support the idea of Sharding, where data is spread across a number of nodes in what is also sometimes called "horizontal partitioning" to allow for greater scalability. The examples we use here are stand-alone, but when you review the architecture, bear in mind the end product is often to be expected to run in a multi-node environment.

Sharding is a Shared Nothing approach to distributed databases. Each node has its own instance of the database running. When well implemented this allows high levels of parallel processing when searching for data. However, there would be a risk that the whole database (the sum of the shards) would become invalid if one node failed. For that reason, these databases will replicate shards to provide redundancy. This in turn needs high powered replication processes to always ensure all shards are always available.

Document databases can be complex. A document can contain arrays and sub-documents. Using JSON-like notation, here are two valid documents which could be used in these databases. Note how the two "documents" do not have the same structure and yet can be stored in the same collection.

```
{
name:{ First: "Penelope", Surname: "Pitstop" },
Birthday: new Date("Jun 23, 1912"),
RacesWon: [ "Alaska", "Charlottesville"]
}
{
name: { First: "Peter", Surname: "Pefect" },
Birthday: new Date("May 23, 1940"),
Hometown: "Miami"
Favourite: "Penelope"
}
```

These two pots of information do not look similar enough to become rows in a standard RDBMS. They don't share all fields for a start. And yet a document-based approach allows that sort of flexibility. The name field in both cases is a container for other fields. This is called document embedding. Embedded documents can be complex. RacesWon, however, with its square brackets, is an array.

5.8.1   Examples of Document-Based Using MongoDB

MongoDB chooses to store its data following the JavaScript Object Notation (JSON) rules. JSON is a data-interchange format. You can read about it at the JSON site: http://www.json.org/ For speed this human-readable format is turned into Binary format and stored as BSON.

Architecturally RDBMS users coming to Mongo might find it helpful to think of these comparisons:

- A Mongo Database is a collection of related data, just as in an RDBMS
- A Mongo Collection is a container for documents. It can be thought of as RDBMS table-like
- A Mongo Document is rather like a RDBMS Row
- A Mongo Field is rather like a RDBS Column
- A Mongo embedded document is rather like a RDBMS Join
- A Mongo Primary key is the same as a RDBMS Primary Key
- A Mongo Secondary index is the same as a RDBMS Secondary Index.

5.8.1.1   Getting Hands-On with MongoDB

The tutorial material in this chapter demonstrates the use of MongoDB on Ubuntu Linux. Mongo will also run on other Linux servers, and can be installed on Windows. These notes were created using Ubuntu Linux 11.10 with release 2.2.2 of MongoDB.

We start with the expectation that the reader has basic Unix skills, and has a version of Linux with MongoDB installed on it.

5.8.2   Data Sources

The data in the follow tutorial material is from the UK Civil aviation Authority, made publicly available as Open Data. Many other data sources are available too, from: http://data.gov.uk/.

5.8.3   Getting Started

Assuming you have followed the default installation of MongoDB, as set out on the MongoDB site: http://docs.mongodb.org/manual/tutorial/install-mongodb-on-ubuntu/ you should open a terminal session and, from your home location, create a script file that we will use to launch MongoDB. It will contain a single line:

```
sudo service mongodb start
```

Save this as startMongo. Then when you call it, it will ask for your root password. After entering the password the database server will be running, waiting for connections from a client. Here we will be using the Mongo client that comes with the installation. In the screenshot (Fig. 5.14) you see us starting the server and then starting a client session by issuing the Mongo command.

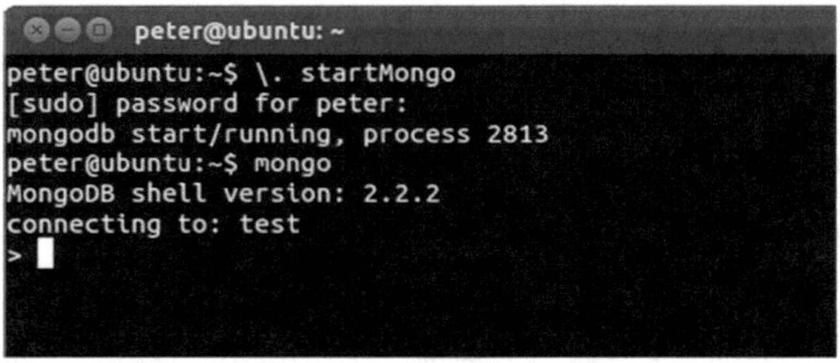

Fig. 5.14 Starting and connecting to Mongo

You will be connected to the default database called "test". As we will see below, the Mongo client is a JavaScript environment and gives the user access to all standard JavaScript functionality.

The service will run until you stop the service:

```
sudo service mongodb stop
```

5.8.4   Navigation

If you need to know what database you are using you can issue the **db** command. In the screenshot (Fig. 5.15) we move to a different db, creating it as we do, by issuing the **use** command—use either changes your working database to an existing database, or creates one of the name you provide. We use a call to **dropDatabase** to remove a database.

If you need further help there is a sizeable manual available online: http://docs.mongodb.org/manual/.

5.8.5   Creating a Collection

The first Collection we are going to work with is a simple list of UK airlines and their domestic flights. The downloaded.csv is bigger than this, but we have edited it down so that it only contains columns we will be using:

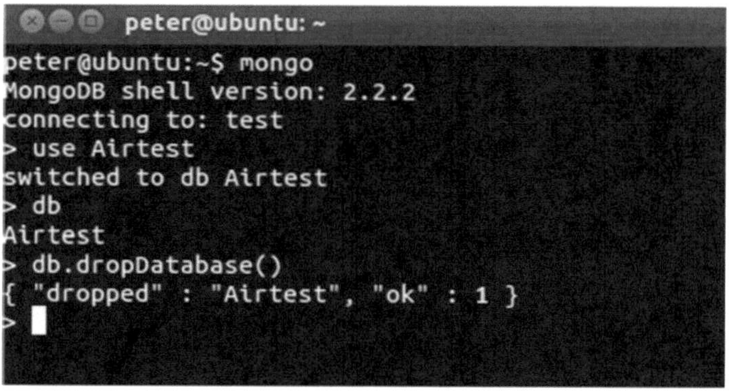

Fig. 5.15 Using and dropping a database

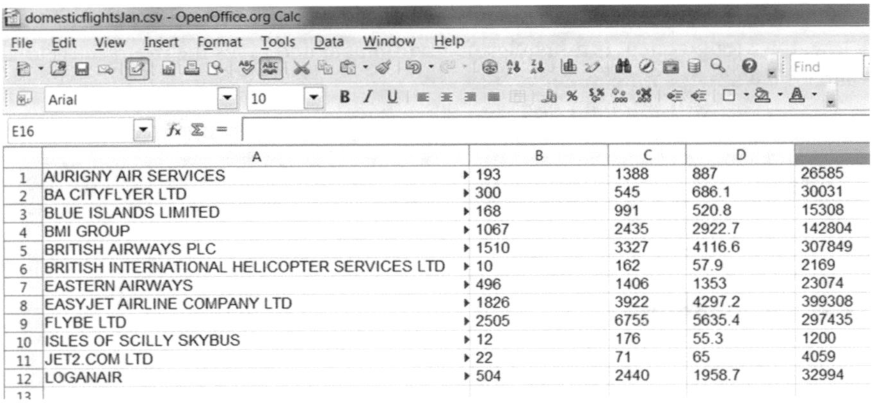

	A	B	C	D	
1	AURIGNY AIR SERVICES	193	1388	887	26585
2	BA CITYFLYER LTD	300	545	686.1	30031
3	BLUE ISLANDS LIMITED	168	991	520.8	15308
4	BMI GROUP	1067	2435	2922.7	142804
5	BRITISH AIRWAYS PLC	1510	3327	4116.6	307849
6	BRITISH INTERNATIONAL HELICOPTER SERVICES LTD	10	162	57.9	2169
7	EASTERN AIRWAYS	496	1406	1353	23074
8	EASYJET AIRLINE COMPANY LTD	1826	3922	4297.2	399308
9	FLYBE LTD	2505	6755	5635.4	297435
10	ISLES OF SCILLY SKYBUS	12	176	55.3	1200
11	JET2.COM LTD	22	71	65	4059
12	LOGANAIR	504	2440	1958.7	32994

Fig. 5.16 Domestic flights data

Airline Name, Km Flown (x1000), Number of Flights, Number of Hours flown, and the Number of Passengers handled. The data is shown in Fig. 5.16.

This is the same data we used in the Cassandra tutorial if you have done that already. It is not that appropriate for a real document-based application but will get us started in using the tool, and we can look at data collection types later.

MongoDB is a document-oriented storage system. Each document includes one or more key-value pairs. Each document is part of a collection and in a database but more than one collection can exist. A collection can be seen as similar to a table in a RDBMS.

Unlike relational databases, MongoDB is schemaless and we do not need to define the datatypes for our incoming values. This can come as a bit of a shock to people with an RDBMS background!

We are going to store our documents in a collection called Flights. As with the **db** name, we do not have to create the collection before we call it. As we see below, if we issue the command to insert and the collection does not yet exist, Mongo creates it. It can do this because there is no schema to worry about.

5.8.6 Simple Inserting and Reading of Data

As we are working in a JavaScript environment we can create variables in memory which we pass to Mongo as parameters when we want to create documents.

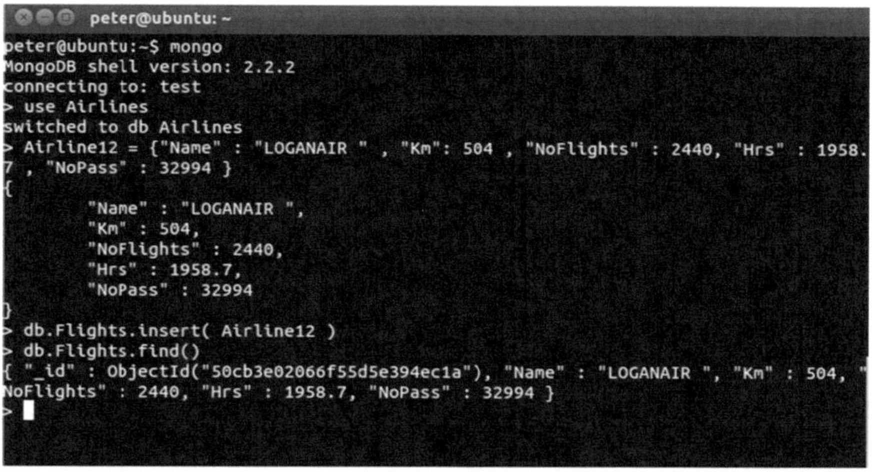

```
peter@ubuntu: ~
peter@ubuntu:~$ mongo
MongoDB shell version: 2.2.2
connecting to: test
> use Airlines
switched to db Airlines
> Airline12 = {"Name" : "LOGANAIR " , "Km": 504 , "NoFlights" : 2440, "Hrs" : 1958.
7 , "NoPass" : 32994 }
{
        "Name" : "LOGANAIR ",
        "Km" : 504,
        "NoFlights" : 2440,
        "Hrs" : 1958.7,
        "NoPass" : 32994
}
> db.Flights.insert( Airline12 )
> db.Flights.find()
{ "_id" : ObjectId("50cb3e02066f55d5e394ec1a"), "Name" : "LOGANAIR ", "Km" : 504, "
NoFlights" : 2440, "Hrs" : 1958.7, "NoPass" : 32994 }
>
```

Fig. 5.17 Adding data to Mongo

In the screenshot (Fig. 5.17) you will see we have:

1. Created a database called Airlines
2. Created a Javascript variable called Airline12 to store information about Loganair.
3. Checked the feedback screen to make sure the variable is correct
4. Used the insert() method of db to add the document to the collection
5. Checked that the data is saved by calling the find() method with no parameters to list all the collection contents

Note the lack of positive feedback from the system after the insert. And the fact that MongoDB has created its own ObjectID to uniquely identify the document.

We can now use find() to look for specific values in the collection. Try this, for example to return the same document which has a Km value of 504:

```
db.Flights.find( {"Km": 504})
```

Naturally we ought to have a few more rows to make finds more interesting, so cut and paste, or type a few, of the following:

```
Airline1 = { "Name": "AURIGNY AIR SERVICES", "Km": 193, "NoFlights": 1388, "Hrs": 887,
"NoPass": 26585 }
db.Flights.insert( Airline1 )

Airline2 = { "Name": "BA CITYFLYER LTD", "Km": 300, "NoFlights": 545, "Hrs": 686.1,
"NoPass": 30031 }
db.Flights.insert( Airline2 )

Airline3 = { "Name": "BLUE ISLANDS LIMITED", "Km": 168, "NoFlights": 991, "Hrs": 520.8,
"NoPass": 15308 }
db.Flights.insert( Airline3 )

Airline4 = { "Name": "BMI GROUP", "Km": 1067, "NoFlights": 2435, "Hrs": 2922.7,
"NoPass": 142804 }
db.Flights.insert( Airline4 )

Airline5 = { "Name": "BRITISH AIRWAYS PLC", "Km": 1510, "NoFlights": 3327, "Hrs":
4116.6, "NoPass": 307849 }
db.Flights.insert( Airline5 )

Airline6 = { "Name": "BRITISH INTERNATIONAL HEL", "Km": 10,
"NoFlights": 162, "Hrs": 57.9, "NoPass": 2169 }
db.Flights.insert( Airline6 )

Airline7 = { "Name": "EASTERN AIRWAYS", "Km": 496, "NoFlights": 1406, "Hrs": 1353,
"NoPass": 23074 }
db.Flights.insert( Airline7 )

Airline8 = { "Name": "EASYJET AIRLINE COMPANY L", "Km": 1826, "NoFlights": 3922,
"Hrs": 4297.2, "NoPass": 399308 }
db.Flights.insert( Airline8 )

Airline9 = { "Name": "FLYBE LTD", "Km": 2505, "NoFlights": 6755, "Hrs": 5635.4,
"NoPass": 297435 }
db.Flights.insert( Airline9 )

Airline10 = { "Name": "ISLES OF SCILLY SKYBUS", "Km": 12, "NoFlights": 176, "Hrs": 55.3,
"NoPass": 1200 }
db.Flights.insert( Airline10 )

Airline11 = { "Name": "JET2.COM LTD", "Km": 22, "NoFlights": 71, "Hrs": 65, "NumPass":
4059 }
db.Flights.insert( Airline11 )
```

Note : all these inserts work but look closely at the Airline11 row. Instead of NoPass, we have NumPass as the field name. This means, for example, that this would return nothing:

```
db.Flights.find({NoPass:4059})
```

This is one of the issues with working without a schema. The overhead of having to check that this was a valid field name would probably mean a relational database would be slower to insert, but the trade-off is that you have to be responsible for the quality of the data.

We can remove the incorrect document:

```
db.Flights.remove({NumPass:4059})
```

Now let us try to insert something else that may not, at first, feel right to a RDBMS person. Try creating this variable and then inserting it:

```
another = { "Name": "Metal Bird", "Km": 112, "NoFlights": 72, "Hrs": 165, "Wings": 2, "Animals":
"Elephants/Hippos" }
```

As we might expect after the previous example, the fact that the 5th Field is called "Wings" rather than "NoPass" does not worry Mongo. But then we add an extra field called "Animals" which does not appear in any other document. Again, this just emphasises the schemaless nature of MongoDB.

5.8.7 More on Retrieving Data

To find out what collections there are in a database, you use the following method:

```
db.getCollectionNames();
```

We can perform some aggregation on the data we now have in the database using some of the methods provided.

The first thing we might like to do is count the number of documents we have stored, which we call the **count**() method to do:

```
db.Flights.count()
```

Then we might want to count particular items. For example, how many of the Airlines in the list fly more than 1000 k Kms?

```
db.Flights.count({ Km: { $gt: 1000 } })
```

So we pass a parameter to the count method which Mongo has to evaluate. Note the syntax, with the use of "{}" pairs to separate out the distinct elements of the expression. $gt means *greater than*.

We saw earlier that **find**() can be used to find specific values. These searches can be **ANDed**, again with the use of "{}". Have a look at the example below and see if you can work out what will be returned. Note the use of "[]" with the $and to pass an array of several expressions.

```
db.Flights.find({ $and: [ { Km: {$gt: 2000} }, { NoPass: {$gt:140000} } ] } )
```

There is also an $**or** operator that works in a similar way. Will the following generate more or less rows?

```
db.Flights.find({ $or: [ { Km: {$gt: 2000} }, { NoPass: {$gt:140000} } ] } )
```

Looking for values from a list is also possible, using the $in operator. In this example we look for two values of Km.

```
db.Flights.find( { Km: { $in: [ 300, 496 ] } } )
```

If you want your output sorted you can use the $sort operator. It needs a sort type to be passed of either −1 (descending) or 1 (ascending).

```
db.Flights.find().sort({Km: -1})
```

A little confusingly you would need to use this sort to discover the Min and Max values in a field since Mongo uses Min and Max in a very different way elsewhere. Here we answer the question Which Airline flew the most Kms?

```
db.Flights.find().sort({Km: -1}).limit(1)
```

So, we sort descending but limit printed output to one row, answering the question in doing so.

Remembering that we can have a variety of field names, we will occasionally need to check if a field actually exists. Using the final insert from earlier for "Metal Bird", we could ask for all documents which contain a field called "Animals":

```
db.Flights.find( { Animals: { $exists: true } } )
```

5.8.8 Indexing

MongoDB allows us to add indexes to fields. As with any database we need to be aware that whilst indexes can speed the retrieval of data, they are a heavy processing overhead during Inserts and Updates, so we should use them with caution.

Indexes in Mongo are stored in B-Trees (see the chapter on Performance for a discussion of index types) and can either be placed on one field, or on multiple fields to form a compound index. They are held on collections. The MongoDB manual suggests that:

In general, you should create indexes that support your primary, common, and user-facing queries. Doing so requires MongoDB to scan the fewest number of documents possible.

Let's assume we decide we will query the collection often using the Km in our queries. To have secondary index on that field we would issue this command (the 1 indicating Ascending)

```
db.Flights.ensureIndex( { Km: 1 } )
```

Queries such as our earlier one to count documents where Km is above a level would automatically use this index. You can also force the optimiser to use the index, as with the example below where we hint to use the index that has been created on the Km field. Note how the data output is sorted in Km order when you use the index.

```
db.Flights.find().hint( { Km: 1 } )
```

You can review the indexes available with the **getIndexes** method on the collection:

```
db.Flights.getIndexes()
```

5.8.9 Updating Data

We can either update the values of a particular field, or alter the fields themselves using the Update() method.

After trying each of these examples, use the find method to check your entry has worked.

Assuming we made a mistake with the entry in the Animals field, we could locate the document using the unique identifier, or as a result of a query, and then pass the change as a parameter. Below, we find the first document for which the Km = 11, and then change the value in the Animals field "Elephants and Badgers":

```
db.Flights.update( { Km: 11 }, { $set: { Animals: "Elephants and Badgers" }})
```

If we wanted to change the name of fields, we could do this by replacing $set with $rename, as below;

```
db.Flights.update( { Km: 112 }, { $rename: { Animals: "Creatures" }})
```

Finally, we may want to add a field, with a value in it:

```
db.Flights.update ( { Km: 112 },{ $set: { Rivers: "Don and Ouse" }})
```

In this case, because there is no field called "Rivers", Mongo creates the field
and then adds the value "Don and Ouse".

5.8.10 Moving Bulk Data into Mongo

CSVs can be input directly using the MongoImport utility This utility can also cope
with JSON data. The utility is called from the $prompt, not within the Mongo
client. Here is an example of how to import a CSV file called AirportLocations.csv,
creating a Database called Airports and a Collection called AllAirports. Note that
we have told MongoImport that the first row contains field names in the header.

Parameters are identified with a leading double minus sign (Fig. 5.18).

The CSV file being input is shown in Fig. 5.19.

Using a freely available dataset showing airport locations and Mongodb, answer
the question:

How many airports are there in Great Britain north of Heathrow?

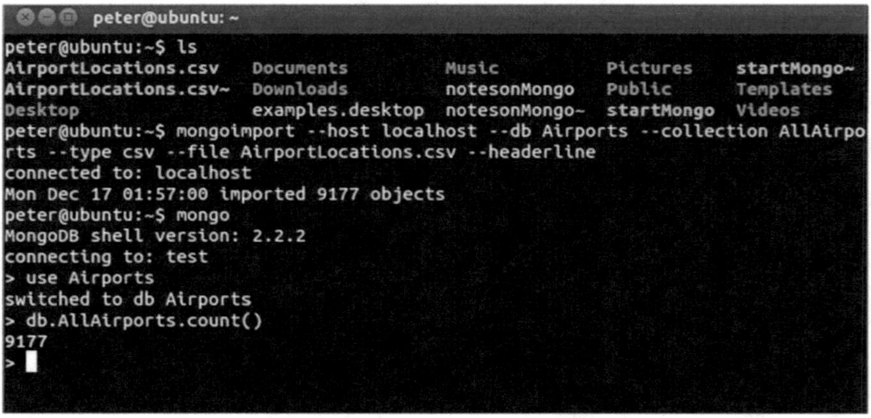

Fig. 5.18 Bulk imports

Fig. 5.19 The dataset used for the bulk import

You can do this with what we have just learned. You need to know that the country code is GB and that Heathrow's code is LHR.

If you get the answer without looking for help, award yourself a pat on the back!

If you need a pointer or two, have a look at the end of this chapter.

5.8.11 Timings

Now we have enough information to be able to begin comparing MongoDB to other databases. You could, for example normalise the AirportLocations data and load it into two related tables (Airport and Country) using MySQL. Using the Linux TIME command, you could do some comparisons of load time, and retrieval time.

Of course MongoDb was designed from the outset as a distributed database and real performance benefits are more likely to come from large volumes of data spread across more than one instance in a distributed document database. Mongo refers to this as Sharding. For now, however, let us just be happy with some elementary reconnaissance!

5.9 Summary

In this chapter we have seen that there are many different data storage methods available for a database. The decision as to which is the right one should be driven by the requirements of the system being supported.

We have examined column-based and a document-based examples of NoSQL databases and seen that they support different types of applications from those transactionally based relational systems we might be used to. There can be no doubt that the advent of Web and Cloud computing generated opportunities and challenges for data professionals and that NoSQL is a potentially useful set of tools to deal with this new era.

5.10   Review Questions

The answers to these questions can be found in the text of this chapter.

- What do ACID and BASE stand for, and what is the most significant difference between them?
- What type of data is best stored using Cassandra?
- What type of data is best stored using MongoDB?
- What is meant by Sharding?
- What do the letters "CAP" stand for and describe what is meant by each letter.

5.11   Group Work Research Activities

These activities require you to research beyond the contents of the book and can be tackled individually or as a discussion group.

Discussion Topic 1 Once you have become familiar with the NoSQL databases in the tutorials above, you should draw up a SWOT analysis to see what strengths and weaknesses, threats and opportunities may be derived from adopting the database in any organisation.

Discussion Topic 2 Try to think of criteria you might use to compare different types of database, including RDBMS and NoSQL examples, to help you decide which might be the most appropriate for a given application. For example, you might think Performance is an important criterion. Having established your criteria, consider how you would measure them. What sort of tests might you need to carry out in order to compare the different databases?

5.11.1   Sample Solutions

Open the spreadsheet you have downloaded (the author used https://ourairports.com/data/). Remember it is Tab separated. Remove the unwanted columns and then save as a CSV file and name it AirportLocations.csv. It should now look like this:

Then, using your editor, create a CQL Script and call it NorthofHeathrow. It should contain:

```
use Flights;
create ColumnFamily Airports
(KEY varchar PRIMARY KEY,
 Lat float,
 Lon float,
 Fullname varchar,
 Country varchar,
 CountryCode varchar
);
Create index on Airports (Lat) ;
Create index on Airports (CountryCode) ;

copy Airports (KEY, Lat, Lon, Fullname, Country, CountryCode) from 'AirportLocations.csv' ;

select Lat from Airports where KEY = 'LHR';
select count(*) from Airports where CountryCode = 'GB' and Lat > 51.5;
```

Run the script:

```
./bin/cqlsh < 'NorthofHeathrow'
```

5.11.2   MongoDB Crib

Open the spreadsheet you have downloaded (the author used https://ourairports. com/data/). Remember it is Tab separated. Remove the unwanted columns and then save as a CSV file and name it AirportLocations.csv. It should now look like this:

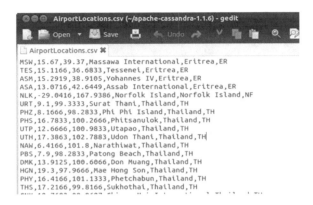

Add a row at the beginning to give the fieldnames:

Use MongoImport, as described earlier to import the data. Then issue the following queries:

db.AllAirports.find({AirportCode: "LHR"})

db.AllAirports.find({Lat: {$gt: 51}, CCode: "GB"})

db.AllAirports.count({Lat: {$gt: 51.47}, CCode: "GB"})

References

Brewer E (2012) CAP twelve years later: how the "rules" have changed. Computer 45(2):23–29. https://doi.org/10.1109/MC.2012.37

Cattell R (2010) Scalable SQL and NoSQL data stores. SIGMOD Rec 39(4)

Chang F, Dean J, Ghemawat S, Hsieh WC, Wallach DA, Burrows M, Chandra T, Fikes A, Gruber RE (2006) Bigtable: a distributed storage system for structured data. In: Proceedings of the 7th symposium on operating systems design and implementation (OSDI'06). USENIX Association, Berkeley, pp 205–218

Gilbert S, Lynch N (2002) Brewer's conjecture and the feasibility of consistent, available, partition- tolerant web services. SIGACT News 33(2)

Hill R, Hirsch L, Lake P, Moshiri S (2013) Guide to cloud computing: principles and practice, Springer, London

Data Sources

UK Government Airline data: https://www.caa.co.uk/Data-and-analysis/UK-aviation-market/Airlines/Datasets/Airline-data/
Airport Locations data: https://ourairports.com/data/

Big Data

6

What the reader will learn:

- That Big Data is not just about data volumes
- That analysing the data involved is the key to the value of Big Data
- How to use tools like Hadoop to explore large data collections and generate information from data
- That the structured data traditionally stored in a RDBMS is not the only valuable data source
- That a data scientist needs to understand both statistical concepts and the business they are working for

6.1 What is Big Data?

1 Terabyte = 1024 Gigabytes.
1 Petabyte = 1024 Terabytes.
1 Exabyte = 1024 Petabytes.
1 Zettabyte = 1024 Exabytes.

And what does a zettabyte of information look like?

A Cisco blog (https://blogs.cisco.com/sp/the-zettabyte-era-officially-begins-how-much-is-that) says:

> If each Gigabyte in a Zettabyte were a brick, 258 Great Walls of China (made of 3,873,000,000 bricks) could be built.

So, we do mean BIG!

© Springer Nature Switzerland AG 2021   141
K. Domdouzis et al., *Concise Guide to Databases*, Undergraduate Topics
in Computer Science, https://doi.org/10.1007/978-3-030-42224-0_6

According to Forbes in 2018 (https://www.forbes.com/sites/bernardmarr/2018/05/21/how-much-data-do-we-create-every-day-the-mind-blowing-stats-everyone-should-read/):

> There are 2.5 quintillion bytes of data created each day at our current pace, but that pace is only accelerating with the growth of the Internet of Things (IoT). Over the last two years alone 90 percent of the data in the world was generated.

But the most obvious trap to fall into is to believe that Big Data, a new term, is only about large volumes of data.

Roger Magoulas from O'Reilly media is credited with the first usage of the term 'Big Data' in the way we have come to understand it, in 2005. But as a distinct, well defined topic, it is younger even than that.

However, Springer's Very Large Databases (VLDB) Journal has been in existence since 1992. It:

> Examines information system architectures, the impact of technological advancements on information systems, and the development of novel database applications.

Whilst early hard disk drives were relatively small, Mainframes had been dealing with large volumes of data since the 1950s.

So handling large amounts of data isn't new, although the scale has doubtless increased in the last few years. Perhaps it isn't really the actual size, but more to do with whether or not we can meaningfully use and interact with the data? This is what Forrester seem to have in mind with the definition suggested on Mike Gualtieri's blog https://go.forrester.com/blogs/13-01-02-big_data_predictions_for_2013/:

> Big Data is the frontier of a firm's ability to store, process, and access (SPA) all the data it needs to operate effectively, make decisions, reduce risks, and serve customers.

They go on to suggest three questions about big data:

> Store. Can you capture and store the data?
> Process. Can you cleanse, enrich, and analyze the data?
> Access. Can you retrieve, search, integrate, and visualize the data?

The Process question is also part of our definition of Big Data. It is often a presumption that Big Data cannot be handled by the standard, RDBMS-based data systems.

Many references to Big Data also come with the word Analytics tagged along somewhere nearby. Analytics may be quite a new term, but again, it has, in reality been with us for decades, sometimes called Business Analysis, sometimes Data

Analysis. We will look at some of the exciting ways Analytics has changed business decisions later in the chapter, but we are really just talking about applying tools and techniques to the large volumes of data now available to an organisation and making some sense of it.

So there seems to be evidence that Big Data is more than just a new buzzword. We can see it as a loose label which covers the storage and accessibility of large volumes of data from multiple sources in a way that allows new information to be gleaned by applying a variety of analytic tools. Interestingly, whilst the phrase "Big Data" appears all over the place on the web, it isn't used much in the jobs market. Instead, people with the required skills are tending to be called Data Scientists.

The rest of this chapter is in three sections. We will look at Big Data from a datacentric perspective, then from an analytics perspective, and then finally quickly review some of the tools being used by Data Scientists.

6.2 The Datacentric View of Big Data

The cost of HDD storage has dropped dramatically over the last few decades, from thousands of dollars to fractions of a dollar per Gbyte. The era when data professionals spent much of their time trying to reduce the amount of data stored in an organisation is fast coming to an end. And Cloud will accelerate the trend as it provides an always available, infinitely flexible store of data.

This super-availability of storage is probably one of the key drivers in the upsurge in Big Data. It is certainly true that data production itself has also grown exponentially over the past few years, but if the cost/Gbyte were currently the same as it was in 1990 there can be little doubt that much of this generated data would be discarded as "not worth keeping".

As we shall see in the Analytics section, significant advances in analysis techniques have allowed useful information to be retrieved from a seemingly meaningless pile of raw data. This means that keeping data just in case it is useful is becoming the norm.

6.2.1 The Four Vs

There are many new data specialists currently helping us get an understanding of big data, and they sometimes disagree. It isn't, of course, unusual for experts to disagree, particularly when a topic is relatively new, but it can make it more difficult for the newbie to come to their own understanding.

An example in point is the number of "V's" that should be considered. Some experts hold with three, others four. On the grounds only that it is easier to ignore one, we have decided to go with the four "V's" (Fig. 6.1). Such acronyms are only useful as an aide-memoir after all, so it is what they are describing that matters.

Fig. 6.1 The 4 "V"s

1. **V is for Volume**

   As we have seen, the most obvious characteristic of Big Data is that it is BIG. It may even be so big that an organisation needs to look for new tools and techniques to store and query it. This volume therefore is likely to be the biggest challenge for data professionals in the near future. It may result in the need for scalable distributed storage and querying, and many will turn to Cloud computing to meet those needs.

   Organisations will also recognise that they have historic data in archives that may help provide analysts with longer time-lines of data to look for trends in. These archives may be tape-based and hard to access and making potentially valuable data available will also be an important part of the data professional's job.

2. **V is for Velocity**

   The devices we carry with us every day, like iPhones, have the ability to stream vast quantities of data of different digital types including geolocation data. A travelling salesman can use an App to report visit information back to head office instantly. Only a couple of decades ago that return of information might have been weekly. Not only is there more data being collected, but it is also being collected instantly.

   But it is the time taken by the decision-making cycle that really matters. Gathering the information quickly is of no benefit if we only analyse it once a week. Real-time analytics is discussed later, but is about using very current data to provide information that will help an organisation improve a service, or respond to demand, in a much swifter way.

3. **V is for Variety**

   For those with a background in using relational databases the idea that data should be anything other than structured may be difficult to grasp. For most of the past three decades we would have models of all the data that a business needed to keep. Whole methodologies grew around storing known specific data items in the most space efficient way.

But one of the interesting aspects of Big Data is that we can use data from a wide range of sources. Perhaps the most frequently quoted example is in analysing the mass of readily available social media data to provide companies with information about how their products are being perceived by the public, without the need for focus groups or questionnaires. They collect and then measure the volume of comments and their sentiment. But the details about their products will be needed too, and they may well be stored in a more traditional RDBMS. Many data sources are now readily available through open data government portals. The data itself can be in many different formats, and the ability to cope with CSV, Excel, XML, JSON and many other formats is one of the skills the Data Scientist now needs.

4. **V is for Veracity**

   Data is just a series of ons-or-offs, usually on a magnetic medium, often squirted around the globe in packets of ons-and-offs. Things go wrong! Organisations need to be able to verify the incoming data for accuracy and provenance.

   But as we begin to hear some astonishing helpful outputs from analytics we also need to be aware that data analysis can get things wrong too. The fact is that when you search for patterns in large data sets it is possible that the patterns discovered are entirely caused by chance.

   We also need to attempt to extract some meaning from the variety of inputs so that we can be accurate about their content. When you have no control over the provenance of data it can become very difficult to ensure its accuracy. Let's say you have mined some social media and discovered the phrase: "Life of Pi is the best film showing in Washington this weekend." Does this mean Washington state, Washington DC or Washington in County Durham in the UK?

6.2.1.1   Non-V

The trouble with helpful terms like "The 4 V's" is that it prevents other equally helpful characteristics from being considered unless you can force them somehow into a V-word. So, for example, there may be an argument that there should be a "U" in there—Usefulness. This can be measured as Potentially Useful, Immediately Useful, and so on. Some analytics experts would counter that all data is potentially useful! Data storage costs have plummeted, but they aren't zero yet. There are occasions when an organisation will decide it's just not worth hanging on to some sorts of data.

6.2.2   The Cloud Effect

Cloud computing brought with it flexible approaches to data storage. Before cloud, if you needed to capture 10 Terabytes of data, then filter it to remove unwanted data, ending up with one Terabyte of data, you actually needed to buy 10 Terabytes of storage. Once the filtering was done that would mean you had over-provisioned by 9 Terabytes. Now, with cloud, you can simply rent ten Terabytes from a service provider for a short period, carry out your filtering and then store only the one Terabyte you need, releasing the unwanted disk space.

If you add this flexibility to the relatively cheap cost of disk storage we can see why the propensity to save data in case it might be useful has risen and the drive to only store what is vital is reducing. If you then add the cloud's worldwide reach and the ease with which datasets can be gathered and analysed we can begin to see how Big Data is so widely talked about.

When organisations begin to use Facebook and Twitter data for data mining purposes, they are, in effect, using the Cloud as part of their data storage strategy. Just as with more traditional database centred approaches, the data professional needs to ensure appropriate levels of availability to the data sources for the business users.

Guaranteed broadband speed connections to the internet are not always available, with availability rates depending upon geography as much as anything else. The most obvious decision is that if the data you need is critical you should store it where you have control and replicate it to ensure Disaster Recovery can happen.

However, it may be the case that it does not really matter to a business that its market intelligence gathered from Twitter does not have to be absolutely current. In that sort of case, bothering with the effort and expense to store the twitter data locally may not make sense, even in the era of cheap data storage. The decision might be to gather the data directly from the internet on an as needed basis, and just live with any gaps caused by lost connections.

In addition to externally sourced data, the Cloud now allows organisations to rethink their backup and DR strategies. As Hill et al. (2013) say:

> "Traditional backup and recovery methods have largely been based around magnetic tape as a medium for storing data. The advantage of this medium is that it is relative cheap. The disadvantage is that it is slow to access and can be quite labour intensive. Systems where the user simply clicks a button to send their backup information to one of several servers somewhere in the Cloud are fast pressuring the traditional approach."

Because of the Pay-as-you-Go approach, Data Storage-as-a-Service has provided organisations with the opportunity to store their data off-site and by storing multiple copies of the data on several servers, these sites have built-in redundancy.

Database-as-a-Service is also becoming an alternative to maintaining your own database server. Microsoft's Azure is one example of this, but there are many others. In terms of Big Data, what this provides is instant scalability and flexibility. As we said above, should you need to store and analyse 1 Petabyte of data as a one-off exercise, you merely buy the space and pay for it only whilst you need it. Traditionally you would have had to ensure you had a free petabyte's worth of disk doing nothing—not a frequent occurrence in even rich organisations!

Cloud can be seen to be, in many ways, an enabler for Big Data. Arguably, we could even say that Big Data would not exist without it.

6.3   The Analytics View of Big Data

Something that comes out clearly from the material written about Big Data is that we are talking about making sense of the data we are storing, not just worrying about the physical aspects of storage.

Moreover, we are also examining data in new, innovative ways to discover new information. Some of this innovation in analysis is to do with the flexibility the new physical storage models allow. For the most part Business Analysts used to concentrate on asking questions of the data within their organisation's control; usually well-structured in format and usually stored in a relational database.

Data warehousing as a discipline is not new. The core idea of capturing a company's OLTP data at certain points of time and storing them in a way that makes querying more efficient has been with us since the late 1980s. The heavy CPU usage caused by the analysis of the data by Business Analysts could dramatically slow down the database server and the core OLTP system would suffer as a result. Indexes can speed up the return of query results, but they always slow the Insert, Delete or Update process. The idea, then, was to extract the data, clean it and filter it, and then store it in a query friendly way, with appropriate schemas and indexes, and store it away from the "live" data.

This process is known by the acronym ETL; Extract, Transform and Load. As we look at the techniques used in Big Data we will see that the process is also a large part of the modern Analytics discipline and the Data Scientist needs to master it as part of their standard toolset.

Data warehousing is a large topic in its own right and outside of the scope of this chapter, but the technologies and techniques we cover here are already beginning to impact upon the area, and there will doubtless be a blurring of the edges between traditional warehousing and Big Data.

6.3.1   So Why Isn't Big Data just Called Data Warehousing 2?

Well, in some ways it could be, but there are differences. Probably the most significant is to do with the analyst's ability to structure the data. As with most relational tasks, a warehouse needs a schema to describe it. To create that schema the designer has to know what data, and data-types, will be stored. They have to have some form of foreknowledge to be able to plan a warehouse effectively.

As we saw earlier, there are two "V" attributes of Big Data that make foreknowledge less likely: Variety and Velocity. Data is now coming into the organisation's purview from many different sources and presented in a variety of formats, such as CSV, Excel, XML, JSON. And that data is coming at the organisation quickly. When a new potentially useful data feed is found there is a need to instantly use it; not to have to define and model it and design a schema to manage it.

The velocity and variety elements are going to be a big challenge. As global research and advisory firm Forrester employee Mike Gualtieri predicted in his blog (https://go.forrester.com/blogs/13-01-02-big_data_predictions_for_2013/):

> Real-time architectures will swing to prominence. Firms that find predictive models in big data must put them to use. Firms will seek out streaming, event processing, and in-memory data technologies to provide real-time analytics and run predictive models. Mobile is a key driver, because hyperconnected consumers and employees will require architectures that can quickly process incoming data from all digital channels to make business decisions and deliver engaging customer experiences in real time. The result: In 2013, enterprise architects will step out of their ivory towers to once again focus on technology—real-time technology that is highly available, scalable, and performant.

But the Volume aspect will also impact upon the analyst. Many data warehouses would archive out, or even delete, data that was beyond the standard reporting time periods—often this year and last. This would be to prevent data storage running out, and also to ensure good performance when querying the data. With these constraints, analysts tended to investigate trends within a relatively short time period— how many tins of beans did we sell last month as compared to the previous month or this time last year—but we are now able to store much more data for longer term analysis.

The ability to store and analyse huge volumes of historic data is likely to make new insights available to the savvy analyst. As always, the hope when looking for new information in a commercial environment is that you can provide some, albeit temporary, competitive advantage. In less commercially focused organisations, such as those in the healthcare area, the hope is to be able to find trends that will help in the identification of causal relationships between lifestyle factors and disease.

As Samuel Arbesman put it in his wired article https://www.wired.com/2013/01/forget-big-data-think-long-data/):

> Datasets of long timescales not only help us understand how the world is changing, but how we, as humans, are changing it—without this awareness, we fall victim to shifting baseline syndrome. This is the tendency to shift our "baseline," or what is considered "normal"—blinding us to shifts that occur across generations (since the generation we are born into is taken to be the norm).

Probably the most high-profile area using long time-scale data at the moment is that of Climate Change, with historic data being used by proponents and doubters alike. And the recent trend in making public data more openly available is also a driver here. The UK Meteorological Office, for example has a selection of weather details back to 1961 available for use by anyone (see Fig. 6.2).

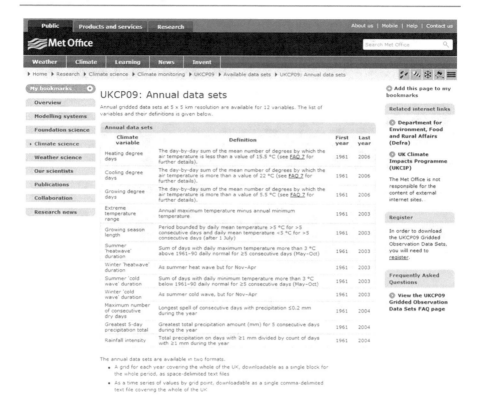

Fig. 6.2 UK Met Office data

Data is also available from organisations like NOAA (National Oceanic and Atmospheric Administration), the US federal agency whose mission is *to understand and predict changes in climate, weather, oceans, and coasts*. They make public, for example, data from ice cores and tree rings which provide palaeoclimatology experts with the ability to deduce how the climate has changed through the earth's history.

So, lots of interesting, detailed new sources of data have recently become available and analysable. Exciting though this may seem for data scientists, it does raise another problem: just how do you select data which might produce useful results after analysis? For data scientists employed by a commercial organisation this question is likely to be framed as "can we contribute to the bottom line as a result of this research?" That constraint will tend to restrict the datasets investigated by any but the least risk-averse analyst as they try to make sure they keep their jobs. Nonetheless, the data scientists' job most certainly includes exploring for new datasets. It is just that it also must include a filtering process that ensures that the outcome is suitably focused.

This issue is well summarised by Vincent Granville on a blog: https://www.analyticbridge.datasciencecentral.com/profiles/blogs/the-curse-of-big-data

> In short, the curse of big data is the fact that when you search for patterns in very, very large data sets with billions or trillions of data points and thousands of metrics, you are bound to identify coincidences that have no predictive power—even worse, the strongest patterns might be:
> - entirely caused by chance (just like someone who wins at the lottery wins purely by chance) and
> - not replicable,
> - having no predictive power but obscuring weaker patterns that are ignored yet have a strong predictive power.
>
> The question is: how do you discriminate between a real and an accidental signal in vast amounts of data?

Two elements of his own answer to the question posed are:

> Being a statistician helps, but you don't need to have advanced knowledge of stats. Being a computer scientist also helps to scale your algorithms and make them simple and efficient.

6.3.2 What is a Data Scientist?

There are many jobs advertised for organisations looking for Data Scientists. The evidence is that this is a booming field and that the shortage of Data Scientists means that those that exist can earn very good salaries. Interestingly there are very few jobs advertised as looking for Big Data expertise, although the Data Scientist is clearly the most obvious user of Big Data techniques in most organisations.

Harvard Business Review published an article in as early as October 2012 (https://hbr.org/2012/10/data-scientist-the-sexiest-job-of-the-21st-century) with the headline:

Data Scientist: The Sexiest Job of the 21st Century.

In a later (2018) HBR article (https://hbr.org/2018/11/curiosity-driven-data-science) says:

> Data science can enable wholly new and innovative capabilities that can completely differentiate a company. But those innovative capabilities aren't so much designed or envisioned as they are discovered and revealed through curiosity-driven tinkering by the data scientists.

One definition of data science used on the Forbes website is:

> "using the accidental output of computing—i.e. data—this new(ish) field uses statistics and coding to do previously difficult things, from understanding customer behavior, to making predictions, to copying human-like 'intelligence.'" https://www.forbes.com/sites/sophiamatveeva/2019/11/29/what-data-scientists-do-and-how-to-work-with-them/?sh=3bda28a04d68

6.3.3 What is Data Analysis for Big Data?

Probably the most important place to start is with questions, not data. Being data driven can occasionally help find unexpected information, but given the need to prioritise a data scientist's tasks, some sort of identification of what an organisation needs to know is essential. This is one reason why some experience in the industry concerned can be a big advantage.

Different industry sectors will tend to want to ask different types of questions. Food retailers, for example, are often looking for buying patterns, both at the individual, and at the market level. Put very simply, if you can use data to evidence the fact that every summer month we sell twice as much ice cream as we do in other months, we know that we should stock more to meet the expected demand.

Many retail store managers would tell you that they make this sort of decision intuitively anyway. And with years of experience in the job they may well be able to "sense" trends rather than precisely discover them. However, they cannot hope to be able to identify trends for all products, especially when the trends are less obvious than "hot weather equals more ice cream".

Production orientated organisations, such as in the coal mining industry, may want to ask similar demand focused questions to help them regulate their supply to the market. However, they may also want to ask questions about the production itself. Historically, for example, can they say that the kilogrammes of coal dug per man-shift is lower on any particular day of the week? Some senior mining engineers might use their gut-feel and say that Friday is always the least productive day. But does the data support that conjecture?

In general, then, big data analytics is about exploring large volumes of data looking for trends, anomalies, previously unknown correlations and obscure patterns which can be used to an organisation's advantage by evidencing some sort of prediction upon which better business decisions are taken.

6.4 Big Data Tools

If you were to doubt that Big Data is really a part of the corporate lexicon, just have a look at some of the vendors who use the phrase prominently:

- Oracle
- SAS
- SAP
- IBM
- EMC

These are all leaders in the field of delivering enterprise scale solutions. All have significant amounts of Web collateral which explain, propose, and sell Big Data products. It is not likely that they have all called this wrong. And they are by no means the only players in the field.

Some of these tools, whilst highly relevant to Big Data, are not Big Data specific and have been around for a while, but it is worth exploring a couple of the newer tools. As with all new areas there are different understandings of what terms mean. Hadoop, for example, is most certainly a frequently asked for skill. In this book the preceding chapter was all about NoSQL databases, but we have decided that Hadoop is so Analytics focused that we would review it here, rather than in Chap. 5.

6.4.1   MapReduce

MapReduce has become a core technique for data scientists. Recognising that analysing high volumes of potentially unstructured data that may be spread across many data nodes is not something that the relational model would be good at handling, people began to turn to a two-stage process. At its simplest this entails:

- looking through all the data and extracting a key identifier and a value, and then storing that in a list.
- Then using grouping, reducing the data thus listed such that you can get information like group totals, averages, minimums and the like.

This process can be shown graphically by referring to Fig. 6.3.

Fig. 6.3 The map reduce process

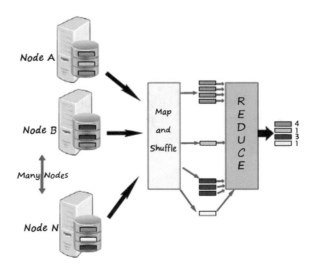

Although the concept is not new, it is as a result of the Google innovators that we are currently seeing such heavy reliance on the technique to cope with large volumes of data. Dean and Ghemawat (2008) tell us that in order to handle the complex and large data analysis tasks they were daily encountering at Google:

> ... we designed a new abstraction that allows us to express the simple computations we were trying to perform but hides the messy details of parallelization, fault-tolerance, data distribution and load balancing in a library. Our abstraction is inspired by the map and reduce primitives present in Lisp and many other functional languages.

NoSQL tools, such as MongoDB have this open source method built into their databases. For examples of using Map Reduce to analyse data, see the MongoDB example in the tutorial section later in this chapter.

6.4.2 Hadoop

Just as MapReduce has become a big feature in the Big Data arena, one of the most frequently used implementations of MapReduce is Hadoop. This is part of the Apache open source suite, and so is freely downloadable from https://hadoop.apache.org/. The website describes it as a:

> ... a framework that allows for the distributed processing of large data sets across clusters of computers using simple programming models.

The two key elements of Hadoop are the distributed file management system (HDFS) and Hadoop MapReduce. The MapReduce examples we provide later are similar except that we use MongoDB to manage the raw data, as opposed to HDFS.

HDFS is distributed and expects to run over several, or many, nodes, although it is possible to run it on a single PC and simulate multi-node operation. It uses replication of data across nodes for both availability and performance reasons. Data nodes are managed by a master node called the NameNode which keeps track of all the files and rebalance data by moving copies around. Client applications, such as MapReduce, talk to the NameNode to locate data. This makes the NameNode a single point of failure and is the potential weakness in terms of High. MapReduce is a separate layer which uses HDFS to source its data requests.

6.4.2.1 If You Should Want to Explore Hadoop...

The examples later in this chapter, using MongoDB, show that MapReduce can be a powerful tool. It is also at the core of Hadoop. At the time of writing there are several example Hadoop installations available for downloading as Virtual Machines, meaning you do not have to go through the pain of installation. That said, if you have access to an Ubuntu (or other Linux) machine, then undertaking the installation journey for yourself will help you get a good understanding of the underpinning architecture.

Amazon's Elastic MapReduce A paid for service. As their website says:

> Amazon EMR is the industry-leading cloud big data platform for processing vast amounts of data using open source tools such as Apache Spark, Apache Hive, Apache HBase, Apache Flink, Apache Hudi, and Presto. Amazon EMR makes it easy to set up, operate, and scale your big data environments by automating time-consuming tasks like provisioning capacity and tuning clusters. With EMR you can run petabyte-scale analysis at less than half of the cost of traditional on-premises solutions and over $3 \times$ faster than standard Apache Spark. You can run workloads on Amazon EC2 instances, on Amazon Elastic Kubernetes Service (EKS) clusters, or on-premises using EMR on AWS Outposts. https:// aws.amazon.com/elasticmapreduce/

6.4.3 Hive, Pig and Other Tools

With computing tools there is often a trade-off between powerfulness and ease of use. This is certainly true of Hadoop which is a very powerful and flexible tool, but for which even its biggest fans do not claim ease of use as one of its attributes. In order to get the best from Hadoop the user should ideally have Java skills and be fully conversant with the Linux operating environment and distributed systems.

As Hadoop is open source there has been a sudden upsurge in Hadoop add-on software to attempt to make the data scientist's job easier. Some, like JasperSoft (https://www.jaspersoft.com/) provide an entire Business Intelligence stack that can plumb into Hadoop (and other data sources). Other vendors, like Oracle, provide their own tools but allow the use of "connectors" to use Hadoop when needed. Two popular open source Hadoop running mates are Hive and Pig.

Hive is, in effect, a data warehousing environment that uses Hadoop behind the scenes. It aims to make data summaries and ad hoc queries against big data sets simpler than it would be using raw Hadoop. One of the ways it does this is with a SQL-like query language called QL. https://hive.apache.org.

Pig uses a programming language called Pig Latin which, when compiled, produces sequences of Map-Reduce programs using Hadoop. It provides a variety of functions and shell and utility commands. Originally developed by Yahoo to provide an ad-hoc way of creating and executing map-reduce jobs, it is now open source and freely usable. https://pig.apache.org/.

6.5 Getting Hands-On with MapReduce

The tutorial material in this chapter demonstrates the use of MapReduce with MongoDB on Linux, and assumes you have carried out the data inserts in the MongoDB tutorial in Chap. 5.

MapReduce as a means of analysing large amounts of data really came to the fore as Google used it to analyse their BigTable data. In the open source world many organisations have turned to Hadoop to perform the same sort of functionality.

Before we move on to those examples, however, you do need to be aware that if you are looking to gain employment as a Data Scientist you will probably have to bite the bullet and become proficient with Hadoop, as it has become the de facto standard in the Big Data area. Even big and powerful vendors like Oracle, SAS and SAP have found no better solution than Hadoop and build it in to their own products. Some examples of how you might get to grips with Hadoop are given at the end of the chapter.

Hadoop would doubtless take a few chapters in a specialist Data Science text-book, and so we feel that its complications, and the need for reasonable Java programming skills, make it unsuitable for this text. Hadoop installation is complex and there are many potential pitfalls in the process, as the author learned to his cost! As we are more interested in using MapReduce itself, and we already have some MongoDB experience (Chap. 5) the easiest solution is for us to use the MapReduce functionality built in to MongoDB to demonstrate its use.

6.6   Using MongoDB's db.collection.mapReduce() Method

As we saw in Chap. 5, MongoDB provides a number of built-in methods in the shell. We used the db.collection.find() method, for example, to search for records.

Another shell method provided is the db.collection.mapReduce() method which is a wrapper around the mapReduce command. We need to write a little bit of code to make this work for us in our environment—in effect creating our own extension to the Map-Reduce process.

Start by re-opening the MongoDB database. Assuming you inserted the Airport data in Chap. 5 you can jump straight to the Airports Database and we will be working with the AllAirports collection. If you did not do this you need to go to the end of the MongoDB tutorial in Chap. 5. The screen dump below reminds us how to do this before starting to build the functions required.

You would probably also need to remind yourself of what the data looks like (again, see Chap. 5). Our first Map Reduce exercise will count the number of Airports each country has.

Remembering that MapReduce is actually a two-stage process we need to create first the **map** function and then the **reduce** function. In this case the Airport-Count_map function adds the number 1 to the output against each instance of every Country Code. The reduce function will use the 1 for its count. The "emit" line is where we define what to output. The reduce function will then add up all the 1 s for each Country Code. Reduce takes the output from Map and creates an Array. The word "this" is used to refer to "the collection currently being operated on". When we call this function you will see that the collection is part of the call.

We have now created the functions (Fig. 6.4) required and the next step is to actually call the functions, using the mapReduce method that MongoDB provides. We have to tell the method which collection we are using, and this is what our map function will use as "this".

The first two parameters to pass are the names of the map and reduce functions that we have just created, and then a third parameter tells MongoDB which collection to write the results to (Fig. 6.5).

As you can see there is some reassurance returned when the method runs successfully. The final step is to look at the results, which we have asked MongoDB to store in the map_reduce_output collection. We need to be aware that if this collection already existed, it would get over-written by this. The opening section of the content of the collection is shown in Fig. 6.6.

So, given that we can discover that AU is the code for Australia we can see that they have 610 airports, whereas Andorra (AD) has just one.

As can be seen from this example the limit of what you can do with map reduce is more to do with the user's programming ability than with the function itself! Just to push this a little further, now let's see if we can use map reduce to tell us how many airfields are on the same parallel.

Firstly, we need to recognise that lines of parallel refer to latitude. Moreover, the data we have is too exact and we will need to use only the units from the latitude stored. So now all we need to do is alter the map method so that it outputs a parallel and a 1. The reduce and output can remain the same.

Try changing the map code to read:

```
var LatCount_map = function() {
var key = Math.floor(this.Lat);
emit(key, 1);
};
```

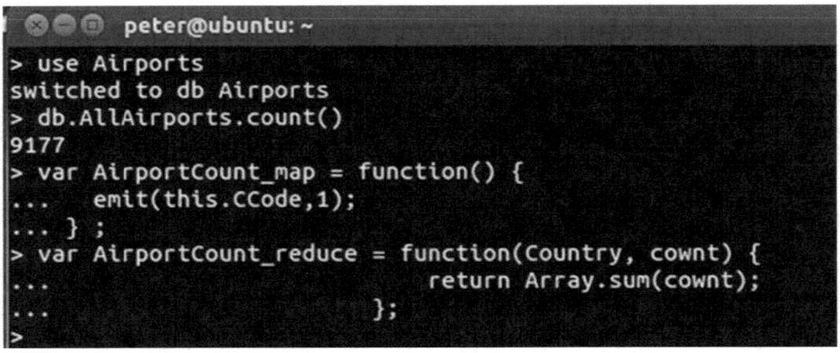

```
😣➖⬜  peter@ubuntu: ~
> use Airports
switched to db Airports
> db.AllAirports.count()
9177
> var AirportCount_map = function() {
...     emit(this.CCode,1);
... } ;
> var AirportCount_reduce = function(Country, cownt) {
...                              return Array.sum(cownt);
...                         };
>
```

Fig. 6.4 Creating the MapReduce functions

```
>
> db.AllAirports.mapReduce(
...                       AirportCount_map,
...                       AirportCount_reduce,
...                       { out: "map_reduce_output" }
...                     )
{
        "result" : "map_reduce_output",
        "timeMillis" : 213,
        "counts" : {
                "input" : 9177,
                "emit" : 9177,
                "reduce" : 303,
                "output" : 234
        },
        "ok" : 1,
}
>
```

Fig. 6.5 MapReduce being called

Fig. 6.6 MapReduce output

```
> db.map_reduce_output.find()
{ "_id" : "", "value" : 26 }
{ "_id" : "AD", "value" : 1 }
{ "_id" : "AE", "value" : 9 }
{ "_id" : "AF", "value" : 27 }
{ "_id" : "AG", "value" : 2 }
{ "_id" : "AI", "value" : 1 }
{ "_id" : "AL", "value" : 1 }
{ "_id" : "AM", "value" : 2 }
{ "_id" : "AN", "value" : 5 }
{ "_id" : "AO", "value" : 39 }
{ "_id" : "AQ", "value" : 1 }
{ "_id" : "AR", "value" : 98 }
{ "_id" : "AS", "value" : 3 }
{ "_id" : "AT", "value" : 14 }
{ "_id" : "AU", "value" : 610 }
{ "_id" : "AUS", "value" : 1 }
{ "_id" : "AW", "value" : 1 }
{ "_id" : "AZ", "value" : 4 }
{ "_id" : "BA", "value" : 4 }
{ "_id" : "BB", "value" : 1 }
Type "it" for more
>
```

But this isn't quite accurate enough since the floor function works the wrong way for negative numbers— −5.5 would become −6 if we used floor. So we need to use ceil with negatives. Here is the revised code, using the appropriate rounding tool depending upon the Latitude passed:

```
var LatCount_map = function() { if (this.Lat > 0)
{
var key = Math.floor(this.Lat);
}
else
{
var key = Math.ceil(this.Lat);
}
emit(key, 1);
};
```

A screenshot of this being called is shown in Fig. 6.7.
Now you could have a go at this task:

Exercise 1
Now see if you can produce a map reduce output that tells us how many airports there are in each of the earth's hemispheres. A worked example is at the end of this chapter. **HINT:** the key in the last example was a number, but it could have been text.

We can also alter the functionality of the reduce function. Let us say we want to discover the furthest north there was an airport. The map function could just send out the list of latitudes and then the reduce could discover the maximum value:

```
var MostNorth_map = function() {
 emit('Lat', this.Lat);
};
```

```
peter@ubuntu: ~
connecting to: test
> use Airports
switched to db Airports
> var LatCount_map = function() {
...   if (this.Lat > 0)
...   {
...     var key = Math.floor(this.Lat) ;
...   }
...   else
...   {
...     var key = Math.ceil(this.Lat) ;
...   }
...
...   emit(key , 1);
... } ;
>
> var LatCount_reduce = function(Lat, cownt) {
...                               return Array.sum(cownt);
...                           };
>
> db.AllAirports.mapReduce(
...                          LatCount_map,
...                          LatCount_reduce,
...                          { out: "map_reduce_output" }
...                        )
{
        "result" : "map_reduce_output",
        "timeMillis" : 192,
        "counts" : {
                "input" : 9177,
                "emit" : 9177,
                "reduce" : 867,
                "output" : 136
        },
        "ok" : 1,
}
```

Fig. 6.7 Airfields on the same Parallel

```
var MostNorth_reduce = function(key, values) {
var max = values[0]; values.forEach(function(val){
    if (val > max) max = val;
  })
  return max;
}

db.AllAirports.mapReduce( MostNorth_map,
    MostNorth_reduce,
    { out: "map_reduce_output" }
    )
db.map_reduce_output.find()
```

Now you could try this:

Exercise 2
Now see if you can produce a map reduce output that tells us which is the most westerly airport from the
Prime Meridian (0°). A worked example is at the end of this chapter.

6.6.1   And if You Have Time to Test Your MongoDB and JS Skills

Only try this if you have some Javascript knowledge! To help, you need to be aware
that what is returned when you use the collection find() method is an array, and the
output can be used programmatically by declaring a variable array to capture the
output values.

Try this task:

Exercise 3
Use the output from Exercise 2 to print all airport details we hold for the most westerly airport. A worked
example is at the end of this chapter.

6.6.2 Sample Solutions

Ex 1 Hemispheres:

```
var HemiCount_map = function() {
if (this.Lat > 0)
{
    var key = "North";
}
else
{
    var key = "South";
}
emit(key, 1);
};
var HemiCount_reduce = function(Hemi, cownt) { return Array.sum(cownt);
    };

db.AllAirports.mapReduce( HemiCount_map,
      HemiCount_reduce,
      { out: "map_reduce_output" }
    )
db.map_reduce_output.find()
```

Ex 2 Most Westerly:

```
var MostWest_map = function() {
      emit('Lon', this.Lon);
};
var MostWest_reduce = function(key, values) {
 var min = values[0];
 values.forEach(function(val){
     if (val < min) min = val;
  })
  return min;
}
db.AllAirports.mapReduce(
     MostWest_map,
     MostWest_reduce,
      { out: "map_reduce_output" }
    )
db.map_reduce_output.find()
```

Ex 3 Most Westerly details:

```
var MRCursor = db.map_reduce_output.find();
var lon = myCursor[0].value
db.AllAirports.find( {"Lon": lon})
```

```
>
> var MRCursor = db.map_reduce_output.find();
> var lon = myCursor[0].value
> db.AllAirports.find( {"Lon" : lon})
{ "_id" : ObjectId("50ceec6b65b30753ebb32bd7"), "AirportCode" : "ONU", "Lat" : -
20.65, "Lon" : -178.7, "Fullname" : "Ono I Lau", "Country" : "Fiji", "CCode" : "
FJ" }
>
```

6.7   Summary

In this chapter we have seen that Big Data is not just about the number of bytes of data we are storing, but about the complexity of the data, and the speed with which it arrives. Organisations need to be able to make sense of more and more data and begin to look outside of their own data sources. Tools that have enabled the change in the way we store and analyse data are also increasing in number and maturity rapidly. At the time of writing Hadoop seems to have become the de facto standard such tool with many leading commercial vendors adopting it and integrating with it. MapReduce is a key part of Hadoop but is a general programming approach and other tools allow MapReduce, as we saw with MongoDB in the tutorial.

6.8   Review Questions

The answers to these questions can be found in the text of this chapter.

- What has become the de facto standard approach for handling large datasets stored across many nodes? Your answer could be a framework or a programming model—or both!
- What do the letters SPA stand for, as used by Forrester talking about big data?
- What are the 4 "V"s?
- What makes Big Data different from traditional data warehousing?
- What is HDFS?

6.9   Group Work Research Activities

These activities require you to research beyond the contents of the book and can be tackled individually or as a discussion group.

Discussion Topic 1 As the CIO of a company you need to come to terms with Big Data. Your board of directors are asking you what it might mean for them. Review the key elements of Big Data, and how they may impact upon any organisation's information strategy, and attempt to report, in terms simple enough for a non-technical executive, what changes to information management might be worth exploring as a consequence of the new technologies becoming available.

Discussion Topic 2 "Big Data is nothing new". Discuss this assertion. You should review the benefits and disadvantages of different approaches to storage and analysis of large volumes of data.

References

Dean J, Ghemawat S (2008) MapReduce: simplified data processing on large clusters. Commun ACM 51(1):107–113. https://doi.org/10.1145/1327452.1327492
Hill R, Hirsch L, Lake P, Moshiri S (2013) Guide to Cloud Computing: principles and practice. Springer, London

Object and Object Relational Databases

7

What the reader will learn:

- The problems with data structures and relational databases
- What is an object
- How objects are handled in a database
- What an object oriented database is
- What is an object relational databases and how it is implemented

7.1 Querying Data

One of the issues with data is that it has become more and more complex. As we saw in Chap. 2 there was a transition from early file-based systems to more complex database systems which could be accessed using a query language. The format of data in these systems was alphabetic, numeric or alphanumeric with some special types such as date. This was stored in independent files which required end to end sequential processing. There was no need for a query language. The second transition was to be able to search and select data directly using so-called random-access files. These files were ultimately joined together to become databases which could be manipulated with a powerful query language. As seen in Chap. 4, relational databases became the de facto standard for this type of data. The next development was the requirement to store complex objects and retrieve them using a query language. Figure 7.1 gives a simple classification of data and queries. As will be seen in the text below, considering object databases to only be associated with simple queries is not correct.

© Springer Nature Switzerland AG 2021
K. Domdouzis et al., *Concise Guide to Databases*, Undergraduate Topics
in Computer Science, https://doi.org/10.1007/978-3-030-42224-0_7

Fig. 7.1 A simple
classification

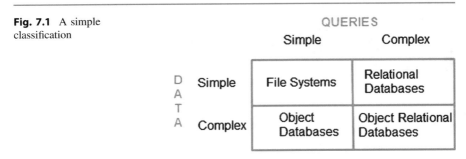

7.2   Problems with Relational Databases

The first big problem with relational databases is that SQL only supports a restricted number of built-in types which deal with numbers and strings. Initially the only complex object was BLOB (Binary Large OBject) but now vendors are including other objects such as CLOB (Character Large OBject) and XML_Type. XML will be discussed later in this chapter. Increasingly there are requirements to deal with different complex objects such as graphics, video, audio and complete documents, all of which can be in a variety of different formats. The volume of this electronic data is rapidly increasing and there is a tendency to store anything that can be stored. Relational databases are not the best structures to store this type of data.

The second problem is that relational tables are essentially flat files linked by joins and do not easily support sets and arrays. Set theory means you can have data which is grouped by some criteria (say people aged between 20 and 29) which can be viewed in terms of its relationships with other groups of data (say smart phone ownership). In this example the intersection of two sets would be the data common to both sets (people aged between 20 and 29 who own a smart phone) while the union would be all the data in both sets (all smart phone owners and all people aged between 20 and 29). Arrays on the other hand bring us back to the first problem in that they store lots of data, often images which have a pixel format.

The third problem is there are certain types of relationships that cannot easily be represented without some kind of work around. For example, in Chap. 4 the concept of a hierarchy was introduced where there was a superclass with one or more subclasses associated with it. Attributes and methods from the superclass were inherited by the subclasses. This structure had to be converted into relational tables to make it work in a relational database. Doing this always introduced some in efficiency either in the form of NULL fields or excessive table joins which has an impact on database performance. In the real-world things are often organised into hierarchies. For example, in a staffing system different classifications of staff will have different attributes, but some data, like staff number, name and address will be common to classes of staff and would be at the top of the hierarchy, to be inherited by the specialist subclass definitions.

The fourth and probably most important issue is that there is often a mismatch between the data access language (SQL) and the host language (for example java). This is termed the impedance mismatch. For example, in object oriented programming one of the main concepts is encapsulation. Some encapsulated objects have their representation hidden. These are called private objects and are at odds with relational database representations where access is relative to need rather than an absolute characteristic of the data. Issues such as these are often solved by a programming work around.

Some vendors have solved at least some of these problems, but in a proprietary way rather than an industry standard way. Oracle, for example, has an implementation for sets and operators to manipulate them.

7.3 What Is an Object?

It is probably best to start with a definition and discussion of objects, then move on to object oriented databases, then look at the disadvantages of pure object oriented databases when dealing with lots of 'traditional data'. We will then look at the disadvantages of using relational databases when there are requirements to include and merge with object oriented technologies.

As we saw in Chap. 2, relational database theory is based in mathematics. Humans however tend to recognize 'objects' immediately in terms of their totality or 'wholeness'. Therefore our original relational example of an invoice would be viewed as a single object rather than being composed of a number of 'relations' by the average person.

From a programming point of view, an object is an encapsulation of data and the process which manipulate it. Only the data and methods which need to be seen on an interface are 'visible' to a user. For example, if we think of a television set as an object there are a restricted number of controls and data entry you as a user can interact with. The rest is 'hidden' inside the device.

In object oriented programming when an object instance ends, the data associated with it is lost. The problem with this definition is that the data may 'outlive' the processes. With a digital television, it 'remembers' the stations it has been tuned to, even when it is switched off. This phenomenon of data outliving the object is known as persistence.

In fact, in a pure object world a relational database is often represented as a single persistent object. This fits with the concept of object orientation where the complexity of the object is hidden and only its 'public' data and processes can be 'seen'.

The discussion so far, that hasn't really defined an object in database terms. The word 'object' is really a shortened version of what we are talking about and there are two interpretations: object class and object instance. Depending on the object definition language you are using an object class is normally a description of the classes attributes, the messages to which the object responds and the methods which manipulate the object. The data itself is called an object instance. So if we have an object class student, an instance of the class could contain the attributes for the student 'Dorian'.

So far we are still looking at attributes which store simple data such as characters and numbers, however a further complication has been the rise of graphics, images, video and other large data items which require storing, linking and retrieving. As already mentioned relational databases deal with these via a single data type— BLOB (Binary Large OBject) although most vendors included other large object data types. Relational databases also include other, normally character based attributes to assign keys. This was OK when dealing with something which fitted the relational structure such as a single image of a stock item. It was not such a good solution when dealing with the data required in a graphic based system of multiple related images. In these systems using the traditional primary/foreign key joins becomes highly complicated.

A solution to this is to assign an object an identity that uniquely identifies the object, but unlike a primary key is not stored as an attribute of the object.

7.4 An Object Oriented Solution

The Object Data Management Group (ODMG) which formed in 1991 and disbanded ten years later in 2001 developed a set of standards, the last of which was ODMG 3.0 in 2000. This formed the basis of an industry standard giving guidelines for a SQL like language to manipulate objects, Object Query Language (OQL).

About the same time the Object Oriented Database System Manifesto was produced by Atkinson et al. (1992). This proposed thirteen mandatory features:

- Complex Objects
- Object Identity
- Encapsulation
- Types and Classes
- Type and class hierarchies
- Overriding, overloading and late binding
- Computational completeness
- Extensibility
- Persistence
- Efficiency
- Concurrency
- Reliability
- Declarative query language Taking each of these concepts in turn.

Complex Objects: these are formed through constructor orthogonality. This means a small set of primitive constructs can be combined in a small number of ways to form more complex structures. In simple terms this means complex objects can be formed from other objects by a set of constructors.

Object Identity: Each object has a unique identity assigned by the system. Objects can be shared through references to their identity. This corresponds to the structure proposed by the ODMG.

Encapsulation: In object orientation an object consists of an interface and implementation. The interface defines the way the object looks to the environment. The implantation defines the object data and methods which are used for internal manipulation. The state of the object can only be altered through its interface although the data structure can have declarative queries applied to it.

Classes: Developers should be able to develop their own classes, for example an 'Employee' class or 'Address' class.

Hierarchies: Many data structures can be regarded as hierarchies. We already saw this in Fig. 4.15 of Chap. 4 where we had a hierarchy consisting of 'Motor Vehicle' as the super class at the top of the hierarchy and a number of subclasses. Objects in the subclass automatically belong to and inherit all the attributes and methods of the superclass although the subclass can have attributes and methods in its own right.

Overriding, overloading and late binding: This is related to hierarchies. In method overriding, a method in the superclass is redefined in the subclass. This allows specialisation in the subclass while preserving the uniform interface defined in the superclass. Overloading is the effect caused by method overriding. This is because it is possible to have multiple methods in the same class that share the same name but have different parameter lists. They must however have the same number of return values. Late binding refers to the overloaded method that is selected at run time and will depend on where you are in the hierarchy.

Computational completeness is a requirement for the method implementation language. Basically, it should be possible to express any computable function.

Extensibility: The database has a set of predefined types which developers can use to define new types. This relates to the mandatory feature of complex objects and constructor orthogonality.

Persistence: The data has to survive the program execution. In all object oriented applications a database is regarded as a persistent object.

Efficiency: The database must have index management, data clustering and data buffering to optimise queries.

Reliability: The database must conform to the principles of ACID (see Chap. 2 for details). In other words, it must be resilient to user, software and hardware failures. Transactions must be all or nothing in terms of completeness and operations must be logged.

Declarative query language: Non-trivial queries must be able to be expressed consistently through a text or graphical interface. The query language must be vendor independent, in other words be able to work on any possible database.

This of course was a manifesto and together with the ODMG served as guide to the development of object oriented databases from the early 1990's. The resulting query language, Object Query Language (OQL) met the requirements of the manifesto and the ODMG. It looks very much like normal SQL but rather than naming tables in the SELECT clause, object classes are named. The language also has a concept of joins, but because the relationships are established with pointers rather than with a primary/foreign key reference, only the key word JOIN is required. Other structures such as hierarchies are also implemented.

In the 1990's a number of vendor implementations of object-oriented databases appeared. These included O2 (now owned by IBM), JADE and more recent open source products such as db4o.

As an example, in the O2 language (which follows ODMG OQL standard) a simple select clause becomes:

```
SELECT c FROM c IN BBB.customer
WHERE date_added < '01 JAN 2013'
```

To retrieve data from two objects:

```
SELECT DISTINCT inv.what FROM cl IN BBB.customer, inv IN cl.invoice
WHERE cl.customer_name = "Felsky"
```

For more details see the ODMG OQL User Manual Release 5.0—April 1998.

There have been a number of ways put forward to get around the impedance mismatch problem. Java Persistence Query Language (JP-QL) is an object query language designed for use with Java and to be platform independent. This is not designed to manipulate object oriented databases, but to allow an interface between java and relational databases. For example:

```
public List getStock() throws StockNotFoundException
  { try {
  return em.createQuery(
  "SELECT st FROM Stock st ORDER BY st.code"). getResultList();
} catch(Exception ex){
throw new StockNotFoundException("Could not find stock:"
+ ex.getMessage());
  }
}
```

which has a relational SELECT clause embedded in the middle.

7.5 XML

A final solution presented here is XML (eXtensible Markup Language) which can be used to structure data. The central design goal for XML is to make it easy to communicate information between applications by allowing the semantics of the data to be described in the data itself. XML was designed to overcome the short-comings of HTML by providing a way to have a domain specific markup language. Many industry specific XML standards have been proposed. In the chemical industry a standard called ChemML has been developed to represent chemicals and their properties. For example in ChemML water (H2O) is described as:

```
<chem><molecule n ="2">
    <atom n ="2"> H < /atom>
    <atom> O < /atom>
< /molecule>< /chem>
```

The primarily purpose of XML is to markup content, but it is claimed to have many advantages as a data format because:

- Utilizes unicode.
- Platform independent
- Human readable format makes which makes it easier for development and maintenance (although this is sometimes contested).
- Extensibility, so new information won't cause problems in applications that are based on older versions of the format.
- There exists a large number of off the shelf XML tools

Therefore it is not primarily a database definition language. However code can then be written to manipulate XML objects in the database. The are two main variants: XML Data Reduced (XDR) and XML Schema Definition (XSD). XDR was an interim standard adopted by Microsoft before the introduction of XSD which is the World Wide Web Consortium (W3C) specification. However, because XDR was introduced first (and by Microsoft) there are still a lot of applications which use it as a base.

The following XML Data Reduced (XDR) is in the Microsoft based version and defines a customer:

```
<Schema name+"customer"
       xmlns="urn:schemas-microsoft-com:xml-data"
       xmlns="urn:schemas-microsoft-com:datatypes">
       <ElementType name="cutomer" model="closed" content="eltOny" order="seq">
         <AttributeType name="CustomerDescription" dt:type="string" required+"yes"/>
         <attribute type="CustomerDescription"/>
         <element type="Customer_Name" minOccurs="1" maxOccurs="*"/>
       < /ElementType>
       <ElementType name="Customer_Name" model="closed" content="textOnly"
             dt:type="string">
         <AttributeType name="Customer_Address" dt:type="string"
             required="yes"/>
       <attribute type="Customer_Address"/>
       < /ElementType>
< /Schema>
```

XML Schema Definition (XSD) looks very similar. Here we have a definition for stock:

```
<xs:element name="stock" maxOccurs="unbounded">
  <xs:complexType>
    <xs:sequence>
      <xs:element name="code" type="xs:string"/>

      <xs:element name="description" type="xs:string" minOccurs="0"/>
      <xs:element name="price" type="xs:decimal"/>
    < /xs:sequence>
  < /xs:complexType>
< /xs:element>
```

To search for a record a typical code fragment would look like:

```
FOR $b IN document("cust.xml")//customer
WHERE $b/name = "Warren Felsky"
AND $b/postcode = "S11 4RT"
RETURN $b/customer_id
```

which would return the customer_id's of any customer called Warren Felsky.

Major vendors have already embraced XML as part of their products. Oracle has developed Oracle XML DB, a native XML storage and retrieval technology which is delivered as part of their standard database system. It provides support for all of the key XML standards, including XML, XML Namespaces, DOM, XQuery, SQL/XML and XSLT. This support enables XML-centric application development.

Although not as advanced, SQL Server provides support for XML including support for the XML data type and the ability to specify an XQuery query against XML data.

There are also a number of free and open source XML database systems available such as Sedna which is a free native XML database. It provides a full range of core database services including persistent storage, ACID transactions and flexible XML processing facilities including W3C XQuery implementation (see https://www.sedna.org/ last accessed 26/07/2013).

Another is BaseX which is also free. This is a scalable light-weight XML Database engine supporting XPath and XQuery Processing. It supports the latest W3C Update and Full Text Recommendations (see https://basex.org/home/ last accessed 26/07/2013).

7.6   Object Relational

Object oriented databases were never really adopted by the vendor community despite a flurry of products in the 1990's, but many of the principles ODMG defined were incorporated into relational database management systems resulting in what is often referred to as object relational databases. Oracle Corporation, for example started incorporating object features in Oracle 9i and steadily expanded them and associated development tools such as J developer. In the following examples Oracle statements will be used. Microsoft's SQL Server also has object relational features but these are not fully developed. For example, constraints are not inherited in hierarchy structures.

PostgreSQL is another popular object relational database management system which was first devised in the 1980's. The advantage of this system is it is cross platform, free and open source. As a result, it is popular with personal computer users. For more information see Obe and Hsu (2012).

It should be remembered that object relational is a work around to give some of the functionality of object orientation by building on top of the existing relational framework. As will be seen, there is always a relational table storing the objects.

7.7   What Is Object Relational?

Figure 7.2 will be used as the basis of the discussion and examples in the rest of the chapter. The code in bold can be typed in as you work through this section so it will be possible to create and experiment with object relational structures as you proceed.

Figure 7.2 shows a number of object classes. An object class consists of a number of attributes and the methods to manipulate them. In the example each of the object classes has a number of methods or operations associated with them. Generally, there is one operation for create, retrieve, update and delete (so called CRUDing operations) but this is not a hard and fast rule. It should be noted that hierarchy under shop_stock contains only one operation (in subclass magazine). This is because each of the subclasses inherits the methods of shop_stock. Magazine is an exception because periodicals are not reordered based on stock levels instead being ordered on expected sales so returns are kept to a minimum. This operation would override the add new stock operation in the shop_stock class. This will be illustrated later.

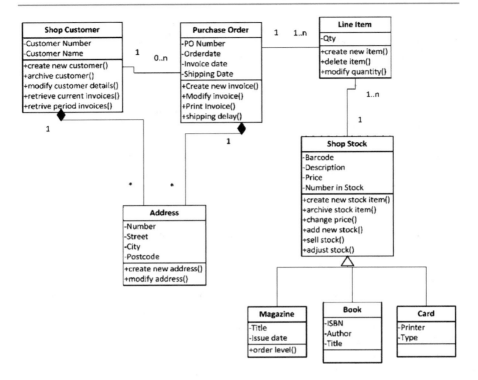

Fig. 7.2 A UML class diagram which will be implemented as an ORDB

It is probably a good idea at this point to define an instance of an object. This is roughly equivalent to a record in a relational database, so purchase order 45,378 of the 3rd December 2012 is an instance of the purchase_order class.

The second thing to note about the class diagram is there are no primary or foreign keys. Classes are linked via associations implemented by pointers.

7.8　Classes

When a class is defined it can be used in any other definition where that class is used. In most commercial databases we often define a table called address, but there are many types of addresses for example: delivery address, home address, billing address. Each of these has the same format, but we define them individually in a relational database system. A much better approach would be to have a single data item called 'address' which we could then use whenever an address is needed.

```
CREATE TYPE addr_ty AS OBJECT
    (street          varchar2(60),
     city            varchar2(30),
     postcode        varchar(9));
```

The address type could then be used in the definition of 'Shop Customer':

```
CREATE TYPE shop_customer_ty AS OBJECT
    (customer_no varchar(9),
     name            varchar2(25),
     address         addr_ty);
```

Obviously you must create something before you can use it in another creation statement so in this example you must create the address type first before you can use it in the shop customer type. Once you have created a type you can use it multiple times, for example address is used in purchase order.

Up until this stage the structure looks object oriented but actual data still needs to be stored in a table, so now we need a table to hold the object structures:

```
CREATE TABLE Shop_Customer OF Customer_objtyp
    (PRIMARY KEY (CustNo))
    OBJECT IDENTIFIER IS PRIMARY KEY;
```

The Shop_Customer table contains Customer objects. Each of these has its own object identifier or OID. You can either allow Oracle to generate this (**OBJECT IDENTIFIER IS SYSTEM GENERATED**) or specify the objects primary key to serve as it OID with **OBJECT IDENTIFIER IS PRIMARY KEY** which is what we have done in this case. **OBJECT IDENTIFIER IS PRIMARY KEY** should only be used if there is a naturally occurring attribute which lends itself to this role. If there is no natural candidate for a primary key, you should not create one but use **OBJECT IDENTIFIER IS SYSTEM GENERATED**.

Once the table has been created it can be populated with object instances:

```
INSERT INTO customer (shop_customer)
    VALUES
        ('0032478FT',
         'Warren Felsky',
         '8 Mien Place, Sheffield',
         'S1 6GH' );
```

The address information does not have to refer to the type (**addr_ty**) which was created. It is just another data type, only one that has been created by the user.

Once you have stored information of this object instance in this structure you need to be able retrieve it again. In this case you must state what attributes you want returned, but not their type:

```
SELECT c.shop_customer.customer_no ID, c.shop_customer.name NAME,
       c.shop_customer.address ADDRESS
       FROM customer c
       WHERE c.shop_customer.customer_no = '0032478FT'
```

We can use any of the selection constructs we saw in Chap. 4's discussion on SQL. In this case we are looking for the details of customer '0032478FT' which will result in the output:

ID	NAME	ADDRESS
0032478FT	Warren Felsky	8 Mien Place, Sheffield.

It is important to note that in Oracle, aliases (in this case 'c') must be used. This allows the substitution of 'c' for 'customer' otherwise the statement would look like:

```
SELECT customer.shop_customer.customer_no ID,
       customer.shop_customer.name NAME,
       customer.shop_customer.address ADDRESS
       FROM customer
       WHERE customer.shop_customer.customer_no = '0032478FT'
```

which is not only longer but messy and confusing. **ID, NAME and ADDRESS** are also aliases for the column headings; otherwise the name of the selected attribute would be used, for example **c.shop_customer.customer_no** would be the column heading instead of the alias ID.

7.9   Pointers

In a traditional relational database, tables are linked via joins. The joins use a common primary key—foreign key attribute to link the two tables together. This is one of the hardest concepts for those new to the database field to master. There are two problems with this, however. One is you may be creating an attribute for no other reason than to give the data a unique identifier (the primary key). Second you may include that data item in another table for no other reason than you want to join them—it may not logically be an attribute of that table.

In our example, the Purchase Order object contains a pointer to the associated customer object. That is a customer can have many orders but the order can only be associated with one customer—a classic one to many relationship. In a relational database this would be implemented with a table join involving the primary key of the customer table as the foreign key in the order table. In an object relational implementation the link must still be established but it is done with a pointer embedded in one class pointing to another. So an instance of purchase order must include a pointer to the instance of the customer class to which it belongs.

Creating the purchase order object is done as follows. Note this object has **Cust_ref** included to reference the customer object. A pointer is generated to the appropriate object instance in the **shop_customer** table. This will be seen later when we create the tables which hold the objects. Also note you could use the syntax **CREATE OR REPLACE** in the creation of **Address_objtyp** and **Customer_objtyp**. This means you do not have to first **DROP** an object before creating its replacement:

```
CREATE OR REPLACE TYPE Purchase_Order_objtyp AS OBJECT
    (PONo varchar2 (12),
    Cust_ref REF customer_objtyp,
    Orderdate        DATE,
    shipdate         DATE,
    shp_address_obj Address_objtyp);
```

Just like the customer table holds the customer object, we need a table to hold the purchase order object. There is a problem here as a foreign key constraint is required. This illustrates the issues of combining relational and object oriented structures. In this case the **Customer Number** needs to be added to **Purchase Order** as a foreign key. When the purchase order object was created we already specified the **Cust_ref** attribute was a pointer, now we specify which table it is pointing to.

```
CREATE TABLE purchase_order OF Purchase_Order_objtyp
    (PRIMARY KEY (PONo),
    FOREIGN KEY (Cust_ref) REFERENCES Shop_Customer) OBJECT IDENTIFIER IS
    PRIMARY KEY;
```

Now we have created the basic structure for Customer, Address, Purchase Order and Shipping Address. It also illustrates the trade-off for having objects in what is still essentially a relational database environment.

The next stage is to add data:

```
INSERT INTO Shop_Customer
    VALUES (1234, 'Warren Felsky',
    Address_Objtyp ('2 Sherwood Place', 'Latrobe', 'L1 1AC'));
```

Adding data to a table with a **REF** construct to allow one object to reference another is more complex than a relational **INSERT** statement and requires the use of a SELECT as shown in the following example where a new purchase order is created. This makes sure that each **Purchase_Order** object instance has a pointer (an object ID or OID) to the associated **Shop_Customer** table object instance.

Once again, the order in which you create things is important. You must create a **Shop_Customer** record before you can create a **Purchase_Order** record. In other words, you can't have a purchase order with no associated customer.

```
INSERT INTO Purchase_Order
    SELECT '1004', REF(c),
        SYSDATE, '10-MAY-1999',
        address_objtyp( '8 Mien Place',
                        'Sheffield',
                        'S1 6GH' )
    FROM Shop_Customer c
    WHERE C.CustNo = 1234;
```

In the above example:

- The literal value "1004" is inserted into the **Purchase_Order** table.
- The **REF** function returns the OID (object identifier) from the query on the selected **Shop_Customer** object.
- The OID is now stored as a pointer to the row object in the **Shop_Customer** object table. This is the link from the purchase order object to the associated customer.
- **SYSDATE** captures the current date from the system clock.
- The delivery date is entered.
- The address details are stored.
- **FROM Shop_Customer c WHERE C.CustNo = 1234** is the query associated with the **REF** function.

The referenced value cannot be seen unless the DREF function is used. The DREF function takes the OID and evaluates the reference to return a value. Any attempt to select objects containing a REF, say with:

```
SELECT * FROM purchase_order;
```

would result in a long alphanumeric string representing the hexadecimal value of the pointer rather than a real value.

In the following example we want the customer's name, purchase order numbers and shipping address:

```
SELECT (cust_ref).custno,
    (cust_ref).custname,
    p.pono,
    p.shp_address_obj.city
FROM Purchase_Order p
WHERE (cust_ref).custno = 1234;
```

If you don't use the (**cust_ref**) and try to use both tables and not put in a table join, we end up with a Cartesian join. **Cust_ref** is following the **REF** pointer to the customer.

Note that using **p.cust_ref** does not give the same value as **c.custno** as **cust_ref** is a pointer to the appropriate record in **Shop_Customer** table, not an attribute that stores 'real' data (try it and see!). To see the real value you must use **DEREF**:

```
SELECT DEREF(p.cust_ref)
    FROM Purchase_Order p
   WHERE p.pono = '1001'
```

7.9.1 Hierarchies and Inheritance

One of the problems in relational databases is you cannot directly implement inheritance. In our example we have items in our shop which share a lot of attributes, for example barcode, price and description. However different types of stock then have very specific attributes.

In the design in Fig. 7.2 we have an object called **shop_stock**. We could populate this with data, but when we consider different types of stock lower in the hierarchy, each has its own unique attributes which need populating.

In a relational structure, as we saw in Chap. 4, we would either include these in description of shop stock which would mean a number of NULL fields or we would create tables which duplicated shop stock but added a few extra attributes. Both of these solutions create either inefficiencies or complexity.

To create the objects involved in a hierarchy, you must start at the top grouping the attributes which are common to all objects. This is the most generalised part of the structure which is then inherited by lower level specialised objects. Therefore the hierarchy involving the **shop_stock** object is created as follows:

```
CREATE OR REPLACE TYPE shop_stock_objtyp AS OBJECT
        (barcode              NUMBER (13),
        description           VARCHAR2(50),
        price                 NUMBER(7,2),
        number_in_stock       NUMBER(6) )
    NOT FINAL;
```

The key words '**NOT FINAL**' means this object has subclasses associated with it. Because the key words '**AS OBJECT**' also appear, it means this is the most generalised type of superclass.

The subclasses are created next. The order is not important and in this case, we will create a subclass to hold information about 'book'. Note: do not use the key words '**AS OBJECT**' here. You must however use the key word '**FINAL**' at the bottom of any hierarchy. This specifies that there are no more subclasses below this class.

```
CREATE OR REPLACE TYPE book_type_objtyp
    UNDER shop_stock_objtyp
    (ISBN                    NUMBER(16),
    Author                   VARCHAR2(50),
    Title                    VARCHAR2(30))
FINAL;
```

The book object will inherit all the attributes of the shop stock. Just like all the examples we have seen so far you must store data in tables, so you still have to create a table to hold the **shop_stock_object**. This will contain the structure for the complete hierarchy:

```
CREATE TABLE shop_stock OF shop_stock_objtyp
    (PRIMARY KEY (barcode))
    OBJECT IDENTIFIER IS PRIMARY KEY
```

You only need to worry about the object at the top of the hierarchy when creating the table. However, all the subclasses need to be created before the table is created.

Once you have created the table to hold the hierarchy you can start to populate it. Here you do need to worry about which subclass you are populating, so to insert a new book:

```
INSERT INTO shop_stock (book)
    VALUES('5023765013141', 'hard back', 12.95, 14,
    book_type_object (9781444712247, 'Marco Vichi', 'Death and the Olive Grove'));
```

The following two examples show how to retrieve data from either the superclass and the selected subclass, or individual attributes from a specified subclass. It is not possible to retrieve all data from all subclasses with a simple SQL statement:

```
SELECT s.barcode, s.price, s.number_in_stock,
    TREAT(VALUE (s) AS book_type_objtyp)
    FROM shop_stock s
    WHERE VALUE (s) IS OF (ONLY book_type_objtyp)
```

Which retrieves all the records which have an instance in the book subclass. The barcode, price and quantity in stock along with all the subclass attributes will be displayed.

```
SELECT s.barcode, TREAT(VALUE (s) AS book_type_objtyp).isbn
    FROM shop_stock s
    WHERE VALUE (s) IS OF (ONLY book_type_objtyp)
```

This retrieves the attribute barcode from the shop_stock superclass and the isbn from the book subclass.

7.9.2   Aggregation

In object orientation, the structure '**is a part of**' is often required. If we go to our example, a line item is a part of the purchase order. Effectively this is a one-to-many relationship. In other words, a purchase order is an aggregation of line items. In an object relational system this is once again created by using REF's to link individual line items to their purchase order. In this example there is also a reference to the **shop_stock** object so line item details can be retrieved.

Therefore, assuming we have both some purchase orders and shop stock we can create line_item by first creating a line item object:

```
CREATE OR REPLACE TYPE po_line_objtyp AS OBJECT
    (PO_ref REF purchase_order_objtyp,
    Qty NUMBER,
    bar_ref REF shop_stock_objtyp)
```

then creating a table to hold the object (and ultimately the data) by:

```
CREATE TABLE line_item OF po_line_objtyp
    (FOREIGN KEY (PO_ref) REFERENCES purchase_order,
    FOREIGN KEY (bar_ref) REFERENCES shop_stock)
    OBJECT IDENTIFIER IS SYSTEM GENERATED;
```

You should note we haven't nominated an attribute as a **PRIMARY KEY**. We could have introduced an attribute **line_item_number**, but its sole purpose would be allow individual lines to be explicitly named. There is no requirement for this. However, because there is no **PRIMARY KEY** we must use the **OBJECT IDENTIFIER IS SYSTEM GENERATED** clause.

Once we have created the table, then data can be added:

```
INSERT INTO line_item
    SELECT REF(p), '2', REF(s)
    FROM purchase_order p, shop_stock s
    WHERE p.pono = '1001'
    AND s.barcode = '5023765013141'
```

This code means insert a new line item which belongs to purchase order 1001 and contains an order for some stock with bar code 5,023,765,013,141 and we want two of them.

7.9.3 Encapsulation and Polymorphism

In a definition of an object oriented system, not only is data defined, but so are the methods to manipulate that data. This is called encapsulation. The method can be stored as part of the definition and then retrieved when required. In the following example a method to calculate a person's age will be demonstrated. Normally only date of birth is stored in a database as age can be calculated. Also, you are now older than when you started reading this section so age is highly volatile and if it is stored, it should be stored with a date/time stamp.

In the example here, the code used is written in PL/SQL, Oracles proprietary language. However, in some of Oracles other products such as J Developer there has been a move towards java.

Creating the method is a two-step process with the first step being to create the object which holds the method or function:

```
CREATE OR REPLACE type newperson_ty as OBJECT
   (firstname       varchar2(25),
   lastname        varchar2(25),
   birthdate       date,
   MEMBER FUNCTION age(birthdate IN DATE) RETURN NUMBER);
```

We have created a member function called **age** and it uses the data stored in the attribute **birthdate**. It outputs a value in **NUMBER** format.

Once the object which is to hold the function has been created, then the function itself can be defined. Note that in the following example the return value has to be divided by 365 or it will return the persons age in days:

```
CREATE OR REPLACE type body newperson_ty as
   MEMBER FUNCTION age(birthdate in DATE) RETURN NUMBER IS
   BEGIN
        RETURN ROUND(SYSDATE - BirthDate)/365;
   END;
   END;
```

Assuming we have created a table called newperson and inserted one record with a birthdate of 25th February 1983 and that today's date (SYSDATE) is 19 January 2013:

```
SELECT p.person.age (p.person.birthdate) AGE IN YEARS
   FROM newperson p
   WHERE p.lastname = 'Felsky';
```

would result in the output of:

AGE IN YEARS

30

Because **age** is a function it can be selected directly like an attribute, but the **birthdate** must be specified as the input parameter.

7.9.4 Polymorphism

When using structures involving hierarchies and inheritance it is possible to implement ad-hoc polymorphism using function and method overloading. This allows a method in a sub type to override a method in a super type. For example, if we had created the **shop_stock_objtyp** with functions:

```
CREATE OR REPLACE TYPE shop_stock_objtyp AS OBJECT
        (Barcode               NUMBER (13),
         Description           VARCHAR2(50),
         Price                 NUMBER(7,2),
         Number_In_Stock       NUMBER(6)
         MEMBER FUNCTION vat() RETURN NUMBER,
         MEMBER FUNCTION printme() return VARCHAR2) )
    NOT FINAL;
```

and we create the card subclass:

```
CREATE OR REPLACE TYPE card_type_objtyp
        UNDER shop_stock_objtyp
        (Printer               VARCHAR2(30),
         Type                  VARCHAR2(50),
         Reorder_level         NUMBER(16)
         MEMBER FUNCTION
           number_before_reorder(number_in_stock, re_order_level)
           RETURN NUMBER,
         OVERRIDING MEMBER FUNCTION printme() RETURN VARCHAR2)
    FINAL;
```

You would have to write the **printme()** function first as you can't override something that does not exist. Assuming you have created the **printme()** function, the **number_before_reorder** function would look like:

```
CREATE OR REPLACE type body card_type_objtyp as
        MEMBER FUNCTION number_before_reorder(number_in _stock, re_order_level)
              RETURN NUMBER IS
        BEGIN
              RETURN (number_in _stock - re_order_level);
        END;
        END;
```

On execution, whenever the **printme** function is called from the superclass the over- riding function **number_before_reorder** will execute whenever a card type object is retrieved.

7.9.5 Support for Object Oriented and Object Relational Database Development

The most common support is in the form of UML (unified modeling language) toolkits. Many of the available UML toolkits claim to have database modeling capabilities. Generally, these do not directly link to databases, an exception being Oracles J Developer. They do however provide a useful modeling tools to help with the design of a database. Arguably the two most useful are:

Use Case: A use case diagram shows how a user will interact with s system. This tool can be used to model what the data requirements are for the system and can even be used to define the requirements for the user interface (Fig. 7.3).

Class Diagram: Fig. 7.2 is a class diagram and shows the components of a class and the links between classes.

Oracle has introduced JDeveloper which includes UML like tools to develop databases. These include a use case modeler to map user interactions and a class

Fig. 7.3 Use Case diagram

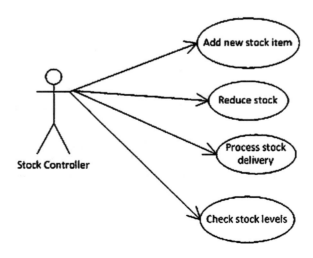

modeling like tool which can dynamically change the structure of underlying tables. It is supports java application development and is offered as an alternative to Oracle's PL/SQL centric development tools.

7.9.6 Will Object Technology Ever Become Predominant in Database Systems?

Object-oriented capabilities have in effect turned the traditional relational model and the traditional view of normalization on its head in terms of design. Despite this, the relational principles of having entities which are complete and encapsulated remain. We are now adding methods to that encapsulation.

One of the biggest issues is the complexity of the SQL needed to manipulate object relational data despite the structure of the data being simplified. In object relational systems it is made more complex by having to store all structures in tables as ultimately data is still stored in tables rather than as true object instances.

A further issue is the number of systems which have been developed using relational database management systems. The cost of converting these would be high as would the retraining of database developers and administrators.

The most likely scenario is there will be a gradual shift from the relational to the object-oriented model. This is already happening in Oracle with object relational features becoming more common. It may be boosted by the need to store non-alphanumeric objects such as images and sound files.

7.9.6.1 Review Questions
The answers to these questions can be found in the text of this chapter.

- What is the difference between and object class and an object instance?
- What does an object class define?
- What is meant by persistent data?
- What is an object identifier and what is it used for?
- What is polymorphism?

7.9.6.2 Group Work Research Activities
These activities require you to research beyond the contents of the book and can be tackled individually or as a discussion group.

Activity 1 If you have not already done so, create the objects and tables using the examples in the text. Then populate and extend the example by reference to Fig. 7.2 and completing the following exercise:

Add two more records to the Shop_Customer table and four more records to the Purchase Order table. Don't forget that a Purchase Order must have an associated customer first, but a customer can have more than one Purchase Order.

The line_Item class in the original design is an association class. To serve its purpose in an ORDBMS it needs to be an object with foreign key links to the Purchase Order and the Shop Stock tables.

- Create the user defined type Line_Item_objtyp.
- Create a table to hold Line_Item_objtyp. This has two foreign keys, PONo to reference Purchase Order and barcode to reference the Barcode in Shop Stock.
- Use the LineItemNo as the primary key as trying to use PONo and barcode as a combined key will cause problems because they are defined with REF.)
- Populate line_Item_objtyp with at least 2 records for each purchase order.
- List all stock items.
- For purchase order 1001, list the shipping address and line items.
- Modify the previous exercise by adding stock item description.
- Create a new customer.
- Create a purchase order for the customer with one line item.
- Modify the customer's name.
- List the customer's name and associated Purchase Order number(s).
- Delete the customer.

Define a function that calculates the number of items left in stock after a line item has been added (Number in Stock – Qty). Store the function in Line_Item even though you require data from Shop_Stock.

Activity 2 Refer to the case study at the end of Chap. 4.

If you have not already done so, download one of the free UML tools available.

1. Draw a class diagram for the scenario. Include both attributes and operations. Include relationships including hierarchies and aggregation.
2. Create the database.

References

Atkinson M, Bancilhon F, DeWitt D, Dittrich K, Maier D, Zdonik S (1992) The object-oriented database system manifesto. In: Building an object-oriented database system. Morgan Kaufmann, San Mateo

Obe R, Hsu L (2012) PostgreSQL: up and running. O'Reilly, Sebastopol. ISBN 1–4493-2633–1 ODMG

OQL (1998) User manual release 5.0. Available at https://db.ucsd.edu/static/cse190/readings/23562262-Odmg-Oql-User-Manual.pdf. Last accessed 29 Apr 2013

Further Reading

Oracle Corporation (2008) A sample application using object-relational features. Available at https://docs.oracle.com/cd/B28359_01/appdev.111/b28371/adobjxmp.htm#BABCCIBC . Last accessed 07 Dec 2012

Visual paradigm for UML community edition. https://www.visual-paradigm.com/. Last accessed 29 Apr 2013

In-Memory Databases

8

What the reader will learn:

- The origins of in-memory databases
- The advantages and disadvantages of in-memory databases
- Different implementations of in-memory databases
- The type of applications suited to in-memory databases
- The use of personal computers with in-memory databases

8.1 Introduction

Disk based database technology has influenced database design since the inception of electronic databases. One of the issues with disk-based media is that the physical design of systems tries to speed up processing by reducing disk access, in other words disk input/output (I/O) is a limiting factor which needs to be optimised. In-memory databases have been described as a disruptive technology or disruptive tipping point because it provides a significant improvement in performance and use of system resources.

In-memory databases systems are database management systems where the data is stored entirely in main memory. There are several competing technologies that implement this. For example, Oracle's TimesTen system is effectively a relational system loaded into memory. Another other big player in the field is SAP with its HANA database which offers column-based storage. In contrast, Starcounter is a OLTP (On Line Transaction Processing) transaction database using its own proprietary object oriented data manipulation language based around NewSQL. A comparison between these technologies will be made later in the chapter.

© Springer Nature Switzerland AG 2021
189
K. Domdouzis et al., *Concise Guide to Databases*, Undergraduate Topics
in Computer Science, https://doi.org/10.1007/978-3-030-42224-0_8

8.2   Origins

In early computers, memory was always the most expensive hardware component. Until the mid-1970's magnetic core memory was the dominant memory technology. It was made of magnetised rings (cores) that could be magnetised in one of two directions by four wires that passed through the centre of them forming a grid. Two wires controlled the polarity, and the others were sensors. This allowed binary representation of data. It's one advantage was that it was non-volatile—when the power went off the contents of memory was not lost.

Core memory was however expensive and bulky. It also meant that programs were written in such a way as to optimise memory usage. One way of doing this was to use virtual memory where data was swapped in and out of memory and onto disk storage. This optimised memory usage but degraded overall performance.

From the mid-1970's memory started to get cheaper and faster. For example, in 2001 the maximum capacity of memory was 256 megabytes. By 2012 that had risen to 16 gigabytes, a 64-fold increase. Cost on the other hand dropped from 0.2 US dollars a megabyte to just 0.009 US dollars per megabyte. But by far the biggest change was in speed where in 2002 response time using hard disk drives was 5 ms, by 2012 using in-memory technology, speed had increased to 100 ns, a 50,000 fold increase.

The last hurdle to overcome was the D—the durability of ACID (atomicity, consistency, isolation and durability) issue of memory. ACID is discussed in more detail in Chap. 2. Early semi-conductor memory had been volatile so when power was lost, so was all data stored in memory. NVDIMM (Non-Volatile Dual In-line Memory Module) solved that problem; initially by battery backup (BBUDIMM) then by the use of super capacitors for power backup.

This increase in speed along with a falling cost and non-volatility lead to a greater interest in in-memory databases from the mid-2000's. Preimesberger (2013) coins the term 'data half-life' referring to data being more valuable in real time and diminishing in value over time. Therefore, speed of processing giving real time insights which can be used immediately is important. In-memory databases therefore allow real-time online analytical processing (OLAP) analysis on data from online transaction processing (OLTP).

It should be noted that an influential paper by Garcia-Molina and Salem (1992) was already talking about the advantages of in-memory databases and the issues in implementing them. The issues raised in this paper seem to have influenced the direction of in-memory databases from that time.

8.3   Online Transaction Processing Versus Online Analytical Processing

One of the issues with management information systems is the various components are often at odds with each other. Business processing for example has different requirements to analytics. As a result it is common for there to be at least two separate systems. The first, usually based around a relational database was for operational systems with lots of update transactions. The second was based around archived data in a data warehouse. Transactions were added to a data warehouse, often with data from other sources. There were inserts, but no updates of records. The database part was usually associated with online transaction processing (OLTP) while the data warehouse was associated with by online analytical processing (OLAP).

In OLTP The data storage tends to be record or row based. Records are stored in blocks which can be cached in main memory. Sophisticated indexing then gives rapid access to individual records. The system slows if lots of records are required. By contrast, OLAP tends to use a column based approach and often works on data sets stored in a data warehouse. Optimisation, where attributes are converted to integers allows rapid processing, but the data is archival rather than operational. Chapter 4 discusses column based approaches and NoSQL in more detail. Plattner (2009) goes further and suggests data warehouses were a compromise with the flexibility and speed paid for by the additional resources needed for loading data, extracting data and controlling redundancy.

Interestingly OLTP was a prerequisite for developing OLAP, however OLAP provides the data necessary to understand the business and set strategic direction. Plattner argues that although data warehouses allow integration of data from many sources, integration of OLAP and OLTP into a single system has the capability of making both components more valuable for real time decision making.

8.4   Interim Solution—Create a RAM Disk

Placing an entire on disk database into memory in the form of a RAM disk where the database management software is treating memory as if it were a disk drive is at best an interim solution to creating an in-memory database. This will speed up reads and writes, but the systems still 'thinks' the data is going to a disk drive and as such will still operate caching and file input output services even though they are not required. This is because the optimisation strategy of a disk-based database is diametrically opposed to an in-memory one. Disk based systems try and reduce the amount of time consuming I/O operations. This is where the primary resource overhead is located with data moved to numerous locations as it is used. The trade-off is using memory for cache which in turn uses CPU cycles to maintain. There is also a lot of redundant data held in index structures which allow data to be directly retrieved from the indexes rather than doing a disk I/O. The time saved therefore, is down to eliminating the mechanical latency of the disk drive rather than any improvement in data access strategies.

Relational databases which are specifically designed to run in memory eliminate the multiple data transfers and strip out redundant caching and buffering. This reduces memory consumption and simplifies processing resulting in reduced CPU demands, potentially showing a dramatic difference in speed between a disk based, RAM based and an in-memory database system.

8.5   Interim Solution—Solid State Drive (SSD)

In many ways this is another type of RAM disk but the technology is different and there are reliability issues after a period of operation. Removable flash memory drives became available in 1995 and after an initially slow take up rate, these devices have become the main type of removal storage media for personal computing. They are fast, reliable and have a high capacity which means you can store an entire database on them. Their advantage over traditional disk drives is they have no moving parts so the issues of seek and latency times are removed. They are not without limitations as the following section will illustrate.

SSD's have a number of components: a processor, cache and NAND chips. NAND chips are named after NAND logic gates (the other type is NOR) and are random access memory chips (NOR chips are used for read only memory applications). In a flash drives the NAND chips are multi-layer chips (MLC) which give a greater capacity for the same area as a single layer NAND.

One disadvantage of SSDs, specifically the NAND chips is they do wear out. This is because they have individually erasable segments, each of which can be put through a limited number of erase cycles before becoming unreliable. This is usually around 3,000 to 5,000 cycles. To reduce the risk of uneven wear where some segments are used more heavily than others a process known as wear levelling is used. This involves arranging data so that erasures and re-writes are distributed evenly across the whole chip. It also means that everything wears out at the same time.

Georglev (2013) gives a summary of the issues involved in using SSDs compared with traditional HDD technology:

Fragmentation This is still an issue with SSD's despite access to all cells being equally fast. This is because if indexes are fragmented, they require more reads than for one which is not. Fragmentation also reduces available disk capacity.

Access Speed There is still a difference between random and sequential reads and writes which also depend on block sizes. They are still faster than HDD's but performance diminishes with writes and particularly updates.

Speed versus Capacity Fragmentation and wear (segments become unreliable) lower capacity, but speed is still greater than with a HDD. The biggest issue is when does the SSD become unusable. Wear levelling means once one segment becomes unreliable, the rest of the segments will soon become unreliable as well. The time it takes this to happen will depend on the number of update operations being performed— the more operations, the sooner the device will fail.

Caching data is held in cache as long as possible to reduce wear, in other words attempts are made to do as many updates as possible before writing to the NAND. The danger here is reliability may be compromised in the event of a power failure as cache tends to be volatile.

Data Most Suitable for SSDs Updates are the biggest issue for SSDs because when data is updated the entire block where the data resides has to be moved to a new block with the update, then the old block has to be erased. This causes both wear and gives a performance overhead. Given this situation SSD are best for static data where there many reads but few updates.

Data Recovery When a HDD fails there are many ways to extract most of the data depending on the nature of the failure. With an SSD once its dead, its dead—it is almost impossible to recover any data. It should also be noted that an SSD has a shelf life of about seven years. This means if it is not powered up for a significant period of time data loss should be expected.

The bottom line is that SSDs are useful as a backup and data transportation medium (as long as you take into account the data recovery issues). They are not an ideal replacement for disk-based databases when lots of transactions involving updates are expected as their life cycle will be curtailed. If you are planning on using this technology you should read the technical specifications relating to the device and ask how many erase cycles can a segment sustain.

8.6 In-Memory Databases—Some Misconceptions

Populating the Database The first misconception is populating a very large in-memory database is a slower process than populating an equivalent database on disk. On disk systems use memory caches to speed up the process, but ultimately the cache becomes full and must be written to disk. This requires moving data from cache to I/O buffers. From there data is physically written to disk and this is relatively slow compared with other processes. As well as writing data to disk indexes mapping the data's storage location are developed. These grow bigger and more complex as more data is added to the system. Also as the size of the database grows the amount of data that can be held in cache memory becomes a smaller and smaller percentage of the total database further reducing performance. Finally, as the database grows the physical size on the disk gets bigger resulting in higher seek times. Basically, as the size of the database grows there is a continual degradation of performance.

By contrast the performance of an in-memory database remains roughly constant as more and more data is added because none of the on disk issues apply.

Single User, Single System In memory databases are not restricted to being single user. The database can be held in shared memory with the database management system handling concurrent access requests. They can also operate with remote servers (nodes). In other words, in-memory databases can be shared by multiple threads, processes and users.

An In-Memory Database Is the Same as an Embedded Database This is not a total misconception, some in-memory databases are the same as embedded databases. These are databases which are part of an application with the database itself being invisible to the end user. However, as seen with the previous point, in-memory databases can also employ the client server model with the use of shared memory.

8.7 In-Memory Relational Database—The Oracle TimesTen Approach

No one technology appears dominant in the in-memory database sphere. There are however several contrasting approaches. The first to be discussed is implementing what is essentially a relational database in-memory. Oracles TimesTen is an example of this. Simply put TimesTen is a relational database where all data resides in memory at runtime.

In a cached relational database management system a lot of processing power is used to manage memory buffers and control multiple data locations on disk and in memory. The in-memory approach only uses disks for persistence and recovery rather than primary storage. This gets over the D-durability issue of ACID. Changes from committed transactions are logged to disk and periodically a disk image of the database is updated (in Oracle's terms, a checkpoint). The timing of this checkpoint is configurable and many applications favour higher throughput over synchronous logging, in other words the period between checkpoints is maximised to improve performance. The trade-off is that there is a small risk that data could be lost although this is unlikely to be due to power failure if NVDIMM is used and more likely to be to a catastrophic hardware failure. Transactions are also logged asynchronously which means if the period between checkpoints is too long, there is a danger of running out of disk space. When a checkpoint is executed, the logs are cleared (For more information see Oracle 2006).

There are five system's components of TimesTen: Shared: libraries, memory resident data structures, system processes, administrative programs and checkpoint files and log files on disk (Fig. 8.1). The memory requirements for this are given by Oracle as PermSize + TempSize + LogBufMB + 20 MB overhead although discussion boards suggest an overhead of 64 MB is more realistic (see https://forums.oracle.com/thread/2547114 accessed 29/07/2013 for example). PermSize is the size of the permanent data and includes the tables and indexes. The permanent data partition is written to disk during checkpoint operations. TempSize is the size of the

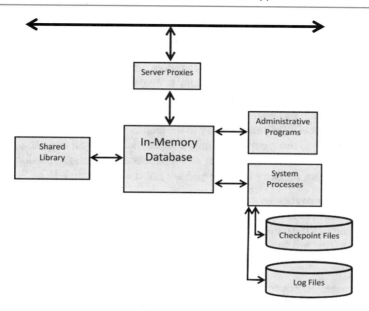

Fig. 8.1 Oracle TimesTen in-memory database

temporary data and includes locks, cursors, compiled commands, and other structures needed for command execution and query evaluation. LogBufMB is The size
of the internal log buffer in MB and has a default of 64 MB (Oracle 2011).

Although TimesTen is a relational database, this refers to the data structure.
Traditionally a relational database management system (RDBMS) assumes the data
it is managing is on disk at runtime. However, with all data in memory the system
optimises its management for that environment. One of the main differences is
query optimisation.

In a disk-based system data might be on disk or cached in main memory at any
given moment. The balance is crucial in reducing disk input/output which from a
resource point of view is expensive. However, this problem goes away if all the
data is in memory. The thing to be optimised now is processing and this can be
influenced in a number of ways.

Indexing The primary function of an index in a disk based system is to locate a
record on disk as quickly as possible based on an index key and record identifier. In
an in-memory system index keys do not need to be stored. Indexes are implemented
as record pointers which point to the corresponding record containing the key. In
effect the record identifier is implemented as the record pointer. Because an index
key is not stored in the index there is no duplication of key values in the index
structure which reduces it size. Also pointers are all the same size so the need to
manage variable length keys goes away making index implementation simpler.

Query Processing A common clause in SQL is ORDER BY. In a disk based system this is fast if the data in the table being targeted by the query is stored in the order requested. Often, in fact usually, this is not the case. The next best option is to use an index scan. This carries the overhead of random access to records which may result in a high input/output cost. The problem is exasperated if sorting is required on multiple columns. In an in-memory database, as seen in the indexing, the only entries in the index are the record identifiers which are implemented as record pointers. In other words index entries point directly to the memory address where data resides, so a random scan is no more expensive than a sequential scan, and of course there is no disk I/O. Buffer pool management is also unnecessary because you don't need to cache data in main memory because you are not doing any disk I/O.

Backup and Recovery as already mentioned the primary means of backing up a TimesTen database is by checkpoints where a snapshot is taken of the permanent data that includes the tables and indexes. These are used with the on-disk log files to recreate the database in the event of a failure.

8.8   In-Memory Column Based Storage—The SAP HANA Approach

Like TimesTen, Hana incorporates a full database management system with a standard SQL interface and ACID. It is geared towards existing SAP users in that applications using its proprietary version of SQL (Open SQL) can run on the SAP HANA platform.

SAP HANA exploits parallel multicore processors, so if a native SQL command is received it is optimised to allow parallel execution by partitioning the data into sections. This scales with the number of available core processors. For 'Big Data', this can be partitioned across multiple hosts.

The libraries shown in Fig. 8.2 contain business applications, for example currency conversion and converting business calendars from different countries. These can be used for processing directly in main memory rather than the traditional way for utilising plain SQL.

HANA optimises memory usage by data compression and by adapting the data store for the task. For applications that are processed row by row, records are placed in sequence for the best performance. If the application is calculation intensive executing on a restricted number of columns, then these are aggregated into a column store. Finally, graphical objects are created by specifying minimal database schema information, such as an edge store name, a vertex store name, and a vertex identifier description (where a vertex is a description of a set of attributes describing a point on a graph). The object body is stored in sequence and the graph navigation based on the schema information is stored as another sequence to support unstructured and semi structured data storage and retrieval. For more information on graphical objects in SAP HANA see Rudolf et al. (2013).

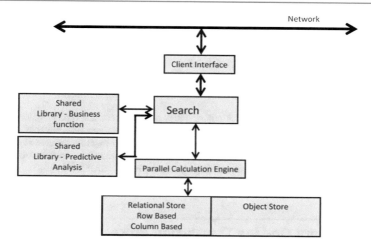

Fig. 8.2 SAP HANA In-memory database

Parallel Execution In SAP HANA sequential processing is avoided. Key to this is aggregation where values such as maximum, minimum, average and mode are required. Aggregation is performed by creating a number of threads that act in parallel. This is done by creating a aggregation function which creates threads that fetch a small partition of the input table which is then processed (for example to find the maximum). The process continues until the whole table is aggregated. Each thread has a hash table where it writes its aggregation results and when the threads are finished the buffered hash tables are merged.

Column Versus Row-Based Storage As mentioned you can specify whether to use column or row storage. Row based storage is recommended when:

- The table has a small number of rows
- Records are processed one at a time
- The complete record is needed
- Column values are mainly distinct, so compression rates would be low
- Aggregations and fast searching are not required Column based storage is recommended when:

  - Calculations are executed on a restricted number of columns
  - Only a few columns are used as the basis of searches
  - The table has a large number of columns
  - There are a large number of records and columnar operations are required
  - The majority of columns contain only a few distinct values (compared to the number of rows) which means a higher compression rate is possible.

Row based tables can be joined with column based tables although master data that is often joined with transaction data (the database versus data warehouse issue) is put in a column store.

The advantages and operation of column based databases are discussed in detail in Chap. 5 and will not be repeated here.

SAP claim increased benefits for using in-memory databases:

> In financial applications, different kinds of totals and balances are typically persisted as materialized aggregates for the different ledgers: general ledger, accounts payable, accounts receivable, cash ledger, material ledger, and so on. With an in-memory column store, these materialized aggregates can be eliminated as all totals and balances can be computed on the fly with high performance from accounting document items. (SAP 2013b)

8.9 In-Memory On-Line Transaction Processing—The Starcounter Approach

So far we have looked at two of the biggest players in the in-memory database field both of which have taken different philosophies to their implementation. Here we will look at one of the smaller players which have taken a very different approach to either of them.

Starcounter is an in-memory object oriented database management system which is focussed on OLTP (Online Transaction Processing). It is designed for "highly transactional large-scale and real-time systems, systems supporting thousands or millions of simultaneous users, such as retail systems, adserve applications, online stores and finance applications" (https://www.crunchbase.com/product/starcounter-in-memory-database accessed 29/06/2013).

A key feature of Starcounter is it integrates an application run time virtual machine with the database, a product they call VMDBMS. Effectively this allows the database data to reside in a single place in RAM and not get copied back and forth between the application and the database. This has been likened to effectively integrating the application with the database management system where you transfer code to the database image instead of data from the database image to the code. The downside of this is the database needs to understand the code of the application so is not universally language compatible.

Like Oracle's TimesTen product Starcounter only writes logs to disk. Reads only happen if and when there is a need to recover the database. Users can query the database using SQL, however Starcounter have created their own proprietary object-oriented data manipulation language called NewSQL (not to be confused with NoSQL discussed in Chap. 5). This is SQL like (in fact it is claimed to adhere to SQL 92 standard) and is embedded in java code, for example:

```
string query = "SELECT e
FROM Employee e WHERE e.FirstName = ?";
Employee emp = Db.SQL(query, "Warren").First
emp.PrintCV();
```

At the time of writing the biggest user of Starcounter is Gekas, a superstore in Sweden with 100,000 different product lines visited by 4.5 million customers each year (https://www.eweek.com/database/newcomer-starcounter-updates-high-performance-database accessed 13/09/2020).

8.9.1   Applications Suited to In-Memory Databases

From the previous discussion it will come as no surprise that systems that need to do OLAP and OLTP simultaneously are those most suited to in-memory database deployment. As an example, Savvis, an IT hosting and colocation service provider uses another of Oracles in-memory products, Exalytics. Here a broad range of users in the organisation need to view a variety of complex data sets to extract data for their specific requirements. This ranges from customer service staff who need to know what products a customer has purchased, service requests in progress and satisfaction survey feedback through to senior management who need financial data for strategic planning. The data all groups use has to be current from the operational database. The analytics are provided by a combination of visualisation and filtering of real-time data. The most effective way to provide this without building parallel systems is with an in-memory database. This particular application also allows various scenarios to be tested (so called what-if scenarios) using the operational data.

Mullins (2015) tells us:

> …the primary use case for an in-memory database management system is to improve the performance of the queries and applications that access the data. An in-memory DBMS can also benefit from a reduced instruction set because fewer activities are required to access data (as opposed to accessing it from disk).

https://searchdatamanagement.techtarget.com/feature/How-to-determine-if-an-in-memory-DBMS-is-right-for-your-company.

8.9.2   In Memory Databases and Personal Computers

The problem with in-memory databases for personal computers is not so much the fact it can't be done (it can) but rather should it be done? The applications which have been described so far have been for corporate systems which want to be able to do analytics on real-time data with multiple simultaneous users. From this standpoint the main usage of a personal computer would be to access an in-memory database located on a server rather than having its own in-memory database.

The place where in-memory database technology is most likely to be found on personal computers is in the form of embedded databases. You will recall from the definition of an embedded database that these are databases you don't see, because they are hidden inside another application managing that applications data. They are typically single application databases that do not share their data with other applications. Some examples are as follows:

Games Systems The technical challenge with persistent games, particular massively multiplayer online (MMO) games is transaction management. Every move and interaction is a transaction. In single user games data corruption can be solved by restarting the session. Persistent games, on the other hand, must react by rolling back incomplete or failed transactions. These manage their view of the games world within a database. Early versions attempted this via a disk-based solution, however disk resident databases have difficulties handling the transaction load required in MMO's. Games vendors also exploit the data streams being generated by MMO's as our earlier example of Bigpoint GmbH showed.

Route Delivery Management The database in this application is used to provide delivery drivers with the best route to the next delivery. Basically it is the database behind most satnav systems. As an example MJC2 (see https://www.mjc2.com/real-time-vehicle-scheduling.htm last accessed 29/07/2013) produces planning and scheduling software, part of which is real-time routing and scheduling for logistics. Their dynamic route planner software is able to schedule and reschedule very large distribution and transport operations in real-time, responding automatically to live data feeds from order databases, vehicle tracking systems, telematics and fleet management systems. The system requires an in-memory solution to allow managers to respond dynamically to a continuously changing operations including optimal responses to variable demand, last minute orders, cancellations and redirections.

Gas and Electricity Consumption Reading This is a sector specific application where the database is used to capture meter readings, often remotely. For example, Australian energy retailer, AGL has adopted an in-memory computing to help it cope with the vast amount of data coming from smart meters. Smart meters measure energy usage at regular intervals, for example every 30 min, and can tell how much electricity is consumed during on and off-peak periods. Instead of one simple reading every three months the meters now provide continuous data streams generating around 4400 readings per quarter instead of the traditional 1. As well as still generating customer bills, the data streams are analysed to separate out base meter data from other data for use in forecasting. The system used is SAP HANA.

Mobile Customer Resource Management (CRM) Marketing and sales need customer resource management applications without wanting to worry about the database driving it. This often relies on replication of a segment of the master database.

It may also be integrated with a satnav application similar to the route delivery management system described above. SAP have developed their CRM system to be deployed on SAP HANA to provide sales people with real-time customer information throughout the sales cycle on a mobile device.

8.10   Summary

Attaining the fastest speed possible has always been the goal of database applications. Unfortunately optimisation efforts in the past have been targeted at disk based systems which have led to duplicating data. One version of data has been placed in a database which is used for operational OLTP systems and the other is placed in data warehouses for applications associated with OLAP. This is because OLTP is I/O heavy while OLAP is computationally heavy and requires diametrically opposite optimisation routines. In this chapter we have seen that in-memory database applications have the capability of combing both requirements in a single system.

Common misconceptions of slow population of in-memory databases and them only being available for single user systems were discussed and dismissed. However there is no one standard approach to their implementation which ranged from Oracles' TimesTen which was an in memory relational system, SAP HANA which used column based storage through to new players exemplified by Starcounter which used an object oriented approach effectively integrating an application with the database management system.

8.10.1   Review Questions

The answers to these questions can be found in the text of this chapter.

- What is NVDIMM and why is it important in the context of in-memory databases?
- What are three misconceptions about in-memory databases?
- What are the performance increases an in-memory database can give compared to a on disk database?
- What approach to implementation of an in-memory database has Oracle taken with its TimesTen product?
- How do SAP HANA and Starcounter differ from Oracle TimesTen approach to in-memory database implementation?

8.10.2   Group Work Research Activities

These activities require you to research beyond the contents of the book and can be tackled individually or as a discussion group.

Activity 1 Wikipedia in its definition of 'embedded databases' seems to have fallen into the trap of considering in-memory databases as being the same thing. Go to https://en.wikipedia.org/wiki/Embedded_database where you will see a list headed 'Comparisons of database storage engines'. Examine the list and determine which are purely embedded (single user) and those which have client/server capabilities.

Activity 2 Look in your wallet or purse and see how many plastic cards you have. What are each of them for? (you may have bank cash cards, phone cards, loyalty cards, membership cards, student card, a driving licence among others). Which of these, when you use them, could be providing data for an OLTP or a OLAP. Make a list of 5 columns headed Card, OLTP, OLAP, Both and Neither and fill it in with an X in the appropriate part of the grid. For those with an X in OLTP, OLAP and both, work out what is happening to your data. For those labelled both—do you think there is a in-memory database behind the processing? (One pointer is do you get targeted advertising before you complete your transaction).

References

Garcia-Molina H, Salem K (1992) Main memory database systems: an overview. IEEE Trans Knowl Data Eng 4(6):509–516

Georglev F (2013) HDDs, SSDs and database considerations https://www.red-gate.com/simple-talk/sql/database-administration/hdds-ssds-and-database-considerations/. Accessed 29 July 2013

Oracle Corp (2006) TimesTen in-memory database recommended programming practices release 6.0, p 28. https://download.oracle.com/otn_hosted_doc/timesten/603/TimesTen-Documentation/goodpractices.pdf. Accessed 24 July 2013

Oracle Corp (2011) Oracle TimesTen in-memory database operations guide release 11.2.1, Part 1 Managing TimesTen databases. https://docs.oracle.com/database/121/TTOPR/toc.htm. Accessed 29 July 2013

Plattner H (2009) A common database approach for OLTP and OLAP using an in-memory column database. In: Proceedings of SIGMOD 09 (special interest group on management of data), Providence, Rhode Island, USA. Available at www.sigmod09.org/images/sigmod1ktp-plattner.pdf. Last accessed 29 June 2013

Preimesberger C (2013) In-memory databases driving big data efficiency: 10 reasons why. e-week, available at https://www.eweek.com/database/dealing-with-the-half-life-of-data-value. Last accessed 14 Nov 2013

Rudolf M, Paradies M, Bornhövd C, Lehner W (2013) The graph story of the SAP HANA database. https://www.researchgate.net/publication/236178288_The_graph_story_of_the_SAP_HANA_database. Last accessed 29 July 2013

Further Reading

Oracle Corp (2013) Oracle TimesTen in-memory database and Oracle in-memory database cache. Available at https://www.oracle.com/technetwork/products/timesten/overview/index.html. Last accessed 29 June 2013

Hierarchical Databases

9

What the reader will learn:

- The definition of Hierarchical Databases
- The Hierarchical Data Models, Paths and Optimization
- About the applications of Hierarchical Databases.

9.1 Introduction

A hierarchical database includes a number of records that are connected to each other through links. Each record is a set of fields (attributes) and each attribute contains only one value. A link is an association between two records. The schema for a hierarchical database is a tree-structure diagram. A tree-structure includes two basic components: boxes which correspond to record types and lines which correspond to links. In the case of a tree-structure diagram, records are organised in the form of a rooted tree (Silberschatz et al. 2010).

An example of hierarchical database is the SCOP database. This is a database of protein structural classification which includes a detailed description of the structural and evolutionary relationships among proteins. The classification of the proteins in SCOP is done hierarchically. Proteins are grouped into families based on a common evolutionary origin. Proteins whose structure and functional features suggest that a common evolutionary origin is probable belong to superfamilies. Superfamilies and families have the same fold if their proteins have the same secondary structures and the same topological connections. SCOP2 is the successor of SCOP. In SCOP2, proteins are organised in terms of their structural and evolutionary relationships but instead of organising a simple tree-hierarchy (such as in SCOP), these relationships form a complex network of nodes (Lo Conte et al. 2000). Each node represents a relationship of a specific type (https://scop2.mrc-lmb.cam.ac.uk/).

© Springer Nature Switzerland AG 2021
K. Domdouzis et al., *Concise Guide to Databases*, Undergraduate Topics in Computer Science, https://doi.org/10.1007/978-3-030-42224-0_9

The hierarchical and the network models are called 'navigational' databases because the reader moves across paths to acquire data. These models were developed by Charles Bachman who received the ACM Turing Award in 1973 for his contributions to database technologies. Except IMS, TOTAL from Cincom was focused on the use of a master record that was pointing to one or more groups of slave records. The Integrated Database Management System (IDMS) generalized the navigational model. The Conference/Committee on Data Systems Languages.

(CODASYL) formalized the navigational model and produced the NDL language specification. The IBM IMS is the most popular hierarchical database in use today. It can be divided into five parts: 1. Database, 2. Data Language I (DL/I), 3. DL/I Control blocks, 4. Data Communications components, 5. Application programs (Celko 2014).

9.2 Hierarchical Data Model

Hierarchical databases are some of the oldest and simplest types of database. Every record in a hierarchical database has one "parent". The hierarchical data model defines hierarchically-arranged data. This relationship is visualised through the use of an upside data tree. In this tree, a table is the 'root' of the database from which other tables branch out. Parents and children are tied together through links called 'pointers'. An arrow can point from a parent to a child and also from a child to a parent (Gaurav and Simmi 2012).

The IBM Information Management System (IMS) is a joint hierarchical database and information management system that uses a number of record access schemes. These schemes are the Hierarchical Sequential-Access Method (HSAM) which is used for physically sequential files, the Hierarchical Indexed-Sequential-Access Method (HISAM) which is an index-sequential organization at the root level of the hierarchy, the Hierarchical Indexed-Direct-Access Method (HIDAM) which is an index organization at the root level with pointers to child records and the Hierarchical Direct-Access Method (HDAM) which is similar to HIDAM but with hashed access at the root level (Silberschatz et al. 2010).

The schema for a hierarchical database is a tree-structure diagram. This diagram includes two basic elements: boxes which correspond to record types and lines which correspond to links. A tree-structure diagram is similar to a data-structure diagram in a network model. In a network model, records are organised in the form of an arbitrary graph while in a tree-structure diagram, records are organised in the form of a rooted tree (Silberschatz et al. 2010).

A hierarchical data model was used during the Mainframe Computers era. Nowadays, a hierarchical data model is used in the storage of file systems and geographic information. A hierarchical data model is simple because of the use of parent–child relationships. In such a model, referential integrity is always maintained and any changes in the parent table are automatically shown in the child table. The hierarchical data model is efficient with one-to-many relationships, it increases specialization and offers high performance. A hierarchical database is also used for Windows Registry (Educba 2020).

9.3 Dimensional Data Model

Data warehouses use multi-dimensional data modelling in order for specific elements of analysis (measures) from different perspectives (dimensions) to be explored. The attributes of dimensions can form a hierarchy or they can be descriptive. A dimensional hierarchy can obtain data views with different granularity (Rozeva 2007).

Dimensional models are used in the overcoming of performance issues for large queries in data warehouses. In this case, data integrity is not affected. The performance results to a cost for extra storage space. A dimensional database requires more space than a relational database. A dimensional model is also commonly called a star schema. It is also easier to understand (Ballard et al. 2006).

9.4 Hierarchical Data Paths

Segments in a hierarchical database is the same as tables in a relational database (IBM Knowledge Center 2020a). Segments in a hierarchical database are accessed based on their sequence in the hierarchy. The storage of segments becomes in a top-to-down order and in left-to-right sequence. The sequence flows from the top to bottom of the leftmost path or leg. When the bottom of the path is reached, the sequence continues till it reaches the top of the rightmost leg. The comprehension of the sequence of segments is important in comprehending the movement and position within the hierarchy. Movement can be forward (from top to bottom) or backward (from bottom to top). Position refers to the current location at a specific segment [Celko,]. Segments are defined by the order in which they occur and by their relationship with other segments. There are the root segment which is the highest segment in the record. There must be one root segment for each record. There are the dependent segments which are all the segments in a database record except the root segment. The parent segment has one or more dependent segments beneath it in the hierarchy while a child segment is dependent of another segment above it in the hierarchy. A twin segment is a segment occurrence that exists with one or more segments of the same type under a single parent (Celko 2014).

9.5 Hierarchical Optimization

A powerful optimization can be implemented at queries because of the hierarchical data structure. The optimization is based on data referenced in nodes and specifies that only the referenced nodes and any nodes on the path to referenced nodes are required for processing. The paths to the referenced nodes are needed to maintain the semantics of the paths to reach the desired data (David 2010).

A data warehouse is a relational database that has been developed for query and analysis rather than for transaction processing. Such a database includes historical data related to transactions but it can also have data from multiple different sources (Oracle 2002). Denormalization offers benefits in relation to performance and it can be applied to hierarchical database tables and the hierarchies of data warehouses (Pinto 2009; Zaker et al. 2009).

Hierarchies are significant aspects of Data Warehouses. There are several types of hierarchies: balanced tree structure, variable depth tree structure, ragged tree structure (Zaker et al. 2009). Denormalization can improve performance through the minimization of joins, the pre-computation of aggregate values and the reduction of the number of tables (Sybase 2009).

9.6 Hierarchical Queries

If a table contains hierarchical data, then rows in a hierarchical order can be selected using the hierarchical query clause. An hierarchical clause includes the clause START WITH which specifies the root row(s) of the hierarchy, CONNECT BY specifies the relationship between parent and child rows of the hierarchy and the NOCYCLE parameter which instructs Oracle to return rows from a query even if a CONNECT BY LOOP exists in the data (Oracle Help Center 2020).

In Microsoft SQL Server, the built-in hierarchyid data type facilitates the storage and query of hierarchical data. This data type is optimized for representing trees. Examples of hierarchical data are file systems, an organisational structure and a graph of links between web pages. The hierarchyid functions in T-SQL are used to query and manage hierarchical data. A value of the hierarchyid data type represents a position in the tree hierarchy. The values of hierachyid are characterised by a number of properties, such as they are in-depth first order and they support random insertions and deletions. The hierarchyid data types is characterised by some limitations. For example, the application defines the generation of hierarchy id in such a way so that the relationship between rows is shown in the values. The application can also enforce uniqueness to the values of hierarchyid by using a unique key constraint or through its own logic (Microsoft 2020a).

Hierarchical queries are implemented through Common Table Expressions (CTEs). CTEs are temporary result sets that are located in memory and they view the underlying data. They can be references within a single SQL statement. These CTEs can be chained together in order for a more complex final query to be developed. Due to the derived nature of CTEs, there is no need to write these temporary result sets to disk, thus reducing I/O requirements to complete each transaction (Harris et al. 2014). There are two types of CTEs: ordinary and recursive. The latter CTEs provide the ability to realise hierarchical or recursive queries of trees and graphs. All CTEs are created by putting a WITH clause in front of a SELECT, INSERT, UPDATE or DELETE statement (SQLite 2020).

9.7   Languages for Hierarchical Queries

In recent years, a number of linguistic query languages have been developed and most of them are focused on linguistic trees. An example is the LPath language that has been proposed as a language for querying linguistic trees. The LPath language has been suggested as a convenient path-based language for querying linguistic trees (Bird et al. 2006). The specific language adds three additional tree operators to XPath and it can be translated into SQL for execution. LPath also takes advantage of relational database technology and it is an extension of XPath (Lai and Bird 2005).

MUMPS (Massachusetts General Hospital Utility Multi-Programming System) is a general-purpose programming language environment that provides ACID database access through the use of arrays and variables. The MUMPS database allows access to data that are organised as trees that can also be viewed as multi-dimensional arrays. MUMPS applies a hierarchical and multi-dimensional database. The trees can be viewed as n-dimensional matrices of unlimited size. It also offers built-in manipulation operators and functions that allow the complex string manipulation. MUMPS can handle Big Data overcoming the capabilities of many RDBMS systems and it is characterised by high performance (O'Kane 2017). UML is a modelling language that can be used for the design and presentation in hierarchical format. UML can be implemented successfully for multi-dimensional modelling in data warehouses. UML can be used in the modelling of hierarchies. Hierarchies include levels (sets of attributes) that collectively form dimensions.

9.8   Applications of Hierarchical Databases

WordNet is a large lexical database for the English language. There is grouping of nouns, verbs, adjectives and adverbs into clusters of cognitive synonym rings (synsets) and each of these clusters express a specific concept. There is interconnection of synsets through conceptual-semantic and lexical relationships. WordNet is used in Natural-Language Processing (NLP) and Artificial Intelligence (AI) applications. ImageNet is an image database organised according to the noun-hierarchy presented by WordNet. Each node in the hierarchy is represented by hundreds and thousands of images. ImageNet does not own the copyright of the images and it only provides thumbnails and URLs of images in a manner similar to what image search engines do (Internet with a Brain 2014). ImageNet uses the hierarchical structure of WordNet (Fellbaum 1998). WordNet includes 80,000 noun synonym sets (synsets). ImageNet uses per average 500–1000 images to depict each synonym set. In ImageNet, there is the provision of an average 500–1000 images that are used to illustrate each synset. ImageNet provides millions of cleanly sorted images. The aim of ImageNet is the inclusion of 50 million full-resolution images (Deng et al. 2009).

IBM Information Management System (IMS) is a hierarchical database management system which is characterised by transaction processing capabilities. The IBM Business Monitor can monitor business events from IMS applications. The IBM Transaction Manager provides an environment for high-performance transaction processing. IMS is applied to a number of banks. IMS can monitor business activities which helps in the definition of business activities and operations, the identification of new business opportunities and more efficient risk management (IBM Knowledge Center 2020b).

The registry is a hierarchical database which includes data necessary for the operation of Windows and the services that run on Windows. The data is structured in a tree format. Each node in the tree is called a key. Each key can contain sub-keys and data entries that are called values. A key can have any number of values and the values can be of any form. Each key has a name that includes one or more printable characters. Key names are not case sensitive. The name of each sub-key is unique (Microsoft 2020b).

Hierarchical databases can be applied to lithology where groupings of different types of rocks (eg. metamorphic, sedimentary) can be developed. Within each of these groups, there would be further subgroups. For example, igneous rocks can be further sub-divided into volcanic and plutonic (Maher 2019).

Hierarchical databases form a tree. Domain Name Servers (DNS) are organised in an hierarchical manner. The root name servers are at the base of the tree while individual DNS entries form the leaves. For example, www.syngress.com points to the syngress.com DNS database which is part of the.com top level domain (TLD) which is part of the global DNS (root zone). From the root, there is another branch down the.gov TLD.

9.9 Summary

In this chapter, the topic of hierarchical databases was explored. A range of definitions were provided for the topic and different aspects of the technology were analysed. Examples of such aspects are the hierarchical data modelling and the hierarchical data paths. Other aspects of these databases are hierarchical queries and their optimization as well as the languages used for such queries. A number of applications of hierarchical databases are also presented.

9.10   Review Questions

The answers to these questions can be found in the text of this chapter.

- Describe the SCOP database.
- Explain the role of Common Table Expressions (CTEs).
- Describe specific applications of hierarchical databases.

9.11   Group Work Research Activities

These activities require you to research beyond the contents of the book and can be tackled individually or as a discussion group.

Explore different applications beyond the limits of the specific chapter in which hierarchical databases can be used. What are the different criteria that define the depth of the hierarchy of the data and how does this hierarchy depend on the application in which an hierarchical database is used?

References

Ballard C, Farrell DM, Gupta A, Mazuela C, Vohnik S (2006) Dimensional Modeling. In: A business intelligence environment. IBM Redbooks [online]. Available at: https://www.redbooks.ibm.com/redbooks/pdfs/sg247138.pdf. Accessed 05 Nov 2019

Bird S, Chen Yi, Davidson SB, Lee H, Zheng Y (2006) "Designing and Evaluating an XPath Dialect for Linguistic Queries". In: 22nd International Conference on Data Engineering (ICDE'06), 2006, pp 52–52. https://doi.org/10.1109/ICDE.2006.48

Celko J (2012) Chapter 15—Hierarchical Database Systems (IMS). In: Celko's J (ed) Trees and Hierarchies in SQL for Smarties, 2nd edn. Morgan Kaufmann, pp 255–270

Celko J (2014) Chapter 13—Hierarchical and Network Database Systems. In: Celko's J (ed) Complete Guide to NoSQL, Morgan Kaufmann, pp 185–201

David MM (2010) 'SQL's optimized hierarchical data processing driven by its data structure'. Database J [online]. Available at: https://www.databasejournal.com/sqletc/article.php/3877281/SQLs-Optimized-Hierarchical-Data-Processing-Driven-by-its-Data-Structure.htm. Accessed 01 Dec 2019

Deng J, Dong W, Socher R, Li, L-J, Li K, Fei-Fei L (2009) ImageNet: a large-scale hierarchical image database. In: Proceedings/CVPR, IEEE computer society conference on computer vision and pattern recognition. IEEE Computer Society Conference on Computer Vision and Pattern Recognition

Educba (2020) Hierarchical Database Model'. [online]. Available at: https://www.educba.com/hierarchical-database-model/. Accessed 05 Dec 2019

Fellbaum C (1998) WordNet: an electronic lexical database. Bradford Books

Harris DR, Henderson DW, Kavuluru R, Stromberg AJ, Johnson TR (2014) Using Common Table Expressions to Build a Scalable Boolean Query Generator for Clinical Data Warehouses. IEEE J Biomed Health Inf 18(5):1607–1613

IBM Knowledge Center (2020a) 'Comparison of hierarchical and relational databases'. [online]. Available at: https://www.ibm.com/support/knowledgecenter/en/SSEPH2_15.1.0/com.ibm.ims15.doc.apg/ims_comparehierandreldbs.htm. Accessed 12 Dec 2019

IBM Knowledge Center (2020b) 'IMS applications'. [online]. Available at: https://www.ibm.com/support/knowledgecenter/SSTLXK_8.0.0/com.ibm.wbpm.mon.doc/intro/intro_ims.html. Accessed 05 Oct 2019

Internet with a Brain (2014) WordNet and ImageNet'. [online]. Available at: https://www.web3.lu/wordnet-imagenet/. Accessed 06 Dec 2019

Jindal G, Bali S (2012) Hierarchical model leads to the evolution of relational model. Int J Eng Manag Res 2:11–14

Lai C, Bird S (2005) LPath+: a first-order complete language for linguistic tree query. In: Proceedings of the 19th Pacific Asia conference on language, information and computation. Taipei, Taiwan, pp 1–12. https://www.aclweb.org/anthology/Y05-1001.pdf, https://www.aclweb.org/anthology/volumes/Y05-1/

Lo Conte L, Ailey B, Hubbard TJP, Brenner SE, Murzin AG, Chothia C (2000) SCOP: a structural classification of proteins database. Nucleic Acids Res 28(1):257–259

Maher Jr HD (2019) Introduction into geoscience database design. [online]. Available at: https://maps.unomaha.edu/Maher/GEOL2300/week8/database.html. Accessed:10 Dec 2019

Microsoft (2020a) Hierarchical Data (SQL Server). [online]. Available at: https://docs.microsoft.com/en-us/sql/relational-databases/hierarchical-data-sqlserver?view=sql-server-2017. Accessed 01 Dec 2019

Microsoft (2020b) Structure of the Registry. [online]. Available at: https://docs.microsoft.com/en-us/windows/win32/sysinfo/structure-of-the-registry. Accessed 06 Oct 2019

O'Kane KC (2017) Introduction to the Mumps Language. [PowerPoint presentation]. Available at: https://www.cs.uni.edu/~okane/source/MUMPS-MDH/MumpsTutorial.pdf. Accessed 05 Oct 2019

Oracle (2002) 1 Data Warehousing Concepts. [online]. Available at: https://docs.oracle.com/cd/B10500_01/server.920/a96520/concept.htm. Accessed 10 June 2019

Oracle Help Center (2020) Database SQL Reference—Hierarchical Queries'. [online]. Available at: https://docs.oracle.com/cd/B19306_01/server.102/b14200/queries003.htm. Accessed 15 Nov 2019

Pinto Y (2009) A framework for systematic database denormalization. Global J Comput Sci Technol 44–52

Rozeva A (2007) Dimensional hierarchies—implementation in data warehouse logical scheme design. In: International conference on computer systems and technologies - CompSysTech'07, pp IIIA.24–1–IIIA.24–6

Silberschatz A, Korth HF, Sudarshan S (2010) Appendix E—Hierarchical Models. In: Database System concepts, 6th edn. McGraw-Hill

SQLite (2020) SQL As Understood By SQLite. [online]. Available at: https://www.sqlite.org/lang_with.html. Accessed 14 Nov 2019

Sybase (2009) Sybase IQ 15.1 > Performance and Tuning Guide Sybase IQ 15.1 > Managing System Resources > Managing database size and structure. [online]. Available at: https://infocenter.sybase.com/help/index.jsp?topic=/com.sybase.infocenter.dc00169.1510/html/iqperf/iqperf128.htm. Accessed 20 Dec 2019

Van Tulder G (2003) Storing Hierarchical Data in a Database. [online]. Available at: https://www.sitepoint.com/hierarchical-data-database/. Accessed 19 Dec 2019

Zaker M, Phon-Amnuaisuk S, Haw S-C (2009) Hierarchical denormalizing: a possibility to optimize the data warehouse design. Int J Comput 3(1)

Distributed Databases

10

What the reader will learn:

- The different types of Distributed Databases
- About Distributed Query Processing
- Examples of Distributed Databases
- About specific issues of Distributed Databases, such as Performance and Security
- About examples of applications of Distributed Databases

10.1 Introduction

A distributed database includes a collection of local databases which are dispersed in different geographical locations and they are related so they can act as a single, global database (Baron et al. 2014).

Distributed, parallel and concurrent computations are related to the collective actions of numerous processing components. Parallel means the use of multiple data-handling elements in order to execute the exact or similar operations on a number of data items. Concurrency involves the realization of any action in any order. Distributed means that the cost of performance of a computation is characterised by the communication of data and control (Wu 1999).

A number of business conditions allow the use of distributed databases. These are distribution and autonomy of different business units in modern organizations that are geographically distributed. Each unit has the authority to develop its own information systems. Business mergers and acquisitions often create this environment. Another business condition is data sharing across the different business units and the costs and the reliability of data communications which can be especially when it involves remote data sources. A distributed database allows the integration of different technologies from different vendors. A number of organizations use

© Springer Nature Switzerland AG 2021
K. Domdouzis et al., *Concise Guide to Databases*, Undergraduate Topics in Computer Science, https://doi.org/10.1007/978-3-030-42224-0_10

software from different vendors that use different database technologies. A distributed database can help in the integration of these technologies. Furthermore, distributed databases can help in the synchronization of data across OLAP and OLTP platforms. The replication of data across multiple computers is a feature of distributed databases and this can result to quick data recovery. Distributed databases allow the storage of data close to where they are needed and this supports the need for quick access to data (Pearson 2020).

A distributed database is a collection of a number of interrelated databases that are found over a network of interconnected computers (Dollinger 1998). In a distributed database system, there is physical storage of data across a number of disperse sites and each site is managed by a database management system which is capable of running independently of the other sites (O'Brien and Marakas 2008). The degree of autonomy of individual sites have a significant impact on many aspects of the distributed system, such as concurrency control and query optimisation and processing (O'Brien and Marakas 2008).

In order to ensure that a distributed database is up-to-date, there are two processes: replication and duplication. The first process involves the checking of the database for any changes. Once there is identification of these changes, the process of replication makes all the databases look the same. The specific process is characterised by high complexity. In contrast, duplication is not characterised by complexity. During duplication, one database is identified as a master and then this database is duplicated. Each distributed location has exactly the same data. During duplication, only changes to the master database are allowed. Both processes can keep the data current in all distributed locations (Raipurkar and Bamnote 2013).

Distributed database is a collection of multiple databases distributed over a computer network. The retrieval of data from different locations is known as distributed query processing. This type of processing realised a number of computations in order to achieve a single result. In query processing, it is necessary to specify the data that are required. An important aspect of query processing is query optimization. In query optimization, the database system identifies the optimal way to execute queries (Raipurkar and Bamnote 2013). Query processing is more complex in distributed environments in comparison to centralized ones as there is a large number of parameters that affect the performance of distributed queries and the query response time may be very high as many sites need to be accessed (Aggarwal et al. 2005). Distributed query optimization is characterised by different problems related to the optimization cost, the set of queries and the optimization interval (Agarwal et al. 2005; Yan et al. 1999). The goal of distributed query processing is the execution of queries in an efficient manner in order for the response time and the cost associated with a specific query to be minimized.

10.2   Homogeneous Distributed Databases

In a homogeneous distributed database, all sites use identical software. The sites are aware of each other and they agree to collaborate in processing user requests. Each site appears to the user as a single system. In a heterogeneous distributed database, different sites may use different schemas and software. Any difference in schema or software can generate problems in query and transaction processing. Each site may not be aware of the other sites (Manegold 2009).

In a homogeneous distributed database system, the sites involved in the distributed DBMS use the same DBMS software at every site but the sites in a heterogeneous system can use different DBMS at every site. It is easier to implement homogeneous systems, however heterogeneous systems are preferred by organizations since these organizations usually have different database management systems installed at different locations and they may want to access them in a transparent manner. Replication is characterised by reliability and increment of the performance (Kumar et al. 2013). Distributed DBMSs can have multiple copies of relations at different locations or have only one copy of a relation (Cellary et al. 1988). The advantages of data replication is high reliability and increment of performance as transactions can realise queries from a local site. However data replication is characterised by reduced performance in the case there are large number of updates as distributed DBMS have to guarantee that there is consistency of each transaction with every replicated data. This adds additional communication costs in order to guarantee that there is update of the copies of the data (Kumar et al. 2013).

10.3   Heterogeneous Distributed Databases

Heterogeneous distributed database systems offer different types of capabilities. These capabilities include distributed query processing, distributed transaction management and schema integration. Schema integration is related to the way users can view the distributed data. Distributed query management focuses on the analysis, optimization and execution of queries that refer to distributed data. Distributed transaction management deals with the atomicity, isolation, and durability of transactions in a distributed system (Thomas et al. 1990).

10.4   Distributed Data Storage

Distributed storage is appropriate for applications such as web hosting. Especially for applications that are characterised by the demand for large amounts of storage, dedicated storage arrays need to be added to the rack. It is possible to share storage resources between servers within the rack for applications that require large amount of processing. Storage access by a CPU on a different server card will use CPU cycles from the local CPU in order for a specific request to be serviced (Lee 2014).

Storage capacity can be scaled through the provision of storage on every server board. Boot loader storage uses a small program that can bring the processor into a state in which the hypervisor or the operating system can be loaded. The hypervisor can be loaded from a drive or from a shared storage location within the rack. This allows a number of servers to be booted from a single drive. It is possible that each server board can offer additional storage and this can be shared with other servers in the rack through specific protocols. This type of resource clustering can add additional traffic. The sharing of storage resources between racks is possible as long as the additional storage request processing in the server and the additional network traffic are accounted for (Lee 2014).

10.5   Distributed Query Processing

Distributed query processing is the process of query answering in a distributed environment in which data are managed at a number of sites in a computer network. Query processing is related to the transformation of a high-level query into a query execution plan (that includes relational algebra-based query operators). The goal of the transformation is the production of a plan which is equivalent to the original query and efficient—that means reduction of resource consumption and response time (Sattler 2009).

In distributed query processing, the user query should be executed efficiently over distributed data. There are two steps between query decomposition and optimization. These steps are data localization and global query optimization. Data localization acquires the algebraic query that is generated as a result of query decomposition and it localizes the data associated with the query by using data fragmentation. In this step, there is determination of the fragments that are associated with the query and transformation of the query into one that operates on fragments rather than global data units. In the global query optimization step, the localized query is taken and the best method of its execution is determined (Kling 2011).

There are aspects of query processing in distributed database management systems. These aspects are query transformation and query optimization. Query transformation is focused on the transformation of a query into fragment queries. Query optimization is focused on the optimization of a query with respect to the cost of execution of the query. In distributed transactions, the portion of a transaction which is executed at a specific site is a sub-transaction associated with that site (Köse 2002).

10.6 Distributed Transactions

A transaction is a unit of atomicity and consistency and it ensures that the integrity of the database is maintained when concurrent accesses and system failures happen. Supporting ACID transactions involves architectural issues that are related to the control and coordination of executing parts of transactions at different sites. This coordination is realised by the Global Execution Monitor at the site where the transaction is firstly initiated. The Global Execution Monitor is responsible for controlling that the ACID properties are maintained (Kling 2011).

Distributed transactions have historically been applied by the database community in the way realised by the architects of System R* (Mohan et al. 1986) in the 1980s. The primary mechanism by which System R* distributed transactions extend latency is an agreement protocol between all participating machines which ensures atomicity and durability (Thomson 2014).

10.7 Examples of Distributed Databases

Apache Ignite is a distributed database that supports a number of data processing Application-Programming Interfaces (APIs) such as key-value, compute and machine learning. The data and indexes can be stored both in RAM and optionally on disk (apache ignite 2015). Apache Ignite was designed as an in-memory data grid. Its core architecture design is different from that of a traditional NoSQL database and it offers a flexible data model and high scalability. Apache Ignite provides a shared-nothing architecture in which multiple identical nodes form a cluster with no single master coordinator. In the Ignite grid, there is addition or removal of nodes in order to increase or decrease the amount of available RAM. All nodes in Ignite can receive updates quickly without the need of a master coordinator. The communication of nodes becomes through peer-to-peer message passing. The Apache Ignite grid is characterised by resiliency and it allows the automated detection and recovery of a single node or multiple nodes (Bhuiyan and Zheldukov 2020).

Apache Cassandra is an open-source distributed database management system which is used for the handling of large amounts of data. This can be realised through the use of a number of servers that provide no single point of failure. Cassandra runs on top of an infrastructure of numerous nodes. It manages to maintain the reliability and scalability of the software systems that rely on it (Kumarasinghe et al. 2015).

There are distributed graph data management systems. InfiniteGraph is a distributed graph database which is based on an object-oriented database developed by Objectivity Inc. InfinitGraph claims to be scalable, however its free version only supports up to one million nodes which make it incapable for the development of social network applications. Also, it does not have a distributed graph data processing system. Orkut includes more than 3 million of nodes and billions of edges

(Ho et al. 2012). HyperGraphDB is a distributed graph database development framework that provides a P2P layer for data distribution (Kobrix 2020). The framework does not support distributed graph data processing. There are also parallel graph processing systems such as Pregel from Google which processes large-scale graphs and Trinity from Microsoft. The operation of Pregel is based on multiple super-steps and in each of these steps, every node of the graph realises a user-defined computation function. After the completion of the computation, there is transfer of messages from nodes to other nodes in the graph. The messages sent by a node at the end of a super-step will be received by the destination node at the beginning of the next super step. When there is agreement between all nodes, then the computation stops. In Trinity, the data model is a hypergraph and this means than an edge can connect a random number of nodes instead of two as in traditional graphs (Ho et al. 2012).

10.8 Performance of Distributed Databases

Cassandra addresses the problem of failures through the use of a peer-to-peer distributed system across homogeneous nodes where there is distribution of data among all nodes in the cluster. Cassandra is designed to optimize availability and partition tolerance. Consistency in Cassandra is related to how up-to-date a row of data is on all of its replicas (Kumarasinghe et al. 2015). Memtables are in-memory structures where Cassandra buffers writes. Cassandra creates a new SSTable when the data of a column family in Memtable is flushed to disk. SSTasble (Sorted Strings Table) is a concept which exists in Google BigTable and it describes the storage of immutable rows based on row keys. Memtables are in-memory structures and each table has one active memtable. When memtables are flushed on the disk, they become immutable SSTables. These files are used by Cassandra for reasons of data persistence. A number of SSTables can be combined together. Also, when a new SSTable has been written, then there is removal of the old SSTables. Cassandra processes the SSTables by logging a write and then it concludes it with compaction which is the merging of many SSTables into a single table (Apache Cassandra 2016).

10.9 Security of Distributed Databases

There are a number of technologies that aim to provide authentication in distributed databases. These are the Open Software Foundation's Distributed Computing Environment and the European Sesame Project. Oracle has introduced support of distributed authentication services in order to control access to distributed databases. The user logs on to the distributed system using a single logon (username and password) and this information is passed to the authentication server. The authentication server will determine whether access should be granted to the system or not. If a client wishes to gain access to specific distributed services such as the Oracle server then he/she requests a connection to an Oracle server. This request is forwarded to SQL*Net and then to the Oracle Authentication Adapter. The Oracle Authentication Adapter on the client enters into negotiation with the Oracle Authentication Adapter on the server in order for the authentication services that have to be shared between the client and the server to be determined. The Oracle Authentication Adapter of the client requests the credentials for that client. Then the adapter forwards these credentials to the server together with a request for a connection to the Oracle server. The Oracle Authentication Adapter on the server receives these credentials and through the use of the API on the server, it asks the shared distributed authentication service to validate these credentials (Harris and Sidwell 1994).

Multi-Level Security (MLS) provides two capabilities to standard environments: labelling and Mandatory Access Control (MAC). Labelling means that all objects and data are labelled with a tag. Mandatory Access Control (MAC) allows a user to access data if the relationship between the user's label and the object's label allows that access. If a user logs into a system with the label 'secret', he/she can read unclassified data but he/she cannot have access to top secret data. This form of access control is called mandatory and it is imposed by the operating system. MLS is appropriate to organizations that need to label their data, such as government and defence organizations. Numerous operating systems have produced MLS versions of their products. MLS database products extend the MAC policy of the MLS operating system on database objects (Harris and Sidwell 1994). In an MLS-DDBMS, users are cleared at different security levels and access and exchange information at different security levels.

Distributed systems use four main security components and these are security authentication, authorization, encryption and multi-level access control. Authentication is realised through the use of a password. The database can store the user's password in the data dictionary in an encrypted format. Authorization is used in order to provide one secured access point that allows users to connect to the network and access authorised resources. Encryption is the technique of data encoding which only authorised users can comprehend. A number of encryption algorithms are used for the encryption and decryption of server data. Examples of such algorithms are DES, RSA and PGP. In a multi-level access system, there are policies that restrict the users from accessing certain parts of the data. In such systems, access policies are characterised as open or closed. In a distributed database system, there is focus on multi-level security (Quasim 2014).

10.10   Examples of Applications of Distributed Databases

Modern applications, especially mobile ones are geo-distributed by nature. Internet of Things (IoT) applications connect devices that could be located anywhere at any time. These applications need a single database that runs on a cluster of database servers in different data centres. That can offer them higher performance and the ability to manage issues of data privacy (NuoDB Inc 2020).

Distributed databases are often applied through 'Sharding'. Sharding has gained popularity due to the large growth in the size of application databases in services such as Software-as-a-Service (SaaS) companies and social networking websites. Sharding can be defined as the partitioning of a database into a number of smaller databases that all together comprise one logical database. Distributed queries allow faster processing because of the realisation of parallel execution on each shard (McObject 2019).

The Observational Health Data Sciences and Informatics (OHDSI) project is an international and interdisciplinary project which is focused to develop applications for the analysis of large-scale observational health data. The collaborative was initiated at the end of the Observational Medical Outcomes Partnership (OMOP) project. The OMOP was a public–private US project responsible for the development of solutions for the realisation of medical product safety surveillance through the use of observational healthcare databases (Hripcsak et al. 2015). The OMOP consortium managed to develop the OMOP Common Data Model (CDM) which standardises the content and structure of healthcare databases through the recognition of the challenges of the realisation of research across disparate databases in both a centralised environment and a distributed research network. A number of analytic tools were developed by the OHDSI community, such as Achilles, HERMES and CIRCLE. In 2016, the community released a web-based platform called ATLAS4. This is a web-based platform that explores databases and analyses observational data converted to the OMOP CDM.

Distributed databases find applicability in different fields, such as data warehousing and On-Line Analytical Processing (OLAP). For example, data related to blood banks can be distributed and medical staff or patients can find the availability of blood from any blood bank (Patil et al. 2011). Distributed databases find also great applicability in telecommunications. The sector of telecommunications is expanding, and the sector is responsible for the satisfaction of customers through the provision of different services efficiently. Customer Relationship Management (CRM), market analysis, the evaluation of call detail records and personalized telecommunication services require very efficient database support [19]. Distributed database systems can guarantee data availability in such environments, even if some nodes crash. Specifically, they can provide efficient response time and continuous round-the-clock availability (Ashraf and Knokhar 2010).

10.11   Summary

The chapter presents definitions of distributed databases emphasizing the definitions of homogeneous and heterogeneous distributed databases. It also presents information on distributed query processing and on the security of distributed databases. The chapter also presents examples of applications of distributed databases.

10.12   Review Questions

The answers to these questions can be found in the text of this chapter.

- Provide the different definitions of distributed databases.
- What are the security components used by distributed databases?
- Describe specific examples of applications of distributed databases.

10.13   Group Work Research Activities

These activities require you to research beyond the contents of the book and can be tackled individually or as a discussion group.

Explore the parameters that affect the security of distributed databases. Explore how these parameters also affect the fault-tolerance capabilities of distributed databases.

References

Aggarwal G, Bawa M, Ganesan P, Garcia-Molina H, Kenthapadi K, Motwani R, Srivastava U, Thomas D, Xu Y (2005) Two can keep a secret: a distributed architecture for secure database services. In: The second biennial conference on innovative data systems research (CIDR 2005), January 4–7, 2005, Asilomar, California

Agarwal A, Charikar M, Makarychev K, Makarychev Y (2005) O($\sqrt{\log}$ n) approximation algorithms for min UnCut, min 2CNF deletion, and directed cut problems. In: STOC '05: Proceedings of the thirty-seventh annual ACM symposium on Theory of computing, May 2005, pp 573–581

Apache Cassandra (2016) Storage engine—commitlog. https://cassandra.apache.org/doc/latest/architecture/storage_engine.html

Baron C, Șerb A, Iacob NM, Defta CL (2014) IT infrastructure model used for implementing an E-learning platform based on distributed databases, vol 15. pp 195–201

Ho L-Y, Wu, J-J, Liu P (2012) Distributed graph database for large-scale social computing. In: 2012 IEEE Fifth Int Conf Cloud Computing, pp 455–462

Hripcsak G, Duke J, Shah N, Reich C, Huser V, Schuemie M, Suchard M, Park RW, Wong I, Rijnbeek P, Lei J, Pratt N, Norén N, Li Y.-C, Stang P, Madigan D, Ryan P, (2015) Observational Health Data Sciences and Informatics (OHDSI): Opportunities for observational researchers. Stud Health Technol Inform 216:574–8

Kling P, Özsu MT, Khuzaima D (2011) Scaling XML query processing: Distribution, localization and pruning. Distrib Parallel Databases 29:445–490

Kobrix (2020) 'HypergraphDB'. [online]. Available at: http://www.kobrix.com/hgdb.jsp. Accessed 05 July 2019

Köse I (2002) Distributed database security, data and network security—Spring 2002, GYTE, Computer Engineering. Available at: https://pdfs.semanticscholar.org/049b/f9271f5b01e0d 1b9fd0379cc9846fd31a21e.pdf. Accessed 30 Aug 2019

Kumar N, Bilgaiyan S, Sagnika S (2013) An overview of transparency in homogeneous distributed database system. Int J Adv Res Comput Eng & Technol (IJARCET) 2(10)

Kumarasinghe CU, Liyanage KLDU, Madushanka WAT, Mendis RACL (2015) 'Performance comparison of NoSQL databases in pseudo distributed mode: Cassandra, MongoDB & Redis'. [online]. Available: https://www.researchgate.net/profile/Tiroshan_Madushanka/publication/ 281629653_Performance_Comparison_of%20_NoSQL_Databases_in_Pseudo_Distributed_ Mode_Cassandra_MongoDB_Redis/links/55f113ba08aedecb68ffd29%204.pdf, https://www. researchgate.net/profile/Tiroshan_Madushanka/publication/281629653_Performance_ Comparison_of_NoSQL_Databases_in_Pseudo_Distributed_Mode_Cassandra_MongoDB_ Redis/links/55f113ba08aedecb68ffd294.pdf. Accessed 19 Oct 2019

Lee G (2014) Understanding cloud-based data center networks. Morgan Kaufmann, Waltham, MA

Manegold S (2009) 'Chapter 19: Distributed database'. [PowerPoint Presentation]. Available at: https://homepages.cwi.nl/~manegold/teaching/DBtech/slides/ch19-4.pdf. Accessed 12 Aug 2019

McObject (2019) 'Distributed database topologies'. [online]. Available at: https://www.mcobject. com/docs/Content/Fundamental_Concepts/Distributed_Database_Systems.htm. Accessed 11 Sept 2019

NuoDB Inc (2020) 'What is a distributed database? And why do you need one?' [online]. Available at: https://www.nuodb.com/resources/content-library/white-paper/why-distributed-database. Accessed 12 Dec 2019

Patil HS, Saheb MY, Pawar SU, Patil DW (2011) Distributed database-an relevance to business organization. JIOM J Inf Oper Manag 2(1):21–24

Pearson (2020) 'Distributed Databases'. [online]. Available at: https://wps.pearsoned.co.uk/wps/ media/objects/10977/11240737/Web%20chapters/Chapter%2012_WEB.pdf. Accessed: 25 Aug 2019

Quasim M (2014) Security issues in distributed database system model. Indian Stream Res J 2

Sattler KU (2009) Distributed query processing. In: LIU L, ÖZSU MT (eds) Encyclopedia of Database Systems. Springer, Boston, MA

Thomson A, Diamond T, Weng S-C, Ren K, Shao P, Abadi DJ (2014) Fast distributed transactions and strongly consistent replication for OLTP database systems. ACM Trans Database Syst 39 (2), Article 11

Graph Databases 11

What the reader will learn:

- The anatomy of Graph Databases
- About Graph Data Modelling
- About Graph Visualization
- About applications of Graph Databases

11.1 Introduction

A graph is a set of nodes and the relationships among them. Graphs represent entities as nodes and the way these nodes are related to each other as relationships. A good example of graph data can be shown in Twitter (Robinson et al. 2015).

Graphs are used in the visualization of relationships and patterns that may be hidden in massive amounts of data. Graph data are different from other data types and this obliges special graph analytics (Abawajy 2014).

Graph technology is based on the idea of developing databases through the use of graph theory used to store data and the links between data as relationships. Graph algorithms are core element of graph analytics. These algorithms use the connections between data to evaluate the dynamics of real-world systems. Figure 11.1 shows how a graph connection can be formed through Twitter.

A graph database is an online database management system which is characterised by CRUD capabilities that expose a graph data model. Graph databases are optimized for transactional performance and they are built for operational availability. Graph databases are characterised by two properties: the underlying storage and the processing engine. Some graph databases use native graph storage that is optimized and it is designed for the storage and maintenance of graphs. Some graph database technologies serialize the graph data into a relational database, an object-oriented database or any other general-purpose data store. A graph database

© Springer Nature Switzerland AG 2021

K. Domdouzis et al., *Concise Guide to Databases*, Undergraduate Topics in Computer Science, https://doi.org/10.1007/978-3-030-42224-0_11

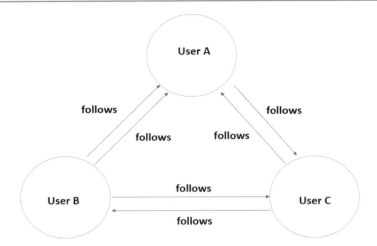

Fig. 11.1 Example of Twitter Graph Data

uses index-free adjacency and this means that connected nodes physically point to each other. There are also performance advantages of index-free adjacency and in this case the term 'native graph processing' is used to describe graph databases that use index-free adjacency t its maximum (Robinson et al. 2015).

Graph database technologies are an f tool for data modelling with a focus on the relationships between entities. The modelling of objects and the relationships between them means that anything can be represented as a graph (Miller 2013). A graph that is supported by most graphs is the property graph. Property graphs have attributes, and they are directed multi-graphs (Rodriguez and Neubaeur 2010). A property graph can model all the other graph types. The graph database is optimized for the efficient processing of dense datasets. In this case, predictive models can be built and correlations and patterns can be detected (Silvescu et al. 2002). This highly dynamic data model allows the fast traversals along the edges between vertices.

The performance of a graph database stays the same even if the dataset grows bigger. The reason for this is that queries are localized to a portion of the graph. As a result, the execution time for each query is proportional only to the size of this portion of the graph which is traversed to satisfy the query rather than the size of the overall graph. Graph databases allow the dynamic growth of the project they are applied to, concurrently to the parallel growth of the knowledge acquired. Graphs are by nature additive; therefore they can accept new nodes, new types of relationships and new sub graphs. Because of the flexibility of graph models, a domain does not have to be modelled in detail at the very beginning and this allows adaptation in the constantly changing business requirements. The additive nature of graphs has as a consequence the realization of fewer migrations, therefore maintenance overhead and risk are reduced (Patil et al. 2014).

Data volume is expected to increase even more in the future and more importantly what will increase are the connections between data points. As the number and depth of relationships increase, the JOINS used in traditional databases will cease to exist while graph databases will stay consistent. With graph databases, IT and data architect teams follow the speed of business as the schema of the graph data model changes. Also, the development which is based on graph databases follows the modern agile, test-driven development practices alongside the changing business requirements (Sasaki et al. 2018).

A number of graph processing systems have been developed in the period from 2003 to 2014 by academic and industry sectors. Angles and Gutierrez (2011) underline the advantages of the use of graphs as modelling mechanisms. Graphs enable users to model data accurately as they are shown in a real-world scenario. There can be development of queries through a graph structure. Graphs can be stored efficiently within databases through the use of graph storage structures and functional graph algorithms (Ismail et al. 2017).

AllegroGraph (Franz Inc. 2020) is an example graph database that it is oriented to meet the Semantic Web standards (e.g. RDF/S, SPARQL). It also provides special features for GeoTemporal Reasoning and Social Network Analysis. DEX (Martinez-Bazan et al. 2007) uses a Java library for the management of persistent graphs. The implementation of this library is based on bitmaps and other secondary structures and it is used in order to ensure the good performance in the management of very large graphs (Angles 2012).

HyperGraphDB (HyperGraphDB 2010; Iordanov 2010) is a database that uses the hypergraph data model. This model allows the natural representation of high-order relations and it is very useful in the modelling of areas such as knowledge representation and bioinformatics. InfiniteGraph (Objectivity 2020) is a database that supports large-scale graphs in a distributed environment. The specific database is used for the efficient traversal of relations across distributed, massive data stores. Neo4J is based on a network-oriented model and it applies an object-oriented API and a framework for the traversal of graphs. Sones (Carnegie Mellon Database Group 2020) is a graph database that provides support for high-level graph data abstraction. It uses its own graph query language.

Two main query languages are used in graph databases. These are the Cypher and Gremlin query languages. Cypher is a SQL-like query language which is based on graph pattern matching while Gremlin is a graph traversal language which is capable of realising complex graph traversals. They achieve similar performance and they both outperform SQL (Malekovic et al. 2016).

Cypher provides capabilities for querying and modifying data and also for specifying definitions of schema. Cypher is a declarative query language for property graphs. It provides capabilities for both querying and modifying data as well as specifying schema definitions. A Cypher query accepts as input a property graph and it outputs a table. These tables provide bindings for parameters of some patterns in a graph. The structuring of queries by Cypher is done linearly. In this case, query processing starts from the beginning of the query text and then progresses linearly to the end (Francis et al. 2018).

11.2   Anatomy of Graph Databases

The simplest graph is a node which has a number of values called 'Properties'. A node can start with a single property and grow to millions. It is logical to distribute the data into a number of multiple nodes connected with each other. Nodes can be connected in an arbitrary manner, thus a graph can resemble a list, a tree, a map or a compound entity. Graph databases use graph theory. The graph model is faster for associative data sets and it uses a schema-less, bottom-up model for the quick change of data (Shimpi and Chaudhari 2012).

Two important issues need to be considered when graph databases are used. These are graph storage and the graph processing engine. The graph storage is designed to store and manage graphs while others use relational or object-oriented databases. Native graph processing is the most efficient means of processing data in a graph because connected nodes point to each other in the database. Non-native graph processing engines use other ways to process CRUD operations (Sasaki et al. 2018).

Graph databases store data in vertices and edge in contrary to relational databases that store data in tables. Graph databases are efficient in identifying relationships between data items, patterns of relationships between multiple data items (Cray 2016).

11.3   Graph Data Modelling

A graph database includes three elements: a set of data structure types, a set of operators and a set of constraints. A graph database can be considered an instance of its schema. Graph schemas are appropriate for comprehending and visualizing the data included in a graph database (Pokorný 2016).

The schema in a graph database is represented as a graph or as a data structure that generalizes the notion of a graph. The manipulation on such a schema is based on graph transformations and operations such as sub-graphs, patterns, connectivity and statistics. The constraints used in a graph database are categorized into schema-instance consistency, identity and referential integrity constraints and function and inclusion dependencies (Dogda 2017).

11.4   Examples of Graph Databases

The World-Wide Web in its whole is a huge graph of data linked together. It is characterised by linked-data movement which allows the dissemination of structured data through the use of Unique Resource Identifiers (URIs), the use of structured data (in the form of Resource Description Framework (RDF) triplets and the provision of links to online resources to connect the data with the purpose of developing data clusters. This huge graph of data results to applications in web data retrieval. An example of a graph algorithm, PageRank, analyses web pages in order for a rank of pages to be determined through the identification of the number of pages that are linked to a specific page. Other examples of graph algorithms are related to web-document clustering and keyword search. Small-scale web applications are characterised by online querying of graph-like data. Larger-scale graph data applications provide offline querying so that the analytics of graph data are realised (Buerli 2012).

Social Networking sites such as Facebook, Twitter and LinkedIn are focused on network-generated social connections. The navigation of these connections is done in real-time because this information is used from online recommendations to parcel routing. An example of a graph database is a flight path analysis database. In such a database, airlines visualize all the flights in and out of various airports and allocate to each route graph factors such as distances and costs in order to identify new routes. A financial traffic analysis database is also a graph database and it is used to show the popular routes between institutions and people. Graph databases are also used on the analysis of transportation networks and telecommunication networks (McKnight 2014).

11.5 Graph Databases Search Algorithms

There are a number of algorithms for graph database searching. An example is the Parallel Breadth-First Search (BFS) algorithm that is used to locate the nearest neighbours and their sub-level neighbours. The algorithm can be used to identify the shortest path between nodes or avoid the recursive processes of depth-first search. The Parallel Depth-First Search (DFS) algorithm is used in deeply hierarchical data and it is a pre-cursor to many other graph algorithms. The specific algorithm can traverse a chosen tree until an optimal solution path is discovered (Hodler 2018).

Another example is the Single-Source Shortest Path algorithm. This algorithm is used in order to acquire directions between physical locations (e.g. Google Maps directions). The All-Pairs Shortest Path algorithm is good in calculating a group that includes all the shortest paths between the nodes in a graph. The algorithm is used for finding alternate routing when the shortest route is blocked or it is used to find call routing alternatives. The Minimum Weight Spanning Tree (MWST) calculates the paths along a connected tree structure with the smallest value associated with visiting all nodes in the tree. It is also used to approximate some NP-hard problems, such as the traveling salesman problem. It is widely used for network designs, such as efficient circuit designs and least-cost logical or physical routing. Real-time applications associated with this algorithm are the processes in a chemical refinery or driving route connections (Hodler 2018).

11.6   Differences Between Graph Databases and Relational Databases

A Relational Database Management System (RDBMS) is based on the relational model invented by E.F. Codd back in 1970. The relational model uses tables to store data. Any relationship between tables are defined during the creation of the tables. Relational databases use a rigid, predefined structure, called schema. Any data inserted to the database must follow the way the schema is formed. That is why the design of a relational database is important from the start. Most graph databases use a flexible data model. A graph database uses vertices and edges to store data. Graph databases have no fixed schema. Any schema of a graph database is driven by the data. The schema is dynamic, in other words it constantly changes as data are entered.

11.7   Graph Visualization

Different types of graphs require different algorithms for clean layouts. Examples of different types of graphs are trees, networks and cyclic graphs. A tree browser is used for the display of a hierarchical tree. If a list of edges is provided based on which a rooted tree is to be displayed, then the parent–child relationships must be formed. The first step is the identification of leaves by finding nodes that appear only once in the list of edges. A value is assigned to each node by finding the longest path to any leaf from the node. Children are grouped by parents. Leaves can move up to the hierarchy so that shorter branches are created. A spanning tree can be laid out by approximating graph-theoretic distance with Euclidean distance. In this case, adjacent vertices (parents and children) are placed close together and vertices separated by many edges are pushed apart. The algorithm that can be used in this case is the springs algorithm. The algorithm uses a physical analogy in order for a loss function to be derived. This function represents the total energy in the system. Iterations use steepest descent to reduce that energy (Chen et al. 2008).

KeyLines is a graph visualization technology. It uses data from any source, such as a graph database, NoSQL data stores, triple stores, SQL databases or even just memory. KeyLines is a fat graph visualization engine. If it collaborates with a graph database which is optimized for deep, complex graph querying, this performance is amplified. Graph format allows the simplification of the data mapping and the data visualization process. The graph representation of data provides a deeper understanding (Tandon 2018).

Amazon Neptune is a graph database service which uses an engine optimized for storing billions of relationships and querying the graph with milliseconds of latency. The database supports two different standards for the description and querying of data. These standards are Gremlin and the Resource Description Framework (RDF). Cayley is a graph database. Thus, it is designed to hold connected, network data. These data are stored in a graph model with index-free adjacency. This is a characteristic that is really good for network visualization tools, such as KeyLines as users can expect high performance and low latency. Cayley is written in Go and it has a RESTful API. It uses a 'Gremlin-based' query language and it works with multiple backend stores, such as MongoDB (Cambridge Intelligence 2020).

Graph visualization and analysis are ripe for research innovation to address the escalating scale and complexity of data and information systems. New methods must address all aspects of network representation, from the fundamental problem of laying out a large graph to graph analytics and simplification for dynamic graphs. Dynamic graph visualization is its very initial stages. Any layout method to develop a node-link diagram of a dynamic graph must consider both the graph stability and stability between time steps. The result is a trade-off between layout quality and stability (Ma and Muelder 2013).

NodeXL for Excel allows the network and graph visualization from inside Excel. Another tool is Gephi which is used as an interactive visualization tool for networks and hierarchical systems. It is characterised by the use of automatic layout algorithms and it can easily handle different types of input files, such as tweets. Cytoscape is another tool which was originally designed for the biological sciences. It is used for complex network analysis and visualization. It supports a rich ecosystem of Java plugins that allow the customisation and extension of the base functionality. Sigma.js is a javascript library that is used for graph drawing. It uses the same formats as Neo4J and Gephi (GovHack 2020).

11.8   Applications of Graph Databases

The application of graphs is important in order to describe a number of scenarios in the real-world. One of the applications of graphs is the provision of a simplified description of complex datasets in way that these data are presented in a simple manner. This resulted to the development of a special form of graph model, the so-called labelled property graph (Robinson et al. 2015). Labelled property graphs are similar to simple graphs. They include nodes and relationships which are expressed as vertices and edges. Labelled property graphs provide additional characteristics in order to facilitate graph understanding (Ismail et al. 2017).

Master Data Management (MDM) is the effort made by an organization to develop a single master reference data source so that less redundancy in business processes is achieved (Informatica 2020). Graph databases can contribute to the realization of Master Data Management though the development of hierarchies and data completeness. In MDM, a recursive hierarchy is necessary and it is derived from a recursive relationship. Furthermore, a graph database can be used to represent master data in the form of a graph and this would make the traversal of these data easier. Graph databases can also be used to discover possible quality issues related to MDM data (McKnight 2018).

The fast development in Information Technology resulted to the adoption of new digital methods such as the Building Information Modelling (BIM) for construction management purposes. BIM models may include a huge number of data that are characterised by complex relationships. These data may be inaccessible because of closed property formats or the absence of appropriate data management tools. Graphs are characterised by large capabilities in the comprehension and access of complex datasets in a number of different domains (Ismail et al. 2017). Graph models are useful in the representation of complex relationships among elements and data within BIMs (Isaac et al. 2013). This allows the conversion of BIM models into an efficient information model which is easily retrievable and it is based on graph databases. The latter characteristic allows the exploration and analysis of BIM connected data.

Khalili and Chua (2015) presented a graph-based schema which is called the graph data model (GDM). The specific schema uses semantic information in order to extract, analyse and present the topological relationships among 3D objects in 3D space and to perform faster topological queries. Tauscher et al. (2016) use the Industry Foundation Classes (IFC) object model which is based on graph theory in order to present another approach towards information retrieval. In this approach, there is generation of a directed graph that facilitates generic queries.

Graph databases can be used to provide a holistic view of customers' data (a Customer 360 application). Customer 360 applications combine data from data sources to help customers decide what they need ahead of time. Graph databases can also help companies sell more and earn online more revenue by delivering real-time personalized recommendations based on the analysis customers' behaviours.

Graph databases can be highly scalable. During periods of high traffic and concurrent use, the technology can provide personalized recommendations to each customer in a fast and reliable manner. Graph data can be used as a fraud detection mechanism. The comparison of real-time transactions within the C360 application to historical behaviour results to the detection of anomalies.

Graph databases can leverage relationships and data in order for the customers' unique behaviours to be learned (Gosnell 2019)

Social networks have been extensively analysed over the last two decades in order to analyse the interactions among people. Social networks can be considered as a graph structure whose nodes represent nodes or other entities and the edges represent the influence and collaboration between the entities. Recently, the research has focused on Online Social Networks (OSNs). OSNs are characterised by few links between content objects, between users and content objects and between users themselves. OSNs are highly dynamic objects that grow and change quickly over time through the addition of new edges. OSNs are characterised by richness of information as they include a very large amount of linkage data which can be exploited in a number of applications such as user profiling, social data privacy and viral marketing (Mezzanzanica et al. 2018).

The majority of Social Network Analytics analyse user-to-user interactions and the graph theory is a significant tool for the examination of the different types of analytics. More advanced forms of analysis have also been provided through the analysis of user-to-content relationships. The SNA techniques are based on two different approaches: the Linkage-based approach and the Structural Analysis approach. In both approaches, the linkage behaviour of the network is built in order for important nodes, communities and links to be determined. Many social networks, such as Flickr, include a really large amount of content which can be used in order for the quality of the analysis to be improved. It has also been observed that the combination of content-based analysis with linkage-based analysis produces more effective results (Wen et al. 2017).

Graph databases are not limited to academia or large data graphs. They can also be used in enterprise data storage. Graphs offer the advantage of representing complex data models and supporting dynamicity in schemas (Buerli). Graph databases have been successful for companies that store hierarchically financial and industrial data. Graph databases are important for the analytics of big data as they allow the collection, the storage and the analysis of such data as well as their visualisation. Graph analytics offer different paths for the analysis of relationships and also, they offer different types of analysis using graphs. Examples of such types are community analysis, connectivity analysis and sub-graph analysis. Graph analytics can be used in Social Medi analytics (Xenonstack 2019).

Graph Algorithms or Graph Analytics are used in a number of applications. These applications are associated with Clustering, Search- and Breadth-First Search, the finding of the Shortest Path and the Widest Path, IP Traffic Routing, and the ranking of web pages. Clustering is related to the grouping of objects based on their characteristics such as the intra-cluster similarity. Applications of clustering can be found in machine learning, data mining and image processing. Also, graph algorithms are used in the identification of weak spots in data and communications networks through partitioning. In social network analysis, transportation logistics and many other optimization problems, graph algorithms are used in the finding of the shortest path between two nodes. The finding of the widest path which is the identification of the path between two vertices in a weighted graph is applied in IP traffic routing. In social network analysis, a strongly-connected graph is one which allows to get to every node in the graph from any starting point. Also, in social-network analysis, there is the use of the Page Rank algorithm. The algorithm is a measure of popularity of webpages and it used by internet search for the ranking of the webpages. Other applications include recommendation systems, the study of relationships between proteins and in ecological networks (Nvidia Corporation 2020).

In the Page Rank algorithm, ranks are assigned to specific web pages. The rank of each page averages at about 1. The rank is usually shown as an integer in the range between 0 and 10 where 0 is the least ranked. The algorithm addresses the problem of Link-based Object Ranking (LOR). The objective of this is the assignment of a numerical rank or priority to each web page. A user starts at a web page and performs a 'random walk' by following random links from the page that he/she started (Samatova et al. 2013).

Graph Analytics are useful for the assignment of page ranks to web pages. This is useful in social media analytics. A well-known algorithm used in Graph Analytics is PageRank which was named after its inventor, Larry Page. The algorithm is used for the assignment of ranks to specific web pages. The rank is usually depicted as an integer in the range [0, 10]. PageRank addresses the problem of Link-based Object Ranking (LOR). Graph Analytics use a number of analysis techniques and these are the path analysis, the connectivity analysis, the centrality analysis, the community analysis and the sub-graph analysis. Path analysis is a technique that is used for the analysis of the connections between a pair of entities. Connectivity analysis evaluates the strength of links between nodes while centrality analysis helps in the identification of the relevance of the different entities in a network. Community analysis is a distance and density-based analysis which is used to identify communities of people or devices in a huge network. Sub-graph analysis is used in the identification of the pattern of relationships (XenonStack 2019).

Graph databases provide the basis for linking diverse data. Specifically, they make it easier for developers, users and computers to comprehend the data and find hidden patterns inside them. This level of comprehension is important for machine-based reasoning and inferencing (Vázquez 2019).

There is modelling of chemical data as a graph through the assignment of atoms as nodes and bonds as the edges between them. The graph data is important for drug discovery and analysis. Graph operations are focused on pattern recognition. This is achieved through the finding of frequent sub-graphs of a given graph. Chemical similarity is identified through other operations such as scaffold-hopping and rank-retrieval (Buerli 2012).

11.9   Summary

This chapter has examined the concept of Graph databases. A number of definitions were provided and specific technical aspects such as the anatomy of Graph databases and Graph Data Modelling were examined. The chapter also focused on graph visualization and the applications of Graph databases.

11.10   Review Questions

The answers to these questions can be found in the text of this chapter.

- Describe the differences between Graph databases and Relational databases.
- Describe the reasons Graph database find significant applicability.
- Describe the Graph Databases Search Algorithms.

11.11 Group Work Research Activities

These activities require you to research beyond the contents of the book and can be tackled individually or as a discussion group.

Examine applications in epidemiology in which Graph databases could be applied.

References

Abawajy J 2014 Comprehensive analysis of big data variety landscape Int J Parallel Emerg Distrib Syst 30 1 5 14

Angles R, Gutierrez C (2011) Subqueries in SPARQL. AMW 749(12):34. https://www.CEUR-WS.org

Angles R (2012) A comparison of current graph database models. In: 2012 IEEE 28th international conference on data engineering workshops, pp 171–177

nBuerli M (2012) The current state of graph databases. Department of Computer Science, Cal Poly San Luis Obispo, California

Cambridge Intelligence (2020) Visualizing graph databases. https://cambridge-intelligence.com/keylines/graph-databases-data-visualization/. Accessed 5 Oct 2020

Carnegie Mellon Database Group (2020) sones GraphDB. https://dbdb.io/db/sones-graphdb. Accessed 27 Oct 2020

C-H Chen W Härdle A Unwin 2008 Handbook of data visualization Springer Berlin

Cray (2016) Graph databases 101. https://www.cray.com/blog/graph-databases-101/. Accessed 10 Sep 2019

Dogda SS (2017) Graph data management a survey on addressing the bigdata challenge with a graph. https://www.cs.helsinki.fi/u/jilu/paper/Sore.pdf. Accessed 20 Aug 2020

Francis N, Green A, Guagliardo P, Libkin L, Lindaaker T, Marsault V, Plantikow S, Rydberg M, Selmer P, Taylor A (2018) Cypher: an evolving query language for property graphs. In: SIGMOD conference, pp 1433–1445

Franz Inc (2020) AllegroGraph. https://franz.com/agraph/allegrograph/. Accessed 20 Nov 2020

Gosnell D (2019) The three main use cases for a graph database. https://www.datastax.com/blog/2019/03/three-main-use-cases-graph-database. Accessed 5 Oct 2019

GovHack (2020) Graph databases. https://govhack.org/competition/handbook/graph-databases/. Accessed 1 Oct 2019

Hodler AE (2018) Graph algorithms in neo4j: 15 different graph algorithms and what they do. https://neo4j.com/blog/graph-algorithms-neo4j-15-different-graph-algorithms-and-what-they-do/. Accessed 6 Sep 2019

HyperGraphDB (2010) HyperGraphDB. https://www.hypergraphdb.org/. Accessed 22 Aug 2019

Iordanov B (2010) Hypergraphdb: a generalized graph database. In: Proceedings of the 2010 international conference on web-age information management (WAIM), Springer, pp 25–36.

Informatica (2020) What is master data management? https://www.informatica.com/gb/services-and-training/glossary-of-terms/master-data-management-definition.html#fbid=X7m-BpgNT6P. Accessed 5 Dec 2019

Isaac S, Sadeghpour F, Navon R (2013) Analyzing building information using graph theory. In: International association for automation and robotics in construction (IAARC)—30th ISARC, pp 1013–1020, Montreal

Ismail A, Nahar A, Scherer R (2017) Application of graph databases and graph theory concepts for advanced analysing of BIM models based on IFC standard. In: 24th international workshop on intelligent computing in engineering (EG-ICE), Nottingham, 10–12 July 2017

A Khalili D Chua 2015 IFC-based graph data model for topological queries on building elements J Comput Civil Eng 29 3 04014046 https://doi.org/10.1061/(ASCE)CP.1943-5487.0000331

K-L Ma C-W Muelder 2013 Large-scale graph visualization and analytics Computer 46 7 39 46

M Malekovic K Rabuzin M Sestak 2016 Graph databases—are they really so new Int. J. Adv. Sci. Eng. Technol. 4 4 8 12

Martínez-Bazan N, Muntés-Mulero V, Gómez-Villamor S, Nin J, Sánchez-Martínez M-A, Larriba-Pey J-L (2007) DEX: high-performance exploration on large graphs for information retrieval. In: Proceedings of the 16th conference on information and knowledge management (CIKM), ACM, pp 573–582

McKnight W (2014) Graph databases: when relationships are the data. In: Mcknight W (ed), Information management, pp 120–131. Morgan Kaufmann, Boston

McKnight W (2018) Three practical uses for graph databases in MDM. https://tdwi.org/articles/2018/05/07/diq-all-three-practical-uses-for-graph-databases-in-mdm.aspx. Accessed 5 Dec 2019

Mezzanzanica M, Mercorio F, Cesarini M et al (2018) GraphDBLP: a system for analysing networks of computer scientists through graph databases. Multimed Tools Appl 77:18657–18688

Miller JJ (2013) Graph database applications and concepts with neo4j. In: Proceedings of the southern association for information systems conference, Atlanta, United States, March 23rd–24th, 2013, pp 141–147

Nvidia Corporation (2020) Graph analytics. https://developer.nvidia.com/discover/graph-analytics. Accessed 01 Dec 2019

Objectivity (2020) Infinitegraph. https://www.objectivity.com/products/infinitegraph/. Accessed 15 Nov 2020

S Patil G Vaswani A Bhatia 2014 Graph databases—an overview Int J Comput Sci Inf Technol (IJCSIT) 5 1 657 660

Pokorný J (2016) Conceptual and database modelling of graph databases. In: IDEAS '16: Proceedings of the 20th international database engineering and applications symposium, July 2016, pp 370–377

Robinson I, Webber J, Eifrem E (2015) Graph databases, 2nd edn. O'Reilly Media Inc

MA Rodriguez P Neubauer 2010 Constructions from dots and lines Bull Am Soc Inf Scie Technol Am Soc Inf Sci Technol 36 6 35 41 https://doi.org/10.1002/bult.2010.1720360610

Samatova NF, Hendrix W, Jenkins J, Padmanabhan K, Chakraborty A (eds) (2013) Practical graph mining with R. Chapman and Hall/CRC

Sasaki BM, Chao J, Howard E (2018) Graph databases for beginners. https://go.neo4j.com/rs/710-RRC-335/images/Graph_Databases_for_Beginners.pdf. Accessed 12 May 2019

Shimpi D, Chaudhari S (2012) An overview of graph databases. In: IJCA proceedings on international conference on recent trends in information technology and computer science 2012 ICRTITCS, vol 3, pp 16–22

Silvescu A, Caragea D, Altramentov A (2002) Graph databases. https://www.researchgate.net/publication/238680382_Graph_Databases. Accessed 20 June 2019

Tandon A (2018) Introducing neo4j bloom: graph data visualization for everyone. https://neo4j.com/blog/introducing-neo4j-bloom-graph-data-visualization-for-everyone/. Accessed 12 June 2019

Tauscher E, Bargstädt H-J, Smarsly K (2016) Generic BIM queries based on the IFC object model using graph theory. In: The 16th international conference on computing in civil and building engineering. Osaka, Japan

Vázquez F (2019) Graph databases. what's the big deal?. https://towardsdatascience.com/graph-databases-whats-the-big-deal-ec310b1bc0ed. Accessed 25 Oct 2019

Wen S, Wu W, Castiglione A (eds) (2017) Cyberspace safety and security. In: Proceedings of the 9th international symposium, CSS 2017, Xi'an China, October 23–25, 2017

XenonStack (2019) Role of graph databases in big data analytics. https://www.xenonstack.com/insights/graph-databases-big-data/. Accessed 1 Dec 2019

Part III
What Database Professionals Worry About

Database Scalability

12

What the reader will learn:

- that the number of concurrent users is one important aspect of scalability
- and that volumes of data stored and accessed is also important, particularly in the era of Big Data
- that scalability brings its own issues for DBAs, such as the cost and performance implications
- that cloud computing's "use when needed" model can be helpful in handling scaling issues
- that there are many approaches to tackling scalability issues and that each has strengths and weaknesses.

12.1 What Do We Mean by Scalability?

As with most chapters in this book we will start by defining what we mean by scalability. And, as with some other chapters there are several possible answers.

Dictionary.com defines it as:

> the ability of something, especially a computer system, to adapt to increased demands.

But even this is debatable. In its literal sense scale can go up (increased demands), but it can go down.

It is far from only computing that uses the term. Here is a definition from a paper in the healthcare area:

> The ability of a health intervention shown to be efficacious on a small scale and or under controlled conditions to be expanded under real world conditions to reach a greater proportion of the eligible population.

© Springer Nature Switzerland AG 2021   239
K. Domdouzis et al., *Concise Guide to Databases*, Undergraduate Topics
in Computer Science, https://doi.org/10.1007/978-3-030-42224-0_12

But this is a database book, so let us narrow this down to what it means for database professionals. Even here, however, there are possible areas of confusion. Hoskins and Frank (2002) define scalability in terms of processing power:

the ability to retain performance levels when adding additional processors

In this MSDN Dunmall and Clarke (2003) article about load testing, scalability is described in terms of:

... the number of concurrent users anticipated at peak load in production.

In the era of Big Data the focus is often more to do with the volumes of data that an organisation needs to store. This is 10-Gen's take on scalability from their MongoDB website:

Auto-sharding allows MongoDB to scale from ingle server deployments to large, complex multi-data enter architectures.

In actual fact these three elements are often closely related: concurrent user count; processing loads; data volume. It is often the case that more data or users will cause more processing, for example. So, for this book, we will describe scalability as:

The ability of a database system to continue to function well when more users or data are added.

We will split this chapter into two main parts as we first examine strategies for coping with increases in the number of users of a system, and then look at the alternative approaches to handling the growth of data being stored and queried.

12.2 Coping with Growing Numbers of Users

As with many Microsoft products, ease of use is a real plus-point for Access. Some relational database concepts are difficult for non-technical users, and yet people are able to use the Wizards to help them create complex databases with apparent ease. And, compared to licenses for products like SQL Server and Oracle, Access is cheap.

So why doesn't everyone just use Access? Well, we can get into a war between vendor's claims and counter-claims if we are not careful, but the more general point in a chapter about scalability is that even Microsoft only claim 255 as the maximum number of users it can cope with. Anecdotal evidence, and the author's experience, leads to the belief that considerably fewer than 255 may be the sensible maximum number of concurrent users.

If you are storing information about your immediate family's addresses, or you are creating an application for the administrators of a small company, then this limit may not matter. However, if you are hoping to be an Amazon, with thousands of concurrent users, Access will clearly not do the job! According to Complete.com (https://www.complete.com/) Amazon.com had more than 129 million users in the month before this chapter was written. Even if every user logged on at different times of day and was logged on for less than a minute, this is roughly 3000 concurrent users at any point in the day. Naturally their systems designers will have to build in re- sources to cope with peak times, so this figure will actually be much, much greater than 3000.

12.2.1 So Why Can't Access Cope with Lots of Users?

Well, because it was never designed to be truly multi-user. Access is a file-server solution. It relies heavily on the operating system of a single file-server (usually a PC) on which it runs and stores its data. Databases like SQLServer and Oracle are Client-Server databases. Architecturally they were designed from the start to be capable of allowing many users to access the system. Client-server solutions can manage their own processes and data placement, including the use of multiple servers to share the load. This is not to say that Access's architecture is second best —it is just different; designed to meet different needs.

Typically the file-server database is designed with a single user in mind. Many Access users will use the PC they sit at to install and run Access. In that unconnected mode, multiple users are never going to be an issue.

Before Access became the success it currently is there was a trend for computers to become connected to one another in a peer-to-peer way. This meant that the Access-like databases on the PC mentioned above could now be available to other PCs in a workgroup. But what actually happens is that Access is installed on all the PCs that are permitted to use the database, and a copy of the data is taken to work on the second PC. This scenario, and the stand-alone PC are both referred to as one-tier architecture (Fig. 12.1).

Allowing multiple users to read data is a relatively trivial task for a database. However, one of the most significant issues for multi-user databases is for the management system to control the write processing that is needed when users want to insert, delete or update data. And one of the control mechanisms used is that of locking rows, or tables—preventing other users from having access to a row whilst

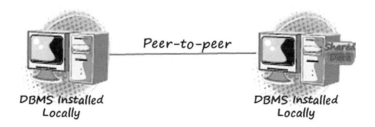

Fig. 12.1 Peer-to-peer database system

it is being changed. We cover locking in more detail in Chap. 3. Locks are often a problem because, to the users who do not own the lock, this just looks like they are having to wait for the data. They tend to see it as a system performance problem.

As with any system that relies exclusively on the resources of one PC, things can go wrong. Information about Access locks is stored in a.ldb file. These files are cleaned up as the system loses users, but occasionally they are left behind and need to be cleared up by the systems administrator.

These problems may not be an issue for smaller systems with few users. However, the more users there are, the more susceptible the system becomes to things going wrong. And this means we can say that Access does not scale well.

12.2.2 Client/Server

Largely in response to the scalability problems associated with the peer-to-peer approach, computer science began to look to a different model. What became apparent was that connecting computers together and allowing them to share processing in some way was a good use of resource. It was also clear, particular at a time when disk, cpu and ram were very expensive, that having some sort of specialisation for particular machines was the best way of maximizing the usage of these resources.

So evolved powerful PC-like computers that became known as Servers. They "served" services to PCs that connected and requested such services. The latter became known as the Client of the Server. The model of high performing machine serving one or many client machines became known as Client/Server (or Client-Server) (Fig. 12.2).

There are all sorts of variations on this theme. The World Wide Web is a form of client/server, for example. Even mainframes, it could be argued, are Client/Server systems with central processes carrying out the work and then returning the results to dumb terminals.

One of the decisions for designers of client/server systems is where to do the processing. In the mainframe example all the processing is carried out at the server end. What made the client/server revolution different to mainframes was that the clients tended to be relatively intelligent PCs. In database terms, the decision then becomes—do you use the server to serve-up the data and then do the manipulation (in the form of sorting, filtering, etc.) at the client end? Or do you do everything at the server end and just send the finished dataset, but use the PC's graphical abilities to present it to the user?

Another pair of oft-used terms here are "thin client" or "fat client". The former can almost be thought of as a more graphically pleasing version the dumb terminal. All the processing is carried out at the server end. At the opposite end we have all the processing carried out by high performance client PCs, and the server merely "serving" requests for data.

There are advantages and disadvantages to both the fat and thin approaches. Perhaps the biggest reason for the client to be a fat client PC is that of user

Fig. 12.2 A client/server
database system

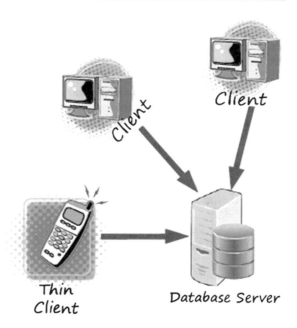

expectation. Users now expect to be able to have some control over their own
computing. In addition, thick clients allow sometimes lengthy data transfer to
happen in the back- ground whilst the user works on other tasks. Simple tasks like
screen refreshes and paging through data can be processed at the PC, whereas, with
a thin client, network traffic would be increased significantly as the keystrokes and
results pass back and forth.

Amongst the advantages of thin client, perhaps the two most significant are those
of cost savings and greenness. Without the need for powerful computing power,
thin clients can be better than half the price of a PC to purchase and can use five- or
six-times less electricity in use.

In addition, thin client supporters claim it to be easier be easier to manage
(software upgrades are easy since they just apply to one machine, for example) and
more secure (since the applications are entirely housed in the data centre, where
strict rules and policies can be applied).

Whichever approach is taken it was clear that the client/server model allowed for
much better scaling than did peer-to-peer. Handling more users could be as simple
as adding more RAM or upgrading the CPU on the server.

However, as pressure rose for more and more users to be able to access an
organisation's data, the single server solution (known as two-tier) showed weaknesses and the next step was to split server-side processing over two servers.
Typically, this would be a Database Server and an Application Server. This became
known as Three-tier architecture. Many organisations now use this approach. Extra
scalability can come in this environment by having users connect to the application

server which then manages connections to the database server, pooling connections rather than requiring the server to have a process for every user. The most recent move has been to n-tier architecture, in which many servers each cope with aspects of servicing the clients (see Fig. 12.4).

The advent of Cloud computing has now brought us the ability to scale either way (up and down) very easily, and this is seen by many as one of the great benefits of Cloud. If you had to buy and maintain a client/server system adequate to support an estimated 200 concurrent users, and then you discovered that the estimate was wildly wrong and you needed only to cope with 20 concurrent users, you would be grossly over resourced (and over spent!). Having bought hardware, it is virtually impossible to downsize. However, Cloud just needs you to change your contract with your service provider. And of course, virtually unlimited and very rapid upward scaling is also available on the Cloud.

12.2.3 Scalability Eras

The different approaches to the scalability issue outline above have all taken place since the PC became a viable business tool and each approach has evolved. A summary of this evolution in shown in Fig. 12.3.

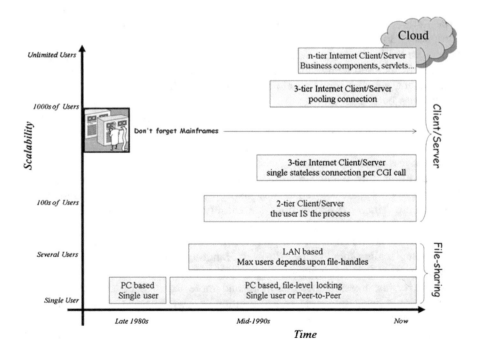

Fig. 12.3 Scalability eras

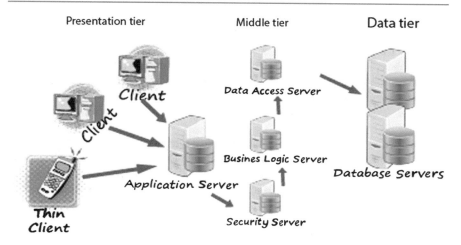

Fig. 12.4 Multi-tier systems

Some of the aspects discussed above also impinge heavily upon the networking domain. Having a server do all of the processing and just sending the final dataset to the client means that network traffic is minimised. But the fat client solution may mean a need for network upgrades when more users begin to use the system. As always, database and networking professionals should ideally be liaising to provide the organisation with an optimal solution.

12.2.3.1   Separating Users from Sessions

In the traditional client/server database system the user connects to the database and the database will then manage a bit of server RAM and some server-based processes on behalf of that user, called a database "session".

Managing sessions is an important and resource heavy task for the RDBMS. Idle sessions need to be continually checked and killed after a certain time since they are using up valuable RAM without doing anything. The activity of every session is recorded in great detail. This information is useful for performance tuning activity, allowing the DBA to ascertain which sessions used most resources. However, its primary purpose is to act to allow audits of activity. But why this activity happens need not concern us here—what we need to know is that the more sessions we have the less well the database will perform.

However, especially in a e-commerce type environment it may well be that users who are logged on to the server for as long as an hour only actually make calls to the database that take less than one minute of database process time. Consider a simplified version of the shopper who asks the site to show him all the gentlemen's trousers available:

1. The SQL is formed which says something like Select * from catalog where item_type = Trouser; The SQL is sent to the server which returns the dataset asked for.
2. The shopping basket may or may not be stored on the server
3. The user then browses the dataset for 50 min, decided to make a cup of tea half way through the process.
4. The user completes the purchasing process.

If we were to kill this session for inactivity whilst the user made their tea we would lose our customer—not a sensible approach to take! On the other hand, tying up resources, especially when multiplied thousands of time over with the potential number of concurrent users accessing the site, could be very costly in terms of having RAM and CPU in the server "just in case" all the users need to access the database at the same time.

The solution is to have an extra layer between the client and the database server that manages the connection process. This extra layer, known as the Application Server, will own the database connection and will manage requests for data access on behalf of clients. This is often called Connection Pooling. In effect, the problem with the fifty minutes of inactivity identified above is lost since the application server will simply service other requests from other clients with the open session.

The application server can do much more than manage sessions. It can, for example, carry out the query processing, such as sorting and filtering, removing pro- cessing load from both database server and client.

12.2.3.2   Adding Tiers

As we saw above, there is a trend towards multiple tier server solutions. In our example above, we are divorcing database server from the need to worry about what happens to the data once it is served to the requesting agent. This means that physical aspects of the server (RAM and CPU) can be optimised for data-intensive processing, whilst the application server can also be optimised.

Three tier architecture is now the norm in enterprise scale architecture. The three tiers are identified as:

1. The Data tier: responsible for writing to and reading from the data store or file system
2. Business Logic: responsible for liaising between the other tiers, including sharing connections. But this layer can also contain rules, business logic and other processes that can work with any extracted data before passing it on to the client
3. Presentation: responsible for turning the information from the second tier into something the user can read.

If the clients are thin clients then the middle tier tends to have to carry out much more work and that tier itself needs to be broken down into different layers, each sitting on a different server. A diagram of such an n-tier architecture is shown in Fig. 12.4.

12.3   Coping with Growing Volumes of Data

As we saw in Chap. 6 we are now working in an era where volumes of data are increasing at an enormous speed. Storing that data load as it grows, in a way that allows it to be accessed efficiently, is what scalability means in terms of data.

One of the reasons to use normalisation was to reduce the amount of data being stored. And one of the key reasons for that was that storage media were very expensive until quite recently. They were also very unwieldy (see Fig. 12.5). The continuing reduction in relative cost and enhanced functionality of computing technologies are key in driving new expectations and requirements. The fact that we can now store 1 terabyte of data for around $100 (under £70) means that the business that wants to store that amount of data can easily do so. Only twenty years ago the cost would have been hundreds of times higher and would therefore have been far more likely to prevent the storage from happening.

The physical performance of data stored on disk, too, has increased significantly. In terms of data transfer rates, today's 6 gigabits per second SATA drives are 4 × faster than when SATA drives started to become available in 2003. There are some who argue that disk speeds are beginning reach the best they can possibly be

Fig. 12.5 What HDD used to look like! Courtesy of International Business Machines Corporation, ©International Business Machines Corporation

as a result of the constraints set by the physical elements that make up the HDD (spinning platters on a spindle and a moving arm).

SSD technology on the other hand has no moving parts and can therefore be much faster. This may well be the way that data storage moves in the future, but, though the cost/Gb of SSD is dropping, it may be a few years before the cost and reliability matches HDD technology.

12.3.1 E-Commerce and Cloud Applications Need Scalable Solutions

The rise of companies whose core business is selling to consumers by using the internet has brought a whole new requirement in terms of scalability. When starting new businesses in this area the entrepreneur does not know how many customers they will have using its site. They can only guess. And guesses can be considerably out (either way!).

But the hope is usually that customers will come flocking in to your new e-commerce site. And once you have your reputation built, even more will come, month on month increasing the number of hits your site receives.

But the worry is that your website is only as good as its ability to cope with peak traffic. As the hits increase you need to be able to be sure that your website, and its underlying database will be able to scale upwards. Failure to scale will result in disgruntled customers who could even ruin the business if it gets that bad!

If your solution is cloud-based then you can afford to worry a little less since you can quickly buy your way out of scaling problems by renting more CPU and disk from your provider.

12.3.2 Vertical and Horizontal Scaling

These two terms have come to the fore recently to describe two completely different approaches to allowing database applications to scale. Vertical is also referred to as Scaling UP and Horizontal as Scaling OUT.

Unfortunately these terms are amongst many in computing that suffer from definition creep. For ease we will here suggest that Vertical Scaling is the act of adding resource, such as CPU or RAM to a database server, and/or using database architectural techniques to assist in allowing more data to be added to the system without degrading performance. Horizontal is the act of connecting several cheap (usually referred to as "commodity servers") computers to share out the storage and processing load.

Both of these scaling techniques have their strengths and weaknesses. There can be little doubt that the complexity involved in managing multiple nodes in an Hadoop cluster might be enough to put even technical experts off from using that approach, especially if their expertise lies in the relational arena. But if the business need is to store and analyse masses of data that can be spread across multiple nodes, it may be that the complexity is worth it. Google, for example, would not have gone to the trouble of creating their own file system if they had thought scaling up a standard RDBMS could have coped.

12.3.3 Database Scaling Issues

So why are there problems in adding more and more data to a database? Surely a table can simply keep growing? Well, yes it can keep growing—provided the under- pinning disk system can keep expanding. There are physical limits to the amount of storage that can be addressed, but the main limit is still likely to be cost. However, even if you have a disk array that will house all of your data, other problems occur as a consequence of constantly adding data.

The most significant problem is the time it takes to access the data in response to SQL queries. There is a pre-retrieval overhead for all queries that will not get slower because there is more data, but the actual retrieval phase could take twice as long if you are reading twice as many rows.

One of the most frequent processes carried out by an SQL query execution plan is a full table scan. In Oracle, for example, if the optimiser calculates that your query will return more than around 15% of the total rows, the execution plan will not include the use of indexes (even if they exist), but will read every row in the table, discarding unwanted ones in memory.

This is quicker because the use of indexes will frequently lead to several read operations per row fetched, and each read may require the disk read head to have to jump to different physical addresses. A full table scan only requires one move—to the address of the start of the table—and then to keep reading until it gets to the end of the table (identified by a High Water Mark). It can also use much larger I/O calls, biting more off with each read. Making fewer large I/O calls is less costly than making many small calls.

Any query that uses a full table scan, then, will take longer the more rows you add to the table concerned. Queries that use index retrieval will also probably take longer as rows are added for a couple of reasons. Firstly, more rows means more leaf blocks to the index and possibly more branches (each requiring a read) to get to those nodes. Secondly, having retrieved the rowid (which contains the hex-address of the row on the disk) it is likely that the disk head will need to move further to access the data concerned.

Bigger datasets also probably mean more data maintenance—things like updates to, or deletions of, rows. Both updates and deletions have effects on any indexes concerned too. Inserts to tables with Foreign Key constraints will take longer if the referenced table is growing significantly.

All this extra work as a result of the volume of data stored will slow the system down. The need to protect against database failure means that Redo Logs activity may well increase significantly with increased usage and may result in the need for more disk space to be devoted to Redo. More data changes also means increased Undo activity as the need to be able to Rollback and provide read consistency expands. Again, this means more disk space and slower access to the contents as it increases in size.

If you have a Disaster Recover policy that relies on a mirrored server in another physical location you will have double the issues of disk space to worry about, as both servers need to be in step. Moreover, the network traffic will increase as more information needs to be passed to the mirror.

Back-up will take longer as you have more data. There may be only slight increases in any incremental backing up carried out, but full, cold backups will take longer. More worrying, the fact that there is more data involved means that the time to recovery will be much slower should you need to use those backups.

All of these are just natural biproducts of a growth in data. Just as it is true that it takes longer to read War and Peace than Of Mice and Men, so it is true that reading lots of data takes longer than reading small amounts.

Even if it the data involved made it appropriate, the database architect may well not be able to make sweeping changes to the infrastructure in response to problems caused by growing data. If your organisation has invested heavily in large, powerful servers running Oracle or SQLServer, it would be a very brave DBA indeed that suggested throwing that all on the waste heap and replacing it with many commodity servers running Hadoop. As always, the constraints on the DBA will not always be technical ones.

For this reason, in the next few sections we will examine possible scalability-related solutions for different environments, recognising as we do, that the current environment is often the given that has to be worked around.

12.3.4   Single Server Solutions

In this section we consider the example of a single server running a Oracle or SQLServer database which is growing and which, as a consequence, beginning to suffer from poor performance. It is taken for granted that the extra data is being handled by extending the storage disk-farm.

It is true that there may be an immediate cure in terms of simply upgrading the CPU or providing more RAM, but they can be costly, and are not always the right solution. There is also the possibility that improvements can be found by changing the underlying operating system, though this latter may have far too many organisation-wide repercussions to be considered realistic.

Extra RAM—lots of it—might seem like the obvious solution to our problem. After all we will discover in the performance chapter later, reading a row from a HDD is far slower than reading from memory. So more RAM means less HDD reading, which means we can scale our database up and ensure our users do not notice any change in performance.

There is some truth in this. As we saw in the In-Memory chapter, there are examples (Oracle Times-Ten, VoltDB) of databases running entirely in memory. How- ever, just having picked at random a cheap 1 Tb HDD and 1 Gb RAM on

Amazon, the cost/Gb difference is very significant; it is around 300 times more expensive/Gb for RAM than it is for HDD. Except for some very time critical applications it is probably that we will need to continue working with HDD technology as the means of making our data permanent.

The other important factor is just what you are doing with the data. If this is a very volatile many user OLTP system, it may well be the case that much of the data that is cached into memory as a result of one users SQL statement will simply time-out and disappear as it isn't needed again before the RAM is needed for other data. In this circumstance performance will not improve at all by adding RAM. As usual we need to understand what the application needs from the database before we make our decisions about how to tackle scalability.

Memory management is a very important part of any RDBMS system. Newer databases will often manage the available RAM automatically, but if the RDBMS is not the only software running on the server, some manual intervention and decision making will need to be carried out.

What we do know is that there will come a time when the benefit accrued from adding RAM, or CPUs, will not seem worth the expense. So are there other, software related, ways of improving performance when our data increases?

12.3.4.1 Partitioning

Partitioning data, also known as vertical scaling, is one approach to extending data storage within the existing schema. At its core the concept is relatively simple: if you are struggling to access large volumes of data, simply break the storage object (usually a table) into smaller objects.

There are several ways of doing this. One is to take a table and attempt to break it into two or more tables, with data that is regularly accessed in one table, and the other tables holding the less active columns. It is sometimes referred to as row-splitting.

The original, unsplit table can be recreated with a view which joins the tables this split. Care needs to be taken however since this activity obviously increases (resource intensive) join activity so, as usual, it will depend upon what activity your database is supporting as to whether the split is worthwhile.

Another way of subdividing the data is by breaking the table into logical portions based upon a key value. For example, in an OLTP system you could partition the data such that data for the current month is stored on one tablespace, whilst data for previous months which can't be updated, is stored on faster to access read-only disks.

As partitioning requires the DBA to identify criteria for breaking up the structures it is not useful in situations where the data distribution changes often. Predictability and some regularity in the distribution of data between the new structures makes partitioning more likely to succeed.

12.3.5 Distributed RDBMS: Shared Nothing Versus Shared Disk

One of the problems with scaling up data storage on a traditional RDBMS sitting on a single server is that the server itself is expensive.

RAID technologies (see Chap. 3) began the process of utilising cheap technology (in that case HDD technology) in enterprise systems that had hitherto feared that reliability would suffer if cheaper hardware was used.

In 2006 Oracle released Version 10g of its database. The "g" stands for grid. Grids are just pools of computers (cheap, off-the-shelf) that can share the processing required to run the database between themselves. Scalability is achieved by permitting extra computers to be added to (or removed from) the grid. Naturally, in order for this to work, there has to be some sort of Grid Control mechanism which manages the flow of tasks and data.

Whilst the term "grid" was the cause of some disagreement in the industry because grid computing was a term already in use by Computer science, the concept is still seen as a sensible approach to the problem of scalability and cost-effective performance.

In the Oracle grid solution, whilst additional nodes can be added to the grid, what they actually provide is extra only places for processing to take place. The data is not owned by any individual node. Rather it accesses a single shared database. This may, in actual fact, reside on many different physical disks in a SAN, but, as far as the RDBMS is concerned, it is treated as a single database which is attached to by the nodes when they need data. All the nodes share the database, hence one of the names for this approach: Shared Disk (see Fig. 12.6).

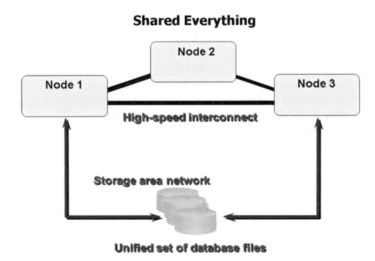

Fig. 12.6 Shared everything (or shared disk)

Confusingly, different manufacturers use different terms to describe concepts. The shared disk approach is also referred to as Clustering. Oracle calls this approach Real Application Clustering (RAC). Its real strength is in enhancing availability since, should one of the nodes fail, the other nodes are available for users to attach to, and thence gain access to the shared data.

Query performance can also be improved since each node can, if appropriate, use its computing resources to return parts of an overall query at the same time; in effect allowing for parallel processing.

Unfortunately, although there are some performance advantages with this approach the fact that each node is accessing the same data means that there will be many more locks in play than on a single server, and those locks need synchronising across all the nodes. It can be argued that this makes this approach less than truly scalable as a result of this.

Shared disk is not the only approach to distribution. A shared nothing approach means that each node also looks after its own data and it has its own memory and disk resource. Examples of this approach are IBM's DB2 and Teradata.

Here the whole database is actually a logical construct made up of the individual databases on each node. This can be its performance weakness since joins across multiple nodes can be very slow. Moreover, if a node fails you lose far more than you do in the shared disk approach—you lose part of your whole database, so availability is an issue which needs to be thought carefully about. However, it is very much easier to scale. You just add another commodity server when you need more resource. This approach is popular for e-commerce sites for which the degree of scaling is unsure, or certain to be high.

There are, as usual, pluses and misuses to each approach. The business needs will need to be the driver in the decision making.

We are now moving into the grey area between shared nothing and sharding. Indeed, it could be argued that sharding is the same as Shared Nothing is the same as horizontal scaling (see Fig. 12.7).

12.3.6 Horizontal Scaling Solutions

As we have seen, there are various names for the basic idea of splitting your data across two or more databases (often referred to as nodes) such that all nodes have a subset of the data. This works well in cases when a query only needs to connect to one node. It can be more cumbersome if many nodes need to be accessed to return data from a query. This is sometimes referred to as "scaling out" as opposed to the traditional approach of "scaling up".

As the data stored for web usage expanded dramatically early in 2000s Google realised that the traditional RDBMS solutions would not cope with workload being placed on them by the various applications like Google Search, Web-indexing, Google Earth, and others. They set about inventing their own file system (GFS) and sat their own database (BigTable) on this platform. The need to scale easily was

Shared Nothing

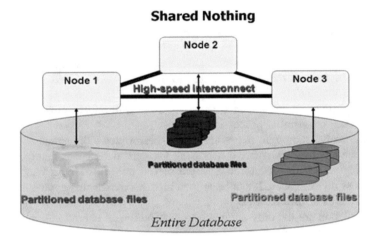

Fig. 12.7 Shared nothing

paramount. They achieved this in a cost-effective way by using cheap, commodity servers which can be easily slotted in and out of the data centre infrastructure.

Google started a trend. GFS and BigTable are proprietary products, but very similar tools began to appear in the open source environment. At the time of writing the industry standard horizontal scaling tool seems to be becoming Apache Hadoop. Other NoSQL databases (see Chap. 5) also adopt this approach. The examples we looked at earlier, Cassandra and MongoDB both shared their data to allow scaling. But it is not just the open source arena that is turning to sharding. Microsoft's Azure allows sharding too.

One of the first problems when designing shared systems is in identifying a key on which to split the data. Let review a simple example:

An application starts by looking up information about a client based upon their surname.
You have two servers available. Perhaps it may be sensible to have two shards, one with all the names beginning with A to L, and the other M to Z.

And whilst the only query asked of the data is about one individual, then this split will reduce the searching that needs to be carried out. But if you were to want to discover all clients who lived in a particular town, this query may well result in joins needing to be carried out and the management of that process may take more time than if all the data were in one single table. It is clear that selection of the sharding key is key to the success, or otherwise of this approach.

The management of the process includes the need to maintain an centrally controlled index of the keys used in the sharding in order to make sure that the request for data is made to the correct database. All this means there is an extra overhead involved in managing the database connections.

There can be little doubt that the use of cheap servers to allow easy scalability is very attractive and this is a significant factor in the recent rise in the use of horizontal scaling. As always in IT, however, we need to be careful not to just jump on the current bandwagon. We should assess every situation individually since Sharding is not a silver bullet.

It may be that Sharding the whole system is overkill. Perhaps only the part that comes under most load—the web front-end, for example—needs sharding whilst the traditional back-office and transactional systems remain on single servers.

As we have seen above, sharding is not the only way of coping with the need to scale. It could be that when or if the price of RAM falls in the future we will look back at this fundamentally disjointed approach to database architecture and laugh. However, for the foreseeable future the scaling out approach is likely to be the de facto standard for large datasets.

12.3.6.1 Cloud Computing

Many texts about Cloud site flexibility and scalability as inherent benefits from adopting a cloud-based strategy. Hill et al. (2013) say:

> It is probably true that a need for scalability is a significant driver towards adopting cloud. If an organisation understands its business well and it is relatively stable, it can plan what capacity is required and purchase as and when required. Many organisations, however, go through unexpected sharp up- and downturns in their OLTP traffic in step with the business performance. Not having to purchase extra capacity 'just in case' in such circumstances can make public cloud more appealing.

It is true that the cost of the physical resources needed to cope with the maximum processing load a database might face can be expensive. Being able to temporarily gain extra resource and pay for it "as used" can be a good way to keep capital expenditure down on a large scale database project. The costs, however, will not disappear, but rather will appear as rental fees in revue costs.

That caveat aside, it is clear that Cloud computing does offer virtually unlimited scalability, provided the costs do not become prohibitive. Some vendors make relational databases available in the cloud, allowing the single (albeit virtualised) server solution that can, almost instantly, be turned into a distributed solution. The NoSQL tools are also used heavily in the cloud. Having a system with multiple data nodes across many geographic regions becomes a relatively simple task for the system designer, if such horizontal scaling is required.

12.3.7 Scaling Down for Mobile

A recent phenomenon that has begun to impact upon the world of database design is that of mobile computing in general, and more specifically the need to integrate mobile devices into enterprise-wide systems. The term being used is BOYD (Bring Your Own Device). It recognises that employees are often willing to work in places other than at their desk and that they want to access data from all sorts of place, at all sorts of times, from all sorts of devices.

The problem with this move is that, despite the continuing evolution and improvement of mobile devices, they suffer from resource poverty (RAM and Storage) compared to desktop PCs. This can be a major obstacle for many applications and means that computation on mobile devices will always involve some form of compromise.

Perhaps the easiest solution to this problem is to treat mobile devices just the same as a very thin client and allow a server to carry the processing and data storage load. Unfortunately, however, this solution requires ubiquitous broadband to be of any use, and even in some developed nations there are places where communications are unavailable, meaning the system is, in effect, unusable for the mobile client.

At the other end of the spectrum, another solution is to have the system run entirely on the mobile device and have a database there to store the data locally. In these systems data responsibility for data persistence is handed to the device in question. There are databases designed to operate with a very small footprint, such as the public domain SQLite. But this also has its own problem; enterprise systems called for sharing data, not lots of independent data stores.

Synchronising with a Cloud-based server whilst communications allow it is one solution used. This can also be a means for ensure vital corporate data is regularly backed-up. Management of availability when there any many different client system types is far more complicated, but if all devices are connecting to the Cloud this can be made easier and automated.

12.4 Summary

This chapter has reviewed scalability in terms of growing data and growing user-bases. We have seen that small, PC based databases have their strengths, but they do not allow scalable systems to be created. We have seen that there are many possible approaches to database design which may help with scalability. We saw that the systems designer needs to consider where the processing should happen (thin/thick client) in a client-Server design. If more scalability is required there is the option to distribute the processing and/or the data and that many of today's Big Data focused databases using sharding to allow them to easily scale.

12.5 Review Questions

The answers to these questions can be found in the text of this chapter.

- What is the maximum number of concurrent users that can log on to Access databases?
- Why is the separation of a database session from a user logging-on to an application an important factor in scalability?

- What does sharding mean?
- Describe the elements of a three-tier architecture
- How does partitioning help when data in a table grows to extent that performance worsens?

12.6 Group Work Research Activities

These activities require you to research beyond the contents of the book and can be tackled individually or as a discussion group.

Discussion Topic 1 You are asked to discuss appropriate database designs for an e-commerce site your organisation is wanting to create. As the application becomes available they expect only a few users, but they believe that, once the word gets round about how good the application is, that the number of concurrent users will dramatically increase in the coming months. Your aim is to architect a scalable back-end to the application being created. What alternative design options can you suggest, and what are their respective strengths and weaknesses?

Discussion Topic 2 What are the arguments for and against thin client solutions for an office-based environment? Review some of the sales material from market leaders in the area and see what they say.

References

Dunmall J, Clarke K (2003) Real-world load testing tips to avoid bottlenecks when your web app goes live. https://msdn.microsoft.com/en-us/magazine/cc188783.aspx

Hill R, Hirsch L, Lake P, Moshiri S (2013) Guide to cloud computing: principles and practice. Springer, London

Hoskins J, Frank B (2002) Exploring IBM EServer ZSeries and S/390 servers: see why IBM's redesigned mainframe computer family has become more popular than ever! Maximum Press, 464 pages

Database Availability

13

What the reader will learn:

- that we should not expect our databases to be always available
- that the more available a system is, generally the more expensive it is
- that there are several approaches to making a system as available as is appropriate to suit the business need
- that Cloud computing changes the way we think about availability
- In some circumstances the expense of a Disaster Recovery strategy is irrelevant as client expectation will drive the decisions

13.1 What Do We Mean by Availability?

As with most chapters in this book we will start by defining what we mean by availability. And, as with some other chapters there are several possible answers.

For an online business, availability is measured mostly by uptime. Because every second the database is unavailable (or "down") to potential customers could cost thousands of dollars in lost income, having the database usable for the magic five nines (99.999% up-time) is a sensible, if difficult to achieve, target. This is around 5 min downtime in a year.

As we shall see, the move from three nines (99.9%) to five nines can be very expensive. Some organisations will not need that level of availability. Three nines is under nine hours per year. If you need to spend an extra $100,000 to get to five nines, those will be a very costly few hours of computing you have bought!

To be more accurate, database up time is not the same as availability. It is possible for a database to be open, but for network problems to prevent access to the database. But there is more to availability than merely keeping a database open and accessible. What happens if your data centre is struck by a meteor? Or flood? If you are a bank, for example, your customers will probably expect you to have an

© Springer Nature Switzerland AG 2021   259
K. Domdouzis et al., *Concise Guide to Databases*, Undergraduate Topics
in Computer Science, https://doi.org/10.1007/978-3-030-42224-0_13

alternative server somewhere else that can kick in to (almost) seamlessly replace the destroyed one. Disaster recovery (DR) is part of the availability mix. A DR strategy like that of the bank would be very, very expensive and there would really need to be a good business case for having an expensive server (or servers) sitting doing nothing "just in case".

And the other important element to availability is recovering from smaller problems cleanly. If a user mistakenly deletes some data and wants to retrieve it, the DBA will have a number of tools available to address the problem. This could even be something the user can affect themselves, like Oracle's Flashback technology. Part of the standard toolkit here is Backup and Recovery. Taking a full copy of the database once every now and then (full backup), and then recording the changes made on a regular basis is one very common strategy that we will examine in this chapter.

In a traditional Client/Server environment a fail-over strategy may also include the use of redundant disks (RAID). Again the downside is the expense is the extra disk and processing required to make the system more robust, and a potential effect on performance.

Cloud has allowed us to change the way we think about availability. Disk Storage as a Service is now commonplace, meaning that you do not need to worry about maintaining an array of expensive disks, but rather you rent the space you need, when you need it. But what Cloud changes is more to do with costs and flexibility than the overall principles involved ensuring optimum availability.

So, what is our definition of Database Availability? How about this:

> Ensuring that the database is open and accessible for as long as possible, by planning for as many eventualities as is reasonable, given the constraint of cost.

In this chapter we will explore three key areas in database availability: Keeping the system running—immediate solutions to short term problems; back-up and recovery; Disaster Recovery (DR).

13.2 Keeping the System Running—Immediate Solutions to Short Term Problems

High Availability (HA) is not a new concept and has been part of every leading database vendor's sales pitches for many years. But before we look at some approaches to ensuring high availability, we need to explore some key concepts.

As we discussed in Chap. 3, databases are primarily about making data permanent. From the earliest days of relational databases that has meant storing ons and offs on some form of magnetic medium, such as a floppy, or hard disk.

Although, in the author's experience, it is true that computers have become generally more reliable over the decades, it is also true that they are far from perfect. Disks can fail, as can CPUs, motherboard elements and a whole host of communications interfaces. Availability is about recognising the less than perfect environment and putting in place processes for coping with such disturbances with minimum effect on the users.

13.2.1 What Can Go Wrong?

There is an apocryphal story that does the rounds with seasoned database professionals. It happens that the DBAs would regularly come in on a Monday morning and find that the database had been down for about half an hour at 4 pm on Sunday afternoon. None of them came in to work on a Sunday, and there was no remote access. The server brought itself up, but nonetheless, this was a worrying event.

One week the lead DBA decided to go in and watch the server for himself and couldn't believe his eyes when at 4 pm the server room door was opened by a cleaner who, after smiling and waving to our DBA, proceeded to unplug the server and plug in the vacuum cleaner.

What this story highlights is that one of the major points of failure in any database system is the humans who interact with it in any way. These events may never have happened, but the database professional should attempt to think about all possible occurrences that might in any way affect the database and work out ways of pre- venting the event, or at least limiting the damage caused by it.

The other significant problem caused by humans is in the writing of the code which makes up the database management system, and any database systems using that database. Any database management system is itself a piece of software that has been written by software engineers. A product like Oracle will have had many software engineers produce many thousands of lines of code to bring us the product we now use. And they still beaver away, generating new releases with improvements (or corrections) to previous versions.

13.2.1.1 Database Software Related Problems

The problem is, humans make mistakes. And software engineers are no different, regardless of the quality assurance mechanisms that are put in place. When products evolve, as Oracle has from Version 6 in 1988 to its current Version 12c, there is potential for mistakes to be built on mistakes. This isn't to say Oracle is an unsafe product—far from it, Oracle's reputation is very strong in the area of reliability. However, if you count the patches that are released every year you can't help but notice that somebody, somewhere, gets things wrong!

Often such problems are caused by software engineers making assumptions about customer's operating environments and data distributions, and so it isn't necessarily an error that is being corrected so much as an omission. But this nicety of definition doesn't help the DBA affected by it.

So potential fault number one is a problem introduced by a change to database software release, or its configuration. As a DBA looking to keep the database available at all times, how can we mitigate the effect of these potential problems?

Most of the approaches we cover in this chapter start with the age-old dilemma: how much are we willing to spend to make the system more robust? One solution to the dangers of errors introduced by upgrades is to run two parallel systems for a period, with the upgraded version running besides the older version. Should anything bad happen the new version can be switched off and the old version can continue.

This approach sounds like a sensible one. But then the question is, how long do we run in parallel? A week; a month; a year? Much will depend upon the type of system this is (OLTP or Decision Support, for example) and the volatility of the data. It will also depend upon how critical not losing the database is to the organisation. Whatever the decision, an accountant may see this as a very expensive safety net.

If you are a bank, however, you will probably be willing to pay very considerable amounts to ensure that there is no outage as a result of an upgrade or change to a system. Your customers would, quite rightly, be very angry if they could not access their cash whenever they wanted to. In these circumstances the servers involved would probably already be mirrored (see later in the chapter about mirroring) with DR stand-by servers involved. These will all probably need to be upgraded at the same time too and will need protecting as they are upgraded. This makes it a very complicated and expensive process with the risk of significant financial damage if it were to go wrong.

13.2.1.2 Systems Design Problems and User Mistakes

RDBMSs are at the heart of many applications and e-commerce systems. Vendors design their applications to interact with the database in many different ways and it is possible for there to be mistakes in the coding. Whilst we should not get involved in the wider discussion of systems testing, DBAs may need to be able to change the values stored because a badly designed system element has caused some values to be mistakenly altered. It might even be as simple as users misunderstanding the input screens and typing wrong numbers into a dialogue box.

DBAs themselves are not infallible. There may be issues like there not being enough disk storage space available to write some inserts, or inappropriate settings on the UNDO which cause processes to fail due to the "snapshot too old" error.

Whatever the cause, it is not unusual for the DBA to be asked to return the row or rows affected to the way they were at a point in time, or a point in a transaction process to allow the correct values or operations to be applied.

This process of reverting to previous values was made easier in Oracle with the development of flashback technology. This was first released in Version 9i and has been built on in subsequent versions. Oracle are not forthcoming about how this technology works, but it is evident that the use of UNDO data, stored in the UNDO TABLESPACE is important. Undo was around before 9i. It was sometime referred to as Rollback segments as it serves as a place to store the values before any change is made so that, should the ROLLBACK command be issued, changes can be undone. It is also used to allow read consistency (see Chap. 4).

Let us take an example of a user who has just accidentally deleted a customer, ID201213, from the CUSTOMER table. They contact the DBA and they can retrieve the missing row by issuing the following command:

```
INSERT INTO CUSTOMER
   (SELECT * FROM CUSTOMER AS OF TIMESTAMP TO_TIMESTAMP('2013-04-04 09:30:00',
    'YYYY-MM-DD HH:MI:SS') WHERE cust_id = 'ID201213');
```

The subquery (within the brackets) retrieves the row for ID201213 as it was at a point of time, as described by the timestamp. This row is then inserted to the CUSTOMER table as it is now.

Even careless dropping of tables can be undone using flashback. Here we retrieve a table called PERSONS that has been accidentally dropped:

```
FLASHBACK TABLE persons TO BEFORE DROP;
```

Perhaps the most powerful is the FLASHBACK DATABASE command which allows you to revert the database to the way it was at a particular point in time, or at a particular System Change Number (SCN). Naturally the database has to be down for this to happen, and you will lose all the data between the point in time and shutting the database down. Replaying data from the Redo logs or archive files would allow some recovery.

13.2.1.3 Technology Failures

As well as human-initiated problems, databases exist in a world of fallible technology. The Hard disks (HDD) that many database management systems use to provide permanency to their data are, at their core, very old technology. They record their data by magnetising a very thin film of ferromagnetic material and this can become corrupted, losing or altering the data as it does. That would result in the partial loss of some data. The mechanisms which allow the disk to be spun and the disk head reader moved to the appropriate place are also vulnerable to failure, and any such failure would result in the loss of all the disk content.

The measure used to describe disk reliability is Mean Time Between Failure (MTBF). The fact that there is even a measurement for this should worry us! Some HDD manufacturers claim 300,000 h between failures. But since this is a mean, many devices could fail well before that time has elapsed. The point is they DO fail, however occasionally. Even the most expensive disks fail; you pay the extra because they fail less frequently. And if they fail in the middle of your company payroll run, you can bet you will have many unhappy employees!

The HDD is the weakest link in a database management system. As Alapati (2009) says in the *Expert Oracle Database 11g Administration*:

The most common errors on a day-to-day basis are hardware related. Disks or the controllers that manage them fail on a regular basis. The larger the database (and the larger the number of disk drives), the greater the likelihood that on any given day a service person is fixing or replacing a faulty part. Because it is well known that the entire disk system is a vulnerable point, you must provide redundancy in your database. Either a mirrored system or a RAID 5 disk system, or a combination of both, will give you the redundancy you need.

We will review RAID later in this chapter.

If you refer back to Chap. 3 you will see that Oracle keeps its data in Tablespaces which are themselves supported by one or more Operating System files. If the area of disk which stores the data gets corrupted, the DBA will need to recover that file, potentially taking the tablespace offline (making it unusable) whilst the copy is restored from a back-up. Naturally, whilst recovery can be relatively trivial in terms of tasks to undertake, the loss of a part of the database can have expensive business repercussions.

Once the backed-up replacement file is in place the DBA will need to "replay" the changes made between the time of back-up and the failure. They do that using the Redo Log files. More on this process follows in the Recovery section of this chapter. But the fact that Redo is required for any recovery, and that Redo is also stored on vulnerable HDDs means that we have to be extra careful with Redo files. Critical elements of the database architecture, such as Redo and Control Files, are stored multiple times across multiple disks to ensure that recovery for a disk failure can be both rapid and, where possible, automatic.

Redo Logs which consist of two or more files that store all the changes made to the database as they occur, are so critical to the recovery task that they are multiplexed. This means at least two identical copies of the redo log are automatically maintained, but on separate locations, ideally on separate disks.

13.2.1.4   CPU, RAM and Motherboards

Other parts of the server architecture are also vulnerable to failure. CPUs are made up from many transistors and failure of one can cause the failure of the processor itself. The failure can be triggered by excesses in temperature, for example.

If your database is running in a single server, as it will be for most smaller scale applications, then failure of CPU or motherboard can mean your database is down. As we keep saying, that outage can be expensive to the company.

Larger systems may well consist of more than one physical server. Oracle Version 10 gained a "g" suffix, becoming Oracle 10g. The "g" stands for grid. In essence grid, in Oracle terms, is about using multiple, relative cheap "commodity servers", all connected together working on the same database to meet an organisation's performance and availability requirements. Oracle have two types of grid, as explained in their online references:

- A Database Server Grid is a collection of commodity servers connected to run one or more databases.
- A Database Storage Grid is a collection of low-cost modular storage ar- rays combined together and accessed by the computers in the Database Server Grid.

They go on to say:

The same grid computing concepts can be used to create a standby database hub that provides data protection, minimizes planned downtime, and provides ideal test systems for quality assurance testing and all for multiple primary databases

Having multiple servers and redundant disks available was, and still can be, an ideal way of managing availability. Some forms of Cloud computing offer this sort of advantage without having to pay for and maintain multiple servers yourself, thus replacing the high capital expenditure costs involved with hardware purchase with a longer term spread of revenue costs as processing is "rented" from cloud providers. Storage as a Service is fast becoming a popular offering by providers. As this allows an organisation to have redundant data spread across the world the service offers potentially more security than having servers in one geographical location.

13.2.1.5 Using RAID to Improve Availability

Some organisations will not be looking to the Cloud for some time to come. Those that worry about security, or which have recently invested heavily in internal infrastructure, will still want to ensure their databases are as available as possible.

A Redundant Array of Independent Disks (RAID) is one way of enabling higher availability. Most external storage devices provide support for RAID. There are several types of RAID types, known as levels. RAID can either improve performance or provide higher availability, dependent upon the level used. As with many aspects of database management there are trade-offs between the different desired outcomes. Replicating data to more than one disk will add redundancy and thus improve availability, but, even if the writes are made in parallel, there will be an overhead involved in ensuring the success of the write that will slow the write process down.

Here we are concentrating on availability, and the RAID levels most often used are RAID 1, also known as Disk Mirroring, and RAID 5. RAID 1 is the simplest form of high availability implementation, and needs two disks. If the pair of disks are available for parallel reading, queries can perform more quickly than against a single disk. However, since it needs double the amount of disk space to store the data it is not the most efficient mechanism.

RAID 5 is a popular RAID level for enterprise systems since it offers better performance than RAID 1 as well as high availability, and although it needs the use of at least 3 disks, it is potentially less space hungry since not all data is replicated.

It manages this by striping both data and parity information across the three (or more) disks (see Chap. 3 for a discussion of Striping and Parity).

Parity arrays work well because they are built on the assumption that a HDD will rarely fail entirely, but may on occasion fail in a sector of the disk. A recovery of that lost sector is made possible by using the parity value, with the data you do have, applying an exclusive or (XOR) and regenerating the missing data.

If you have a system with n disks, you will need n × 2 disks for RAID 1, and n + 1 for RAID 5. In addition to using less disk resource, RAID 5 can be better performing than RAID 1 since your data is striped across more disks and therefore, with parallel reading enabled, potentially able to return data faster. The downside however is that writes will be slower than RAID 1 since the parity calculation will need to occur for all data being written.

As usual there is no simple answer for the DBA. They need to know the systems they are supporting well to be able to select the most appropriate availability mechanisms. Write-heavy OLTP systems, for example, might find RAID 5 too slow, whereas it may be very suitable for a non-volatile Decision Support System.

13.2.1.6 Recovery at Startup

Failures to write data can happen at any time. They can even be as a result of a DBA's actions if they issue the SHUTDOWN ABORT command, for example. This might be the only way they can get the database to close, but it has to be a last resort since any live SQL statements are terminated immediately.

If the database has terminated un-cleanly, either because of an ABORT, or some system generated fault, Oracle's STARTUP command will try and carry out an automatic recovery. The process which looks after this is called SMON (System Monitor) and this is a core process, which will cause the database to terminate if it were to fail.

The DBA may be lucky and the system may be able to get back to the last consistent state, or they may have to recover files manually before opening the database for wider access. They would do the latter by issuing the STARTUP NOMOUNT command. This starts the database and allocates memory structures, but does not connect to the disks, allowing changes to be made at the operating system level. Once the recovery has happened the DBA can make the database attached to disks and available to all users by issuing the **ALTER DATABASE OPEN** command.

13.2.1.7 Proactive Management

You could, of course, greatly reduce the risk of disk failure on your system by simply having a rolling replacement program that replaces your HDD resources every three months, or perhaps six. Using the MTBF measure, at least statistically, you will have a more robust system. However, against that possible improvement in availability you have to recognise the actual cost of excess HDD purchasing.

Silly though the above example may seem, if your data is core to your business's success, you may well be willing to pay good money to reduce the risks of failure.

System maintenance should indeed be an important aspect of keeping a system available. Replacement of servers and disks should be part of the strategy, with replacements being timed to cause least disruption.

13.2.1.8 Using Enterprise Manager

Most of the main RDBMS vendors have some form of management console. Oracle's is called Enterprise Manager. It has a dashboard home screen on which appears warnings of various types, some of which the DBAs will have set up for themselves. You can configure it, for example, to warn you when a particular tablespace is get- ting to 75% full. That may give you time to go and buy some more disks to allow for more expansion later. You can also have warnings emailed to the DBA team to ensure that they are not overlooked.

Since the database will, at the very least, reject inserted rows if the file supporting the tablespace is full, and at worst, abort, taking a proactive approach to disk usage is very much a key part of availability management.

13.3 Back-Up and Recovery

As we have seen, we can't rely on the database platform being error free. To safeguard against unexpected data loss we need to take copies of the data known as Back-ups. If you should lose any data, then you use the copies stored as a backup to replace the lost data.

Before we begin looking at backing up, we should just remind ourselves that the logical data we see in our RDBMS is made permanent using physical media, such as HDDs. There are, therefore, two types of back-up: Physical, which is the primary concern of this chapter and which will be dealing with operating system level files, and Logical which is more often to do with taking temporary copies of data, often of tables, as a precaution when applying changes to the original data.

Dealing with Logical first, let us follow an example. The user wishes to apply a 5% pay rise to all employees with a Grade of 'B'. Because things can go wrong our cautious user wants to take a copy of the Employee table before applying the changes. They are, in effect, backing up the table. This code might be what they use:

```
Create Table oldEmployee as select * from Employee;
... . do the processing
... . When happy that you no longer need the Table back-up:
Drop Table oldEmplyee;
```

As we have seen with the Flashback command, there is more than one way of getting to the way the data was at a point in time, but this could be one solution.

All the logical application data in the database, and all of the data dictionary data, will actually be stored in operating system files. These files are precious and regular copying will allow the database to be restored in the event of corruption to the files used by the database. In Oracle these files can be either copied (backed up) directly from the operating system, known as User-Managed back-up, or through an Oracle process called RMAN which helps with the management of the back-up process by collecting meta-data about what is being copied.

Some important back-up concepts and terms used need exploring first:

1. **Consistent Back-up**

   A consistent backup is one where datafiles and control files are in agreement with the system change number (SCN). The only way to ensure a consistent Back-up is to issue a SHUTDOWN command other than SHUTDOWN ABORT, and then take the back-up. An open database may well have important data in memory rather than written to disk, so all files have to be closed. This of course means the database is unusable whilst it in down and the back-ups are being taken. This is also referred to as a cold back-up.

2. **Hot Back-up**

   Shutting down the database is clearly not a good thing to do if users are being refused access as a result. The irony is that you are, albeit temporarily, making the database unavailable to help with future availability.

   Hot back-ups are taken when the database is still open. If it is supporting a 24/7 operation you may have very little choice but to use online backups. However, the risk is that a datafile is being written to whilst the back-up is being taken and this will result in an inconsistent back-up. This means that using a Hot Back-up to restore from always runs the risk of needing to apply redo data to remove the inconsistency.

   If you are in ARCHIVELOGS mode (that is, storing the redo logs so they do not get overwritten) then Oracle can help manage the problem by placing a table-space being hot-backed up in a special status whilst the data is being copied, in which no users can write data to the tablespace. Assuming the copy is quite rapid users will see this as little more than a glitch in system performance. However, there is always a slight risk with hot backups that you do not account for changes being made at the moment of back-up. These risks can be limited, and so many DBAs will take the risk rather than bring the whole database down to enable a consistent cold back-up. Backing up tablespaces one at a time, rather than backing up all datafiles at once also spreads the overhead of back-up processing, often allowing the user to see no adverse effect from the back-up process.

3. **Whole Database Back-up or Partial Back-up and Incremental Back-ups**

If we take a backup of the whole database whilst it is down we will have a consistent and immediately usable copy of the data. If the back-up finishes and then one second later, once the database is restarted, it collapses, the DBA will simply need to restore the back-up they have just taken.

Unfortunately, that sort of luck rarely happens! Full back-ups can take hours, depending upon how much data is being stored. And unless you are fortunate enough to work in an environment which doesn't mind the database being down for a day, full back-ups are not going to be a popular move.

So, one option is that you take a full back-up on one day, and then every day thereafter you store only the changes that have been made to the data. These are called incremental back-ups and they save only data blocks that have changed since the previous back-up.

The good thing about incremental is they are so much faster to store the back-up. The bad thing is that, should you need to recover the database, it will be so much slower since you will need to restore the last full back-up and then apply the changes as stored in the incremental back-ups.

The trade-off between time to back-up and time to restore is again typical of the DBAs balancing act. For different organisations, different back-up strategies will be appropriate. In terms of the lifespan of the backed up data, the final decision is to have a retention policy which specifies which backups need to be retained to meet the organisation's recovery requirements. Probably the minimum would be the last full back-up plus subsequent incremental ones, but there may be legal obligations on the company to keep data much longer than this would enable. A generalised view of the back-up process can be seen in Fig. 13.1.

Fig. 13.1 Generalised view of back-up process

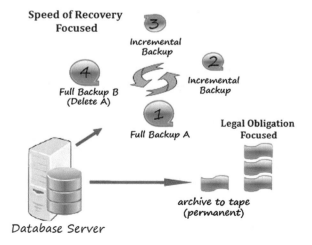

13.3.1 MTBF and MTTR

Two key metrics when deciding on availability strategies are:

- Mean Time Between Failures (MTBF) which is a measurement of how long elapses between failure. This will be influenced by both the hardware in use (which may fail) and the software systems and human interaction with it and so will be different for every organisation. Historic failure data is often used to estimate this by dividing a given period (say a month) by the number of times the system was unavailable.
- Mean Time To Recover (MTTR) which is a measure of how quickly your database will be available in the event of a failure.

Oracle allows you to set a target time for MTTR and will automatically calculate what it needs to do to ensure that this happens. The FAST_START_MTTR_ TARGET initialization parameter controls the duration of recovery and startup after instance failure.

However, as always, there is a trade-off. Oracle speeds up the MTTR by forcing the system to checkpoint more often. This ensures that the consistent data (which can therefore be used immediately) is as big a proportion of the total data as possible, and that there is very little Redo data (with SCN greater than that at the check- point) to apply to bring the database back to its position at failure. The increased checkpoint activity is, however, detrimental to performance as it forces more write activity, and if your system is an active OLTP system this could be quite a problem.

13.3.1.1 Recovery

The other half of Back-up and Recovery is just as important as taking the back-ups. A DBA needs to know where the most current back-ups are and how to apply them. Typically this will mean the use of tape storage devices and the retrieval of tape cartridges from a fire-proof safe. The cloud now offers a cleaner alternative, with the back-up being retrieved from a Storage-as-a-Service provider.

Two key terms are used in bringing a database back to as close to its state at failure as possible;

- Restore: Copying datafiles from a back-up to the server.
- Recovery: "replaying" the changes since the last back-up by applying the redo logs.

The first, and most critical part of any recovery is the notification of failure. Modern dashboard systems like Oracle's Enterprise Manager will automatically notify the DBA, sometimes by sending emails, when there is some error or warning from the database. If the DBA is out on a picnic in an area with no telecoms available, the recovery may take longer than it could, so having policies in place to ensure DBA access between team members is an important starting point!

Assuming the DBA gains actual, or remote, access to the database terminal the next task is to establish the type of problem. SQL errors may require no intervention other than talking to the user responsible. An error with one of the key processes may require the database to be "bumped"—shutdown and restarted.

But in terms of restoring data it is more likely that the DBA will be responding to a disk failure or similar media related problem. If Oracle tries unsuccessfully to read a data file on a disk it will flag the problem and the DBA can restore from a back-up and replay any redo information to bring the file up-to-date. The database will continue to run and be accessible to any processes not accessing that file.

If Oracle can't write to a data file it takes it offline It is the datafile that is taken offline—the tablespace remains online and can be used. If Oracle can't write to the SYSTEM Tablespace (which contains the data dictionary) however, the database will shut down automatically and a restore will be required from the last available back-up.

13.3.1.2   RMAN and Enterprise Manager

As usual we will use an Oracle database to provide examples of the tasks that make up back-up and recovery. And again, as usual, Oracle provides two key approaches: the GUI Enterprise Manager with built-in wizards; and the command line utility called RMAN (**R**ecovery **Man**ager). You will need special privileges to issue these commands, either granted to a specially created Backup Manager user, or using SYS or SYSTEM DBA privileges.

Newcomers may wonder why DBAs don't just use the far simpler interface. But the fact is that many Oracle systems have grown from earlier versions of Oracle, and many DBAs have years of experience of writing scripts to do the important maintenance tasks in the database, and so the command line tool remains very popular.

Let us start by comparing the approaches to resetting the MTTR. The Enterprise Manager approach is shown below, and is followed by the command line equivalent (Fig. 13.2).

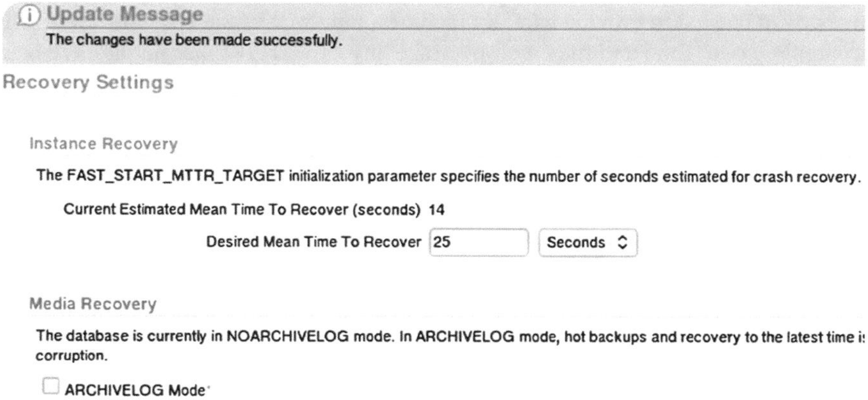

ⓘ **Update Message**
The changes have been made successfully.

Recovery Settings

Instance Recovery

The FAST_START_MTTR_TARGET initialization parameter specifies the number of seconds estimated for crash recovery.

Current Estimated Mean Time To Recover (seconds) 14

Desired Mean Time To Recover 25   Seconds ◇

Media Recovery

The database is currently in NOARCHIVELOG mode. In ARCHIVELOG mode, hot backups and recovery to the latest time is corruption.

☐ ARCHIVELOG Mode·

Fig. 13.2 MTTR setting in enterprise manager

```
SQL> ALTER SYSTEM SET fast_start_mttr_target = 25 SCOPE=BOTH
```

The Availability management page of Enterprise manager (11g) is shown in Fig. 13.3, showing the sorts of tasks that can be controlled.

And these are the commands required to do a full backup of a database called orcl using RMAN (Fig. 13.4).

13.3.1.3   Storing the Back-Ups

Whatever your back-up strategy you will need to decide on which medium you will select to store the data. As usual there are good and bad points about most of the alternatives.

Solid State Drives (SSD) are becoming relatively cheap and can store large volumes of data and because back-ups write few times, it could be argued this makes SSD a good medium for back-ups. HDD are also dropping significantly in price/Gb and are therefore a reasonable suggestion for storing back-up.

Both of these media would be far quicker at the restore stage than would the more traditional medium of magnetic tape, but, even at today's prices, they would also be more expensive. As tape is a sequential read medium access time to any specific section of a back-up is likely to be far slower to the HDD which allows random access.

Tape drives are relatively simple and not over-used and so they tend to last a long time. Many organisations who invested in databases more than a few years ago will therefore already have invested in a (tape oriented) back-up system which they will not need to replace for a long time. The cost of the alternatives, therefore, is only likely to be borne should there be a good business case for speeding recovery times.

In the last couple of years Storage as a Service has meant that HDD storage has become more popular by default as Cloud users access disk farms made available by the service providers. As the service is rented there is no up-front capital investment needed to provide back-up facilities, but the revenue cost will eventually accumulate over time and may well overtake any capital cost that might have been incurred instead.

13.4   Disaster Recovery (DR)

Whilst Back-ups ensure the longevity of an organisation's data, they are not really a means of keeping a database readily available. Should a major event, such as an earthquake or tsunami destroy your company's data-centre, the presence of a set of back-up tapes stored off-site will allow you to get your database back—but only eventually, and only to the point of the last back-up!

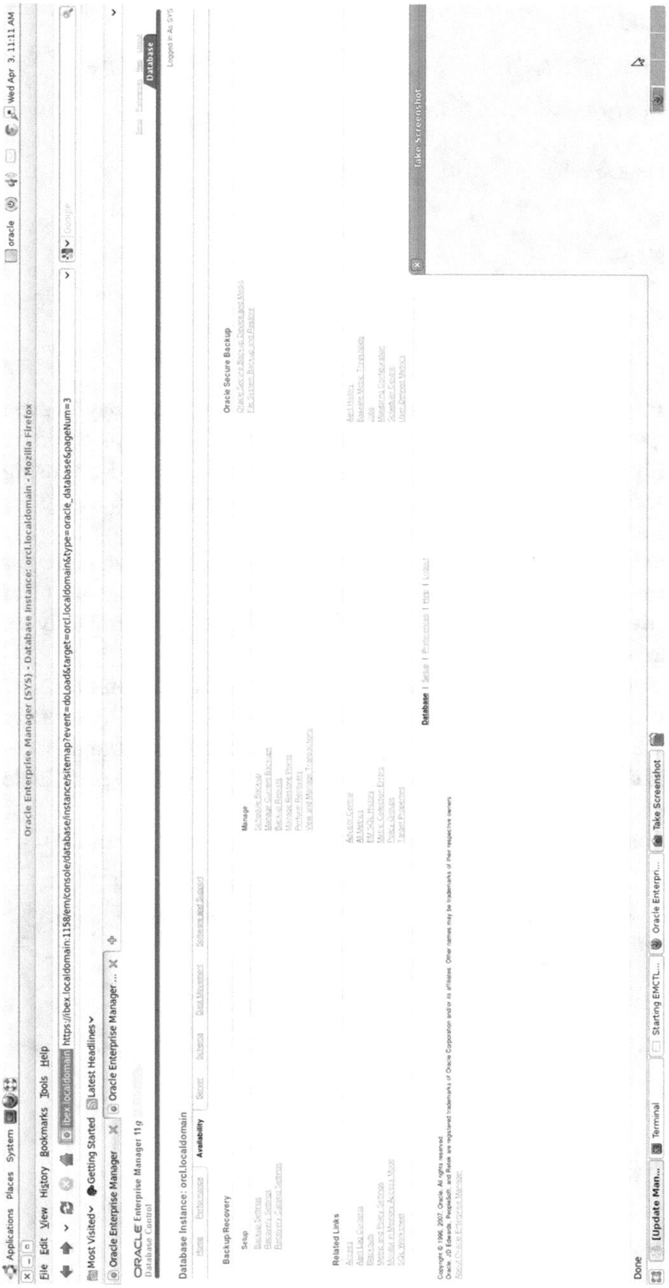

Fig. 13.3 Using enterprise manager to control back-up tasks

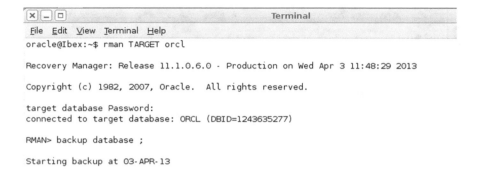

```
 [x][_][□]                                              Terminal
 File  Edit  View  Terminal  Help
oracle@Ibex:~$ rman TARGET orcl

Recovery Manager: Release 11.1.0.6.0 - Production on Wed Apr 3 11:48:29 2013

Copyright (c) 1982, 2007, Oracle.  All rights reserved.

target database Password:
connected to target database: ORCL (DBID=1243635277)

RMAN> backup database ;

Starting backup at 03-APR-13
```

Fig. 13.4 Using RMAN from the command prompt

Finding and procuring replacement IT infrastructure will take time, maybe even weeks. And then the process of rebuilding the database from the back-ups could be lengthy too, especially on a large database which has been backed-up using incremental back-ups. The back-up medium can also slow things down as tape is not the fastest (but is among cheapest) storage method.

In our often quoted example of a bank, having your system unavailable for weeks is going to do you a lot of damage—maybe even enough to put you out of business. When the disaster happens you need to be able to, as seamlessly as possible, get the system up and working again.

An example of the sort of damage that happens to businesses the Bank of New York (BONY) immediately post 9/11. The oldest bank in the US had a DR strategy but found that because most operations were heavily concentrated around Manhattan, and because of the scale of the disaster, they were unable to keep in reliable contact with customers.

As the Wall Street and Technology online journal (2001) said (Guerra 2001):

> But the temporary loss of an entire data centre and a damaged telecommunications network left BONY struggling to connect with its customers and industry utilities like the DTC.
>
> BONY's difficulties during the hours after the attack gain gravity when its vital role in world of securities processing is understood, making the fact that it could regroup from the disaster—and do it quickly—of intense interest to more than just the firm's shareholders.

Demonstrating how short-lived can be feelings of sympathy where money is concerned, the article goes on to say:

> Starting just days after the attack, BONY began to be pilloried in the press for systems malfunctions and other technological failures which had purportedly left billions of dollars in securities transactions unsettled. Articles cited angry customers who were misled about the status of BONY systems, demanding the facts on unsettled orders.

And yet it is clear that the Bank did have a disaster recovery strategy and that it worked. However, it did not work well enough to meet expectations of some customers and commentators.

13.4.1   Business Impact

It is assumed that some level of difficulty would follow the loss of an organisation's database. After all, why incur the expense of having one if it isn't that vital? However, it may be that your business will not suffer unduly if you lose access to your database for a few days. In other words, not everyone needs to spend lots of money on HA.

So, one of the first steps required when considering your DR strategy is to measure the potential impact of the loss of your database systems. This will involve tangible (for example, lost production) and intangible costs (for example, loss of goodwill) and discovering just which records are vital and time-critical. As usual, the more broadly robust you make your systems, the more expense you will incur, so you will need to balance the potential losses against real costs.

One key variable in the size of the costs is the time you are willing to be without your database. This is referred to as the Recovery Time Objective (RTO). In general, the shorter the RTO the more expensive the solution. So, the decisions about DR tend to be business driven, not technology led, although there are alternative approaches available as we shall see in the next section.

13.4.2   High Availability for Critical Systems

We have already discussed a couple of key methods of maintaining availability. In some circumstances—let's stick with banks as a good example—Availability is of critical importance to the business and expense is much less of a barrier.

These are the circumstances in which the term High Availability (HA) tends to get used. There are several approaches the database architect can take:

- Stand-by databases which are copies of the Master database and which kick-in in the event of failure of the Master

- Cloud-based stand-by services
- Clustering the database, using several servers to provide some redundancy. Different vendors use different approaches to clustering:
  - Shared Disk (for example, Oracle) where separate nodes each run an instance of Oracle but share the same database (that is data, redo logs, control files). The database must sit on a Storage Area Network (SAN), which provides the capability to connect to many servers, usually through high-speed fibre connections. Having multiple servers allows for automatic fail-over to happen and connections seem to persist, even if, in the background, another instance has taken over. Disk redundancy is managed by the SAN.
  - Shared nothing (for example MySQL) where multiple servers and their disks save copies of the same database. Data within each node is copied to at least one other data node. If a node fails, the same information is always to be found in at least one other server.
- Distributed databases, providing the copies of the same database on multiple sites, allowing continuous operations even if a catastrophic event happens in one geographic location.

A standby system is the traditional form of providing DR. Having one, or several identical servers running an exact copy of your live system allows the organisation to switch between servers in the event of a failure to one.

The most significant issue with stand-by servers is when and how you do the copy process. If money is no object and you can manage your connections in-house, the speediest way to bring a standby server up is to use an approach similar to RAID 1, with two servers mirrored. This solution requires good network connectivity and the required infrastructure can be expensive to provide. The standby server is on and running all required applications. This is often referred to as Hot Standby.

A less costly solution is to send packets, for example a day's worth, of archived redo logs to the standbys and then apply the changes. The downside to this solution is that it can take time to replay the redo information so fail-over, whilst it can be automated, is not instant. This is known as Warm Standby.

A Cold Standby is the least complex solution which differs little from a Back-up and Recovery strategy except that the recovery is to a different server in a different location. The standby server, when needed, is started. A valid backup may need to be applied and as much redo history as can be replayed is used to bring the database to as close to current as possible. This approach will be much slower that the other two approaches.

Having a standby system available is not a new idea by any means. But using the cloud as a DR solution is newer. Specialist services providers are beginning to appear in this area. Some suggest a 4 h restore time for a standby server is much cheaper in the cloud than on in-house owned hardware. The basis of the saving is that the database server is built and then taken off-line. As with most cloud solutions, the highest rental cost is for CPU and RAM usage, which are clearly zero whilst the database is offline. Should a disaster happen the server can be restarted and restored and connected to by users. Since Storage As A Service is becoming relatively affordable and convenient even smaller organisations can provision their own DR using a provider's disk space and just start-up a server and restore the data for themselves.

13.4.3 Trade-Offs and Balances

As we saw in Chap. 5, CAP theory has it that we can't have everything: out of Consistency, Availability, and Partition Tolerance, we can only have two. NoSQL databases, and Big Data systems like Hadoop, are built to be massively distributed. Availability comes as a result of the built-in redundancy from replicating the data across many nodes.

If always being able to access the data, regardless of network breakages is the most important thing to your organisation the theory tells us we can't guarantee anything other than eventual consistency. If both availability and consistency is critical (that is all the data across nodes agrees) then you have to live with the fact that your systems may be vulnerable to network problems to the degree that a network outage means your database is unavailable. This approach is what happens in many traditional RDBMS systems. Replication is used for availability and protocols such as the two-phase commit are used for consistency.

13.4.4 The Challenge or Opportunity of Mobile

As more organisations encourage employees to use their own devices such as smart phones and tablets, there is a danger of critical information being spread out in an unmanageable way. Data collected on a tablet but not synchronised with a server is exceptionally vulnerable, and yet could be business critical in nature.

This is a new challenge for information professionals. Adopting appropriate Bring Your Own Device policies which include synchronisation and back-up is clearly one useful step.

But the fact that some of these devices have relatively large storage available on-board, and the very fact that they are mobile means they are likely to be in a different geographical location to the central servers, or even other devices. A natural distributed system which perhaps could be used as part of a DR strategy? At the time of writing this technology is still new and this may end up being the section of this book that future readers laugh at... but who knows!

13.5   Summary

This chapter has reviewed the need to keep databases available for as long as possible. We discussed the trade-off between seeking Five Nines availability and the expense that that sort of robustness can incur. We then went on to talk about Back-up and Recovery types, and finished by looking at alternatives for limiting the down- time a database may suffer because of some sort of disaster.

13.6   Review Questions

The answers to these questions can be found in the text of this chapter.

- What is meant by "Five Nines" in terms of database availability?
- What element in a typical database server is most vulnerable to failure?
- What is meant by MTTR? And MTBF?
- Describe how RAID 1 and RAID 5 can be part of an availability strategy.
- How does Shared Nothing differ from Shared Disk?

13.7   Group Work Research Activities

These activities require you to research beyond the contents of the book and can be tackled individually or as a discussion group.

Discussion Topic 1 You are asked to consider what can be done to mitigate against a potential disaster, such as an earthquake or flood, hitting your organisation's data centre. Discuss some different approaches there are to Disaster Recovery whilst relating your discussion to the business requirements being addressed by each approach. Consider drivers like stakeholder expectation, cost, technical capability.

Discussion Topic 2 Keeping copies of the organisation's database is obviously a sensible precaution. There are, however, pluses and minuses to each potential approach. Imagine you are a DBA faced with implementing a back-up strategy. What options will you have before you, and what factors would impact your final strategy selection?

References

Alapati S (2009) Expert oracle database 11g database. Apress, New York

Guerra A (2001) The buck stopped here: BONY's disaster recovery comes under attack. https://wps.prenhall.com/bp_laudon_essmis_6/21/5556/1422339.cw/content/index.html

Database Performance

What the reader will learn:

- that the different physical and logical aspects of database performance make tuning a complex task
- that optimising for read and write performance is not the same thing and the this can cause conflicts when tuning
- that database tuning is an ongoing requirement in an active OLTP system
- that there are several types of index, each aimed at returning specific kinds of data more rapidly
- that disk operations are amongst the slowest element of any database operation

The examples we deal with in this chapter are primarily based on Client/Server RDBMS technology. Of course, as we saw in Chap. 5, other types of database technology do exist, and do claim to bring high performance in certain scenarios.

The worked examples and diagrams rely heavily on Oracle. We have used Oracle 11 g. However, much of what is covered holds true for versions back to 8i. Many architectural diagrams will hold true in principle for SqlServer, MySQL and most other true Client/Server databases.

14.1 What Do We Mean by Performance?

For users—very important stakeholders in any system—database performance is often simply measured in terms of how quickly data returns to their application. And they will often intuitively know when that is "too slow" despite not having timed the process.

Returning data can be a very important element of a database system's requirements. In a Decision Support System (DSS), for example, the system may well spend more than 90% of its processing time serving out results sets and only

© Springer Nature Switzerland AG 2021

K. Domdouzis et al., *Concise Guide to Databases*, Undergraduate Topics
in Computer Science, https://doi.org/10.1007/978-3-030-42224-0_14

ever have data loads occasionally. OLTP systems, on the other hand are often writing new rows, or updating existing ones, whilst relatively less frequently answering queries. Heavy use of indexing to speed query output will be very likely to slow inserts and updates (since the system has more information to store). The need, therefore, whether your system is read- or write-intensive is a very good starting point.

So performance is not only about the speed with which queries are answered. As we look further at the building blocks of RDBMS we will need to come to a more rounded view. *Performance is about ensuring you use all the system resources optimally in the process of meeting the application's requirements, at the least cost.*

Modern database systems are typically built on several layers of technologies. When running a SQL query, the physical parts of the host server can be just as important in determining how quickly we get the result report runs as any of the processes within the RDBMS itself (see Fig. 14.1).

We can divide the elements that might impact database performance into the following broad, interrelated categories:

- Physical layer, such as disks and RAM
- Operating System (OS)
- Database Server processes

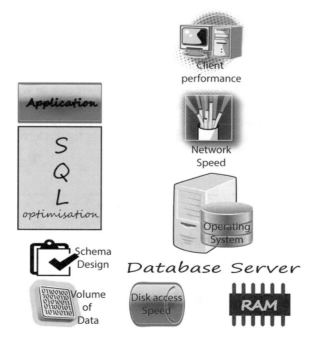

Fig. 14.1 Elements which influence database performance

- Schema level: Data types, location and volumes
- SQL optimisation
- Network
- Application

Typical production databases are dynamic, growing entities, which means that yesterday's perfectly tuned database can become today's performance dog just because it is being used. We will review the influence the data itself can make on performance later in the chapter.

A good database professional needs to understand all the factors that impact upon the performance of their databases. Proactive performance tuning can save a DBA time in the long run as reactive problem chasing can be both time consuming and detrimental to the business.

Before we start, we should clarify some of the important aspects of database performance:

Workload is the combination of all the online transactions, ad hoc queries, data warehousing and mining, batch jobs, and system-generated commands being actioned by the database at any one time. Workload can vary dramatically. Sometimes workload can be predicted, such as peaks with heavy month-end processing, or lulls after the workforce has gone home. Unfortunately, however, DBAs do not always have the luxury of such predictability. This is especially so in a 24/7 environment, such as an e-commerce system. Naturally, workload has a major influence upon performance.

Throughput is a measure of the database's capability to carry out the processing involved with the workload. There are many factors that can impact upon throughput, including: Disk I/O speed, CPU speed, size of available RAM, the effectiveness of any workload distribution such as parallel processing, and the efficiency of the database server operating system.

Contention is the condition in which two or more components of the workload are attempting to use a single resource. Multiple users wanting to update a single row, for example. As contention increases, throughput decreases. Locks are placed on resources to ensure that tasks are completed before the resource is made available again, resulting in waits. The user notices this and calls it poor performance.

14.2   A Simplified RDBMS Architecture

Before we look at the individual performance factors, it would be good to have some idea of what happens when a user interacts with a database, so that we know where to look for improvements (Fig. 14.2).

Review Fig. 14.1 and, with this diagram in mind, let us walk through one interaction, which is a simple fetch of data:

Fig. 14.2 Phases in
processing an SQL query

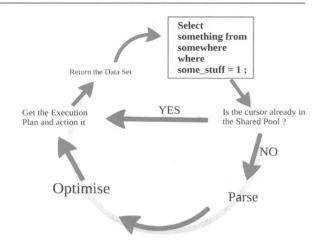

1. The user starts their client-side application process. This could be a simple command-line process, like SQLPLUS, or a full-blown application.
2. The client process connects to the RDBMS server process.
3. An area of RDBMS managed RAM is set aside to hold inputs and outputs, and to allow server-side processes on behalf of the client, such as sorting
4. The request for the RDBMS to process some SQL is passed over the connection from client to server.
5. The SQL string is then compared with the SQL which has been run by the server before, which is stored in the library cache. If this query has been run before the execution plan can be recalled from cache and reused, saving hefty processing on parsing and execution plan generation.
6. If this is a new piece of SQL then the string needs to be parsed. This checks that the objects (tables, indexes etc.) referred to exist and that the user has access rights. It checks that the statement is syntactically correct. It will also gather run-time values if there are bind variables involved in the query.
7. So now we have a valid, new query that we have sufficient privileges to run, we then pass over to the optimiser (see section on optimisation below) to determine the best way to gather the information.
8. The optimiser will generate an execution plan
9. The SQL processor will then carry out the instruction in the plan
10. As this is a query which requires data to be fetched, then the RDBMS will have to maintain read consistency to ensure that data it returns is from a certain point in time and not affected by any changes made by other users during the fetch.
11. If the data has been fetched by another user recently enough for it not to have dropped out of the buffer cache, and it and is clean (it has not been changed), the RDBMS will gather the data from the data buffer rather than use a time consuming disk read.

12. If this data isn't in the cache, it will be read from disk and placed into the buffer cache.
13. If there are any post fetch tasks, such as sorting, these can be carried out at the server or at the client.
14. Once all gathered the requested dataset will be returned to the client for use in the user application.

With this set of core processes in mind, we will now examine each of the layers we outlined above.

14.3   Physical Storage

Unlike RAM, the medium used to store permanent data in a database has to be non-volatile—the data stored must remain the same regardless of whether the device has power to it or not. Most database servers are dependent upon a disk, or array of disks, to enable the permanency of the data. This is a weak point in terms of performance since disk operations are amongst the slowest elements of any database process. The DBA's task, therefore, is more about accepting that there will be some delays as a result of I/O latency, and finding ways to minimise it.

Much of the database's inbuilt processing will already be automatically attempting to minimise the disk I/O. Where possible data that has been fetched from disk will be kept in the server's RAM for as long as possible in case other users may want the same data. Naturally, in a very busy production system this can mean either a huge (and therefore expensive) bank of RAM, or a volatile data pool which has to swap out data from memory frequently, thus causing more disk reads.

14.3.1   Block Size

Of course, we should never lose sight of the fact that we are storing ons and offs on a magnetic material when we store our data. The operating system is given the job of managing the disk handling required to seek a piece of information, but what it will return will be a "block" of ons and offs which the RDBMS will have to manipulate. It may have to extract a small part of what is returned. Or it might have to send the disk head reader to several places, extract data from each read, and then glue the portions together.

In an Oracle database objects are stored in a Tablespace. This is a container for tables, indexes Large Objects, and is a continuous area of physical disk that is under Oracle's control and can't be used by other applications. The Tablespace is the Logical-Physical boundary since one of the parameters passed when issuing the Create Tablespace command is the physical o/s file(s) being used to store the contents. What the operating system will deal in is a block. Block size is set at the OS level. Db block, which is what the RDBMS deal in, needs to be a multiple of that figure in order that we do not waste time retrieving or writing O/S blocks which are only part full of the data we want to collect.

The Oracle Tuning Guide offers this advice:

> A block size of 8 KB is optimal for most systems. However, OLTP systems occasionally use smaller block sizes and DSS systems occasionally use larger block sizes.

Now we have another circumstance when the DBA needs to understand the type of database he is managing. In two extremes, for example, we could have a Data Warehouse which rarely has data added and is always causing the SQL engine to read large datasets from disk. On the other hand we might have an OLTP system recording only small amounts of data from a sales line, and nearly always serving small datasets back to queries.

The task we want to help the HDD avoid is spinning the disk and moving the read-head to a new position, since this is a really slow part of the overall process. If, in the data warehouse example, all the data is physically all together in adjacent disk blocks it would be good if we could "suck up" all those with only one head-positioning movement. This is why Oracle controls an area of disk in a Tablespace. It attempts to manage that portion of disk such that data is most likely to be adjacent to similar data.flash.

14.3.2 Disk Arrays and RAID

The main database vendors all support reading and writing to multiple disks. There can be different reasons for doing this (such as robustness and performance), but in recent years the driving force has probably been the low cost nature of HDD, and the ease with which they can be slotted into a rack.

RAID technology is aimed to either improve the I/O performance of the disk subsystem or to make the data more available. There is usually a trade-off to be had, but some RAID configurations attempt to do both. The other variable to consider is cost, since, generally speaking, the more complex the RAID management system needs to be, the more it will cost.

These storage options can impact on a system's performance. Striping your data such that subsequent data writes are made to different disks in a round-robin, can have a large effect on read speed if parallel processing is enabled since data can be read from all disks at once and then glued together in memory. More information about RAID and arrays can be found in Chap. 3.

14.3.3 Alternatives to the HDD

All of this section so far has been written with the standard HDD as the permanent storage device in mind. There are alternatives. In more recent times mobile computing has come to the fore, and the shock-resistant, lightweight and power efficient nature of flash memory makes it a sensible addition to embedded systems or portable computing devices. RAM is still faster than flash, but in read operations flash can outperform a HDD by factors of several hundreds. This is primarily because there is no spinning platter to add the mechanical resistance the HDD suffers from. One drawback however is that erasing, and therefore effectively managing the disk content, is considerably slower for flash. At the time of writing, flash is also considerably more expensive/Mb than a HDD.

Whilst the need to be mobile can excuse the weaknesses of flash in some applications, it is unlikely that many large scale commercial applications will rely on flash just yet, and research papers are being published which identify hybrid solutions which attempt to take advantage of flash to speed certain operations, whilst maintaining the traditional virtues of the HDD.

Perhaps the most extreme form of performance enhancement is to have a totally in-memory database.

One example is SAP HANA, used for hefty analytics, business processes, and predictive analysis this combines columnar data storage (see Chap. 5) with parallel processing and in-memory computing. Another example is Oracle's Times Ten in-memory database which can be used for any time-critical database processes as well as analytics.

The similarity for both is that performance comes as a result of processing entirely in memory. In order to do this they are likely to need large amounts of RAM. The downside to this approach is that RAM is nowhere near as cheap as HDD storage, so these are expensive systems for specialist use.

They have to provide durability and this is achieved by some form of logging transactions to disk, so they are not truly disk-free solutions. However, persistence is probably the most important attribute of a database system, so this can't be avoided.

14.3.4   Operating System (OS)

Modern commercial databases run on a variety of OS platforms. The OS platforms supported by Oracle, for example, can be seen from this screen shot of their documentation page (Fig. 14.3).

The major player which bucks the trend of having multiple versions is Microsoft's SQL Server which runs only on a Windows platform. However, although overall they are behind Oracle on sales, on the sale of databases to run on Windows platforms, Microsoft performs much better.

The perception amongst professionals can to be that the Unix OS was always built for true multitasking and is therefore a more robust starting point for any critical production system. Microsoft, naturally, would disagree with this. In actual fact, all OSs have their own strengths and weaknesses. A database professional may indeed have to work in an environment where there is a mix of server OS systems. To a degree, modern RDBMS systems, once installed and running, make the OS invisible. This is especially so since GUI-based management consoles have come

Documentation errata are in the README. Extra installation information for each platform is in the Release Notes.

Readme	HTML	PDF
Release Notes for AIX 5L Based Systems (64-Bit)	HTML	PDF
Release Notes for Apple Mac OS X (Intel)	HTML	PDF
Release Notes for HP OpenVMS	HTML	PDF
Release Notes for HP Tru64 UNIX	HTML	PDF
Release Notes for HP-UX Itanium	HTML	PDF
Release Notes for HP-UX PA-RISC	HTML	PDF
Release Notes for IBM z/OS on System z	HTML	PDF
Release Notes for IBM zSeries Based Linux	HTML	PDF
Release Notes for Linux Itanium	HTML	PDF
Release Notes for Linux on POWER	HTML	PDF
Release Notes for Linux x86	HTML	PDF
Release Notes for Linux x86-64	HTML	PDF
Release Notes for Microsoft Windows (32-Bit)	HTML	PDF
Release Notes for Microsoft Windows (x64)	HTML	PDF
Release Notes for Microsoft Windows Itanium (64-Bit)	HTML	PDF
Release Notes for Solaris Operating System	HTML	PDF
Release Notes for Solaris Operating System (x86)	HTML	PDF
Release Notes for Solaris Operating System (x86-64)	HTML	PDF
Retail Data Model Release Notes	HTML	PDF

Fig. 14.3 Operating Systems supported by Oracle

along to re- place the script-based maintenance. However, even with GUI management consoles, in order to be more employable, a mixture of OS experience improves any CV.

14.3.5   Database Server Processes

Whatever the OS, the RDBMS has to perform a number of processes in order to enable all the rich functionality available in most modern client/server systems. Some of these may not seem likely to have an impact upon performance, but they can cause problems if ignored or misunderstood by the DBA.

The connection process and how that works for example, may not seem immediately likely to be a cause for performance problems. However, taking Oracle as an example, there are a number of parameters which can be altered, depending upon the connection workload and the types of tasks being undertaken at the client end.

The default is for a client session to be given their own server-side process once the connection is made. This, in effect, reduces the server's available RAM, since a portion is now given over to the client. When you have thousands of concurrent users attaching to your system, this can mean that RAM gets used up and swapping to (slow) disk will occur more regularly.

This one-to-one relationship between client and server is the standard connection type in Oracle. If you create such a connection and then go and make a cup of tea the area of RAM is needlessly occupied when it could be used elsewhere. You can, however, opt for a shared server setting in your start-up parameters. This will mean that a large area of RAM is set aside for shared use by all users, with the expectation that pauses and delays that are a natural part in any SQL process will even out the load across the users.

Another RDBMS background process is a process manager. This constantly checks to make sure that all open connections, with their associated server sessions, are active. Any timed-out sessions are killed by this monitor, since every connection takes some resource, even if it isn't active, thus affecting overall performance.

14.3.6 Archive Manager

As we have seen elsewhere there are often conflicting needs that a DBA needs to balance. Availability vs Performance is one area of regular tension. Writing data to the Redo Log is an essential part of making sure the database is not compromised during any outage and ensuring that the service, when it comes back up, needs minimum manual correction.

In the default mode, a number of redo logs, which are preallocated files, are filled in a round-robin fashion such that when the last disk is filled, the Log Writer writes the next value to the first disk, overwriting what is there.

All of this is fine in a development environment, but in a production database you would normally want to be able to recover a database to any point in time, and to do that you need to store all the redo information. In Oracle you do this by issuing this SQL command:

Alter database Archivelog;

You need to be aware, however, that this will also slow your system down. Usually, large redo log files provide better performance, but obviously they take up more disk space.

14.3.7 Schema Level: Data Types, Location and Volumes

The whole relational thing of relating connected tables, of normalising to reduce data duplication, was largely a response to the expense of disk storage. At the time when Codd's model was beginning to be used in earnest a "big" HDD was around 1 Mb to 5 Mb and would cost about 1/10th of the average annual wage. Today the average weekly wage would allow you to buy a large HDD and have lots of change! The Per Gb cost of HDD storage has dropped in the same period from thousands of dollars to fractions of a dollar. In short, it made sense to reduce the amount of data being stored.

As HDD have become much less expensive, and able to hold so much more data, this driver has become less important. Whereas most database courses stress the im- portance of normalisation, practitioners began to realise that the join which enabled related data to be reconstructed in user queries was one of the most time-consuming tasks undertaken by the database. De-normalisation—purposefully allowing data to be repeated to avoid joins—became a useful performance tool.

To an extent the new wave of NoSQL databases (see Chap. 5) recognises this. MongoDb, for example, is completely schemaless and allows any old mix of data and datatypes and does not have a mechanism equivalent to normalisation.

With the advent of XML as the de facto medium for data exchange between heterogeneous databases DBA's have had to find ways to store and manipulate XML. Oracle created a new datatype to cope with this. XMLTYPE is an extension to the existing Character Large Object (CLOB) type and it provides functionality to the user, such as XQuery if the data is stored in that datatype.

However, yet again, our DBA needs to know what actually is going to happen to the data when it is stored. If there will be many Xqueries to search and manipulate the data then the performance overhead of using the XMLTYPE might well be justified. However, data loads can be many times slower for the same data being stored as XMLType as compared to CLOB. And Xquery has been tested as slower than SQL in a number of circumstances. Another alternative is to map the incoming XML into relational tables, allowing users to access the data using SQL.

As we can see the decisions taken at design time can have a considerable effect upon performance and these decisions need care.

14.3.8   SQL Optimisation

Imagine you need to get this information from your RDBMS:

Select a.X, a.Y, b.Z from employee a, department b where a.deptid = b.departmentno and b.departmentno = 22;

Could you have written this SQL any better? Will this bring back the data you want in the quickest way possible?

The good news is that in most cases you don't need to worry about the performance aspects of your query. The parser will pass the requirements over to something called an Optimiser. This inbuilt process is responsible for, in effect, re-writing any query into the most efficient possible. And it often surprises newcomers to optimisation that there are likely to be hundreds of ways to return the data you are looking for.

In actual fact the optimiser will not re-write your query. It will simply try and work out which access paths are the most efficient in terms of returning the dataset. Naturally it will depend upon the design of your database and the data distribution within it. Some of the most straightforward options before it might include:

- Using an index on table a
- Using an index on table b
- Doing a full table scan on b followed by using an index on a
- Using a full table scan on both

This would get more complicated depending upon:

- Whether there is more than one index to choose from
- Whilst b.departmentno = 22 may be likely to return less than 15% of the rows and therefore be a good candidate for the use of an index, the optimiser needs to estimate the proportion of all rows that will be returned from table a, before it can decide on whether or not to use an index

Once these decisions are taken the optimiser will create a Query Plan. You can usually examine the choices made (in Oracle there is **Explain Plan**—see Tools section below). And you can force the database to do something different if you know better (see **Hints** in the Tools section).

In order to make sensible decisions, the optimiser needs to do better than just guess. In earlier versions of Oracle the process was one of following rules (Rule-based Optimisation—RBO). At their most basic the rules say things like:

- Only do a full table scan if there is no option
- Use a single row fetch using a Rowid rather than a Primary Key if possible

These rules are simple to implement and therefore the processing involved is relatively trivial. However, Oracle moved away from RBO and it has been obsoleted since 10 g. The default optimiser is now a cost based one (CBO). The CBO approach is a response to the fact that the RBO does not pay any regard to the type and distribution of data being queried, but rather blindly applies a single set of rules.

CBO works by estimating the resources (primarily disk I/O and CPU usage) that will have to be used for each of the possible access paths and then selects the least "expensive" access method. In order to do this estimation, the optimiser must have an understanding of the data stored. It does this by gathering statistics for every table and storing these in the data dictionary.

The use of statistics is, in its own right, a balancing act for the DBA. The statistics stored are about the size, cardinality and distribution of the data stored. But the statistics are only useful if they are reasonably current, allowing accurate estimates to follow. However, the process of gathering the statistics is, itself, an intensive one and slows the database down. A DBA needs to know how regularly to update the statistics. Of course, if the database isn't used at certain periods, such as weekends, this is a job that can be scheduled to run then. But in a 24/7 environment this is more tricky.

14.3.9 Indexes

Perhaps the most well-known, and often over-used performance tool used by database creators is the index. In its most usual form, the B-Tree index is fundamentally just the same as the key/value pair that we saw in Chap. 5. It's just that the value being stored against the key is the hex address of the row containing the column or columns being referenced (see Fig. 14.4).

Fig. 14.4 B-Tree index

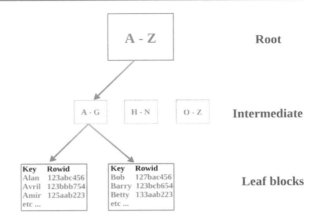

14.3.9.1 B-Tree Indexes

There are many different possible ways to locate a series of rows. If an index is available, and we are searching for a small percentage of the total number of rows in the table, then the RDBMS may choose to look up the key from the index, and then pass the required hex address to the disk reader so that it can retrieve the required row.

But this needs at least two extra reads (to get to the right leaf node of the index) and more processing than would be required to just read the entire table and disregard unwanted rows (known as a full table scan). In Oracle, if there you are retrieving over 15% of the rows Oracle will ignore an index, preferring instead the relative simplicity of a full table scan.

Which columns are best suited for an index? The most obvious is the primary key of a table. Most RDBMS will automatically create an index to support your primary key constraint. Oracle does not, however, index a foreign key. Generally foreign keys should be indexed provided the child table is big enough to warrant this. This is because there is an inferred likelihood of some joining going on in queries between tables related in this way.

Small tables should not be indexed. A full table scan is much the speedier way to gather a row from a table containing just a few rows. Indexing would be overkill— even if you were only ever returning one row.

When looking for suitable candidates for secondary indexes, a DBA should be looking for columns that are often involved in selection or join criteria. Yet again, the DBA needs to understand the application the database is supporting. If users are frequently accessing data with a WHERE clause of a non-primary key column, and that query returns fewer than 15% of the total rows stored, then a secondary index may well help with speeding up reads. However, if that query we have just described runs just once a year, whilst the table itself gets written to many times a minute, it may be that the slowing effect during the writes (caused by having to create and update rows in the index and the consequential need to maintain the index's structure) far outweighs the advantage of having an index. Of course, it could be that the once-a-year report is run by the Managing Director, and therefore the political dynamic changes the decision making process yet again! The DBA's balancing act can be a difficult one!

There are workarounds to the tensions between write- and read-performance effects available to DBAs if they know their system well enough. For example, updating secondary indexes during write operations can slow the entire system due to the extra locking it generates. To avoid this the DBA could store the inserts and updates into a temporary table during the working day, and then apply them all overnight in a single batch job. This is would be unreasonable in a 24/7 operation, but may well work in some circumstances.

Loading large amounts of data can slow the database down. Oracle's bulk loader, SQLLDR, for example, if used in default mode, will generate an insert statement for each row to be loaded. This will generate Redo and Undo and might significantly increase the amount of locking. The workaround may be to delete any indexes before loading, then load the data, then recreate any indexes—preferably at a time when the database is less active anyway. This is another balancing act for the DBA: will the decrease in query response times against the tables when they are without indexes cause sufficiently little overall disruption to justify this approach?

14.3.9.2   Non B-Tree Indexes—Bitmap Indexes

B-tree indexes have been around for decades. Many databases only have this type of index available. Sometimes, however, this form of physical address lookup is not the best. This is particularly true of column data which has low cardinality (very few possible values). Columns containing only values such as Yes/No, for example, or Male/Female, or even colours of the rainbow, are not well suited to B-tree indexes. This is because many valid keys will be stored across potentially many leaf blocks, which will mean many reads per row returned, and the index leaf blocks may well be well distributed across the tablespace, slowing the read process.

To get around this problem the Bitmap Index type was created. The SQL syntax is the same as for a B-tree standard index, but with the addition of the keyword; Bitmap:

Create Bitmap Index Gender_idx on Person(Gender);

In effect the index for each possible key value for this index looks like this:

Male, Start ROWID, End ROWID, 1,000,110,100,010,100,010,010.

Female, Start ROWID, End ROWID, 01,110,010,111,101,011,101,101.

Bitmap indexes use arrays of bits to record whether or not a particular value is present in a row, and answers SQL queries by performing bitwise logic against these arrays. Because these indexes use fast, low level bitwise logic they can significantly reduce query response times and may also reduce storage requirements.

Bitmap indexes can substantially improve the performance of queries in which the individual predicates on low cardinality columns return a large number of rows. It can be especially useful when queries need to use two or more bitmaps to select rows since bitwise logic can rapidly select matches. The downside however, is that the mapping mechanism can be slow during updates and inserts. For this reason, bitmap indexes are often used in decision support environments. These environments usually have large amounts of data but few writes.

14.3.9.3 Non B-Tree Indexes—Reverse Key Index

A physical problem that Indexes can cause is that of "hot disk". This is exactly what it sounds like. If the disk head is constantly accessing a particular sector of the disk, perhaps because lots of similar key values are being written into the same index leaf block, then the HDD's capacity to execute I/O will be exceeded which can cause performance problems as users wait for their turn to get to that area of disk.

As an example, think of a relatively straightforward concept of creating a composite index on three columns: date, branch_id and saleperson_id. The scenario is that this is a chain of stores recording its sales information and to speed the monthly reports this index is created.

On Thursday 15th Sept 2013, Store 44, during a busy period, sends this series of rows to the server:

Transaction_ID	143434
Date	15092013
Store	44
Salesperson	11
Item_id	732
Qty	4
Transaction_ID	143435
Date	15092013
Store	44
Salesperson	11
Item_id	861
Qty	1

and so on.

Perhaps during a very busy period all their sales assistants are sending very similar information. In the space of a few seconds the server may have to write the following leaf key value pairs:

150920134411 hex address of the row with this composite value.

150920134412 hex address of the row with this composite value.

150920134421 hex address of the row with this composite value.

150920134411 hex address of the row with this composite value.

150920134405 hex address of the row with this composite value.

150920134411 hex address of the row with this composite value.

150920134411 hex address of the row with this composite value.

150920134407 hex address of the row with this composite value.

150920134412 hex address of the row with this composite value.

The point here is that all these keys are so similar that they will end up being written to the same leaf block. This may mean some waiting occurs as each key/value takes its turn to take a lock on the leaf so they can write to it, and, even worse, because the head is virtually constantly over the same physical spot on the disk, we may end up with hot disk.

Oracle came up with a solution to this problem called the Reverse key index. A simple algorithm works to transpose what the application wants to write to the system (using the first row in the above example: 150,920,134,411) and reverses it at the point of storage, in this case to: 114,431,029,051. The benefit becomes clear when we look at what happens to the next key value pair: 214,431,029,051. This is significantly different and will very probably need to be written to a different branch/leaf, reducing contention for blocks and minimising the likelihood of hot disk.

This is clearly a specialist solution. The reverse algorithm has to apply when applications try and retrieve data, and there will have to be an overhead in terms of performance for applying this process to every read and write. However, it is probably much better than destroying your HDD!

14.3.9.4   Non B-Tree Indexes—Function-Based Indexes

Sometimes we have occasions when we are not sure what a user is going to input—all we know is that they are always right! Think of an employee table containing a column called last_name which USER A inserts to:

Insert into Employee (id, last_name) values (12, 'Jones');

Meanwhile User B inserts:

Insert into Employee (id, last_name) values (12, 'JONES');

What would USER C expect to see if he issues this:

Select * from Employee where last_name = 'Jones';

The answer is that they would not see the row entered by User B.

One solution would be to put a CHECK constraint on the column to ensure all names are inserted in uppercase. However, this would force McEwan to be written as MCEWAN, and this may upset the name's owner.

However, if we do not have a CHECK constraint any mix of case will be allowed, and as the Jones example shows, that leaves us with a problem when attempting to find all people called Jones.

Oracle provide a solution to this, and other problems, by allowing us to create an index which is made from altered source data, whilst not actually changing the source itself. The syntax is not dissimilar to creating an ordinary index. In this example we turn the value in last_name to uppercase before it is stored in the index.

CREATE INDEX upperlastname_idx ON employees (UPPER(last_name));

This will sort the 'Jones' problem for us without us having to change the column data.

14.3.9.5   Indexes—Final Thoughts

As with other elements of tuning, index use needs ongoing review. Reports are avail- able which show how well used indexes are. If you discover an index is rarely used that index is a candidate for dropping since the overhead cost of keeping it active is generating no reward.

The distribution of the actual data which is being indexed may also change significantly over time. A small table, initial deemed unworthy of an index, may, for example, grow into a large table, which would benefit from an index. Or a column which the designers thought would contain many different values may, it turns out, contain very few, making it worth considering for a bitmap index.

14.3.10   Network

There is often little the DBA can do about network speed. Database clients are often distant, or sometimes very distant from the server and this means there are many places where bottlenecks on the network layer can happen. A DBA needs to work closely with his networking colleagues.

There are, however, a few things a DBA can affect in terms of networking performance. Oracle, for example, encapsulates data into buffers sized according to the DEFAULT_SDU_SIZE parameter. (SDU is session data unit.) The default is for this size to be 8192 bytes or less. However, if your application is typically bringing back bigger chunks of data you can consider making this larger so that fewer packages need to be sent on the network for each query.

14.3.11   Application

14.3.11.1   Design with Performance in Mind

Without pointing an accusatory finger at developers, it is true that many database systems are written by developers who know SQL well but don't understand the physical aspects of database design. Many IDEs have SQL generators allowing com- plex joins to be written by merely drag-and-dropping. Worse, the developer can fall into the trap of only worrying about system outputs. This can result in excessive use of indexes, with the consequent hit on write performance.

One sensible solution, if the organisation can afford it, is to include DBAs in a development team. They can ensure that the design process is implementation focused, and not merely "well designed". There are a number of less well-known structures available for specialist use which can speed query responses. But because they are non-standard they often get overlooked.

Indexed Organised Table (IOT) If a table is very frequently, or solely searched via the primary key it is a candidate for being stored as an IOT. In effect the table information gets stored in an B-tree-like index structure, which means that searches for a particular primary key will be faster than a standard table+index structure since there is no need to look up the rowid from the index to gather the row data as it is stored in the leaf block itself. Unlike an ordinary table where data is stored as an unordered collection, data for an index-organized table is stored in a primary key order so range access by the primary key involves minimum block accesses. Because of this storage mechanism secondary indexes become difficult to maintain and are probably best avoided.

Wide tables are not ideal candidates, although there is an ability to overflow data that is seldom required into a separate, non-b-tree area. The syntax for creating an IOT is the same as for an ordinary table with the exception of the ORGANISA-TION INDEX clause. There has to be a Primary Key. Here is an example:

CREATE TABLE WardReqIOT

(

        WardID NUMBER,

        RequestDate DATE,

        Grade NUMBER,

        QtyReq NUMBER,

        AuthorisedBy VARCHAR2(30),

        CONSTRAINT PK_WardReqIOT PRIMARY KEY

(WardID, RequestDate, Grade)

)

Organization Index Including QtyReq Overflow Tablespace Users
Here all the columns up to and including the one named in the INCLUDING option of the OVERFLOW clause (QtyReq) are stored in primary key order in a B-tree structure. The other data is stored in a table structure in a tablespace called Users.

Partitioning Oracle can manage very large tables comprising many millions of rows. However, performing maintenance operations on such large tables is difficult, particularly in a 24/7 environment. There can be performance issues associated with inserting into, or reading from tables this large. Indexes can help, of course, in reducing the number of full table scans required, but another solution might be to partition the data (see Fig. 14.5).

A Partition will be assigned according to defined criteria for a key column(s).

Two examples are:

Range Slices the data according to which range a partitioning key is in. For example you could partition rows where the Transaction_Date column contains data from different months, with partitions for January, February and so on.

List Instead of a range you can partition by creating a list of values. For example all rows where the column Location is any of: Edinburgh, Glasgow, Montrose, or Inverness could be in a partition called Scotland.

Fig. 14.5 Partitioning data
across disks

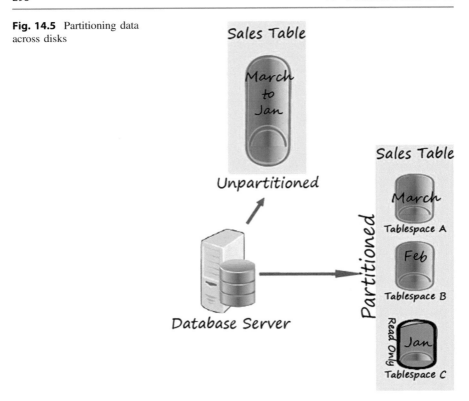

Depending upon the type of data being kept rows may be divided into a series of key ranges, such as ones based on date. Although each partition will have the same logical structure as the others, they may have different physical storage properties.

Data may be stored in different tablespaces, or even disks, enabling a sort of striping potentially speeding up data access by allowing parallel reading to occur.

Furthermore, if the historic data is unlikely to be updated, the majority of the partitions in a history table can be stored in a read-only tablespace (good for performance). This approach can also reduce back-up times.

14.4 Tuning

14.4.1 What is Database Tuning?

There are several steps in the process of ensuring a database is performing adequately. This is often called tuning. Different professionals have different thoughts about what the process should be. Is it an Art or a Science?

At its most abstract, however, the steps will usually be:

1. Monitor
2. Analyse
3. Select the appropriate type of action, which could be any or all of:

   (a) Make changes to the hardware, usually by adding RAM or disk
   (b) Alter the RDBMS parameters to allocate resources more efficiently
   (c) Modify the SQL to run more efficiently.
   (d) Change the application and the way it interacts with the RDBMS

4. Go back to step 1 to assess the success of the actions taken

Ideally this should be an ongoing process. As we have already highlighted, the data that is loaded today may well have made the database less well tuned. Sometimes production systems start off performing well. Any slowing that happens may happen slowly over a number of months. This can make the analysis phase much lengthier. However, in a busy DBA section, when your users aren't complaining, it is very easy to lose sight of the need to constantly monitor.

Modern RDBMS can help (see Tools section below). They have inbuilt performance monitoring and can flash alert on the DBA dashboards when thing begin to go wrong. There may well be situations, however, where there is no forewarning. The DBA who receives a call from some irate user saying their report is taking ages to complete needs to be able to review many possible causes very quickly:

System-Wide What else is happening? Is there a large batch job running now which doesn't usually run? Is a tablespace offline because it is being backed-up or moved to a new device? Is the network functioning normally?

Application-Specific Can we see which SQL is causing the problem? It may not be that belonging to the report in question... it could be that the report is waiting because some rows have been locked by another user. Is the report SQL suitably tuned? Does the client process any of the returned dataset, and if so, what else is happening at the client end?

14.4.2 Benchmarking

Especially when it comes time to decide upon which RDBMS to purchase, people begin to ask questions like: which is the best database for performance? But we have seen throughout this chapter that database performance is a slippery thing. The simple act of inserting data to the most finely tuned database tends to worsen its performance.

The truth of the matter is that all the databases currently on the market have their own strengths and weaknesses and some perform better in some ways, whilst others perform better in other ways. That isn't, however, to say that we simply use a pin to decide—nor allow ourselves to be beguiled by the smoothest sales pitch!

A series of realistic tests is a sensible approach, using examples of each possible alternative database to run some realistic processes against the sort of data your application will be collecting. This is a sensible approach if you have the time and the skills available to set up suitable test scenarios. However, this isn't always possible and you may need to rely on data gathered by others.

It almost goes without saying that test results provided by vendors are to be treated with a degree of scepticism. What is really needed is a fair, standard set of tests against a known dataset. This is what is used in benchmarking.

Probably the most well-known impartial agency for this sort of thing is the Transaction Processing Council (TPC). On their website (https://www.tpc.org/) there are the results of a number of different tests against different types of data. Their mission is declared as:

> The TPC is a non-profit corporation founded to define transaction processing and database benchmarks and to disseminate objective, verifiable TPC performance data to the industry.

An output from one of their tests at the time of writing is given in Fig. 14.6.

14.4.3 Another Perspective

As we saw in Chap. 5 we have, in more recent times, been re-examining some of the assumptions we have worked with since the advent of the client/server RDBMS. Indeed, it is sensible for any IT professional to constantly review the current appropriateness of a technology. This is true of database tuning too.

In their paper, Rethinking Cost and Performance of Database Systems, Florescu and Kossmann (2009) argue that the traditional question, which they saw as:

> Given a set of machines, try to minimize the response time of each request.

should be reshaped to be:

> Given a response time goal for each request, try to minimize the number of machines (i.e., cost in $).

Of course, minimising cost has always been a major objective for any DBA, but recasting the tuning question to provide this focus helps us recognise what our priorities need to be. This is especially useful in the era of cheap computing grids and the ultimate flexibility offered by Cloud provisioning. Indeed, in the era of cloud database perhaps their question could be reworked again to:

> Given a response time goal for each request, try to minimize the cost (in $) of provision.

14.5 Tools

14.5.1 Tuning and Performance Tools

In this section we have a tutorial exploring some of the tools that are available to help tuning the database. We are using Oracle as an example. In order for this to work you need to have admin rights on an Oracle 10 g or 11g instance with the sample HR schema installed (which is there by default unless you ask not to have it).

In order to give ourselves some meaningful data to experiment with we will also use a further table called EmpHours which should have about 15 Mb of data in it

Rank	Company	System	Performance (tpmC)	Price/tpmC	Watts/KtpmC	System Availability	Database
1	ORACLE	SPARC SuperCluster with T3-4 Servers	30,249,688	1.01 USD	NR	06/01/11	Oracle Database 11g R2 Enterprise Edition w/RAC w/Partitioning
2	IBM	IBM Power 780 Server Model 9179-MHB	10,366,254	1.38 USD	NR	10/13/10	IBM DB2 9.7
3	ORACLE	Sun SPARC Enterprise T5440 Server Cluster	7,646,486	2.36 USD	NR	03/19/10	Oracle Database 11g Enterprise Edition w/RAC w/Partitioning
4	IBM	IBM Power 595 Server Model 9119-FHA	6,085,166	2.81 USD	NR	12/10/08	IBM DB2 9.5
14.**	Bull	Bull Escala PL6460R	6,085,166	2.81 USD	NR	12/15/08	IBM DB2 9.5
5	ORACLE	Sun Server X2-8	5,055,888	.89 USD	NR	07/10/12	Oracle Database 11g R2 Enterprise Edition w/Partitioning
6	HP invent	HP Integrity Superdome-Itanium2/1.6GHz/24MB iL3	4,092,799	2.93 USD	NR	08/06/07	Oracle Database 10g R2 Enterprise Edition w/Partitioning
7	IBM	IBM System p5 595	4,033,378	2.97 USD	NR	01/22/07	IBM DB2 9
8	IBM	IBM eServer p5 595	3,210,540	5.07 USD	NR	05/14/05	IBM DB2 UDB 8.2

Fig. 14.6 TCP Test Results

and will therefore make timings improvements more noticeable than with smaller tables. Details about how to create the table and generate these rows are in at the end of the chapter.

14.5.1.1 SQLPLUS Tools

For years Oracle has shipped with a command line tool called SQLPLUS. It is part of Oracle whatever the Operating System which means that a DBA who masters it can ply his or her trade on any platform.

It isn't a friendly environment, being invented before the GUI environments became the norm, but it is very functional, and has some built-in tools that can assist with basic performance tuning.

Timing When users say things like; "that sql report took a long time to run" there are a number of responses a DBA could give—some of which are not polite! But the good DBA will know that what they need is hard, cold measurement. In this case, measurement of the time it takes to get the data back to the user.

From your Oracle working directory, log in as HR and select all the rows from the Departments table where Department_id is less than 100 (Fig. 14.7).

How quickly did that answer come back? Chances are it will have been so quick you might say it responded instantaneously. We can find out how long the query took by using the built-in facility within SQLPLUS to time events. If we issue the **set timing on** command and then re-run the query we now get some information. Don't worry that you don't get any message back after issuing the command. You will get an error if you issue a bad command (Fig. 14.8).

Yes, almost instantaneous: 0.01 of a second! But, we didn't really stretch the optimiser with that query, so let's try something with a join in it that runs against our big table: EmpHours. **The set timing on** will remain the default action now whilst the session lasts, or you issue the set timing off command.

Try running this query:

```
select a.employee_id, a.last_name, b.work_date, b.hours
from employees a, emphours b
where b.emp_id < 105 AND b.emp_id = a.employee_id AND b.fee_earning
= 'Y';
```

Use a text editor to type this in, or copy it in the save it in your working folder and call it something like q1.sql.

On the author's server this takes over 3 s (Fig. 14.9). Now run the same query immediately again (Fig. 14.10).

It may not have looked any quicker, but it is almost half a second quicker. Was yours the same? I would guess it would be. If you remember we said reading from disk was a bottleneck. The first time the query ran Oracle will have had to gather the data from the disk. The results would be kept in RAM until they were flushed out by other data. So the second time we asked the question Oracle could get the answer from memory, saving disk access time. The rule then must be to always run

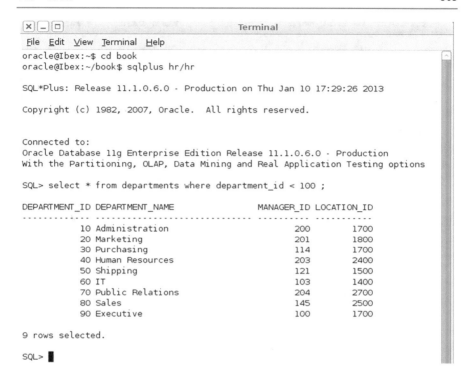

Fig. 14.7 SQL query where department_id < 100

```
SQL> set timing on
SQL> select * from departments where department_id < 100 ;

DEPARTMENT_ID DEPARTMENT_NAME                   MANAGER_ID LOCATION_ID
------------- ------------------------------   ---------- -----------
           10 Administration                          200        1700
           20 Marketing                               201        1800
           30 Purchasing                              114        1700
           40 Human Resources                         203        2400
           50 Shipping                                121        1500
           60 IT                                      103        1400
           70 Public Relations                        204        2700
           80 Sales                                   145        2500
           90 Executive                               100        1700

9 rows selected.

Elapsed: 00:00:00.01
SQL>
```

Fig. 14.8 Turning timing on

```
EMPLOYEE_ID  LAST_NAME                      WORK_DATE     HOURS
-----------  ------------------------       ---------  ----------
        104  Ernst                          04-JAN-13        27
        104  Ernst                          08-JAN-13        25
        104  Ernst                          10-JAN-13        45

21464 rows selected.

Elapsed: 00:00:03.21
SQL> █
```

Fig. 14.9 Test output showing elapsed time

```
EMPLOYEE_ID  LAST_NAME                      WORK_DATE     HOURS
-----------  ------------------------       ---------  ----------
        104  Ernst                          04-JAN-13        27
        104  Ernst                          08-JAN-13        25
        104  Ernst                          10-JAN-13        45

21464 rows selected.

Elapsed: 00:00:02.74
SQL> █
```

Fig. 14.10 Second run—usually will be quicker

tests several times to get an average, and always exclude the first time from that calculation.

Autotrace Statistics Let's now use another SQLPLUS tool: **set autotrace on**.

In order to use this as HR we will need to create the PLUSTRACE role as SYS-DBA and then grant its privileges to HR. Here are those steps to be carried out as SYSDBA (Fig. 14.11).

Now, after moving back to your working directory and logging on to SQLPLUS as HR, we can issue the command; **set autotrace on**. As this generates a report that is wider than the default line width we also need to issue the set linesize 200 command to allow for the output to format nicely.

Now re-run the q1 query and see what we get. There is a lot of extra information now appended to the end of the output. We will examine what the key items are, but first, just to emphasise the point about disk reads being slow, just note the statistics section below which was run after restarting Oracle (and therefore emptying the buffers) (Fig. 14.12).

Now, unless you restarted your instance, what you would be more likely to get is shown in Fig. 14.13.

Note that one line of the Statistics report shows how many physical reads there have been. This tells you how many blocks Oracle has had to read from disk in

```
┌─────────────────────────────────────────────────────────────────────────┐
│ [×][_][□]                          Terminal                               │
├─────────────────────────────────────────────────────────────────────────┤
│ File  Edit  View  Terminal  Help                                          │
│ oracle@Ibex:~$ cd $ORACLE_HOME                                            │
│ oracle@Ibex:/u01/app/oracle/product/11.1.0/orcl$ cd sqlplus               │
│ oracle@Ibex:/u01/app/oracle/product/11.1.0/orcl/sqlplus$ cd admin         │
│ oracle@Ibex:/u01/app/oracle/product/11.1.0/orcl/sqlplus/admin$ ls         │
│ glogin.sql  help  libsqlplus.def  plustrce.sql  pupbld.sql                │
│ oracle@Ibex:/u01/app/oracle/product/11.1.0/orcl/sqlplus/admin$ sqlplus /nolog │
│                                                                           │
│ SQL*Plus: Release 11.1.0.6.0 - Production on Fri Jan 11 15:26:22 2013      │
│                                                                           │
│ Copyright (c) 1982, 2007, Oracle.  All rights reserved.                   │
│                                                                           │
│ SQL> conn / as sysdba                                                     │
│ Connected.                                                                │
│ SQL> @plustrce                                                            │
│ SQL>                                                                       │
│ SQL> drop role plustrace;                                                 │
│                                                                           │
│ Role dropped.                                                             │
│                                                                           │
│ SQL> create role plustrace;                                               │
│                                                                           │
│ Role created.                                                             │
│                                                                           │
│ SQL>                                                                       │
│ SQL> grant select on v_$sesstat to plustrace;                             │
│                                                                           │
│ Grant succeeded.                                                          │
│                                                                           │
│ SQL> grant select on v_$statname to plustrace;                            │
│                                                                           │
│ Grant succeeded.                                                          │
│                                                                           │
│ SQL> grant select on v_$mystat to plustrace;                              │
│                                                                           │
│ Grant succeeded.                                                          │
│                                                                           │
│ SQL> grant plustrace to dba with admin option;                            │
│                                                                           │
│ Grant succeeded.                                                          │
│                                                                           │
│ SQL>                                                                       │
│ SQL> set echo off                                                         │
│ SQL> grant plustrace to HR ;                                              │
│                                                                           │
│ Grant succeeded.                                                          │
│                                                                           │
│ SQL> exit                                                                 │
│ Disconnected from Oracle Database 11g Enterprise Edition Release 11.1.0.6.0 - Pr │
│ oduction                                                                  │
│ With the Partitioning, OLAP, Data Mining and Real Application Testing options │
│ oracle@Ibex:/u01/app/oracle/product/11.1.0/orcl/sqlplus/admin$ █          │
└─────────────────────────────────────────────────────────────────────────┘
```

Fig. 14.11 Setting up autotrace

```
Statistics
-----------------------------------------------------------
        447  recursive calls
          0  db block gets
       3221  consistent gets
        175  physical reads
          0  redo size
     604747  bytes sent via SQL*Net to client
      16150  bytes received via SQL*Net from client
       1432  SQL*Net roundtrips to/from client
         10  sorts (memory)
          0  sorts (disk)
      21464  rows processed

SQL> █
```

Fig. 14.12 Autotrace first time through

```
Statistics
-----------------------------------------------------------
          1  recursive calls
          0  db block gets
       3050  consistent gets
          0  physical reads
          0  redo size
     604542  bytes sent via SQL*Net to client
      16150  bytes received via SQL*Net from client
       1432  SQL*Net roundtrips to/from client
          0  sorts (memory)
          0  sorts (disk)
      21464  rows processed

SQL> █
```

Fig. 14.13 Autotrace with no physical reads

order to be able to answer the query. We can see that the first time we needed 175 block to be read from disk, but the second time we needed none, since all rows were already in the buffer (i.e. in RAM).

When looking for tuning problems, looking to reduce disk reads is an obvious place to start. The point here, however, is that the first time you run a query is not a sensible time to look at tuning data since, in the normal course of events, an active production system is likely to be able to service some, or all, data requests from memory. To reiterate the rule:

Always run tests several times to get an average, and always exclude the first time from that calculation.

Now we will review the other useful information presented when we turn on Autotrace. Firstly, continuing in the Statistics area we have, we can particularly note:

- **recursive calls**: these are internal SQL statements that Oracle needs to issue to service the request. There isn't much you can do about this. Note, in the example above, that the first time through this number was a lot higher. This is probably because of the extra parsing work that Oracle will have had to carry out
- **consistent gets**: this is probably the most useful item to keep an eye on when tuning. It is the total number of blocks Oracle needed to read from disk and memory to service the query. The bigger the number, in general, the slower the query.
- **sorts**: Sometimes you can't avoid having data sorted by Oracle, but sorts can slow the query considerably. You could try rewriting queries to reduce sorts if you know the client will be processing the data. In any case we should aim for memory sorts rather than disk sorts.

We are now going to be playing around with the same query to demonstrate the effect of changes. However, we need to remember our rule about never trusting the first run of a query when we make changes to queries since the second time the revised query runs is likely to be faster than the first time.

In this case let us add an ORDER BY to the query so that our output is sorted by hours worked and then by date worked. Try saving this as q2.sql and then run it twice:

```
select a.employee_id, a.last_name, b.work_date, b.hours
from employees a, emphours b
where b.emp_id < 105 AND b.emp_id = a.employee_id AND b.fee_earning
    = 'Y'
ORDER BY b.hours, b.work_date;
```

The second time, this ran on the author's server the run time returned to just a little longer at 2.82 s as compared with 2.22 for q1. The thing that has changed in the Statistics section is the Sorts (memory) which is now 1. Because the rows were already in RAM from the previous query, Oracle could carry out the sort in one operation, all in memory—hence the only slight performance hit of 0.6 of a second.

The query generates many rows which makes comparing Statistics difficult so, since we know what the query output looks like, we can turn off query row output by issuing set **autotrace traceonly**. Once you have issued that command, before running the next query, run q2 one more time so we have the information we need to compare with the next query. But now look at the time to run. In the author's case it has shrunk from 2.22 secs to a mere 0.22. Why is this? Because writing the results to the screen takes time. The traceonly results are the times for the answers to be generated rather than delivered and this is fairer since writing output will take different times on different platforms.

To give SQL more rows to work with we can now remove the b.emp_id predicate to see what effect that has. Try saving this as q3.sql and then run it twice (see Fig. 14.14).

```
select a.employee_id, a.last_name, b.work_date, b.hours
from employees a, emphours b
where b.emp_id = a.employee_id AND b.fee_earning = 'Y'
ORDER BY b.hours, b.work_date;
```

As usual, the first run through would probably be slower. On the author's server the output from the second run looked like in Fig. 14.14.

```
SQL> @q3

313015 rows selected.

Elapsed: 00:00:02.02

Execution Plan
----------------------------------------------------------
Plan hash value: 2217401640

--------------------------------------------------------------------------------
| Id  | Operation           | Name      | Rows  | Bytes |TempSpc| Cost (%CPU)| Time     |
--------------------------------------------------------------------------------
|   0 | SELECT STATEMENT    |           | 315K| 8625K|       | 2851   (2)| 00:00:35 |
|   1 |  SORT ORDER BY      |           | 315K| 8625K|  24M| 2851   (2)| 00:00:35 |
|*  2 |   HASH JOIN         |           | 315K| 8625K|       |  389   (3)| 00:00:05 |
|   3 |    TABLE ACCESS FULL| EMPLOYEES | 107 | 1284 |       |    3   (0)| 00:00:01 |
|*  4 |    TABLE ACCESS FULL| EMPHOURS  | 315K| 4929K|       |  383   (3)| 00:00:05 |
--------------------------------------------------------------------------------

Predicate Information (identified by operation id):
---------------------------------------------------

   2 - access("B"."EMP_ID"="A"."EMPLOYEE_ID")
   4 - filter("B"."FEE_EARNING"='Y')


Statistics
----------------------------------------------------------
          0  recursive calls
          0  db block gets
       1332  consistent gets
          0  physical reads
          0  redo size
   10134177  bytes sent via SQL*Net to client
     229957  bytes received via SQL*Net from client
      20869  SQL*Net roundtrips to/from client
          1  sorts (memory)
          0  sorts (disk)
     313015  rows processed

SQL> █
```

Fig. 14.14 Screenshots of the output for q3.sql

We can note that we now have 313,015 rows returned as compared to 21,464 in q2. So the report is returning about 14 times more rows. And then if we compare **bytes sent via SQL*Net** to client 10,134,177 for q3 and 604,542 for q2 we see that we are sending nearly 17 times more data. However, look at the comparison in runtime: 2.02 for q3 and 0.22 for q2. The response is only 9 times slower.

So another useful thing to remember is that the volume of data is not the only factor in the speed of a query, although it will plainly have an effect. There are some processes that will need to happen only once, or a few times only, in the overall task, regardless of the number of rows being returned. Parsing, for example, is not dependent upon likely row count, and it must happen for every query. These "overheads" can be demonstrated by creating q4 as shown in Fig. 14.15. Note, there are no rows with a fee-earning value of 'Q'.

```
SQL> @q4

no rows selected

Elapsed: 00:00:00.05

Execution Plan
----------------------------------------------------------
Plan hash value: 2217401640

---------------------------------------------------------------------------------------
| Id  | Operation           | Name      | Rows  | Bytes |TempSpc| Cost (%CPU)| Time     |
---------------------------------------------------------------------------------------
|   0 | SELECT STATEMENT    |           | 59282 |  1620K|       |   851   (2)| 00:00:11 |
|   1 |  SORT ORDER BY      |           | 59282 |  1620K|  4664K|   851   (2)| 00:00:11 |
|*  2 |   HASH JOIN         |           | 59282 |  1620K|       |   387   (3)| 00:00:05 |
|   3 |    TABLE ACCESS FULL| EMPLOYEES |   107 |  1284 |       |     3   (0)| 00:00:01 |
|*  4 |    TABLE ACCESS FULL| EMPHOURS  | 59282 |   926K|       |   383   (3)| 00:00:05 |
---------------------------------------------------------------------------------------

Predicate Information (identified by operation id):
----------------------------------------------------------

   2 - access("B"."EMP_ID"="A"."EMPLOYEE_ID")
   4 - filter("B"."FEE_EARNING"='Q')


Statistics
----------------------------------------------------------
          0  recursive calls
          0  db block gets
       1332  consistent gets
          0  physical reads
          0  redo size
        460  bytes sent via SQL*Net to client
        409  bytes received via SQL*Net from client
          1  SQL*Net roundtrips to/from client
          1  sorts (memory)
          0  sorts (disk)
          0  rows processed

SQL> █
```

Fig. 14.15 Output from q4.sql demonstrating overheads

```
select a.employee_id, a.last_name, b.work_date, b.hours
from employees a, emphours b
where b.emp_id = a.employee_id AND b.fee_earning = 'Q'
ORDER BY b.hours, b.work_date;
```

Despite not returning a single row this process took 0.05 of a second and needed to read 1332 blocks.

Autotrace Execution Plan: The other significant section in the autotrace outputs is the execution plan. We will use q2 and q3 again so either find the output, or run them again.

Execution Plan for Q2 is shown in Fig. 14.16.

The first thing to mention about these plans is that you need to read them from the inside out. The Operation column tells you what Oracle will be doing to deliver the required dataset. The name tells you any objects Oracle will be using. It will help to note that SYS_C0010205 is the system generated index to support the primary key in EMPHOURS, whilst EMP_EMP_ID_PK is the index used to support the primary key in EMPLOYEES.

The columns to the right of Name are all estimates that Oracle generates, based upon the statistics in the Data Dictionary. Cost is how Oracle Cost-Based Optimiser decides which plan to use since lowest cost will typically also be most efficient in terms of resource usage. The cost estimates the IO, CPU, and network resources that will be used to answer the query.

Start reading this plan with the one that has the most indentation as this will probably be the first one to be executed. (If two statements have the same level of indentation read top down.)

In this case we have an Index Range Scan using the EMP_EMP_ID_PK index. This means that Oracle will read that index to get the ROWIDS for what it estimates is 5 rows. (It is right, isn't it? Ids 100–104 meet the query WHERE b.emp_id <

```
Execution Plan
----------------------------------------------------------
Plan hash value: 700587718

----------------------------------------------------------------------------------
| Id  | Operation                      | Name          | Rows  | Bytes | Cost (%CPU)| Time     |
----------------------------------------------------------------------------------
|   0 | SELECT STATEMENT               |               |   483 | 12075 |    73   (2)| 00:00:01 |
|   1 |  SORT ORDER BY                 |               |   483 | 12075 |    73   (2)| 00:00:01 |
|   2 |   NESTED LOOPS                 |               |       |       |            |          |
|   3 |    NESTED LOOPS                |               |   483 | 12075 |    72   (0)| 00:00:01 |
|   4 |     TABLE ACCESS BY INDEX ROWID| EMPLOYEES     |     5 |    60 |     2   (0)| 00:00:01 |
|*  5 |      INDEX RANGE SCAN          | EMP_EMP_ID_PK |     5 |       |     1   (0)| 00:00:01 |
|*  6 |     INDEX RANGE SCAN           | SYS_C0010205  |   191 |       |    13   (0)| 00:00:01 |
|*  7 |    TABLE ACCESS BY INDEX ROWID | EMPHOURS      |    96 |  1248 |    14   (0)| 00:00:01 |
----------------------------------------------------------------------------------
```

Fig. 14.16 Execution plan for q2.sql

105). Operation ID 4 and 6 are equally nested, so next comes the earlier operation; **Table Access by Index Rowid**. Oracle uses the ROWID to read the block(s) that contain the Employee data it needs for the query. It estimates that will be around.

Next comes the **Index Range Scan** on the EMPHOURS primary key index. It will use the emp_id number discovered in operation 4 to lookup the ROWID from the index of all the rows in EMPHOURS that have this emp_id. Finally Oracle can access EMPHOURS and return the rows selected by Operation 6.

These operations are in nested loops. First all the rows from Employees are returned and then EMPHOURS index information each row is returned from Employees. Once completed Oracle can sort the data in memory.

Operation 0 is the finished output. Note how poor the estimated number of rows is. Oracle doesn't know how many EMPHOURS rows are likely to be returned for each EMPLOYEE row.

To see the optimiser use an alternative approach to getting similar data, let's now run q3—which removes the emp_id < 105 predicate and generates many more rows (Fig. 14.17).

Because we are returning more than 15% of the rows from both tables Oracle now decides that it will not use indexes. Instead it will read all the rows from the two tables straight into memory in an operation called a Full Table Scan (here described as TABLE ACCESS FULL). Thus, two sets of rows are then joined on the join key.

Two common means of joining are:

- **Merge Join**: Outputs from both scans are sorted by the join key and then merged together
- **Hash Join**: A hash join iterates through the rows of the smaller table and performs a hash algorithm on the columns for the joined columns and then stores the result. It then iterates through the rows of the other table performing the same hashing algorithm on the joined columns. It then compares with the first result and if they match it returns the row.

Once the rows are output Oracle sorts. Because it has estimated how many rows will be output it also suggests it will need 15 Mb of Temporary Space to perform the sort. Note that the estimated row count is a lot more accurate this time.

```
Execution Plan
----------------------------------------------------------
Plan hash value: 2217401640

---------------------------------------------------------------------------
| Id  | Operation          | Name      | Rows  | Bytes |TempSpc| Cost (%CPU)| Time     |
---------------------------------------------------------------------------
|   0 | SELECT STATEMENT   |           |  217K |  4874K|       |  1879   (2)| 00:00:23 |
|   1 |  SORT ORDER BY     |           |  217K |  4874K|   15M |  1879   (2)| 00:00:23 |
|*  2 |   HASH JOIN        |           |  217K |  4874K|       |   388   (3)| 00:00:05 |
|   3 |    TABLE ACCESS FULL| EMPLOYEES |   107 |  1070 |       |     3   (0)| 00:00:01 |
|*  4 |    TABLE ACCESS FULL| EMPHOURS  |  217K |  2755K|       |   383   (3)| 00:00:05 |
---------------------------------------------------------------------------
```

Fig. 14.17 Revised execution plan output

What we sometimes need to do when testing is to run several scripts and then want to compare the outputs, saving them for future reference. We can use the SQLPLUS Spool command to send output to a file. We also need to close the file when we have finished recording. Before we run this test script it is a good idea to make sure that the data dictionary has up-to-date statistics. To force this you can issue this command:

```
analyze table emphours compute statistics;
```

We shall now create such a script, run an SQL query twice, then create an index and then run the same query twice again to see what difference it makes to the Execution plan. The query returns employees who have recorded more than 40 h which was non-fee-paying in the previous 30 days.

Save the follow to q6.sql and then run it, after making sure you understand what the script is doing.

```
set timing on
set autotrace traceonly set linesize 200
spool test.txt

drop index hrs_idx;
select a.employee_id, a.last_name, b.work_date, b.hours from employees a, emphours b
where b.emp_id = a.employee_id AND b.fee_earning = 'N' AND hours > 40 AND work_date
> (SYSDATE -30);

select a.employee_id, a.last_name, b.work_date, b.hours from employees a, emphours b
where b.emp_id = a.employee_id AND b.fee_earning = 'N' AND hours > 40 AND work_date
> (SYSDATE -30);

create index hrs_idx on EMPHOURS(hours);

select a.employee_id, a.last_name, b.work_date, b.hours from employees a, emphours b
where b.emp_id = a.employee_id AND b.fee_earning = 'N' AND hours > 40 AND work_date
> (SYSDATE -30);
select a.employee_id, a.last_name, b.work_date, b.hours from employees a, emphours b
where b.emp_id = a.employee_id AND b.fee_earning = 'N' AND hours > 40 AND work_date
> (SYSDATE -30);

spool off
```

You can now read the results by opening the file test.txt in your working directory.

Our developers have said that they think that there will be several queries, like this one, which use the hours field to select and filter on. So, they have suggested, we should have an index on that column. Sounds reasonable?

Well, if we look at the result, we can see this isn't such a good idea. With or without an index on the Hours column Oracle uses the same Execution Plan (Fig. 14.18).

```
Execution Plan
-----------------------------------------------------
Plan hash value: 1656800177
```

```
---------------------------------------------------------------------------------------
| Id  | Operation                    | Name         | Rows | Bytes | Cost (%CPU)| Time     |
---------------------------------------------------------------------------------------
|   0 | SELECT STATEMENT             |              |   22 |   506 |   114  (1)| 00:00:02 |
|*  1 |  HASH JOIN                   |              |   22 |   506 |   114  (1)| 00:00:02 |
|*  2 |   TABLE ACCESS BY INDEX ROWID| EMPHOURS     |   22 |   286 |   110  (0)| 00:00:02 |
|*  3 |    INDEX SKIP SCAN           | SYS_C0010205 |   65 |       |   109  (0)| 00:00:02 |
|   4 |   TABLE ACCESS FULL          | EMPLOYEES    |  107 |  1070 |     3  (0)| 00:00:01 |
---------------------------------------------------------------------------------------
```

Fig. 14.18 Execution plan showing the index is not used

In other words, the Primary Key is used (at Id3) to filter on date first and there is no need for Oracle to use the new index.

The bad news is that having that index sitting there doing nothing is costing the system performance for every insert and update since it needlessly continues to maintain the index. So not a good idea after all.

Since we are filtering on the Y/N field you could try the same script again, but this time create a bitmap index on the fee_earning column:

create bitmap index fee_bit_idx on EMPHOURS(fee_earning);

What did this last experiment tell you? We now know indexes aren't always a good thing. So when would we use them?

Here is advice from the Oracle Tuning Guide:

> *(You should...) index keys that have high selectivity. The selectivity of an index is the percentage of rows in a table having the same value for the indexed key. An index's selectivity is optimal if few rows have the same value.*

The problem with indexing hours is that it has low selectivity. Prove this by running the following query:

> select hours, count(hours) from emphours group by hours order by hours;

Actually, if we had bothered to understand our data better, we could have guessed that 30 different values which were randomly allocated for 400,000 + rows are likely to generate many rows with the same value.

The reverse case, when we have low cardinality data, calls out for a bitmap index, but only really if the data is non-volatile.

To see when Oracle might use an index, have a look at this slightly reworked query from q6.sql above:

```
select a.employee_id, a.last_name, b.work_date, b.hours from employees a, emphours b where b.emp_id
= a.employee_id AND b.fee_earning = 'N' AND hours > 40 AND work_date > (SYSDATE -30) AND
a.last_name = 'Kumar';
```

We are now asking for the same information for only one particular employee. The Execution plan now uses indexes only—no table scans (Fig. 14.19).

To prove how useful bitmap indexes can be, let us assume the **emphours** table is a read-only table within a data warehouse. You have to write a report that lists all rows where no fee has been earned and yet the employee has claimed 50 h.

The query might now look like this:

```
select a.employee_id, a.last_name, b.work_date, b.hours from employees a, emphours b where b.emp_id
= a.employee_id AND b.fee_earning = 'N' AND hours = 50;
```

We can note that two columns which are in the WHERE clause are low cardinality, and the data is not volatile, so bitmap indexes might help. Placing this within our test template in the same way that we did with q6.sql, we get:

```
set timing on
set autotrace traceonly set linesize 200
spool test2.txt

drop index hrs_bit_idx; drop index fee_bit_idx;

select a.employee_id, a.last_name, b.work_date, b.hours from employees a, emphours b where b.emp_id
= a.employee_id AND b.fee_earning = 'N' AND hours = 50;
select a.employee_id, a.last_name, b.work_date, b.hours from employees a, emphours b where b.emp_id
= a.employee_id AND b.fee_earning = 'N' AND hours = 50;
```

```
-----------------------------------------------------------------------------------------------
| Id | Operation                           | Name          | Rows | Bytes | Cost (%CPU)| Time     |
-----------------------------------------------------------------------------------------------
|  0 | SELECT STATEMENT                    |               |   2  |   46  |   5  (0)| 00:00:01 |
|  1 |  NESTED LOOPS                       |               |      |       |         |          |
|  2 |   NESTED LOOPS                      |               |   2  |   46  |   5  (0)| 00:00:01 |
|  3 |    TABLE ACCESS BY INDEX ROWID|      | EMPLOYEES     |   1  |   10  |   2  (0)| 00:00:01 |
|* 4 |     INDEX RANGE SCAN                | EMP_NAME_IX   |   1  |       |   1  (0)| 00:00:01 |
|* 5 |    INDEX RANGE SCAN                 | SYS_C0010205  |   6  |       |   2  (0)| 00:00:01 |
|* 6 |   TABLE ACCESS BY INDEX ROWID       | EMPHOURS      |   2  |   26  |   3  (0)| 00:00:01 |
-----------------------------------------------------------------------------------------------
```

Fig. 14.19 Execution plan using an index to get at a single row

Elapsed: 00:00:00.08

Execution Plan

Plan hash value: 1594556531

```
--------------------------------------------------------------------------------
| Id  | Operation           | Name      | Rows  | Bytes | Cost (%CPU)| Time     |
--------------------------------------------------------------------------------
|   0 | SELECT STATEMENT    |           |  7001 |  157K |  387   (3)| 00:00:05 |
|*  1 |  HASH JOIN          |           |  7001 |  157K |  387   (3)| 00:00:05 |
|   2 |   TABLE ACCESS FULL | EMPLOYEES |   107 |  1070 |    3   (0)| 00:00:01 |
|*  3 |   TABLE ACCESS FULL | EMPHOURS  |  7001 | 91013 |  383   (3)| 00:00:05 |
--------------------------------------------------------------------------------
```

Fig. 14.20 Without Bitmap

Elapsed: 00:00:00.04

Execution Plan

Plan hash value: 1594230613

```
----------------------------------------------------------------------------------------------
| Id  | Operation                      | Name        | Rows  | Bytes | Cost (%CPU)| Time     |
----------------------------------------------------------------------------------------------
|   0 | SELECT STATEMENT               |             |  7001 |  157K |  315   (1)| 00:00:04 |
|*  1 |  HASH JOIN                     |             |  7001 |  157K |  315   (1)| 00:00:04 |
|   2 |   TABLE ACCESS FULL            | EMPLOYEES   |   107 |  1070 |    3   (0)| 00:00:01 |
|   3 |   TABLE ACCESS BY INDEX ROWID  | EMPHOURS    |  7001 | 91013 |  311   (0)| 00:00:04 |
|   4 |    BITMAP CONVERSION TO ROWIDS |             |       |       |           |          |
|   5 |     BITMAP AND                 |             |       |       |           |          |
|*  6 |      BITMAP INDEX SINGLE VALUE | HRS_BIT_IDX |       |       |           |          |
|*  7 |      BITMAP INDEX SINGLE VALUE | FEE_BIT_IDX |       |       |           |          |
----------------------------------------------------------------------------------------------
```

Fig. 14.21 With Bitmap indexes

Try this and see what the effect is. On the author's server the difference was striking in that the query time was halved (Figs. 14.20, 14.21).

14.5.2 Using the Built-In Advisers

The testing suggested above is fine during system builds, especially if we have realistic data to test against. However, once an optimised system is in place. It may well cause problems in the future due to changes in data. Assuming we want to be proactive and not just wait for complaints from users, how does a DBA establish which SQL might be worth investigating? Logged on as a DBA we can see what SQL has run recently using a DBA-only view called V$SQL.

Fig. 14.22 Example Enterprise Manager tuning recommendation

```
select sql_text from v$sql;
```

Unfortunately this can list all sorts of system generated SQL and in an operational production system there may be thousands of different SQL statements being run at any time. It is possible to join other v$ views to restrict the rows returned to those that might be of interest, but the easiest solution is to use the Enterprise Manager's advisors.

If you have Enterprise Manager open, move to Advisor Central and then select Automated Maintenance Tasks, and then run the Automatic SQL Tuning and finally review the Automatic SQL Tuning Result Details. On the author's server there was a recommendation for an index to support one of the queries that has recently run (Fig. 14.22).

14.5.3 Over to You!

14.5.3.1 Scenario One

We have been asked to create a report that counts the number of entries in EM-PHOURS where no fee was earned. It should have a count for Hours < 30, one for 30–40, and one for >40.

This could be tackled by having two UNIONS join three queries, or by using the CASE statement. You need to establish which is quicker.

NOTE: You should still have your bitmap index on the two columns from earlier for this to work well.

14.5.3.2 Scenario Two

Your developers are suggesting that some reports would benefit from there being a bitmap index on the fee_earning column. You need to get an understanding of how much slower your database would become in writing new records in a write-intensive period if you were to implement a bitmap index on the fee_earning table. As a suggestion, slightly rewrite the emphours creation and insertion script to:

1. Create an identical table, called emphours2
2. Time the INSERTEMPHOURS process
3. drop the table
4. create it again, this time with an index
5. time INSERTEMPHOURS again

If you put this all in one script you might find it useful to name your timers so they are easy to read when you are looking at your spooled outputs. You do this in sqlplus like this:

```
Timing start InsertsNoIdx
do some processing ....
Timing stop InsertsNoIdx
```

Is the insertion process any longer with an index?

14.6 Summary

In this chapter we have reviewed the impact each of the tiers in any database system can have on overall performance. We have seen that CPU usage and Disk I/o are important, but that so are some of the less physical aspects of a system, such as its design, how the indexes are used, and which types of indexes and tables are used.

We have seen that performance problems can be hard to diagnose because of the complexity of the tiers. Moreover, even if we do find the cause and resolve the problem, there is no guarantee that it will remain solved because, as we add data to our system, the data distribution may make some of our previous design assumptions invalid.

14.7   Review Questions

The answers to these questions can be found in the text of this chapter.

- What is the difference between Throughput and Workload?
- Which physical element of a database system is generally the slowest
- Why might a DBA decide not to update the CBO statistics often?
- What effect does a B-tree index have on inserts and updates?
- Why will a query which returns 20% of a table's rows probably not use an index, and what will it use?
- Name at least two alternative types of index, other than B-Tree, and explain when they might best be used

14.8   Group Work Research Activities

These activities require you to research beyond the contents of the book and can be tackled individually or as a discussion group.

Discussion Topic 1 *Indexes are a nuisance in a volatile OLTP system which manages many writes per second.* Discuss this assertion. You should review the benefits and disadvantages of different types of indexes in doing so.

Discussion Topic 2 Normalisation is often seen as a required process in the design of a database. Explain why this is so, and then go on to discuss scenarios when no normalisation is required, or indeed, when data should be denormalised.

Appendix: Creation Scripts and Hints

To create the EMPHOURS table and add the rows, save this code to a file in your Oracle working directory and call it something like CreateEmpHours.sql. Then Log in as hr/hr and run the script. This generates 400,000 + rows and so it will take up to a minute or so to complete.

```
drop table emphours;

create table emphours ( emp_id number, work_date date,
        hours number, fee_earning varchar(1),
        FOREIGN KEY (emp_id) REFERENCES HR.EMPLOYEES (EMPLOYEE_ID),
        PRIMARY KEY (emp_id, work_date) );

        create or replace

  PROCEDURE INSERTEMPHOURS AS BEGIN

    DECLARE
    eid employees.employee_id%TYPE; hdate
    employees.hire_date%TYPE; fee
    emphours.fee_earning%TYPE; howrs
    emphours.hours%TYPE;
    rnd Integer;

    CURSOR c1 IS
      SELECT EMPLOYEE_ID, hire_date FROM EMPLOYEES;

  BEGIN
    OPEN c1;
    -- loop through each of Employee rows LOOP
      FETCH c1 INTO eid, hdate; EXIT WHEN
      c1%NOTFOUND;

      -- loop through every day since they started to sysdate LOOP
        EXIT WHEN hdate > sysdate; hdate := hdate
        +1;
        -- check if weekend
        IF to_char(hdate, 'D') > 1 AND to_char(hdate, 'D') < 7
          THEN
            -- make fee_earning a random Y or N but with more Y values
            rnd := DBMS_RANDOM.value(low => 1, high => 10);
            IF rnd > 7 THEN
              fee := 'N'; ELSE
              fee := 'Y';
            END IF;

            -- generate a random number of hours works between 20 and 50 howrs :=
            round(DBMS_RANDOM.value(low => 20, high
            => 50));
            INSERT INTO emphours (emp_id, work_date, hours, fee_earning)
             values (eid, hdate, howrs, fee ); END IF;
             END LOOP;
             END LOOP;
       CLOSE c1;
  END;
  END INSERTEMPHOURS;
  /

  begin
    INSERTEMPHOURS;
  end;
  /
```

```
SQL> @createEmpHours Table dropped.
Table created. Procedure created.
PL/SQL procedure successfully completed. SQL> select count(*) from
emphours;
   COUNT(*)
                     --------
                      434068
```

Hints on the Over to You Section

Scenario One

set timing on set autotrace on set linesize 200 spool test19.txt

set timing on SELECT COUNT (*)

FROM emphours

WHERE fee_earning = 'N' AND hours < 30 UNION

SELECT COUNT (*)

FROM emphours

WHERE fee_earning = 'N' AND hours BETWEEN 30 AND 40 UNION

SELECT COUNT (*)

FROM emphours

WHERE fee_earning = 'N' AND hours > 40;

SELECT COUNT (case when fee_earning = 'N' AND hours < 30 THEN 1 ELSE null END) lessthan30,

COUNT (case when fee_earning = 'N' AND hours BETWEEN 30 AND 40 THEN 1

ELSE null END) betwix3040,

COUNT (case when fee_earning = 'N' AND hours > 40 THEN 1 ELSE null END) gt40

From EMPHOURS;

spool off

The CASE fails to use the index and so is much slower.

Scenario Two

drop table emphours2;

create table emphours2 (emp_id number, work_date date,

hours number, fee_earning varchar(1),

FOREIGN KEY (emp_id) REFERENCES HR.EMPLOYEES (EMPLOYEE_ID),

PRIMARY KEY (emp_id, work_date));

create or replace

PROCEDURE INSERTEMPHOURS AS BEGIN
    DECLARE

eid employees.employee_id%TYPE; hdate employees.hire_date%TYPE; fee emphours2.fee_earning%TYPE; howrs emphours2.hours%TYPE; rnd Integer;

CURSOR c1 IS

SELECT EMPLOYEE_ID, hire_date FROM EMPLOYEES;

BEGIN

OPEN c1;
    – loop through each of Employee rows LOOP.

FETCH c1 INTO eid, hdate; EXIT WHEN c1%NOTFOUND;

– loop through every day since they started to sysdate LOOP.

EXIT WHEN hdate > sysdate; hdate: = hdate + 1;

– check if weekend.

IF to_char(hdate, 'D') > 1 AND to_char(hdate, 'D') < 7 THEN.

– make fee_earning a random Y or N but with more Y values rnd: = DBMS_RANDOM.value(low = > 1, high = > 10);

IF rnd > 7 THEN

fee: = 'N'; ELSE

fee: = 'Y'; END IF;

– generate a random number of hours works between 20 and 50 howrs: = round (DBMS_RANDOM.value(low = > 20,   high = > 50)); INSERT INTO emphours2 (emp_id, work_date, hours, fee_earning).

values (eid, hdate, howrs, fee); END IF;

END LOOP;

END LOOP;

CLOSE c1;

END;

END INSERTEMPHOURS;

/

Timing start InsertsNoIdx begin

INSERTEMPHOURS;

end;

/

Timing stop InsertsNoIdx

– now drop the table and recreate with an index drop table emphours2;

create table emphours2 (emp_id number, work_date date,

hours number, fee_earning varchar(1),

FOREIGN KEY (emp_id) REFERENCES HR.EMPLOYEES (EMPLOYEE_ID),

PRIMARY KEY (emp_id, work_date));

create bitmap index fee_bit_idx on Emphours2 (fee_earning);

Timing start InsertsWithIdx begin

INSERTEMPHOURS;

end;

/

Timing stop InsertsWithIdx spool off

Reference

Florescu D, Kossmann D (2009) Rethinking cost and performance of database systems. SIGMOD Rec 38(1):43–48

Security

15

What the reader will learn:

- The importance of database security
- Physical security considerations
- Database security risks and how to mitigate them
- Security issues in the cloud
- How to develop a Security Policy

15.1 Introduction

As mentioned in Chap. 2, data is one of organisations most important assets, therefore steps need to be taken to protect it. Security generally has three aspects to it: physical security, software security and procedures. In each case precautions need to be in place along with a risk assessment and a recovery plan. Security is also closely linked with availability which was discussed in Chap. 13. The simple difference is that availability refers to making sure the systems don't shut down, whereas security is keeping the 'bad guys' out. However, if you have a security breach it may mean your database is not available, or your data has been corrupted.

In the case of physical security, the main question to ask is how to protect the servers and infrastructure from damage or loss. This may range from a catastrophic event in the data centre through to someone stealing the actual server. Physical security is not only an issue of restricting access to a computer centre, but how to recover operations if there is a major incident. In other words, it is closely linked to the question of availability.

A more recent physical security threat has emerged from the increase in use of mobile devices. These include smartphones, laptop and tablet computers as well as removal storage devices such as pen drives. Loss and theft of these devices which

© Springer Nature Switzerland AG 2021
K. Domdouzis et al., *Concise Guide to Databases*, Undergraduate Topics
in Computer Science, https://doi.org/10.1007/978-3-030-42224-0_15

may contain sensitive information or have the ability to automatically connect to sensitive systems has been a growing problem for some time.

Although physical security is important, software security is the more important security consideration on a day-to-day basis. Many databases have internet access to them, although this is usually through another server. It is however where most threats come from. The nature of these threats and what can be done to mitigate them will be discussed in this chapter.

The final aspect is the procedures which are in place. These will also have an impact on how physical and software security is implemented and maintained. Questions to ask are what procedures are in place, are they adequate and how are these audited. A major component of this is a risk register which needs to be regularly updated and reviewed.

15.2 Physical Security

Physical security is probably the easiest aspect of security to deal with, but it is potentially the most catastrophic when things go wrong.

A review by Scalet (2009) gives a comprehensive 19 point guide to physical security including building a secure centre capable of surviving explosions. A lot of this is in response to the aftermath of the terrorist attacks of 9/11 and much of it is beyond the capability of an average company. However, as the following Bunce-field example shows, there needs to be a contingency plan as to what to do if the processing centre is destroyed. On 11th December 2005 as a result of an industrial accident there was an explosion at the Buncefield oil storage terminal at Hemel Hempstead just north of London in the UK. The resultant fire was still burning on the 14th December. There were a number of businesses in the adjacent business park which were also damaged or destroyed. One of these was Northgate Information Solutions whose headquarters were badly damaged by a wall being blown out, it was rendered completely unusable.

Northfield hosted systems for other organisations including the payroll system for the author's university. As a result of the explosion, it was not possible to process the payroll for the next payday (18 December and just before Christmas). Although the company had other processing sites it was impossible to completely set the system up in time for the next payday. As a result a stop gap measure where staff were paid the same as they were paid the previous month was instituted. The system was backed up at another site in time for the January 2006 payday.

This illustrates the need of having a contingency plan for when something does go wrong. It is extremely rare that a data centre gets completely destroyed, but floods and fire do happen as the example shows. One question that needs to be asked is how much an organisation is willing to spend on disaster proofing physical infrastructure—it is probably impossible to make a building totally indestructible. A better question is how will operations continue if it does happen and how will the database be recovered.

The other component of physical security is access control where physical access to sensitive hardware and parts of a building are restricted. A 3-line security system consisting of something you are, something you know and something you have gives the best level of security for access to both building space and access to systems:

- Something you are: iris recognition, fingerprint recognition;
- Something you know: password or code;
- Something you have: passkey or other device (see Federal Financial Institutions Examination Council Authentication in an Internet Banking Environment https://www.ffiec.gov/pdf/authentication_guidance.pdf accessed 28/07/2013).

Oracle's Security Guide for Oracle 10g (Oracle Corp 2012a, 2012b) gives a physical and personnel control checklist. At its most basic, the policy should be that no one should be able to walk into a data centre without proper authorisation and identification (which is checked). It should be noted that although this list is not included in the Oracle 11g security guide it is still valid. Scalet (2009) suggests that there should be a minimum of 3 separate checks of personnel—on entering the building, on entering the employee area and on entering the data centre 'core'. She further points out that access to the core should be strictly controlled and on a needs only basis.

Oracle adds that the elaborate measures documented by Scalet are probably not needed by the majority of organisations. Factors such as organisation size, risk of loss, access controls and frequency of external visitors will determine the level of measures needed. They also add that the visibility of security measures such as video surveillance will act as a deterrent. Oracle say: 'Make it difficult to get in, difficult to remain or leave unobserved or unidentified, difficult to get at sensitive or secure areas inside, and difficult not to leave a trace.' (Oracle® Database Security Guide 10g Release 2 (10.2) B14266-09 p 2–2). Even a small company should restrict access to their server, even if that means keeping it locked in a cupboard.

Shinder (2007) in her article lists 10 physical security measures every organization should take which add a few more concerns to the list we have already seen. Workstations, particularly any which are left logged on in an unattended are a potential security risk. The machine at the front receptionist's desk can be a particular risk. Related to this is the physical removal of workstation components such as the hard disk drive. A case lock is a low-cost solution to this problem.

A classic television and cinema scenario is the good (or bad) guy breaks into an office and downloads the information on a workstations hard drive to a memory sick or pen drive. In practice it is more likely an employee who is going to do this—often not for malicious intent (it may be they want to work on data at home). It is how-ever a security risk and many organisations take measures to prevent unauthorised downloading by disabling USB ports and any device capable or writing to removal media.

A final, often forgotten risk in physical security is disposal of equipment. It is essential hard drives are properly erased. This is more than just deleting files because in most cases only directories which point to data are deleted. The actual data often remains and there have been cases of machines being bought at auction and their hard drives being reconstructed. In some cases even a simple delete had not been carried out. Free utilities such as Active@Kill Disk—Hard Drive Eraser from LSoft Technologies (see https://www.killdisk.com accessed 30/07/2013) exist for overwriting disks. Disks can also be cleared magnetically—a process known as degaussing.

15.3 Software Security—Threats

On line access security is the area which is arguably of greater concern to businesses and potentially a much more of a serious risk than the physical securing of a database. Once a building is physically secure, assuming there are no lapses in protocol, the issue is solved. Problems associated with software tend to be more on going and continually evolving, particularly unauthorised access and changes to data.

Therefore, this type of security includes access to software systems (rather than physical access to hardware discussed earlier) and data integrity measures. Data integrity is ensuring the accuracy, reliability and consistency of data in a database. There also needs to be a decision as to where security protocols are enforced. It is not normal for an internet user to directly interact with a database, there is usually some middleware handling security and checking transactions before a database is updated. For example, some banks require up to three security questions to be answered before a user is allowed access to on-line banking. The Yorkshire Bank requires a user ID, then a password followed by a security question followed by verification code (delivered to a smartphone). The password itself is not entered but randomly selected characters from it are requested. This is also done when purchases are made on-line. Only when these security measures have been passed is the user (in this case a customer) able to carry out on-line financial transactions.

There are number of types of threats to databases: privilege abuse, platform weaknesses, SQL injection, weak audit, protocol vulnerabilities, authentication vulnerabilities, backup data exposure and mobile device-based threats, each of which we will review below.

15.4 Privilege Abuse

Users of a database will require different levels of access known as privileges. For example, a database administrator will need to be able to modify the database definition using data definition language and perform database management tasks such as brining the server down or starting it. At the other end of the spectrum there will be users who should only be able to view a restricted subset of the data in the database. Between these extremes there will be users who will need various levels of access to manipulate data to fulfil their roles.

Database Privileges can be arranged in the following way with progressive capabilities to make changes to the database. They are arranged by user: those who are concerned with data and administrator: those who are concerned with management of the databases structure:

User

Read—the basic level most users require to access data. Modification is not allowed.

Insert—add new data, but no modification of existing data. This may not automatically give read privilege.

Update—modify, but not delete data.

Delete—ability to delete a complete record.

Administrator

References—an extension to update where foreign keys can be created Index—create or drop indexes.

Create—ability to create new tables Create a new database Modify—add or delete attributes.

Drop—delete a table.

Grant—ability to grant privileges including create new users start and stop a database.

The way these privileges are maintained depends on the system. For example, on IBM systems these privileges are held in an access control list (ACL). Privilege abuse occurs when users or administrators are given privileges which exceed their requirements and then proceed to exploit these 'excess' privileges.

To mitigate against this type of problem the ACL or its equivalent needs to be developed and maintained. A precursor to this is that the role of the user must be considered and only the minimum rights should be granted to enable the user to carry out their roll. This is not a trivial task in terms of its creation and maintenance. IBM divides the ACL into three parts:

- Access
- User
- Privilege.

Basically the first two determine the third. In terms of access, IBM visualises the hierarchy as an inverted pyramid with Manager at the top and 'No Access' at the bottom.

MANAGER   Can access everything.
DESIGNER   Can modify all design elements.
EDITOR   Can create documents and edit all documents.
AUTHOR   Can create documents and edit those documents they have created.
READER   Can only read documents, but not create or modify documents.
DEPOSITOR   Can only create documents, but not read those documents.
NO ACCESS   No access to anything.

(Adapted form 'The ABC's of using the ACL' at https://www.ibm.com/developerworks/lotus/library/ls-Using_the_ACL/index.html accessed 04/06/2013.)

No Access, Reader and Depositor access is fairly straight forward, but when you get to Author there are a number of options available. For example, you might be designated an author of a document, but you might not have a 'delete' right for the document (even though you created it). The same is true for Editor access.

As well as access, IBM considers five user types.

PERSON   You as an individual.
PERSON GROUP   List of names belonging to a group.
SERVER   Individual server.
SERVER GROUP   Servers in a group.
MIXED GROUP   Combination of server and person groups.

The user types are a means of assigning an ID for accessing the database and all vendors have an equivalent system although they vary widely in implementation. An individual ID will not give a user access to a database that requires a group ID. Likewise if a server or server group is specified, a user will not be able to access the database unless they use specified server. The final option only requires you to be a member of a group and you can be either a server or a client.

These settings allow a database administrator to have a structured approach to privileges. It should also be noted that a user may be another server rather than a human. Once created the ACL needs to be maintained. Users roles change and when this happens their privileges must be reviewed.

Even when you have established privileges and keep the ACL up to date, there can still be an issue with legitimate privilege abuse where legitimate access privileges are used for unauthorised purposes. Examples of this kind of abuse include:

- Accessing confidential data unnecessarily. There was a case where a tax official was viewing a celebrities records for no other reason than they were a fan.
- Retrieving large quantities of data for no legitimate reason causing performance degradation.
- Downloading data and storing it locally. This often happens when someone sets up their own bespoke system—typically on a spreadsheet. The issue is compounded if it is sensitive data and it gets lost. How many times have you read about laptops and pen drives with sensitive information on them getting lost or stolen?

This kind of abuse is more difficult to control but could be aided by more granular ACL policies and firm personnel management.

The final type of privilege abuse is privilege elevation where a user who has legitimate access exploits a vulnerability to gain administrative privileges. This will be discussed further in the next section on platform vulnerabilities.

As already discussed, the primary way of dealing with privilege abuse is through a ACL or an equivalent and we have seen the philosophy behind IBM's approach. However different vendors set this up in different ways. For example, Oracle does not have an ACL but has privileges grouped into roles which are placed in a hierarchy. There are 52 predefined user roles in Oracle 11g and new roles can be created, assuming you have the privileges to do it. Some roles like sys also need to have root privileges for the operating system.

SQL Server on the other hand does not have a dedicated ACL but, instead has a series of operations which can be applied to define privileges and give the same resource as an ACL. This is held as a hierarchy with the top-level user being identified as the principle. Below that there are the operating system, SQL Server and database level permissions.

The other way to restrict access to data is via views. A view is in effect a virtual table which may allow only certain attributes to be viewed and manipulate. Views can include joins so the virtual table a user is working with is made up of columns from two or more tables. As well as restricting access to data it makes complex queries easy by hiding the original (complex) SQL query. It also allows the same data to be presented in different ways to meet user requirements.

In ORACLE and SQL Server a simple view can be created by:

CREATE VIEW phone_contact_vu

    AS SELECT customer_name, customer_phone, customer_mobile

    FROM customer;

This would create a view to retrieve telephone details ignoring other columns such as address details. A WHERE clause can be added to further restrict data:

CREATE VIEW phone_contact_vu

    AS SELECT customer_name, customer_phone, customer_mobile FROM customer

    WHERE customer_city = 'Sheffield';

Once the view is created it can be used to retrieve data as if it was a table, for example:

    SELECT * FROM phone_contact_vu;

You can add restrictions, for example if this was to be used only for reference and the user did not have permission to change details:

CREATE VIEW phone_contact_vu

> **AS SELECT customer_name, customer_phone, customer_mobile FROM customer**
>
> **WHERE customer_city = 'Sheffield' WITH READ ONLY;**

Any attempt to alter the table with either a DELETE FROM, INSERT or UPDATE statement would result in an error. An alternative to the READ ONLY clause is WITH CHECK OPTION where any DELETE, INSERT or UPDATE must conform to the definition of the view. So if you created the view with:

CREATE VIEW phone_contact_vu

> **AS SELECT customer_name, customer_phone, customer_mobile FROM customer**
>
> **WHERE customer_city = 'Sheffield' WITH CHECK OPTION;**
>
> **and then tried an UPDATE of the form:**
>
> **UPDATE phone_contact_vu SET customer_city = 'Leeds';**

you would get an error because the view is defined such that the customer city can only be Sheffield.

A complex view has more than one table in its definition, for example:

CREATE VIEW outstading_invoice_vu

> **AS SELECT customer_name, invoice_id, invoice_date FROM customer**
>
> **INNER JOIN invoice**
>
> **ON customer.customer_id = invoice.customer_id WHERE invoice_status <> 'paid'**
>
> **ORDER BY invoice_date;**

which can be used to retrieve customers who have an outstanding invoice. One problem with complex views in ORACLE is that you cannot perform data manipulation with them. To achieve this requires a procedure or trigger needs to be written.

Not all mistakes in data entry are deliberate, so integrity checks should be set up which are enforced by the database management system. These include check constraints to limit the chances of wrong data being entered. For example, to add a constraint:

ALTER TABLE customer

> **ADD CONSTRAINT customer_city_ck**
>
> **CHECK (customer_city IN ('Sheffield', 'Rotherham', 'Doncaster'));**

In the above example it should be noted that each of the city names has to be in the format described. 'SHEFFIELD', for example would generate an error. A better way to limit invalid data entry is to use lookup tables so the user has to choose from a list rather than entering raw data. This would also reduce the possibility of mistyping data on entry. To implement this would require a simple program known as a procedure or trigger to be written.

Where possible, rules to trap transcription and transposition errors should always be implemented. A typical example of a transcription error is entering a zero in place of the character 'O'. Transposition errors are harder to trap, for example entering 547,619 instead of 546,719.

Some database management systems such as those following CODASYL conventions use a concept of subschemas instead of views. A subschema is part of the database that a user can access and manipulate. This was quite common in early mainframe databases with hierarchical and network structures which were described in Chap. 2.

Ultimately the guiding principle for privileges is to only give a user the bare minimum they require to be able to complete their tasks. When a new user is added to the system unnecessary privileges (often added as defaults) should be removed. If a user's responsibilities change, their privileges should be reviewed.

15.5   Platform Weaknesses

Unfortunately, most products and their underlying operating systems and services have weaknesses and unresolved issues. That is why regular patches are issued by vendors. These have two roles. The first and of most concern here are to fix reported security weaknesses and bugs in a product. The second is to improve usability and performance. It is always a good idea to install these as soon as possible otherwise your system could be vulnerable.

An example of what can happen was posted on 14th January 2013: (https://eu.usatoday.com/story/tech/2013/01/14/oracle-says-java-is-fixed-feds-maintain-warning/1834355/).

"Oracle Corp. said Monday it has released a fix for the flaw in its Java software that raised an alarm from the U.S. Department of Homeland Security last week. Even after the patch was issued, the federal agency continued to recommend that users disable Java in their Web browsers.

"This and previous Java vulnerabilities have been widely targeted by attackers, and new Java vulnerabilities are likely to be discovered," DHS said Monday in an updated alert published on the website of its Computer Emergency Readiness Team. "To defend against this and future Java vulnerabilities, consider disabling Java in Web browsers until adequate updates are available."

The alert follows on the department's warning late Thursday. Java allows programs to run within websites and powers some advertising networks. Users who disable Java may not be able to see portions of websites that display real-time data such as stock prices, graphical menus, weather updates and ads. Vulnerability in the latest version, Java 7, was "being actively exploited," the department said. Java 7 was released in 2011. Oracle said installing its "Update 11" will fix the problem.

Security experts said that special code to take advantage of the weakness is being sold on the black market through so-called "Web exploit packs" to Internet abusers who can use it to steal credit card data, personal information or cause other harm. The packs, sold for upwards of $1,500 apiece, make complex hacker codes available to relative amateurs. This particular flaw even enables hackers to compromise legitimate websites by taking over ad networks. The result: users are redirected to malicious sites where damaging software can be loaded onto their computers."

Oracle issue regular security alerts (https://www.oracle.com/security/) which includes critical patch updates. Likewise Microsoft issues SQL Server alerts (for an example, see https://support.microsoft.com/kb/959420).

It is beyond the scope of this book to discuss intrusion and virus threats in detail. New viruses are released constantly so updates to anti-virus software are released almost daily and sometimes more often. Likewise attempts to gain unauthorized access to systems are getting more sophisticated. It goes without saying you should have firewall and virus detection software in place that is regularly updated. There are both free (for example Avast, www.avast.com, last accessed 08/12/2020) and commercial (for example McAfee, www.mcafee.com, last accessed 08/12/2020) solutions readily available.

15.6   SQL Injection

In some ways this is an extension to the previous topic on system vulnerabilities, but it is a common way of compromising databases. It refers to the insertion of SQL statements in a data entry field. It is the most common type of attack on web connected databases. If the attack is successful it can result in access to unauthorized data and manipulation of that data or privilege elevation which we have already discussed under privilege abuse. SQL injection comes in four main forms: SQL manipulation, code injection, function call injection and buffer overflow.

SQL manipulation is the most common form of SQL injection and involves an attacker attempting to modify existing SQL by adding elements to the WHERE clause and seeing if any records were returned. If the original statement was:

SELECT * FROM users
WHERE username = 'Dorian' AND password = '&mypassword';

and the attacker added an OR clause so it became:

SELECT * FROM users
WHERE username = 'Dorian' AND password = '&mypassword' OR 'a' = 'a';

then the WHERE clause would always be true because of operator precedence and the attacker would have gained access to the application.

Another variation is to use the UNION operator to try and return rows from another table, so if the original query was:

SELECT item_description FROM stock_item WHERE price < 10;

the attacker might attempt:

SELECT item_description FROM stock_item WHERE price <10
   UNION
   SELECT username FROM admin_user WHERE username like '%';

which returns not only a list of items but also all database administration users.

Code injection tends to be more of a problem with Microsoft SQL Server and PostgreSQL (Kost 2007) because it involves adding an extra SQL statement to an existing statement. Oracle does not support multiple SQL statements per database request so it is afforded some protection. However, underlying platform weaknesses as already discussed may allow a java program in a web application to execute multiple requests.

Function call injection is a variation on SQL manipulation where a database function (either a built in one or a custom written one) is added to vulnerable SQL code. Oracle supplies some functions which perform network communication which could be exploited as well as over a thousand other functions which would have no use in an attack.

Buffer overflow occurs when a program writes data to an area of memory and overwrites adjacent memory. A buffer is a temporary area in memory storage space where data is kept prior to writing to another device. In the case of databases, that device is disk storage. Some Oracle functions are susceptible to buffer overflows and this can be exploited through a SQL injection attack.

It is easy to protect against SQL injection attacks so it ultimately comes down to enforcing a series of methods to every web accessible procedure and function as even one unprotected SQL statement could cause problems. The following are a minimum:

- Always use bind variables (substitution variables that are used in place of literals). In any SQL statement where a variable is required, for example in a SELECT statement, the variable should have been declared as a bind variable. It also improves system performance because statements are reused rather than reparsed at every execution.
- Always validate every passed string parameter.
- Restrict all functions that are not absolutely necessary.

15.7   Weak Audit

Database auditing is at the core of any database security policy. Database systems generate an audit log that captures a record of all data access and alternations. This log is managed internally by the database management system and is the most accurate source of monitoring activity. However, there is a possibility of issues arising if an organisation bases all of its audit policies on the built-in database mechanisms. The main problem here is that the system will generate a large amount of data as each transaction is logged. The sheer volume of data requires knowledge of what to look for to make sure there have been no security violations, for example privilege elevation. There are five things that should be monitored for suspicious activity:

- Who accessed which systems when and how. If there is evidence of failed logins there is a high probability someone is trying to break into your system. This is particularly important when you consider most users do not directly log in to a database but go through other applications which automatically connect.
- User and administrator activity should be examined. Failed queries should be taken seriously as they may be an indication of an attacker probing known vulnerabilities in a system including assuming specific features or structures will be present. The error details which are returned when a query fails should be logged rather than displayed to the user as they may use the details to refine their attack. Even if the failed query is not a result of an attack it should still be checked because it may be an indication of a flaw in a script which in turn could lead to application failure.
- Abnormal activity such as unusual access to sensitive data should be logged and investigated. This may require identifying what is sensitive data then applying filters to audit logs to isolate activity on such data.
- All databases should be audited for vulnerabilities and threats. This relates back to platform weaknesses. If you know about weaknesses, you can monitor activity attempting to exploit them.
- Changes to metadata should be monitored. Changes to the databases structure can lead to new vulnerabilities. It is essential to establish a baseline policy for monitoring changes to database configuration. If there are any deviations from that baseline, they should be tracked back to establish their source.

Recording everything in an audit log provides lots of useful information, but there is an impact on performance. Therefore it is necessary to understand the audit settings on your system and implement them in a way that will capture critical information without overly degrading performance. Oracle allows generation of '... audit records that include information about the operation that was audited, the user performing the operation, and the date and time of the operation. Audit records can be stored in the database audit trail or in files on the operating system. Standard auditing includes operations on privileges, schemas, objects, and statements.' (Oracle, '12c Traditional Database Auditing', https://www.oracle.com/database/technologies/security/db-auditing.html, accessed 28/07/2013). Oracle suggests that the audit records should be stored on the operating system as this has the least overhead compared to storing it on the host database system. It should also be noted that every write to the audit files is a system overhead that will reduce system performance. This has to be balanced with the need to recover a system or look for evidence of security breaches.

15.8   Protocol Vulnerabilities

A communication protocol defines the methods of exchanging messages between computer systems and there can be weaknesses. As an example, in 2003 the SQL Slammer Worm exploited a weakness in Microsoft SQL Server and Desktop Server protocol. It was small and resident in memory. Its effect was to generate random IP addresses and send itself to those addresses. It should be noted the worm did not use SQL code, but exploited a buffer overflow problem. It was used to execute denial of service attacks severely compromising performance. Interestingly a patch was available to guard against the problem six months before the worms launch, but many systems did not have it installed.

Although this example features SQL Server, communication protocol vulnerabilities have been identified for every vendor's products. Basically, a communication protocol is how components of a system communicate and if a component can be impersonated, then there is a security issue.

It is therefore essential that protocol validation is enabled. This technology breaks down database traffic, a process known as parsing, and looks for anomalies. Only normal client generated messages should be allowed through with requests using hidden features blocked. Obviously know attacks (like the SQL Slammer Worm) should be checked for which means implementing security patches as they become available.

15.9   Authentication Vulnerabilities

What you are trying to defend against here is someone guessing account names and passwords. In a large English language western organisation, the chances of there being a 'John Smith' with legitimate access rights is quite large. Some organisations have a standard which is used for both e-mail addresses and userid's for example, J. Smith@somecompany.org and then J.Smith as a userid. Combine this with a predictable choice of password ('password' is the most common password) and you have access. Unfortunately, many people use the same password for multiple systems, so once you have access to one system, you may have access to multiple systems. This type of knowledge is used in so called 'brute force' attacks were attacking systems use common names then a list of common passwords in an attempt to break in.

Measures to mitigate these problems include using a different standard for e-mail addresses and userids with the userids avoiding real names. There should be a strong password policy. The authors' institution requires passwords to be changed on a regular basis, the password to be at least eight characters long, the password to contain a mixture of alphabetic and other characters and the password not to have been used recently. The authors' bank doesn't enforce a password change but requires random characters from it to be entered along with a 'secret' word randomly selected from a list provided by the user. Most systems now disable an account if three unsuccessful attempts are made to log in.

Even with these authentication measures in place, unsuccessful access attempts should be logged and investigated, particularly if there is a pattern of related attacks.

15.10   Backup Data Exposure

Backup and recovery are topics dealt with in the chapter on availability. However, it is worth emphasising that databases and in fact any data should be regularly backed up. Most database management systems supply utilities to do this. However there have been many incidents where backup media has been lost or stolen. This has become an escalating problem with the proliferation of mobile devices and memory sticks. Often the data on these is not encrypted meaning there is a potential for large amounts of sensitive data to be compromised.

Encryption of data won't stop devices being lost, but it will keep the data secure. There are however costs, the most noteworthy being performance degradation. Encryption is also often application dependent sometimes with complex key management.

To mitigate backup data exposure, some organisations have banned the use of none encrypted devices to transport data. The authors organisation requires staff transporting sensitive data on memory sticks to use IronKey devices. IronKey is a proprietary device with built in encryption. It can be configured to delete all data stored on it if the maximum number of failed password entry attempts is exceeded.

15.11   Mobile Device Based Threats

Most of the threats mentioned above also apply to mobile devices, especially backup data exposure. Loss or theft of an unsecured mobile device is a major concern. For example, loss and theft of mobile devices cost the BBC over £750,000 between 2010 and 2012 (ComputerWorld UK 2013). This was just the value of the hardware and did not include the cost of data loss and security exposure related to stored passwords. Many mobile devices require a user to activate password security, the default being it is off meaning if this was the case with the BBC devices there was a major security breach. As already mentioned, many systems including Microsoft Windows will offer to remember passwords. That should always be declined and password security to the device should be enabled.

There is another aspect which relates to distributed databases. Most mobile databases are distributed among wired components which are accessed by mobile devices rather than being held on the devices themselves. This is the thin client approach where the mobile device is the thin client and all the processing is done on the host system. Following the rules of never let your device store the passwords and always activate the password security on the device, this should be secure. But in a second scenario data is distributed among both wired and wireless components with active data being distributed to the mobile device. Data management involves data fragmented between mobile devices and fixed servers or base stations. In this scenario base stations and mobile devices must all be secure.

Something that can be regarded either as a threat or a security tool is a wireless sniffer. This is a form of packet analyser. Data is transmitted in packets and this tool decodes the packet's raw data, showing the values of various fields in the packet, and analyses its content. On the positive side it can be used to analyse network problems and detect network intrusion attempts and network misuse. However wireless sniffers can also be used to gain information for executing a network intrusion and to spy on network users and gather sensitive information. To guard against these threats router security should be activated and 'data should be encrypted.

15.12 Security Issues in Cloud Based Databases

Cloud computing is a technology that gained prominence in 2006 when Amazon introduced the Elastic Compute Cloud (EC2) and was at the peak of Gartner's hype cycle for emerging technologies from 2009 onwards (see Chap. 2 for a description of the Gartner Hype Cycle). Since 2012, Gartner published an annual snap shot of the hype cycle specifically for cloud computing. One aspect of this is using the cloud as a database service platform.

The idea of cloud computing is that an organisation does not have to store its own data, or even applications. Instead they are stored on a provider's servers and accessed via the internet. This has many advantages for a user but introduces some new security issues and threats.

Because a user is no longer directly responsible for database security, there is the possibility of failure to provide adequate security by the provider. The provider controls the servers, network and security regime therefore the user must trust the provider's security. It follows that when choosing a cloud provider an organisation should verify the providers security measures before signing a contract with them and to monitor the provider's security performance. It should be noted however that a cloud provider often has security measures that far exceed those of most small to medium sized enterprises.

A second issue is attacks by other users. This process was documented by Ristenpart et al. (2009) where a method of stealing data from Amazons cloud was demonstrated. It was based on the fact that if you hired multiple virtual machines from Amazons cloud, they had similar IP addresses. If you knew an application was cloud based, an attacker could bombard a victim site with requests forcing the target organisation to hire more virtual machines. At the same time the attacker would hire more virtual machines themselves. It was found that 40% of the time the attackers and victims ended up on the same server where the attacker could monitor the victim's virtual machine. Although they didn't actually steal any data, the authors said outright data theft was possible. It comes about because provider resources are shared with other parties, therefore the provider must take measures to separate users data and applications. Amazon has since closed this security loophole.

A related issue is data sanitization. Cloud computing is dynamic with data constantly being moved as demand on servers fluctuates. When data is moved, the physical location where the data is moved from needs to be overwritten rather than just being flagged as 'free'. This differs from an in-house application where pointers to data are removed and the disk space is flagged as being available rather than data being physically removed. In a cloud environment this is not sufficient as other clients of the cloud provider may (and probably will) use the space and could potentially see residual data. On in-house systems not physically deleting data has the advantage that if the 'accidental' delete is recognised soon enough the data can be 'un-deleted'. In a cloud environment with multiple organisational users, it is a security risk.

An area of vulnerability for data in the cloud is during data transfer. Standard communication protocols and procedures such as Hypertext Transfer Protocol Secure (HTTPS) and Secure Shell (SSH) should be implemented. The data should be encrypted to guard against data sanitisation failure.

Although not directly a security threat, there is an issue with regulatory compliance. For example, if an organisation in the United Kingdom is using cloud resources and the servers supplying that resource are in the United States, then the resource is subject to US law and regulation—in other words location matters. This has resulted in many organisations adopting a policy of only non-critical systems with data that is not sensitive being deployed in the cloud.

A lot of the security issues associated with databases in the cloud come down to the service provider. Before embarking on a project to move data to the cloud the provider should be thoroughly vetted. Questions to ask related to the issues raised in this section to provide an idea of risk should include:

- What is the providers security policy including segregation of users?
- What is the providers' backup and recovery policy?
- What are the providers' encryption procedures?
- Where is the physical location of the data (although this could be several locations)?
- Conduct a risk assessment of the providers viability (how likely are they to go bust or get taken over?).

15.13   Policies and Procedures

Unfortunately, the greatest online security threat comes from within an organisation from personnel who have legitimate access to a database. We have already looked at some of the issues here in the section on privilege abuse. To reduce the internal threat to an organisations database system there needs to be policies and procedures in place which are enforced and monitored.

Personnel This comes down to good personnel management and monitoring. All personnel should have a profile detailing what access level they need to carry out their duties. This should be set at a minimum and relates to both physical access to parts of the building and system access. Any attempts, whether deliberate or accidental to circumvent this must be followed up. In the event of an employee leaving, their privileges and access must be immediately revoked. This often means paying out an employee's notice period rather than letting them remain on the organisation's premises. If an employee is fired or disgruntled, this becomes even more critical.

Software Upgrades These should be carried out as soon as practical, particularly security upgrades relating to firewalls, viruses and system vulnerabilities. This needs to be monitored to make sure it is happening. If you have deployed a database in the cloud you also need to check the provider has those policies in place and is adhering to them.

Building Maintenance There is little point having CCTV surveillance if the cameras or recording devices are not working. The same goes for access controls, for example secure doors should never be wedged open, even during cleaning operations. If any part of the physical security of the organisation's infrastructure develops a fault it should be fixed immediately.

15.14 A Security Checklist

The following is based on Oracle's checklist, but is generalised to include other platforms. It details software and configuration security rather than physical security of a system.

- Disable default user accounts. Most database management systems come with preconfigured user accounts—Oracle has some 20 of these. They are a common first place an attempt to break into a system will occur. Other proprietary systems may have a 'guest' user or other default accounts.
- Change default passwords. This is a trivial issue, but one that can leave a system vulnerable if not implemented. It is crucial for administrative accounts. This is important for any system—not just databases (how many of you still have a default password set on your broadband hub?). Passwords should also be changed regularly. If your system does not have a feature to enforce this, develop and enforce a procedure for your users.
- Protect the important resource of your database data dictionary. This stores the name, meaning, relationships to other data, usage, and format of all components

of your database. Protection must therefore be enabled and access restricted to those with DBA roles.

- Give users the lowest level of privilege possible. This means granting only necessary privileges, but also revoking unnecessary privileges if a user's role changes. Monitor employee's roles and review and update privileges if their roles change.
- Create and maintain a Access Control List or its equivalent for your system.
- Authenticate client systems properly—in other words there needs to be stringent authentication of any client system trying to access the database.
- Protect any database gateway to the network. Particularly do not let any gateway software read or write files in the database or sever address space. This is another favoured way of attacking systems via SQL injection.
- Monitor who accesses your system. This should be done at the user rather than server level as servers may be compromised.
- Apply all security patches as soon as they are available. In most cases there is an automatic update, but it is worth regularly checking your vendors web site to check for security alerts and patches. Related to this is to inform the vendor if you become aware of a vulnerability so a patch can be developed.
- If you are using a web interface to your database consider including a CAPTCHA (Completely Automated Public Turing test to tell Computers and Humans Apart) test where a string of characters are presented in a deformed way and the user is asked to enter them. This stops attacks where a computer program attempts to access a website. Recent reports suggest that ways are being found to negate this test.
- Enforce a minimum access security regime of a userid and a password. Make sure there is a password policy which vets passwords to make sure they are not easily guessable. In a database environment there needs to be several levels of security so you may wish to include further security checks.
- If you are using a cloud service provider for your database verify that they have a security checklist and enforce it.

15.15   Review Questions

The answers to these questions can be found in the text of this chapter.

- What are 8 types of threats to database security?
- What are the three basic things you should have for physical access to a secure part of a building?
- What is privilege abuse and what measures can be taken to mitigate it?
- Why are mobile devices a particular security threat and what measures can be taken to reduce that threat?
- What is an SQL injection attack?

15.16   Group Work Research Activities

These activities require you to research beyond the contents of the book and can be tackled individually or as a discussion group.

Activity 1 Create a table of four columns. In the first list the devices you own or have administrative rights to. Don't forget mobile devices such as phones and tablets. In the second column place a tick if you have changed the default password (and remember, the default may be no password). In the third column place an X for devices you have the same password for. If you have several passwords you use regularly, use other letters of the alphabet. Leave a blank if the password is unique. In the fourth column write the date of the last time you changed the password. If you have never changed it, put an X there.

You have a security issue if there is no tick in column two, anything in column three and an X or a date older than 30 days in column four.

If you have no security risks identified congratulations!

If you have any security issues identified take steps to rectify them including a schedule to change passwords. You should also ask yourself if the password is easily guessable (like 'password').

You might consider repeating this exercise for online services (including bank accounts) and fix them as well.

Did you remember to include your wireless hub?

Activity 2 This exercise deals with security software.

What virus checking and firewall software do you run? Does it automatically download and install updates?

When did it last install an update?

When was the last time you did a full system check? It is possible that you had a virus last time you did a full scan that wasn't detected by what was then the most up-to-date version.

Is your product licence current?

Do you subscribe to a service that regularly gives news of security threats?

If any of your answers are 'none', 'don't know' or 'no' you need to take urgent action as your system may be exposed.

References

ComputerWorld UK (2013) Loss and theft of mobile devices costs the BBC over £750,000 in three years. https://www2.computerworld.co.nz/article/458762/loss_theft_mobile_devices_costs_bbc_over_750_000_three_years/. Accessed 28 Jul 2013

Kost S (2007) An introduction to SQL injection attacks for Oracle developers. Integrity white paper. https://www.integrigy.com/files/Integrigy_Oracle_SQL_Injection_Attacks.pdf . Accessed 30 Jul 2013

Oracle Corp (2012a) Oracle® database security guide 10g Release 2 (10.2) B14266–09. Available on line at https://docs.oracle.com/cd/B19306_01/network.102/b14266.pdf. Accessed 02 May 2013

Oracle Corp (2012b) Oracle® database security guide 11g Release 1 (11.1) B28531–19. https://
    docs.oracle.com/cd/B28359_01/network.111/b28531.pdf. Accessed 28 Jul 2013
Ristenpart T, Tromer E, Shacham H, Savage S (2009) Hey, you, get off of my cloud: exploring
    information leakage in third-party compute clouds. In: Proceedings of the 16th ACM
    conference on computer and communications security, pp 199–212. https://www.cs.cornell.
    edu/courses/cs6460/2011sp/papers/cloudsec-ccs09.pdf. Accessed 15 May 2013
Scalet SD (2009) 19 ways to build physical security into a data center. https://www.csoonline.com/
    article/2112402/physical-security-19-ways-to-build-physical-security-into-a-data-center.html.
    Accessed 09 Apr 2013
Shinder D (2007) 10 physical security measures every organization should take. https://www.
    techrepublic.com/blog/10-things/10-physical-security-measures-every-organization-should-
    take. Accessed 28 Jul 2013

Database Adaptiveness and Integration

16

What the reader will learn:

- What Database Adaptiveness is
- The factors that impact Database Adaptiveness
- Specific examples of adaptive capabilities in databases
- About Database Integration Capabilities
- Specific examples of Dynamic Applications in Databases

16.1 Introduction

Adaptation depends on the addition of adaptive and intelligent functionalities to a system (Brusilovsky and Christoph 2003). In modern computer systems, adaptability refers to the provision of options to the users to customise a system according to their preferences. Adaptive technologies refer to the different ways with which intelligent functionalities are added to a system. These functionalities can be further integrated to the system and they can find different ways of implementation (Soflano et al. 2015).

An example of adaptation in databases is the use of adaptive indexes. These indexes allow the creation and optimization of incremental indexes. As the information workflow becomes constantly dynamic and unpredictable, the adaptive indexing technology has emerged as an important technology. In this type of indexing, there is constant reorganisation of the index based on the query workload. The adaptive indexing approaches can be classified into three categories: database cracking, adaptive merging and a series of hybrid approaches. Database cracking reorganises index through a low initialisation cost and the adoption of partitioning logic. Adaptive merging uses merging logic to reorganise the index and achieve a fast convergence speed. However, these two approaches do not achieve good results in relation to initialisation cost and convergence speed. To achieve a balance

© Springer Nature Switzerland AG 2021

K. Domdouzis et al., *Concise Guide to Databases*, Undergraduate Topics
in Computer Science, https://doi.org/10.1007/978-3-030-42224-0_16

between cost and speed, hybrid approaches are realised. In the hybrid approaches and depending on the re-organisation manner, multiple hybrid adaptive merging approaches (e.g. hybrid crack sort, hybrid sort, hybrid crack crack) are generated. Especially, the hybrid crack sort uses database cracking to re-organise the data in each initial partition and then it sorts the data in final partitions.

16.2   Factors that Define Database Adaptiveness

There are a number of factors that define database adaptiveness. These factors are described below.

16.2.1   Changes in User Requirements

There are a number of different requirements which specify the adaptiveness of databases. Examples are operational, functional or design requirements (Dick et al. 2017). Requirements engineering is significant for the development of an information system and it is responsible for the provision of an accurate requirement specification. The requirements are used for the definition of a conceptual model that will lead to the development of a database or a data warehouse (Boukhari et al. 2016).

The requirements associated with the development of a database can be classified into a number of different categories, such as general, data-specific, processing-specific, application-specific, technical, and cost-related. General requirements are related to who will be responsible to the modification of the data included in the database, to who will provide support to the database, and who will be responsible for the maintenance of the database. Data requirements are related to the volume of the data stored in the database, the sensitivity of these data and how long they will be kept to the database. Processing requirements are focused on whether there are special processing requirements, special data formats or any data compression schemes. Application requirements are related to the number and type of users that use the database system while technical requirements are associated with the technical platform that hosts the database system and whether there are any technical standards related to the use of the specific system.

There are also operational requirements that specify the environments of operations in which a system must perform and how these environments evolve in certain time periods. These environments can be information and operating systems but also the physical environment of the system (Dennis et al. 2012).

Any changes in the requirements set by users can affect the database schema. Requirements analysis is an important stage for database design and development. It is based on continuous discussion with clients. During these discussions and depending on the dynamic conditions of a business and the challenges this business has to face, it is possible that the requirements will continuously change.

16.2.2   Change of Users' Rights

Users' rights define different levels of adaptiveness. Depending on the application in which a database is applied to, different users can have different rights. The roles provided for the different users can define the way a specific application or problem to which a database is applied to is handled. If there are many users that have full administrative rights, then these users can define how the system is applied to a specific situation and what type of characteristics and/or functions of the database system are useful for the resolution of specific issues.

16.2.3   Change of Database Technology

Different database technologies have different characteristics. These characteristics must conform to the requirements of the problem to which a specific database technology is applied.

16.2.4   Change of Overall Technology

Any change in the overall technologies that are used for the realization of a specific application may affect the database used for it.

16.3   Examples of Adaptive Capabilities of Databases

Automatic tuning is an intelligent performance service that uses built-in characteristics to monitor the queries realized in a database and it automatically improves the performance of these queries. This is achieved through the dynamic adaptation of the database of the changes of the workloads. Automatic tuning can lead to better performance (Microsoft Azure 2020a). There are two examples of automatic tuning and these are the automatic index management that identifies which indexes should be added to or removed from the database and automatic plan correction which identifies problems related to SQL plan performance (Microsoft Azure 2020b).

There are a number of techniques associated with adaptive query processing. Such techniques are the Batch Mode Memory Grant Feedback, the Batch Mode Adaptive Join and the Interleaved Execution. The first technique allows the allocation of memory to all the returning rows. This technique provides the possibility of selecting a specific algorithm and the query plan dynamically switches to a better strategy for handling joins. In this case, the adaptive join operator is used in order for a threshold in the selection of joins to be defined. Interleaved execution is applicable to multi-statement table valued functions (MSTVFs) in SQL Server 2017. During the interleaved execution, whenever the SQL Server identified MSTVFs, there is pause of the optimization, execution of the applicable subtree first, the acquisition of accurate cardinality estimates and finally the resume of optimization. This technique acquires actual row counts from MSTVFs. This has as a result the improvement of performance (Kumar 2020).

16.3.1 Triggers

A database trigger typically comprises instructions that are executed in response to an event that has occurred on the database. A database trigger may, for example, be associated with a table maintained by a database management system and executed whenever an insert, update, or delete command is performed on the table. Triggers may be used for various purposes, such as validating data, maintaining relational integrity, and other functions. Conventional approaches to implementing database triggers may involve the database management system storing the trigger definitions and executing the triggers when an applicable event occurs (Pol et al. 2017).

16.3.2 Version Control on Databases

Two command-line tools for automating database schema version control have been developed. These tools are db_dump and db_diff. The db_dumo tool is responsible for exporting the database schema into a human-readable text format. In order to get detailed tracking of changes, it exports the definition of each element of the schema into a separate text file. In order for false conflicts to be avoided, db_dump must keep timestamps for files. The db_diff tool compares two sets of configuration items (dumps) created by db_dump and produces the SQL script which is responsible for transforming the database from the state represented by one dump to the state represented by the other dump (Ploski et al. 2007).

The most basic method for managing database changes is the maintenance of a script that includes an ALTER command and its management through a file-based version control system. This script must know the status of its environment and it should be able to handle any conflicts and merge them. Deployment scripts are generated and they include database dependencies. If a single script is used, then this results to many changes to the same objects. If a number of scripts are used, then the order of the scripts plays an important role (Margalit 2014).

Another approach is the use of XML files through Liquibase which is an abstract language used for database refactoring. This language divides the logical from the physical change. At execution time, it converts the XML to a specific RDBMS language to perform the change. Changes are grouped into a changelog and they can be in a single XML file or many XML files referred by a major XML file which includes the order of the changes. Liquibase can also know which changelog(s) have already been deployed or which changelog(s) were not yet deployed and should be deployed (Margalit 2014).

Corwin et al. (2007) describe how they used column-storage architecture in order to store biomedical data. Both column and row storage architectures can use traditional query languages (eg. SQL) but the use of column-storage architecture allows the more precise finding of data since it avoids the scanning of a whole database. This approach is very good in the storage of heterogeneous data, such as biomedical data (eg. protein expression data, genomic sequences). Biomedical databases are characterised by schema changes, the use of sparse and heterogeneous data and the large use of metadata. Examples of such databases are the TrialDB which stores information related to clinical patient data and the SenseLab which stores information related to properties of neurons. The use of a column-storage architecture (also known as dynamic tables or decomposed storage) is the combined use of vertical storage along with the maintenance of clarity and maintainability of querying a horizontal schema. Dynamic tables can be integrated to horizontally stored tables in queries.

16.4   Database Efficiency as Data Change

Data evolve and the databases as they are the major storage element in an Information System, they need to evolve too. A number of mechanisms and techniques characterise modern databases that allow databases to be efficient in the dynamic changes of data.

16.4.1   Indexing Strategies

A number of strategies associated with the use of indexes result to database efficiency. Indexes are different depending on the applications that use them. Different applications may frequently search for a particular attribute or they may require data in a particular format.

Another strategy to improve database efficiency is the use of indexes in predicates in JOIN, WHERE, ORDER BY and GROUP BY clauses. Without the use of proper indexing, SQL queries can cause full table scans which can impact on performance. It is recommended that all predicate columns. The exception occurs when column data have very low cardinality (IBM Knowledge Center 2020).

An indexing strategy is the design of an access method to a specific set of attributes. It facilitates information retrieval and it shows how data are organised in a storage system. Examples of indexing strategies are the Hidden Markov Model (HMM), the Latent Semantic Indexing, the Tree-based indexing strategies and the Hash Indexing Strategy. The Hidden Markov Model (HMM) includes a number of states which are connected by transitions where future states depend only on the present state and they are independent of historical states. The HMM uses pattern recognition and data associations. In the HMM indexing approach, there is categorization of data and characteristics in which a query depends on. Latent Semantic Indexing (LSI) is an indexing strategy that identifies patterns between the terms in an unstructured data set. It is based on the use of a mathematical approach called Singular Value Decomposition (SVD) for pattern or relationship identification. The main feature of LSI is the ability to extract semantic content of data sets and to establish relationships among terms with similar context. In the Tree indexing strategy, the retrieval of data is realised in sorted manner. This satisfies the nearest neighbour queries. The Tree indexing strategies are outperformed by simple sequential scans (Adamu et al. 2016).

16.4.2   Hardware Upgrade

GPUs are useful in realising DBMS operations that are data intensive. Databases that use GPUs are GPUDB and CoGaDB (Gurumurthy et al. 2018). The processing cores of GPUs are valuable for the realisation of complex analytics operations which traditional databases struggle to perform. Aggregations, sorts and sorting operations can be performed effectively using GPUs (kinetica 2020).

Most GPU databases are characterised by open designs and this allows them to execute a variety of data analytics operations. Examples of open design elements are the use of connectors in order to simplify the integration with a number of open-source frameworks, such as Accumuo, H2O, Kafka, Hadoop, NiFi and Spark and the use of drivers for Open Database Connectivity (ODBC) and Java Database Connectivity (JDBC). Also, the use of Application Programming Interfaces (APIs) allow the integration with a number of programming languages, such as C++, SQL, Java and JavaScript. GPU databases use in-memory data structures and processing optimization in order to take full advantage of the parallelization that is available in modern GPUs for the purpose of realising vector and matrix operations necessary for Machine-Learning operations (Biery and Mizell 2017).

16.4.3   Handling Data Variety

There is diversity in terms of data sources and data types. There is also an increment in data variety due to the emerging of new applications, especially related to social network analysis. Data variety indicates the richness of data representation and semantics. A number of new technologies have enabled the collection of a variety of data from a huge set of different sources. Data variety plays a major role in data analytics. An example of data diversity is the structural diversity. Data are categorized into structured, semi-structured and un-structured. Examples of structured data are those data that are stored in Enterprise Resource Planning (ERP) and Customer Relationship Management (CRM) systems. Relationships among data are simple while the management of these data is simple. Unstructured data are data that lack any structure. Examples of unstructured data are data streams and website log files. Data that are not structured or unstructured are semi-structured. The are also different types of Big Data, such as machine-generated, human-generated and process-mediated data. Process-mediated data include transactions as well as metadata that characterise these transactions. Human-generated data are data produced through online human interactions while machine-generated data are data collected by sensors (Abawajy 2014).

16.4.4   Data Transformations

Data Transformation is related to the process of converting data from one format to another. It is an important element of data wrangling and data integration. Data transformation is of two kinds: syntactic data transformation and semantic data transformation. Semantic transformations involve understanding the meaning of the data while syntactic transformation is related to the changing of data formats (Chu 2018).

Oracle defines data transformation as the conversion of data from a source data format into a destination data format. Data transformations are based on two steps: data mapping and code generation. A mapping describes the sequence of operations that are needed in order to extract data from sources, transform these data and load these data into one or more targets (Oracle Help Center 2014).

Examples of data transformations are cross-tabulation and data set flattening. In this case, aggregation and pivoting are combined in order for the data set to be developed. These transformations transform the input table to a "flattened" data set while several values are cross-tabulated (Ordonez 2011). There are certain interesting points in relation to data transformations. These are the points of adaptive data loading, storage and indexing. Adaptive data loading refers to the fact that database users can query the database without all the data been stored in it or even if some parts of these data are left unloaded (Idreos et al. 2015).

16.4.5   Normalization and ER Modelling

Normalization is the process of structural re-organising a database so that there are not any redundant data in it. In other words, it is process of providing logic to the data that will be included in the database. The purpose of Normalization is to resolve database anomalies caused by insertions, deletions or updates of data.

The use of keys is very important especially in relational databases. Keys ensure the integrity of the database and they may change as the data requirements change. The use of keys specify the types of relationships among entities. As entities change, so do keys. As new entities are added to the database, new keys have to be formed. Keys maintain the integrity of the database and they ensure that security and filtering of data is achieved.

16.4.6   Scalability

Relational databases are located on one server which can be scaled by adding more hardware elements, such as memory, processors and storage elements. If there are many relational databases that are located on a number of different servers, then replication is used to maintain database synchronization. Also, a new family of scalable DBMS has been developed. These systems scale linearly with the addition of additional servers. This is because of data partitioning. There is also the method of distributed hash tables in which keys and value are hashed into buckets. Furthermore, horizontal data distribution enables the division of computation into concurrent tasks (Pokorny 2013).

Large relational database installations deal with large amounts of data. Such databases require much processing power and much memory. Solid-State Drive (SSD) data storage technology can provide the capability of processing large amount of information. SSD storages are characterised by larger speeds in random read/writes and the improvement of a shared disk database architecture that is beneficial for cloud databases (Pokorny 2013).

Shared-disk database architecture considers the database as a single unit that is stored on a Storage Area Network (SAN) or a Network Attached Storage (NAS) and this unit is shared by all the nodes of the network. Such architecture requires few low-cost servers. It is easy to virtualize these servers and a middleware is not required to route data requests to specific servers as each node has access to the data.

16.5   Database Integration Capabilities

Databases can be integrated to different environments and technologies. Examples of such integration are provided below.

16.5.1   Heterogeneous Database Systems

The heterogeneous system is useful as it allows the users to handle a database without the concern of data distribution. Also, a heterogeneous system allows the incorporation of an existing database in a DDBMS without any changes of the database and of the applications (Ferrier and Stangret 1982).

Heterogeneity is a major characteristic of Big Data. These data may be interconnected and/or interrelated and they may be characterised by different types and forms. Heterogeneity also refers to the acquisition and analysis of structured, semi-structured and even unstructured data at the same time. Big Data relates large-volume and complex datasets with a number of independent data sources. Non-relational databases such as NoSQL are used to store unstructured data and they aim to developing data model flexibility (Wang 2017).

Semantic Web technologies can be used for the expressive representation of heterogeneous data sources. Appropriate ontological models are used in order to model data streams. These models capture the relevant domain knowledge. The ontologies acquire physical entities and the interrelationships among them. They also capture associated data, metadata and derived data. Once all there is identification of all the entities, the next step is the development of linkages among records of data streams. Different types of data may be recorded for the same asset in a number of different databases. Different data from multiple sources are integrated into a central repository from which any useful knowledge can be retrieved (Sheng et al. 2017).

16.5.2   Integration of Databases with Other Technologies

Database integration is related to the aggregation of data from a range of different sources and their sharing across a range of users of an organization. Database integration offers a number of benefits, such as reliability in the handling of business data, the management of business intelligence in such a way so that any faults in the system are identified, simplified security and more flexible compliance to standards such GDPR and HIPPA. There are specific Apache tools that are used for database integration. These are the Apache Hadoop which allows distributed processing, therefore allowing huge numbers of data to be distributed over a really large number of physical or virtual servers. Apache Hadoop is characterised by linear scalability while parallel nodes allow the resolution of any possible failovers. Another tool is Apache Cassandra which removes the constraints imposed by traditional relational databases and thus allowing the storage of heterogeneous data. In this case, the integration between different data formats, such as images and multimedia is more possible (Talend 2020).

16.5.3   Transparency of Database Systems

Complexity is an important issue especially in a distributed database management system (DDBMS). The complexity should be hidden from the users that use the database system. This is called transparency (Kumar et al. 2013).

16.5.4   Database Virtualization

Database-based application projects must combine database release versions with corresponding datasets. The Delphix Engine includes a technology element, called the DataVisor which provides data synchronization, transactional consistency and continuous versioning. The Delphix Engine can provide synchronization with a number of source applications in near real-time and automatically version all changes. Deplhix uses a time slier in order to deliver a virtual version of a database at any specific time and it can also enable faster testing and error detection. A library of previous versions of the database can be developed and quickly roll back to a previous version during data conversion and mapping (Yueh 2013).

There is also the state-based database versioning approach in which developers declare the ideal database state and then they use tools to generate SQL scripts based on a comparison between the ideal database state and a target database. An alternative technique for database versioning is the migration-based approach in which any changes to the database schema and to the associated SQL code are traced from development to production (Liquibase 2021).

There are a number of database versioning tools, such as the dbForge Source Control, the ApexSQL Source Control, Datical and the DB Ghost Change Manager (DBMS Tools 2020).

16.6 Examples of Dynamic Applications of Databases

There are a number of dynamic applications of databases. Examples of such applications are provided below.

16.6.1 Social Media Applications

Social media data influence the design of the database and each social media platform has very specific rules on how data should be stored. The types of databases that are used in social media are flat files which are two-dimensional databases that include data which have no structured relationship, relational databases which include a set of tables and NoSQL databases that are distributed, non-relational, open-source and horizontally scalable (Batrinca and Treleaven 2015).

Middleton et al. (2014) present a social media crisis mapping platform which is divided into a set of offline and real-time services. The offline services provide a geospatial database and they estimate baseline statistics for a historical period. The real-time element crawl live Twitter tweets, they identify mentions of known locations and they display them on a crisis map. The offline phase uses a set of geospatial data mining tools in order to download geospatial data. A number of geospatial data extraction tools are used during the offline phase in order for geospatial data to be mined. OpenStreetMap is used to access data related to streets and GooglePlaces API is used to access volunteered geographic information (VGI) related to local features. Global gazetteers such as Geonames and GEOnet Names are used to get local region names. The geospatial database is stored in a MySQL database together with OpenGIS shape data for further map visualization (Middleton et al. 2014).

16.6.2   Real-Time Sensor Databases

CrateDB is a 'NewSQL' database that surpasses time-series restrictions of traditional SQL databases. It uses a distributed SQL engine that is built on a dynamic NoSQL foundation. CrateDB can scale horizontally in order for millions of data inserts per second to be handled. CrateDB is characterised by distributed processing and the use of in-memory column indexes that allow the processing of time-series in a minimal amount of time (eg. milliseconds) even when there is concurrent insertion of data. CrateDB uses NoSQL storage and indexing technology and this allows the evolvement of the data model without any recoding. It also allows geospatial, IP address and user-defined functions for analytics within the database (Crate.io 2020).

16.6.3   Engineering Databases

WEB-CONS is a web-based knowledge management and communication system that includes both knowledge at project and corporate level. The development of the system is based on database technology and it allows the storage of huge amount of data. WEB-CONS allows the classification of whole document information. The database also allows the management of the knowledge through the assignment of time, title and revision to the documents and their placement to specific locations. The elements of the system include project progress, equipment management, inventory management and corporate information of the company. WEB-CONS is a web-based database system which allows organizations to make better decisions through the use of codified knowledge of past experiences (Ozorhon et al. 2014).

16.7   Summary

This chapter has focused on database adaptiveness, the factors that affect it and the mechanisms offered by databases in achieving it. Database efficiency has also been examined and specific mechanisms that affect database efficiency are described. Specific dynamic applications of databases are mentioned.

16.8   Review Questions

The answers to these questions can be found in the text of this chapter.

- Describe the significance of Normalization.
- Describe the role of indexing strategies in achieving database efficiency.
- Describe the term 'scalability' in databases.

16.9   Group Work Research Activities

These activities require you to research beyond the contents of the book and can be tackled individually or as a discussion group.

Explore further the topic of database scalability. Identify the impact of the type and the amount of data on scaling different types of databases.

References

Abawajy J (2014) 'Comprehensive analysis of big data variety landscape', Int J Parallel Emergent Distrib Syst, pp 5–14

Adamu FB, Habbal A, Hassan S, Cottrell RL, White B, Abdullah I (2016) A survey on big data indexing strategies, In: 4th International Conference on Internet Applications, Protocols and Services (NETAPPS2015), Cyberjaya, Malaysia

Batrinca B, Treleaven PC (2015) Social media analytics: a survey of techniques, tools and platforms. AI & Soc 30:89–116

Biery E, Mizell E (2017) Introduction to GPUs for Data Analytics. O'Reilly Media, Inc

Boukhari I, Jean S, Ait-Sadoune I, et al. The role of user requirements in data repository design. Int J Softw Tools Technol Transfer 20, pp 19–34

Brusilovsky P, Christoph P (2003) Adaptive and intelligent web-based educational systems. Int J Artif Intell Educ (IJAIED) 2003(13):159–172

Chu X. (2018) Data Cleaning. In: Sakr S, Zomaya A (eds) Encyclopedia of Big Data Technologies. Springer, Cham

Corwin J, Silberschatz A, Miller PL, Marenco L (2007) Dynamic tables: an architecture for managing evolving, heterogeneous biomedical data in relational database management systems. J Am Med Inform Assoc 14(1):86–93

Crate.io (2020) CrateDB for industrial time series data how CrateDB compares to time series data stores. https://go.cratedb.com/rs/832-QEZ-801/images/CrateDB-vs-Specialized-Time-Series-Databases.pdf Accessed 12 Mar 2020

DBMS Tools (2020) Version control tools. https://dbmstools.com/categories/version-control-tools Accessed 10 Mar 2020

Dennis A, Wixom BH, Roth RM (2012) System analysis & design. 5th edn. John Wiley & Sons

Dick J, Hull E, Jackson K (2017) Requirements engineering. 4th edn. Springer

Ferrier A, Strangret C (1982) Heterogeneity in the distributed database management system Sirius-Delta, In: Proceedings of the Eighth International Conference on Very Large Data Bases, Mexico City, pp 45–53

Gurumurthy B, Drewes T, Broneske D, Saake G, Pionteck T (2018) Adaptive data processing in Heterogeneous hardware systems, Grundlagen von Datenbanken

IBM Knowledge Center (2020) Techniques for improving the performance of SQL queries under workspaces in the Data Service Layer https://www.ibm.com/support/knowledgecenter/en/SSZLC2_7.0.0/com.ibm.commerce.admin.doc/refs/rsdperformanceworkspaces_dup.htm Accessed 14 Oct 2020

Idreos S, Papaemmanouil O, Chaudhuri S (2015) Overview of data exploration techniques SIGMOD '15. In: Proceedings of the 2015 ACM SIGMOD International Conference on Management of Data, pp 277–281

Kinetica (2020) Extreme analytics made possible on a GPU database. https://www.kinetica.com/gpu-database/ Accessed 11 Dec 2019

Kumar N, Bilgaiyan S, Sagnika S (2013) An overview of transparency in Homogeneous distributed database system, Int J Adv Res Comput Eng Technol 2:2278–1323

Kumar A (2020) Adaptive query processing in SQL server, Database Journal. https://www.databasejournal.com/features/mssql/adaptive-query-processing-in-sql-server.html Accessed 22 July 2019

Liquibase (2021) 'Intro to application release automation'. [online]. Available at: https://www.liquibase.com/resources/guides/database-version-control. Accessed 10 April 2021

Margalit U (2014) The definitive guide to database version control, InfoQ https://www.infoq.com/articles/Database-Version-Control/ Accessed 22 Aug 2020

Microsoft Azure (2020a) Automatic tuning in Azure SQL Database, https://docs.microsoft.com/en-us/azure/sql-database/sql-database-automatic-tuning Accessed 12 Dec 2019

Microsoft Azure (2020b) What is the Azure SQL Database service? https://docs.microsoft.com/en-us/azure/sql-database/sql-database-technical-overview Accessed 7 Dec 2019

Middleton S, Middleton L, Modafferi S (2014) Real-time crisis mapping of natural disasters using social media. Intelligent Systems, IEEE. 29:9–17

Oracle Help Center (2014) 6 Data Transformation. https://docs.oracle.com/cd/E11882_01/owb.112/e10581/datatransform.htm#WBCON4591. Accessed 15 Mar 2019

Ordonez C (2011) Data set preprocessing and transformation in a database system, Intell Data Anal (IDA Journal), 15(4)

Ozorhon B, Karatas CG, Demirkesen S (2014) A web-based database system for managing construction project knowledge. Procedia-Social Behav Sci 119:377–386

Ploski J, Hasselbring W, Rehwinkel J, Schwierz S (2007) Introducing version control to databasecentric applications in a small enterprise, IEEE Software, pp 38–44

Pokorny J (2013) NoSQL databases: a step to database scalability in a web environment, In: iiWAS Proceedings of the 13th International Conference on Information Integration and Web-based Applications and Services, pp 278–283

Pol PS, Subramanian SS, Loganathan RT, Pokkunuri RKS, Duddi G, Vig A, Mohiuddin S, Narasimhan S (2017) Distributed stream-based database triggers. US 2017/0093755A1

Sheng QZ, Qin Y, Yao L, Benatallah B (2017) Managing the web of things—linking the real world to the web. Morgan Kaufmann

Soflano M, Connolly TM, Hainey T (2015) An application of adaptive games-based learning based on learning style to teach SQL. Comput Educ 86:192–211

Talend (2020) What is database integration?. https://www.talend.com/resources/what-is-database-integration/. Accessed 29 Dec 2019

Yueh J (2013) How database virtualization works. https://www.infoworld.com/article/2607260/how-database-virtualization-works.html?page=2. Accessed 20 Dec 2019

Wang L (2017) Heterogeneous data and big data analytics. Autom Control Inf Sci 3(1):8–15

Part IV
Advanced Applications of Specialised Databases

Blockchain

17

What the reader will learn:

- What Blockchain is
- About the architecture of Blockchain
- About Blockchain Protocols
- About issues related to Blockchain Performance, Security and Data Analytics
- About the applications of Blockchain in different fields

17.1 Introduction

Blockchain is a digital ledger of economic transactions that is constantly updated by an unlimited number of users and it is considered impossible to corrupt. It is a list of continuous records in blocks. Blocks hold sets of transactions and they connected to the previous blocks. A block is also time stamped (Carlozo 2017). Blocks are chained with each other through hash identifiers. The complete blockchain is copied in a number of places in the network and this makes blockchain a distributed database (Bozic et al. 2016).

Such a database has a network of users, each of which store their own copy of the data. Blockchain technology is thus characterised a distributed ledger technology (DLT). Basic elements of DLT include a digital ledger, a consensus mechanism which is used to confirm transactions and a network of node operators (Lewis et al. 2017).

There is quick validation of transactions and it is nearly impossible to transactions once they are included in the blockchain. There is interaction of each user with the blockchain with a generated address that does not reveal the true identity of the user (Zheng et al. 2017).

© Springer Nature Switzerland AG 2021

K. Domdouzis et al., *Concise Guide to Databases*, Undergraduate Topics in Computer Science, https://doi.org/10.1007/978-3-030-42224-0_17

Blockchain is characterised by a number of principles. On the blockchain, there is not a single party that controls the data. Each party can verify the records of its transaction's partners directly without any intervention from an intermediary. The communication between peers happens directly instead through a central node. Every transaction and its associated value can be seen by anyone who has access to the system. Each blockchain node uses an alphanumeric address that is used for its identification. There is anonymity between users while transactions happen between blockchain addresses. Once a transaction is entered in the database, there cannot be any alteration of records because these records are linked to previous records that came before them. Blockchain transactions are checked by computational logic and algorithms and these algorithms are responsible for setting transactions between nodes that are chronologically ordered and available to all the users on the network.

Blockchain technology is characterised by a number of advantages and disadvantages. One of the most important advantages is data integrity. This is achieved through the use of public key cryptography and the use of hashing in block construction. Also, blockchain is characterised by availability as the geographical distribution of nodes allows blockchain to be considered superior than centralized databases. Another feature that characterises the blockchain technology is fault-tolerance. In blockchain, many nodes have a copy of the ledger. In the case of network failure, there is updating of transactions thanks to the distributed nature of the blockchain system (Bozic et al. 2016).

A block includes the block header and the block body. The block header includes the block version which shows the block validation rules that need to be followed, the parent block hash which is a 256-bit hash value that points to the previous block, and the merkle tree root hash which is the hash value of all the transactions in the block. The block has also a timestamp and the 'nBits' which is the current hashing target in a compact format. The block also has a 4-byte field which starts with a 0 and increases for every hash calculation. The block body includes a transaction counter and transactions. The maximum number of transactions that a block can contain depends on the block size and the size of each transaction (Zheng et al. 2018).

Blockchain technology has attracted interest from a large variety of stakeholders related to healthcare, real estate and financial organisations. Blockchains are distributed and fault-tolerant databases that every participant in the network can share. Blockchain technology is designed to function in a contested environment in which adversaries are willing to compromise. The information that is exchanged is resilient to any manipulation (Liang et al. 2017).

17.2 Blockchain Architecture

The blockchain is a distributed database that does not require a central authority and it eliminates the need for third-party verification. The blockchain includes a number of blocks and each block contains a hash of the previous block. This creates a chain of blocks. This chain starts from a genesis block and it continues until it reaches the current block. When two blocks are generated with a difference of few seconds, then forks are created. When this happens, the latest block in the chain is always chosen. The blocks in shorter chains are considered invalid chains and they are often called orphan chains. Blocks include a set of transactions. A transaction is a transfer of values between different entities that are included into the blocks. All the transactions are visible in the blockchain. They are mined into a block by pool or solo miners. The pool miners is a mining approach where multiple devices called miners contribute to the generation of a block. Mining is resource-intensive. Figure 17.1 shows the architecture of a blockchain.

Blockchain technology uses a set of cryptographic mechanisms, such as digital signatures, asymmetric-key cryptography and hash functions. These mechanisms are combined with databases, such as ledgers. Blockchain technology also uses hash functions. In hashing, a cryptographic hash function is implemented to data and it calculates a unique output for an input of any type and size. Even a small change to input data will result to a totally different output (Yaga et al. 2018).

The main characteristics of blockchain technology are decentralisation, persistency, anonymity and auditability. In the blockchain network, a transaction can be realised without the authentication of a central server. In this case, blockchain can reduce the operation and the development cost of the central server. Each transaction is spread across the network and it needs to be confirmed and recorded in blocks distributed in the whole network. Each block is validated by other nodes and any possibility of tampering is detected. Each user can interact with the blockchain network through the use of a generated address. In this case, a user can generate numerous addresses in order to avoid identity exposure. This mechanism maintains certain privacy on the transactions that are realised on the blockchain. Since there is validation of each transaction and recording of it with a timestamp, users can verify and trace previous records through the access of any node in the distributed network. In Bitcoin blockchain, there is tracing of each transaction to previous transactions. This improves data transparency in the blockchain (Zheng et al. 2018).

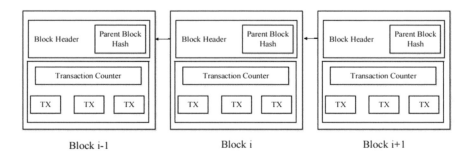

Fig. 17.1 Architecture of a Blockchain (Novo 2018)

17.3   Blockchain Protocols

In blockchain, in order to reach a consensus among the untrustworthy nodes is a transformation of the Byzantine Generals problem. In this problem, a group of generals who command part of the Byzantine army circle the city. A number of generals prefer to attack while others prefer to retreat. The attack would fail if only part of the generals attack the city. In this case, an agreement has to be made whether an attack should happen or not. To reach an agreement in a distributed network such as blockchain is a challenge. There are some protocols that are required in order to make sure that there is consistency of ledgers in different nodes (Zheng et al. 2017).

Proof of Work (PoW) is a consensus strategy used in the Bitcoin network. In such a network, someone has to be selected to record any transactions. This selection is random and it is vulnerable to attacks. If a node wants to publish a block of transactions, much work has to be done in order to ensure that the node will not attack the network. This means computer calculations and especially each node of the network should calculate the hash value of the block header. When a node reaches the target value, it broadcasts the block to other nodes and there must be a mutual confirmation of the correctness of the hash value by the other nodes. When there is validation of the block, then this block is appended to the other nodes' blockchains. Nodes that calculate the hash values are called miners (Zheng et al. 2017).

Proof of Stake (PoS) is an alternative to PoW and its main focus is energy management and saving. In PoS, the ownership of a specific amount of a currency has to be proved by miners. The selection of a miner based on their stake is characterised by unfairness as the person who has the biggest stake is also dominant in the blockchain. PoS also focus on the saving of energy in comparison to PoW. In PoS, miners have to prove the ownership of the amount of currency. Again, the single richest person will be dominant in the network. There has been propositions for different solutions based on the combination of the stake size (Zheng et al. 2017). Blackcoin (Vasin 2014) employs randomization in order to predict the next generator. It uses a formula that focuses on the lowest hash value in combination with the size of the stake. In Peercoin (King and Nadal 2012), older and larger sets of coins are more likely to mine the next block. PoS saves more energy than PoW, however because the mining cost is close to zero, this might result to attacks. Many blockchains adopt PoW at the beginning and transform to PoS gradually. For instance, Ethereum is planning to move from Ethash (a kind of PoW) (Wood 2014) to Casper (a kind of PoS) (Zamfir 2015).

The design of PoS algorithms is focused on overcoming the disadvantages of PoW algorithms in relation to the consumption of electricity in mining operations. There is replacement of the mining operation with a different approach that involves a user's ownership of virtual currency in the blockchain system. Naïve PoS algorithms are characterised from a problem called Nothing-at-Stake. The

Nothing-at-Stake problem needs to be handled so that the implementation of PoS is efficient (Baliga 2017).

17.4 Blockchain Performance

Ethereum and Hyperledger Fabric are two popular Blockchain platforms. Ethereum is an open-source, public blockchain-based distributed platform which offers smart contract functionality. Specifically, it allows users to get Ether which is a digital currency. Hyperledger Fabric applies private blockchain technology that is used as a basis for the development of blockchain applications for a number of industries. The architecture of Hyperledger Fabris is modular and that means that the consensus and membership services are plug-and-play. It uses container technology (docker) in order to enable smart contracts called 'chaincode' that include the application logic of the system. Pongnumkul et al. (2017) have compared Ethereum and Hyperledger Fabric in terms of execution time, average throughput and latency and throughput of one trial of a large workload. There are differences in the time of execution of a number of transactions. The execution times increase as the number of transactions increases. The execution time in Hyperledger is lower than Ethereum's in all datasets. The gap in the execution times between the two blockchain platforms grows as the number of transactions grow. Also, at low number of transactions, the latency of Ethereum is double that of Hyperledger's. As the number of transactions in the dataset grows, the latency of the Ethereum becomes worse than that of Hyperledger's. Hyperledger has higher throughput than Ethereum in all of the data sets (Pongnumkul et al. 2017).

Performance in blockchain depends on the latency, bandwidth and distribution size of the consensus nodes. Blockchain technology's performance when used in the medical field, may degrade because of the large amount of healthcare data and clinical datasets. These datasets may include historical information and data from multiple institutions. Each time a new transaction is realised, then there is accumulation of information and this can result to performance degradation (HIMSS 2020).

Throughput is another factor that affects the performance of a blockchain network. Throughput is expressed in terms of blocks that appended to the blockchain every second. This action depends on the implemented consensus algorithm. This algorithm specifies how the communication between nodes is realised in order for the validity of the appended transaction to be ensured. The factors that impact throughput will be the design, size of data and scope of the blockchain (HIMSS 2020).

In comparison to centralized solutions, blockchain networks will always be slower. The reason for this is the nature of blockchain. Specific characteristics of this nature that affect the blockchain performance are the signature verification, the consensus mechanism and redundancy. In every transaction, there must be verification of every transaction signature and this verification is computationally complex. In contrast, in centralized databases, this verification is not required. A blockchain has to ensure that consensus is reached by nodes. This requires a huge amount of computational power, however this long time which is needed to reach consensus is necessary in order to have a highly secure system. A centralized database does not need to reach this consensus as it is owned and controlled by the same organization. In blockchain networks, transactions must be processed independently by every node in contrast to centralized databases which process transactions once (Scherer 2017).

17.5 Blockchain Security

Blockchain is a decentralized ledger and as a result, there is not any weak point which potential hackers can surpass. If there was any intention of overriding such a point, a huge amount of power would be needed in order to alter every node simultaneously. This becomes extremely difficult especially if nodes are distributed anywhere in the world. Blockchain uses advanced public key cryptography in order to secure the data included in it and this type of cryptography relies on users that use two cryptographically-matched keys. If a user wants to send a message to another user, then they can do it by using a user's public key. The file can then be opened by the user's correlating key. There is low risk of data tampering or data interception and this makes blockchain an efficient risk management system (Salmon and Myers 2019).

The members of the blockchain network are its nodes. A node can create and propose a transaction, validate it and undertake mining in order to support data integrity. When nodes create transactions, they are signed by nodes using their private keys and in order to ensure that they are the true owners of these transactions. In a blockchain, a P2P is needed as well as consensus algorithms in order to ensure that replication is achieved (Minioli and Ochiogrosso 2018).

The first secure chain of blocks was developed using cryptography in 1991 (Haber and Scott Stornetta 1991). In 1993, there was a proposal to improve the efficiency of the cryptographic chain of blockchains (Bayer et al. 1993) through the incorporation of Merkle trees and multiple documents into one block. The construction of the blockchain is based on a number of security attributes such as pseudoanonymity and resistance to a Distributed Denial-of-Service (DDoS) attack. In Bitcoin blockchain, there are three important capabilities that are supported and these are the hash-chained storage, the digital signature, and the consensus that is used for the addition of new blocks to the globally-chained storage. These security mechanisms allow any modification of any transaction-related data in a block after the successful commitment of the block into the blockchain. The hash-chained storage is based on the use of hash pointers and Merkle trees. The hash pointers point to the location in which the data are stored. These pointers can be used to check whether there is any intervention to the data. The hash pointer points to the predecessor block and each block shows the address where its data are stored.

Tampering cannot be realised on the chain's head (the genesis block) which is generated once the system has been built. Merkle trees are defined as binary search trees with their tree nodes linked to one another using hash pointers. This data structure has the ability to protect data from tampering through the traversal of hash pointers. In the case, an intruder tries to intervene on the data of a leaf node, then the hash value of its parent node will change and as a result, all the nodes on the path from bottom to top need to change. The tracking of any possible intervention since the hash pointer of the root node does not match with the hash pointer which has been stored. Merkle trees are characterised by the advantage that it can prove effectively the membership of a data node by showing this data node and all its ancestor nodes on its path to the root node. A digital signature is also used in order to establish the validity of a piece of data through the use of a cryptographic algorithm. There are three elements in the digital signature. These are the key generation algorithm, the signing algorithm and the verification algorithm. The key generation algorithm produces two keys, one that is used to sign messages and the other which is made available to the public. The second element (signing algorithm) produces a signature on the input message. The third element is the verification algorithm. This algorithm takes a signature, a message and a public key as inputs and it validates the message's signature using the public key. The blockchain used in Bitcoin adopts the Elliptic Curve Digital Signature Algorithm (ECDSA) as its digital signature for the realisation of transactions (Zhang et al. 2019). The specific algorithm has been proven to provide resiliency against potential forgeries.

A good consensus mechanism in blockchain is based on transactions that are characterised by two important properties: persistence and liveness. Persistence ensures the consistent response from the state in relation to the state of a transaction. Liveness indicates that all nodes or processes agree on a decision or a value. The role of blockchain in the Bitcoin system is the replacement of the centralised database with authoritative access control. When data are put into the global ledger block chain, then it is impossible for the blockchain to change (Zhang et al. 2019).

There are some aspects that make security difficult to implement in a blockchain network. The different consensus algorithms and the different blockchain types as well as the complex nature of cryptographic protocols make difficult for security practitioners to comprehend security weaknesses.

Furthermore, there is evaluation of the large number of Blockchain platforms on their suitability for a specific application. The lack of regulations related to the Blockchain technology has resulted in legal uncertainties. Moreover, there is the widespread belief that a blockchain is secure by design. The cryptographic protocols used by blockchain are characterised by limitations and also, holistic security included not only technology but also people and operations (Deloitte 2019).

The blockchain technology has emerged as a strong solution to address performance and security issues in distributed systems. Blockchain's distributed peer-to-peer ledger capability can benefit cloud computing services which require functions such as auditing and distributed consensus. There are verifications of the transactions that happen on a blockchain network by a set of miners. The use of strong cryptographic methods allows the chaining of blocks of transactions and this in turn allows the immutability of records (Tosh et al. 2017).

Blockchain technology enables secure transfer of data through a number of cryptographically-secure keys across a distributed system. Keyless signatures separate the processes used for the identification of signer and integrity protection from the processes that are responsible for the maintenance of the secrecy of the keys (Buldas et al. 2013). An example of keyless cryptography is the one-way-collision-free hash functions. Keyless signature processes include hashing, aggregation and publication. A Keyless Signature Infrastructure (KSI) is required for the realization of keyless signatures and this infrastructure includes an hierarchy of aggregation servers which generate global hash trees (Tosh et al. 2017).

17.6 Legal Issues in Blockchain

Certain copyrightable objects such as music and photos are characterised by lack of transparency. Information about different copyright owners are stored in a variety of databases that are owned by publishers or record companies. This unclear legal status creates costs for users of digital content who sometimes have events cancelled from using specific copyrighted work. Blockchain can increase visibility and data availability in relation to copyright ownership. Such information can be provided by means of the so-called 'Trusted Timestamping'. This is a process of securely keeping track of the creation and modification time of a document. Timestamping is an electronic trust service which is a key enabler for secure cross-border electronic transactions. Blockchain can be useful in the definition of the presumption of authorship and the resolution of any disputes (Savelyev 2018).

Blockchain can be used for the development of 'smart contracts'. These assets can be used for the automatic transfer of assets once specific conditions are satisfied. A system like this can resolve disputes quickly and efficiently. This would possibly result also to the end of escrow accounts (Altman 2018).

As blockchain technology is a very new technology, the US Chair of the Federal Reserve mentioned that there should not be any development of regulatory rules so that innovation is ensured. The Chinese government states that regulatory rules should be formulated especially for the financial blockchain technology. The UK originated the regulatory sandbox which intends to provide flexibility in innovations. Using the sandbox, FinTech companies can apply rapidly innovative operations. Also, Australia and Singapore have managed the establishment of FinTech regulatory sandboxes. Even though China has proposed ideas for flexible regulation, these ideas have not been formally standardised. The development of these ideas should be accelerated so that a controlled testing environment for the growth of blockchain technology is created. Standards are also required in order for the security of blockchain technology to be researched. Standards Australia has submitted a request to the International Organization for Standardization in order for the development of global standards for blockchain technology to progress. The R3 blockchain consortium has explored the development of industry standards for interbank applications. In China, the Interbank Market Technology Standards Workgroup (established in 2016) conducts research on interbank market blockchain technology and regulations (Guo and Liang 2016).

17.7   Blockchain Data Analytics

Blockchains can be classified to unspent transaction output (UTXO)-based (e.g. Bitcoin) and account-based (e.g. Ethereum). In both types of blockchain, a finite number of transactions is included in each data block, however the transactions are characterised by different characteristics. In UTXO blockchains, each data block includes a financial transaction which is responsible for the encoding of a transfer of coins between multiple parties. Specifically, each transaction consumes (spends some coins from) some inputs and creates (directs coins to) new outputs. In UTXO, the coin supply is connected to a block creation. A certain amount of coins are created and given to the block miner as a block reward. In account-based blockchains, a transaction has exactly one input and one output address. A single address is used to receive and send coins numerous times. There are three rules that shape the data on UTXO transactions. This is the source rule in which there is merging of input coins from a number of transactions. In this case, the merged coins are spent in a single transaction. There is also the mapping rule in which each coin payment must show proof of funds through the referencing of previous outputs. The third rule is the balance rule in which coins received from one transaction must all be spent in a single transaction (Dixon et al. 2018).

Blockchain data analysis can be summarised into seven aspects: entity identification, privacy risk analysis, network portrait, network visualization, transaction pattern recognition, market effect analysis, illegal behaviour detection and analysis. In Bitcoin transactions, there is anonymity of users. A user can participate in a number of transactions simultaneously. The problem is whether users can be identified through transaction records or which addresses belong to the same user. It is therefore not possible to confirm identification of a user, however it is possible to identify entities. Entities are users or organizations and a user or organization can control a number of entities simultaneously. Heuristic methods can be used in the identification of entities and these methods can be divided into common input method and change address method (Yang et al. 2019).

Machine learning and AI algorithms are executed within smart contracts in Algorithmia [29], Neureal [30], and TraneAI [25]. In Algorithmia [29], there is submission of a data set and a fee for anyone who can develop a model which will be characterised by the highest accuracy on the data set. Models submitted by users are tested through the use of a smart contract and there is release of the fee to the winning model. Neureal [30] provides a platform for realising AI predictions on live data.

Predictive models can be developed through the use of historic data that are held in a Blockchain. An example involves supply chain analytics based on data collected by the IBM Blockchain Platform and the use of a Machine Learning model that predicts shipping delays (Dillenberger et al. 2019). Through the IBM's data science tool IBM Watson Studio, essential Data Science elements are achieved [34].

17.8 Blockchain Applications in Banking

Several components of blockchain such as cryptographic hashes, distributed databases and the consensus mechanism can be combined and create a new form of data sharing and asset transfer which is capable of eliminating intermediaries and central third parties (Accenture 2017). A trading platform can be set-up by a bank based on blockchain technology. The specific technology offers a new way to exchange assets without the need of centralised trusts or intermediaries and without the risk of increased spending. When there is creation of a high-value item, a digital token is issued by a trusted central authority which is used for the authentication of the item's origin. Every time the item is bought and sold, the digital token is moved in parallel so that a real-world chain of ownership is created and mirrored by the blockchain history of that digital token. The digital token acts a virtual 'certificate of authenticity' which is harder to steal or forge than a piece of paper. The final recipient of the token will have to verify the chain of custody all the way to point of creation (Shumsky 2019). Blockchain technology provides the benefit of distributed and verifiable trust Since the technology is decentralised, it is less prone to this type of fraud. Through the use of blockchain, there can be complete transparency which enables real-time fraud analysis and prevention. This is because there is real-time analysis and verification of all the information related to blockchain transactions. The blockchain ledger can provide a historical record of all the documents shared and the compliance activities realised for each banking customer.

17.9 Blockchain Applications in Healthcare

Guardtime is a Netherland-based data security firm which together the Estonian government has developed a blockchain-based framework in order to validate patient identities. All citizens are issued a smartcard which is used for the linkage of their EHR (Electronic Health Record) data with their blockchain-based identity.

Any update in the EHR is assigned a hash and it is registered in the blockchain. In this case, the data within the EHR cannot be modified. These data also use an immutable audit trail that can archive different states of information from existing healthcare databases. Any update in the healthcare database is given a time stamp and it is signed in a block. Such a system provides advantages in the safety against any modifications of healthcare records (Hung et al. 2017).

17.10   Blockchain Applications in Education

A number of Universities apply blockchain technology in order to support the management of academic degrees and the evaluation of learning outcomes (Sharples and Domingue 2016; Skiba 2017). A blockchain network can include information about students' achievements and academic certificates as well as skills and learning experience. Sony Global Education uses the blockchain technology in order to develop a global assessment platform for the provision of services for the storage and management of degree information (Hoy 2017). The Massachusetts Institute of Technology (MIT) and the Learning Machine company collaborated in order to develop a digital badge for online learning based on blockchain technology (Skiba 2017).

17.11   Blockchain Applications in the Transportation Industry

Commercial transportation companies face increasing needs as the expectations of their customers have risen. Advanced tracking technology is already used in such companies but the scaling of this technology is characterised by difficulties especially when it comes to authentication. The current systems used for authentication reply on EDIs and APIs and they are subject to misinterpretation and bad manipulation and these actions can have severe consequences in the global supply chain. Increased reliability of tracking information can impact the conservation of the goods that are shipped. This reliability can only be achieved through blockchain. Also, blockchain in partnership with the Internet Of Things (IoT) can be useful for capacity monitoring. IoT sensors can be placed in trucks and other shipping vehicles, detect the space which is acquired in a shipment and send this information to the blockchain so that the exact cost of shipment is determined. Swiss firm SkyCell has created air-freight containers for refrigerated bio-pharmaceuticals that monitor temperature, humidity and location. The firm also uses its cloud platform to record all the documentation (e.g. custom forms) throughout the whole process on a blockchain ledger. Blockchain technology can also help in the identification of the previous performance of a second-hand delivery vehicle which is about to join a feel of vehicles used for shipping and its maintenance history. The technology can also validate the driver records of a new vehicle. The combined use of Internet of Things (IoT) and blockchain can help companies streamline their operations through the implementation of Vehicle-to-Vehicle (V2V) communications which allow for freight vehicles to communicate with each other and improve their safety and fuel efficiency. Finally, shippers can post timestamped loads that are recorded and verified by the decentralized network. In this case, there cannot be any duplication of data related to a specific load. This eliminates the need for a middleman who would act as a broker because the blockchain can authenticate load data and prevent any duplication (Winnesota Regional Transportation 2020).

17.12   Blockchain Applications in Human Resources

Blockchain could be used in order for a comprehensive record of education, training and workplace performance is maintained. Potential employers can have access to a 'value' passport in which individuals could turn their skills and experience into a genuine value in the job market. The application of analytics to data would allow companies to identify better matches of individuals to specific roles. In this case, small and medium-sized enterprises (SMEs) may benefit as the cost of finding the right people for the right posts is extremely difficult (pwc 2020).

Blockchain can also be used for background and employment-history checks through the acquisition of virtual credentials which point to the record of their work history. On a blockchain, there is encryption of records and this important for medical conditions or performance history. There is sharing of records with participants who have been given the necessary authorization. Smart contracts can be used to release payments once workers have completed tasks. In addition, Human Resources can use blockchain in order to make sure that employees have control over their own data. In other words, employees can delete the encryption key and hide their personal information. Blockchain offers reliability and this allows enhanced auditing. Blockchain no longer requires for payees to depend on intermediaries (Gartner 2020).

17.13   Summary

This chapter examined the very interesting topic of Blockchain. Different definitions were provided together with the examination of specific aspects of the technology, such as protocols, security and legal issues associated with it. There were also descriptions of the applications of blockchain to different industries.

17.14   Review Questions

The answers to these questions can be found in the text of this chapter.

- Describe Blockchain applications in Banking.
- Explain the security in Blockchain.
- Provide different definitions of the Blockchain technology.

17.15 Group Work Research Activities

These activities require you to research beyond the contents of the book and can be tackled individually or as a discussion group.

Explore different applications beyond the limits of the specific chapter in which blockchain technology can be used. What are the limitations in implementing the technology and what are the levels of efficiency offered by blockchain?

References

Accenture (2017) Banking on blockchain. https://www.accenture.com/_acnmedia/Accenture/Conversion-Assets/DotCom/Documents/Global/PDF/Consulting/Accenture-Banking-on-Blockchain.pdf#zoom=50. Accessed 01 Dec 2019

Altman I (2018) How blockchain will transform business and the law. Forbes. https://www.forbes.com/sites/sap/2020/04/09/how-supply-chain-leaders-minimize-risk-and-maximize-opportunities/#3023874f6819. Accessed 11 Dec 2019

Baliga A (2017) Understanding Blockchain Consensus Models. https://www.persistent.com/wp-content/uploads/2018/02/wp-understanding-blockchain-consensus-models.pdf. Accessed 12 July 2019

Bayer D, Haber S, Stornetta WS (1993) Improving the efficiency and reliability of digital time-stamping. In: Capocelli R, De Santis A, Vaccaro U (eds) Sequences II. Springer, New York

Bozic N, Pujolle G, Secci S (2016) A tutorial on blockchain and applications to secure network control-planes.In: 2016 3rd smart cloud networks & systems (SCNS), Dubai, pp 1–8

Buldas A, Kroonmaa A, Laanoja R (2013) Keyless signatures infrastructure: How to build global distributed hash-trees. In: Nordic conference on secure IT systems. Springer, pp 313–320

Carlozo L (2017) What is blockchain? J Account 224(1):29

Deloitte (2019) Blockchain security – protecting the distributed ledger. https://www2.deloitte.com/content/dam/Deloitte/ch/Documents/risk/deloitte-ch-en-risk-blockchain-security.pdf. Accessed 05 Dec 2019

Dillenberger D, Novotny P, Zhang Q, Jayachandran P, Gupta H, Mehta S, Hans S, Chakraborty S, Walli M, Thomas J, Vaculín R, Sarpatwar K, Verma D (2019) Blockchain analytics and artificial intelligence. IBM J Res Dev 63(2/3):5:1–5:14

Dixon M, Gel Y, Kantarcioglu M, Akcora C (2018) Blockchain data analytics. IEEE Intell Syst 20 (1)

Gartner (2020) 5 Ways Blockchain Will Affect HR. https://www.gartner.com/smarterwithgartner/5-ways-blockchain-will-affect-hr/. Accessed 01 Nov 2019

Guo Y, Liang C (2016) Blockchain application and outlook in the banking industry. Financ Innov 2. Article No: 24

Haber S, Scott Stornetta W (1991) How to time-stamp a digital document. J Cryptol 3(2):99–111

HIMSS (2020) Blockchain performance, throughput and scalability. https://www.himss.org/blockchain-performance-throughput-and-scalability. Accessed 10 Nov 2019

Hoy MB (2017) An introduction to the blockchain and its implications for libraries and medicine. Med Ref Serv Q 36(3):273–279

Hung J, Yen NY, Hui L (eds) (2017) Frontier computing theory, technologies and applications (FC 2017). Lecture notes in electrical engineering. Springer. https://www.springer.com/gp/book/9789811073977

King S, Nadal S (2012) PPCoin: Peer-to-peer crypto-currency with proof of-stake. Self-Published Paper, vol 19, 19 August 2012. https://decred.org/research/king2012.pdf. Accessed 04 Nov 2019

Lewis R, McPartland J, Ranjan R (2017) Blockchain and financial market innovation. Econ Perspect 2–12

Liang X, Shetty S, Tosh D, Kamboua C, Kwait K, Njilla L (2017) ProvChain: a blockchain-based data provenance architecture in cloud environment with enhanced privacy and availability.In: CCGrid '17: Proceedings of the 17th IEEE/ACM international symposium on cluster, cloud and grid computing, May 2017, pp 468–477

Minioli D, Ochiogrosso B (2018) Blockchain mechanisms for IoT security. Internet of Things 1–2:1–13

Novo O (2018) Blockchain meets IoT: an architecture for scalable access management in IoT. IEEE Internet of Things J 5(2):1184–1195

Pongnumkul S, Siripanpornchana C, Thajchayapong S (2017) Performance analysis of private blockchain platforms in varying workloads. In: 26th international conference on computer communication and networks (ICCCN), Vancouver, BC, pp 1–6

pwc (2020) How blockchain technology could impact HR and the world of work. https://www.pwc.co.uk/issues/futuretax/how-blockchain-can-impact-hr-and-the-world-of-work.html. Accessed 01 Aug 2019

Salmon J, Myers G (2019) Blockchain and associated legal issues for emerging markets. International Finance Corporation (IFC). https://www.ifc.org/wps/wcm/connect/da7da0dd-2068-4728-b846-7cffcd1fd24a/EMCompass-Note-63-Blockchain-and-Legal-Issues-in-Emerging-Markets.pdf?MOD=AJPERES&CVID=mxocw9F. Accessed 02 Dec 2019

Savelyev A (2018) Copyright in the blockchain era: promises and challenges. Comput Law Secur Rev 34(3):550–561

Scherer M (2017) Performance and scalability of blockchain networks and smart contracts. Degree Project in Computing Science and Engineering, Umea University https://umu.diva-portal.org/smash/get/diva2:1111497/FULLTEXT01.pdf

Sharples M, Domingue J (2016) The blockchain and kudos: a distributed system for educational record, reputation and reward. In: Proceedings of the European conference on technology enhanced learning, Lyon, France, 13–16 September 2016, pp 490–496

Shumsky P (2019) Blockchain use cases for banks in 2020. https://www.finextra.com/blogposting/17857/blockchain-use-cases-for-banks-in-2020. Accessed 06 Dec 2019

Skiba DJ (2017) The potential of blockchain in education and health care. Nurs Educ Perspect 38 (4):220–221

Tosh DK, Shetty S, Liang X, Kamhoua CA, Kwiat KA, Njilla L (2017) Security implications of blockchain cloud with analysis of block withholding attack.In: CCGrid '17: Proceedings of the 17th IEEE/ACM international symposium on cluster, cloud and grid computing, May 2017, pp 458–467

Vasin P (2014) BlackCoin's Proof-of-Stake Protocol v2. https://blackcoin.co/blackcoin-pos-protocol-v2-whitepaper.pdf. Accessed: 04 Nov 2019

Winnesota Regional Transportation (2020) How blockchain is revolutionizing the world of transportation and logistics. https://www.winnesota.com/blockchain. Accessed 06 Nov 2019

Wood G (2014) Ethereum: a secure decentralised generalised transaction ledger. Ethereum Project Yellow Paper

Yaga D, Mell P, Roby N, Scarfone K (2018) Blockchain technology overview. NISTIR 8202. https://nvlpubs.nist.gov/nistpubs/ir/2018/NIST.IR.8202.pdf. Accessed 16 Oct 2019

Yang X, Liu J, Li X (2019) Research and analysis of blockchain data. IOP Conf. Ser.: J. Phys.: Conf. Ser. 1237(2019):022084

Zamfir V (2015) Introducing Casper "the friendly ghost". Ethereum Blog https://blog.ethereum.org/2015/08/01/introducing-casperfriendly-ghost. Accessed 01 Nov 2019

Zhang R, Xue R, Lui L (2019) Security and privacy on blockchain. ACM Comput Surv 1(1). Article 1

Zheng Z, Xie S, Dai H, Chen X, Wang H (2017) An overview of blockchain technology: architecture, consensus, and future trends. In: 2017 IEEE international congress on big data (BigData congress), Honolulu, HI, pp 557–564

Zheng Z, Xie S, Dai H-N, Chen X (2018) Blockchain challenges and opportunities: a survey. Int J Web Grid Serv 14(4):352–375

Biological Databases

18

What the reader will learn:

- The definition of Biological Databases
- The significance of Biological Databases
- About the features of Biological Databases
- About the different types of Biological Databases
- About the different types of data in Biological Databases
- Specific examples of Biological Databases

18.1 Introduction

Bioinformatics is the application of computing in the storage and analysis of vast amount of biological data. These data are available as sequences and protein and nucleic acid structures. Sequences are represented as single dimensions while a structure includes three-dimensional data of sequences. A biological database organises its data in such a way so that they can be easily accessed and analysed. Biological databases can be classified into sequence and structure databases. Sequence databases are applied to both protein and nucleic acid sequences while protein databases are applied only to proteins. The first database was developed after the insulin protein sequence was made available back in 1956. Insulin was the first protein to be sequenced. During the sixties, the first nucleic acid sequence of Yeast tRNA was developed. There was development of three-dimensional structures of proteins and the Protein Data Bank was established with only 10 entries. This database has evolved to a large database with over 10000 entries. In 1986, the SWISS-PROT protein sequence database was developed and it has about 70000 protein sequences that cover more than 5000 model organisms (Babu 1997).

© Springer Nature Switzerland AG 2021
K. Domdouzis et al., *Concise Guide to Databases*, Undergraduate Topics in Computer Science, https://doi.org/10.1007/978-3-030-42224-0_18

Databases are significant for metabolomics. There are different types of databases and they can satisfy different purposes for metabolomics (Manach 2016). The complexity of biological systems requires the use of a variety of experimental methods in order for cellular processes at atomic scale to be examined. Biological databases were developed as part of the technologies that were used for the analysis of the nucleic acid sequences of genes. The application of high-throughput sequencing in biology and medicine for analysis of genomes, transcriptomes, epigenomes and microbiomes has resulted to the generation of a huge volume of sequence data. A significant amount of research on Bioinformatics is based on the use of biological databases. Examples of this research have been published to leading international journals such as PLoS, BMC and NPG series publications. Some of these databases are highly accessed as shown by the number of citations. The capabilities of these databases expand further beyond the fields of Medicine and Biology. For example, the India-centric databases on Mycobacterium tuberculosis can have practical implementations in Agriculture. Many of these biological databases have also contributed in the development of novel data mining methods (Yadav and Mohanty 2017).

Relational database concepts and information retrieval concepts are significant for the comprehension of biological databases. The design, development and management of biological databases are a core element of Bioinformatics (Bourne 2005). The contents of data include gene sequences, attributes and ontology classifications and tabular data. These are often described as semi-structured data and they can be represented as tables and XML structures (Riad et al. 2009; Henneges et al. 2009). The use of database accession numbers allows cross-referencing among databases (Karthick and Muthukumaran 2008; Liu et al. 2009). A biological database is a data collection, the contents of which can be easily accessed and handled. The preparation of such a database is based on collecting data in a form that can be easily accessed and making these data available to multiple users (Toomula et al. 2011).

Databases can be classified into primary, secondary and composite databases. A primary database only includes information on the structure or the sequence of biological information. Examples of primary databases are the Swiss-Prot & PIR for protein sequences, GenBank and DDBJ for genome sequences and the Protein Databank for protein structures (Singh et al. 2010). A secondary information includes data that are extracted from the primary database. A secondary sequence database contains data related to different types of sequences (conserved, signature) as well as active site residues of a group of related protein families (Varsale et al. 2010). A secondary structure database (Shanthi et al. 2009) includes entries of the Protein Data Bank (PDB) in an organised manner. These include entries that are categorised based in their structure. These entries also include data on secondary structure motifs of a specific protein. Some examples of secondary databases include SCOP, developed at Cambridge University; CATH developed at University College of London, PROSITE of Swiss Institute of Bioinformatics, eMOTIF at Stanford (Toomula et al. 2011). Figure 18.1 shows the different categories of databases used in the handling of biological data.

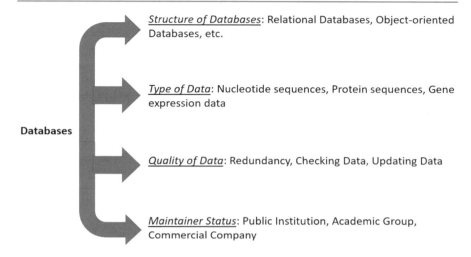

Fig. 18.1 Different databases for biological data (Adapted from: Toomula et al. 2011)

18.2   Significance of Biological Databases

Biological databases contribute significantly in the field of Bioinformatics. They allow scientists to access a wide range of biological data, such as genomic sequences of a broad range of organisms (Baxevanis and Bateman 2018).

There is a requirement for the development of computational tools that can systematically extract useful biomedical information in order to enhance the discovery of new genes (Moreau and Tranchevent 2012). During the last 24 years, a number of innovative 'knowledge-discovery in databases' methods have been developed that include methods to pre-process, integrate, analyse and explain complex biological data. It is very important to recognise the contribution of the users into the knowledge discovery process with the purpose of enriching human intelligence with machine intelligence (Holzinger and Jurisica 2014). The collaborative use of human and machine intelligence can lead to the increment of the efficiency of the discovery of candidate genes.

As there is increment of biological data at larger scales and this is because of the high-throughput and lower-cost DNA sequencing technologies, the number of biological databases that have been developed to manage such increment grows at even faster pace. The major operations of biological databases are not the storage, organization and sharing of data and also the automated exchange of information through the provision of application programming interfaces (APIs). The development of databases to store huge volumes of biological data is a task of bioinformatics. Biological databases integrate huge amounts of data and they serve as significant resources for biologists and bioinformaticians (Zou et al. 2015).

18.3   Features of Biological Databases

Biological databases are characterised by complexity, heterogeneity and dynamicity, still they are inconsistent. This is because of the lack of standards at the ontological level. There is direct submission of data to biological databases for the purpose of indexing, organization and optimization. The databases help researchers identify biological data by making them available in a format that is machine readable (Enago Academy 2019).

Biological data are characterised by high complexity. The definition of such data requires the representation of the complex structures of data and the assurance that not any information is lost during the modelling of biological data. The data model must represent any level of complexity in any data schema ore relationship. The NCBI biological data model considers a biological sequence as a simple integer coordinate system in which there are associations of different types of data. Biological data are characterised by high amount and range of variability. Therefore, there must be flexibility in the handling of data types and data values. There may also be overlap in the data types of different organisms and genome projects. The schema in biological databases changes very quickly. Different biologists will represent the same data differently even when the same system is used by them. Because of the complexity of biological data, there are different ways to model a specific entity. Despite the fact that individuals may produce different data models whenever they asked to interpret the same entity, these models will be characterised by similarities. It is useful for scientists to realise queries across these similarities in order for the connections between unrelated concepts to be understood. This can be achieved through the linkage of data elements in a network of schemas (Oswaldo Cruz Institute 2001).

18.4   Types of Biological Databases

In data-intensive research fields, there is categorisation of databases to primary and secondary. Primary databases include experimentally-produced data such as nucleotide and protein sequence data. Once the data are stored in the primary database, they are given a database accession number and they never change. Secondary databases include data that are the results of the analysis of primary data. Secondary databases are also referred as curated databases. These databases include data from different data sources such as other databases (primary and secondary) and the published scientific literature. These databases often use a complex combination of algorithms and manual data analysis in order to generate new knowledge (EMBL-EBI 2020).

18.5   Types of Data in Biological Databases

The data stored in biological databases include two types: raw and curated. Biological databases are complex, dynamic but also inconsistent. The inconsistency is because of the lack of standards at ontological level. Depending on the scope of the data, there is classification of the biological databases to comprehensive and specialized (Zou et al. 2015). Comprehensive databases include a range of different data. Examples of comprehensive databases are EMBL, DDBJ and GenBank. The establishment of these databases was done for the purpose of collecting and analysing DNA and RNA sequences. Specialized databases include data or data types from specific organisms. Examples of such databases are WormBase and RiceWiki (Enago Academy 2019).

Based on the level of data curation, biological databases can include raw data while secondary databases include curated ones (Zou et al. 2015). An example of a biological database that includes raw data is the NCBI Sequence Read Archive (SRA) (Kodama et al. 2012) while an example of a biological database that includes curate data is the NCBI RefSeq (Pruitt et al. 2014). Biological databases can also be classified as expert-curated databases and community-curated databases. Based on the types of data managed in different databases, biological databases can roughly fall into the following categories: (1) DNA, (2) RNA, (3) protein, (4) expression, (5) pathway, (6) disease, (7) nomenclature, (8) literature, and (9) standard and ontology (Zou et al. 2015).

Examples of biological data are sequences, graphs, high-dimensional data, patterns, geometric information, scalar and vector fields, constraints, images and spatial information. The growth of automated sequencing technology has led to the identification of sequence data such as those that characterise the DNA of various species. Sequence data include strings that indicate bases but there must also be identification of the lengths of any gaps in the sequence data. The relationships among biological data can be captured as graphs as in the case of metabolic pathways, genetic maps and structured taxonomies. The high dimensionality of biological data depends on the comparison of various biological units. For example, gene expression experiments can compare the expressions of thousands of genes and these expressions are affected by the dynamicity of environmental conditions. Data related to the molecular structure are very important and the way to represent these data is through the use of graphs. Biological data can also be characterised by scalar and vector fields. These fields are associated with the chemical concentration and the electric charge across the volume of a cell and chemical fluxes across cell membranes.

Other data are related to hydrophobicity and other properties that can be specified over the surface or within the volume of a molecule. The genome includes patterns that are related to genes and with sequences that are responsible for specific genes' expressions. Proteins are characterised by specific genomic sequences. Patterns are useful in the analysis of data related to protein structure, proteomics and metabolomics. Biological databases should also be characterised by consistency. For example, in thermodynamics databases, reaction cycles must satisfy global energy conservation constraints. A number of different images are used as part of biological research. Examples of different types of images used in biological research are radiographic images, fluorescent images and images generated by electron and optical microscopy. There is not spatial homogeneity among biological entities and there is the need of acquisition of spatial relationships in machine-readable form. There must be comparison and evaluation of computational models. This comparison is facilitated through the use of machine-readable data types. Annotations in biological data are a form of metadata. Annotations are used in order to provide meaning to biological data. As the complexity of a number of biological systems is revealed, the exploration of the relationships in this huge amount of data requires the development of machine-readable representations of data and the development of inferential chains (Wooley and Lin 2005).

18.6 EMBL Nucleotide Sequence Database

The EMBL Nucleotide Sequence Database contains and distributes nucleotide sequences from a range of available public sources. EMBL-Bank is located at the European Bioinformatics Institute (EBI) near Cambridge, United Kingdom. Through the establishment of an international collaboration with the United States (GenBank) and Japan (DDBJ), there is daily exchange of data among collaborating databases. The preferred web-based submission system is Webin while a number of automatic procedures allow the integration of sequence data from large-scale genome sequencing centres and from the European Patent Office (EPO). EBI's Sequence Retrieval System (SRS) which is a network browser, allows the integration of the main nucleotide and protein databases. Various tools such as Fasta and BLAST allows users to compare their own sequences with the latest data in the EMBL Nucleotide Sequence Database and SWISS-PROT (Kulikova et al. 2004).

18.7 GenBank

GenBank is a genetic sequence database and it is a collection of all available DNA sequences. GenBank exchanges data with the DNA DataBank of Japan (DDBJ) and the European Nucleotide Archive (ENA). GenBank is located at NIH and at NCBI. Each GenBank entry includes a description of the sequence, the name and the taxonomy of the source organism as well as bibliographical references and a table of features that includes significant biological information (GenBank 2020) .

The files included in GenBank have been categorized into divisions which correspond to bacteria (BCT), viruses (VRL), primates (PRI) and rodents (ROD). Additional divisions support specific sequencing strategies, such as high-throughput genomic (HTG), high-throughput cDNA (HTC) and environmental sample

(ENV) sequences, making 20 divisions. Also, the GenBank data are partitioned into multiple files, currently more than 1800 (release 173), for the bi-monthly GenBank releases on the NCBI FTP site (Benson et al. 2013).

18.8   DNA Data Bank of Japan

The DNA Data Bank of Japan (DDBJ) is a public database that includes information about nucleotide sequences that was established by the National Institute of Genetics (NIG). Since 1987, the DDBJ collects annotated nucleotide sequences. This is done in collaboration with GenBank (Clark et al. 2016) at the National Centre for Biotechnology Information (NCBI) and with the European Nucleotide Archive (ENA) (Gibson et al. 2016) at the European Bioinformatics Institute (EBI). The collaborative framework is called the International Nucleotide Sequence Database Collaboration (INSDC) (Cochrane et al. 2016) and the product database from this framework is called the International Nucleotide Sequence Database (INSD). The DDBJ Center operates the NIG supercomputer which specializes in analysis of large-scale sequence data. The NIG supercomputer provides computational infrastructure for the development of DDBJ databases and it allows researchers to perform large-scale data analysis. This supercomputer includes two computer systems, the Phase 1 system which was introduced in 2012 and the Phase 2 system which was introduced in 2014 (Mashima et al. 2017).

18.9   UniProt

UniProt is a collection of databases that enable scientists to access the huge amount of sequence and functional data related to proteins. The UniProt Knowledge Base (UniProtKB) combines UniProtKB/Swiss-Prot and UniProt/TrEMB. UniProtKB/Swiss-Prot includes over 550000 sequences. UniProtKB/TrEMBL provides a further 60 million sequences that have been generated from high throughput sequencing of DNA. These entries are annotated by our rule based automatic annotation systems (The UniProt Consortium 2017).

UniProtKB/Swiss-Prot includes high-quality manually annotated and non-redundant protein sequence records. Manual annotation includes the analysis, the comparison and the merging of all the available sequences for a given protein. It also includes critically-analysed experimental data. UniProtKB/Swiss-Prot describes provides all the necessary information about proteins that are produced from specific genes. UniProtKB/TrEMBL includes high-quality records that are characterised by automatic annotation and classification. Different annotation priorities allow different records to be selected for integration into UniProtKB/SwissProt. UnitProtKB includes data from DDBJ/ENA/GenBank coding sequence translations, from sequences from

Ensembl and RefSeq as well as data derived from amino-acid sequences (UniProt Consortium 2020).

18.10 Protein Data Bank

The Protein Data Bank is the single worldwide archive of structural data of biological macromolecules. It was developed at Brookhaven National Laboratories (BNL) in 1971 and it is an archive for biological macromolecular crystal structures. During the 1980s, there was a dramatic increment of the deposited structures of the archive. This was because of the improvements in the technology that was used in the crystallographic process, the addition of structures specific by nuclear-magnetic resonance (NMR) methods and the changes of views expressed by the scientific community in relation to information sharing. In the early 90 s, many journals required a PDB accession code. The mode of access to PDB data has been modified over the years as a result of the progress of data management systems (Berman et al. 2000).

The Protein Data Bank (PDB) serves as a single data archive for 3D structures of proteins and nucleic acids. The Worldwide PDB (wwPDB) organization manages the PDB and it makes sure that the PDB is freely available to the global scientific community (wwPDB 2020).

18.11 Summary

This chapter was focused on biological databases. It analysed the significance, specific features and types of biological databases. It also provided the descriptions of specific biological databases such as the EMBL Nucleotide Sequence database, GenBank and the DNA Data Bank of Japan.

18.12 Review Questions

The answers to these questions can be found in the text of this chapter.

- Describe the different types of data in biological databases.
- Describe the different features of biological databases.
- Describe GenBank.

18.13 Group Work Research Activities

These activities require you to research beyond the contents of the book and can be tackled individually or as a discussion group.

Explore further the topic of database adaptiveness. Identify whether different types of databases have different mechanisms for database adaptiveness.

References

Babu MM (1997) Biological databases and protein sequence analysis. https://www.mrc-lmb.cam.ac.uk/genomes/madanm/pdfs/biodbseq.pdf. Accessed 13 Sept 2019

Baxevanis AD, Bateman A (2018) The importance of biological databases in biological discovery. Curr Protoc. Bioinform 50(1):1.1.1–1.1.8

Benson DA, Cavanaugh M, Clark K et al (2013) GenBank. Nucl Acids Res 41(Database issue): D36–D42

Berman H, Westbrook J, Feng Z, Gilliland G, Bhat T, Weissig H, Shindyalov IN, Zhuang P (2000) The protein data bank. Nucl Acids Res 28:235–242

Bourne P (2005) Will a biological database be different from a biological journal? PLoS Comput Biol 1:179–181

Clark K, Karsch-Mizrachi I, Lipman DJ, Ostell J, Sayers EW (2016) GenBank. Nucl Acids Res 44:D67–D72

Cochrane G, Karsch-Mizrachi I, Takagi T (2016) The international nucleotide sequence database collaboration. Nucl Acids Res 44:D48–D50

EMBL-EBI (2020) Primary and secondary databases. https://www.ebi.ac.uk/training/online/course/bioinformatics-terrified-2018/primary-and-secondary-databases. Accessed 12 Dec 2019

Enago Academy (2019) Biological databases: an overview and future perspective. https://www.enago.com/academy/biological-databases-an-overview-and-future-perspectives/. Accessed 06 Dec 2019

GenBank (2020) GenBank Overview. https://www.ncbi.nlm.nih.gov/genbank/. Accessed 07 Nov 2019

Gibson R, Alako B, Amid C, **Cerdeño-Tárraga** A, Cleland I, Goodgame N, Hoopen PT, Jayathilaka S, Kay S, Leinonen R et al (2016) Biocuration of functional annotation at the European nucleotide archive. Nucl Acids Res 44:D58–D66

Henneges C, Hinselmann G, Jung S, Madlung J, Schutz W et al (2009) Ranking methods for the prediction of frequent top scoring peptides from proteomics data. J Proteomics Bioinform 2:226–235

Holzinger A, Jurisica I (2014) Knowledge discovery and data mining in biomedical informatics: the future is in integrative, interactive machine learning solutions. Lecture notes in computer science, pp 1–18

Karthick RNS, Muthukumaran J (2008) 'Prediction of three dimensional model and active site analysis of inducible serine protease inhibitor -2 (ISPI -2)', Galleria Mellonella. J Comput Sci Syst Biol 1:119–125

Kodama Y, Shumway M, Leinonen R (2012) International nucleotide sequence database collaboration. The sequence read archive: explosive growth of sequencing data. Nucl Acids Res 40(Database issue):D54–D56

Kulikova T, Aldebert P, Althorpe N, Baker W, Bates K, Browne P, Broek A, Cochrane G, Duggan K, Eberhardt R, Faruque N, García-Pastor MP, Harte N, Kanz C, Leinonen R, Lin Q, Lombard V, Lopez R, Mancuso R, Apweiler R (2004) The EMBL nucleotide sequence database. Nucl Acids Res 32:D27–D30. https://doi.org/10.1093/nar/gkh120

Liu Z, Liu Y, Liu S, Ding X, Yang Y et al (2009) Analysis of the sequence of ITS1-5.8S-ITS2 regions of the three species of fructus Evodiae in Guizhou Province of China and identification of main ingredients of their medicinal chemistry. J Comput Sci Syst Biol 2:200–207

Manach C (2016) Metabolomics databases. In: Max Rubner conference, 10–12 October 2016. Max Rubner-Institut, Karlsruhe, Germany

Mashima J, Kodama Y, Fujisawa T, Katayama T, Okuda Y, Kaminuma E, Ogasawara O, Okubo K, Nakamura Y, Takagi T (2017) DNA data bank of Japan. Nucl Acids Res 45(D1): D25–D31

Moreau Y, Tranchevent L-C (2012) Computational tools for prioritizing candidate genes: boosting disease gene discovery. Nat Rev Genet 13:523–536

Oswaldo Cruz Institute (2001) Characteristics of biological data. http://www.dbbm.fiocruz.br/class/Lecture/d17/db_overview/characteristics_of_biological_data.htm. Accessed 01 Nov 2019

Pruitt KD, Brown GR, Hiatt SM, Thibaud-Nissen F, Astashyn A, Ermolaeva O, Farrell CM, Hart J, Landrum MJ, McGarvey KM, Murphy MR, O'Leary NA, Pujar S, Rajput B, Rangwala SH, Riddick LD, Shkeda A, Sun H, Tamez P, Tully RE, Wallin C, Webb D, Weber J, Wu W, DiCuccio M, Kitts P, Maglott DR, Murphy TD, Ostell JM (2014) RefSeq: an update on mammalian reference sequences. Nucl Acids Res 42(D1):D756–D763

Riad AM, Hassan AE, Hassan QF (2009) Investigating investigating performance of XML web services in real-time business systems. J Comput Sci Syst Biol 2:266–271

Shanthi V, Ramanathan K, Sethumadhavan R (2009) Role of the cation-π interaction in therapeutic proteins: a comparative study with conventional stabilizing forces. J Comput Sci Syst Biol 2:051–068

Singh S, Gupta SK, Nischal A, Khattri S, Nath R et al (2010) Comparative modeling study of the 3-D structure of small delta antigen protein of hepatitis delta virus. J Comput Sci Syst Biol 3:001–004

Toomula S, Kumar A, Kumar DS, Bheemidi VS (2011) Biological databases-integration of life science data. J Comput Sci & Syst Biol 4(5):088–092

The UniProt Consortium (2017) UniProt: the universal protein knowledgebase. Nucl Acids Res 45 (D1):D158–D169

UniProt Consortium (2020) The universal protein resource – UniProt. [Flyer obtained online]. Accessed 06 Mar 2019

Varsale AR, Wadnerkar AS, Mandage RH, Jadhavrao PK (2010) Cheminformatics. J Proteomics Bioinform 3:253–259

Wooley JC, Lin HS (eds) (2005) Catalyzing inquiry at the interface of computing and biology. National Research Council (US) Committee on Frontiers at the Interface of Computing and Biology. National Academies Press, Washington (DC)

wwPDB (2020) Worldwide Protein Data Bank (PDB). http://www.wwpdb.org/. Accessed 23 Aug 2019

Yadav G, Mohanty D (2017) Databases developed in India for biological sciences. J Proteins Proteomics 8(3):159–167

Zou D, Ma L, Yu J, Zhang Z (2015) Biological databases for human research. Genomics Proteomics Bioinform 13(1):55–63

GIS Databases

19

What the reader will learn:

- What GIS databases are
- About the different types of GIS databases
- About the different data formats used in GIS databases
- About the applications of GIS databases in different fields

19.1 Introduction

Geographical Information Systems apply computer technology for the purpose of capturing, storing, handling, modelling and analysing information related to the surface of the Earth. The purpose of GIS is to help different specialties focused on nature to perform their operations better. Biologists examine the changes in the populations of amphibian species in forests and natural hazard analysts identify the risk areas generated by monsoon-related flooding through the examination of rainfall patterns and terrain features. GISs can help geological engineers to identify the best areas for the construction of buildings in earthquake-prone areas through the examination of the characteristics of the formation of rocks. A mining engineer is interested in the determination of which mines should be selected for further exploration while a geoinformatics engineer may use GISs in order to specify which are the best sites for the placement of a telecommunications company's relay stations. GIS may be used by geological engineers in order to identify the best locations for the construction of buildings in an area affected by earthquakes. Also, geoinformatics engineers can determine the best locations for a telecommunications company's relay stations. A forest manager can optimize timber production through the use of data on soil and tree stand distributions while trying to preserve species diversity in the area (Goodchild 2007).

© Springer Nature Switzerland AG 2021
K. Domdouzis et al., *Concise Guide to Databases*, Undergraduate Topics
in Computer Science, https://doi.org/10.1007/978-3-030-42224-0_19

19.2   Significance of Geographical Information Systems (GISs)

GIS contribute significantly in the telecoms and network services through the planning, collecting, analysis and storage of complex network designs. GIS are also used in urban planning and GIS are used in the analysis of urban growth. GIS are used in the area of transportation in order for the transportation facilities that are needed in a congested city to be clarified. GIS can be used in the identification of the areas where transportation facilities will be built in order for any congestion to be avoided. GIS contribute in the process of environmental impact analysis. The data from this analysis can be used in order for the effects of the actions realised by humans on a specific land and which cause environmental degradation to be reduced. GIS are also used in agricultural planning so they can provide in which areas of a farm, crops need to grow depending on specific characteristics, such as the soil structure and composition. GIS systems can play a major role in the determination of how each part of a land should be used. In other words, it is important to know which crops will be most appropriate for what part of a land and this will help in crop improvement. GIS systems can also be used for the determination of the nature of the soil and its structure. These systems can also be used for the storage of data that are relevant to community development (Grind GIS 2018).

19.3   Types of GIS Databases

Table 19.1 compares three different types of geodatabases.

In recent years, geodatabases (or spatial databases) have emerged. These databases can store representations of real-world geographic phenomena that they can be used in a GIS. A geodatabase is not the same as a GIS but they are characterised by common features (Huisman and de By 2009).

GIS applications are based on the use of both hardware and software systems. These applications may include data of different types, such as cartographic, photographic and digital. Cartographic data include information related to the location of rivers, hills and valleys. Photographic interpretation is related to the analysis of aerial photographs. There can be inclusion of digital data into the GIS. An example of such data are the data collected by satellites that show land use. Remote sensing data includes imagery and other satellite or drone data that can be entered into a GIS (National Geographic 2020).

Table 19.1 Different types of geodatabases (Esri 2019)

Key characteristics	Enterprise geodatabase	File geodatabase	Personal geodatabase
Description	A collection of various types of GIS datasets held as tables in a relational database	A collection of various types of GIS datasets held in a file system folder	Original data format for ArcGIS geodatabases stored and managed in Microsoft Access data files which are limited in data size
Number of users	Multiple readers/writers	Many readers or one writer per feature dataset. Concurrent use of any specific file eventually degrades for large numbers of readers	Some readers and one writer. Concurrent use eventually degrades for large numbers of readers
Storage format	• Oracle • Microsoft SQL Server • IBM DB2 • IBM Informix PostgreSQL	Each dataset is a separate file on disk	All the contents in each personal geodatabase are held in a single Microsoft Access file
Size limits	Up to DBMS limits	One TB for each dataset. Each file geodatabase can hold many datasets. Large image datasets can raise the 1 TB to 256 TB	Two GB per Access database
Versioning support	Fully supported across all DBMSs	Only supported as a geodatabase for clients who post updates using check-out/check-in and for clients who use one-way replication	Only supported as a geodatabase for clients who post updates using check-out/check-in and for clients who use one-way replication
Platforms	Windows, UNIX, Linux	Cross-platform	Windows only
Security and permissions	Provided by DBMS	Operating File System Security	Windows File System Security
Database administration tools	Backup, Recovery, Replication, Security	File System Management	Windows File System Management

19.4   GIS Databases Data Formats

GIS use a variety of data. The Drawing Interchange (or Exchange) Format (DXF) is a CAD data file format that was developed by Autodesk in order to enable data interoperability between AutoCAD and other programs. Other types of data are those included in comma-separated value (CSV) files that store tabular data in plain text. Each line of the file is a data record and each record includes one or more fields separated by commas (Open Data Team 2020).

Esri uses geodatabase extensible markup language in order to represent the exchange of data between geodatabases and other external systems. Esri keeps the complete geodatabase schema as an XML specification (Esri 2016). XML is a mark-up language that specifies a set of rules for the encoding of documents in a format that is both human and machine readable through the use of tags generated by users (Open Data Team 2020). Geography Markup Language (GML) is the XML grammar which is defined by the Open Geospatial Consortium (OGC) in order to describe geographical features. This is a modelling language that describes geographic transactions over the Internet. GML integrates a variety of data including sensor data. GeoJSON is an open-standard format that is used for the representation of simple geographical features together with their non-spatial attributes, based on JSON. These features include points (e.g. Locations), line strings (e.g. boundaries), polygons (e.g. countries, provinces) and combinations of these types. GeoJSON can also be used to describe mobile routing (Open Data Team 2020). Keyhole Markup Language (KML) is an XML notation used for the description of geographic data within 2D maps and 3D Earth browsers. KML was developed for use with Google Earth. Furthermore, GISs use map packages (.mpk) which allows the sharing of map documents with other. A map package includes a map document (.mdx) and the data referenced by the layers that this document includes. Map packages are used for the exchange of maps among ArcGIS users through the use of ArcGIS Online (ArcGIS is a package developed by ESRI https:// www.esri.com/en-us/home accessed 09/12/2020). Map packages can act as archives that store snapshots of the actual status of data of a specific map. MapInfo Corporation has developed the MapInfo TAB format which is a popular geospatial vector data format. A Shapefile is an ESRI vector data storage format used for the storage of attributes of geographic features. Shapefiles often include large features with a number of associated data and they have been used in numerous GIS desktop applications such as ArcMap.

Vector tiles (or vectiles) are geographic data packets that can be transferred over the web. They are used for the delivery of styled web maps and the combination of specific benefits of pre-rendered raster map tiles with vector map data. Map data are requested by clients as a group pf 'tiles' that correspond to square areas of land of a pre-defined size and location. In contrast to raster tiled web maps, there is return of vector map data from the server and these data have been clipped to the boundaries of each tile (StackExchange 2020).

The Web Map Service (WMS) is a standard protocol for transferring over the Internet georeferenced map images which are generated by a map server through the use of a GIS database. This protocol was published back in 1999 by the Open Geospatial Consortium (Vysocina Region 2011). A WMS server usually serves the map in a bitmap format (e.g. png, gif, jpeg). Also, vector graphics such as points, lines and curves in the format of SVG or WebCGM can be included (Open Data Team 2020).

The Open Geospatial Consortium Web Feature Service (WFS) Interface Standard provides an interface that allows requests for geographical features across the web through the use of platform-independent calls. The geographical features can be considered as the 'source code' behind a map while the WMS interface or mapping portals such as Google Maps generate only an image (Vardhan 2017).

19.5   Geospatial Data Analysis

GIS perform geospatial data analysis. Geospatial analysis is used for the analysis, handling and presentation of geospatial data. Spatial analysis refers to the techniques and models that use spatial referencing of each data case. Spatial analysis makes assumptions on data that describe spatial relationships between cases (Goodchild and Haining 2004). There are three main types of geospatial data: raster data, vector data and point clouds. These data are published in different data formats along with appropriate metadata. Raster data include data related to remote sensing, satellite imagery and scanned maps. Vector data represent data in 2- or 3-dimensions in the form of points, lines and polygons. Point data include individual objects, such as post boxes. Lines can describe road and river networks and polygons can be used to describe property boundaries. Point clouds represent data as points in 3D space and they are collected by using 3D scanners that can be placed on planes, drones and cars (Open Data Institute 2018).

19.6   GIS Water Erosion

The process of soil erosion is affected by soil, terrain and climate parameters. Erosion is a geological phenomenon that results from the removal of soil particles through water or wind while a number of human activities such as agricultural practices increase erosion rates (Ganasri and Ramesh 2016). Erosion is caused by a combination of factors such as steep slopes, climate and inappropriate land use (Renschler et al. 1999). Effective modelling provides data about current erosion and its trends. Fernandez et al. (2003) present a methodology that integrates erosion models, geographic information systems and sediment delivery concepts for estimating water erosion.

19.7   Landslide Risk Mapping

Landslide risk is the loss of life and the damage of properties caused by a landslide in a specific area and for a specific time period (Varnes 1984). There is quantification of the risk depending on probability of occurrence, vulnerability and the number of elements at risk (Van Westen et al. 2006).

The evaluation of landslide risk evaluation is based on the assessment of susceptibility which is the tendency of an area to generate landslides. The mapping of landslide susceptibility aims to highlighting the spatial distribution of potentially unstable areas. A GIS is very important in the management of data with high spatial variability and they are used for the processing of territorial data that are required for the realisation of a susceptibility predictive model (Van Westen 2000). Methods such as inventory-based methods, qualitative heuristic analyses, semi-quantitative heuristic analyses, semi-quantitative index methods and quantitative models can be used for the assessment and mapping of landslide susceptibility. These methods depend on the available data, the scale of the study and the aims of the analysis (Pellicani et al. 2017).

19.8   Urban Planning

Urban planning can help local governments specify policies for the use of land in order to enhance sustainable development (Eraydin and Tasan-Kok 2015; Etingoff 2016). GIS have been used over the last 20 years in urban planning in order to acquire and store spatial data based on their geographical coordinates. From the perspective of urban planning, sustainable development requires the selection of measures in the context of conflicting objectives (Cajot et al. 2017; Della Spina et al. 2017). For example, the selection of the most appropriate priorities in order to optimize energy consumption requires the collection, sorting and joining of spatial and non-spatial information (Pedro et al. 2019).

19.9   Weather Forecasting

GIS are used in different aspects of meteorological and marine applications. Dyras and Serafin-Rek (2005) showed the use of GIS for precipitation mapping. Specifically, they showed how GIS can be used to evaluate data from meteorological measurements into web images. Ustrnul and Czekierda (2005) applied GISfor the development of climatological air temperature maps. Luna et al. (2006) used GIS for the evaluation of maps of extreme temperatures. GIS can be implemented to climate change through the use of meterological statistics (Dou and Zhao 2011). A large amount of meteorological and marine datasets can be optimised for

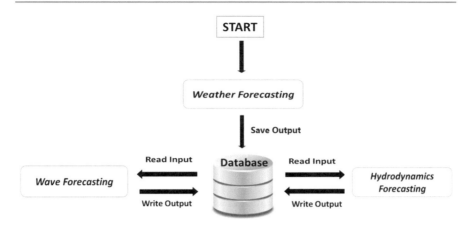

Fig. 19.1 Weather data processing system (Shareef 2012)

effective use in GIS, the development of automatic meteorological and marine maps and of an interactive map for the querying of data at a specific geographical location (Shareef 2012). Figure 19.1 describes such a system.

19.10   Military Operations

All the information associated with a specific battlefield needs to be integrated into a user interface. The reason that this integration is needed is because army commanders need to re-examine past military information. Specialist GIS tools can be used for the integration of data from different sources. Track management software has been used by naval systems in order to generate the tracks of ships on navigational displays. This is related to the processing of speed and direction-related data at different times in order for the positions of vessels to be predicted. This functionality needs to migrate to the battlefield where the conditions are more complex and dynamic and the position, speed and direction are characterised by unpredictability. This required the use of advanced GIS systems in collaboration with advanced distributed visualisation tools (Swann 2010).

19.11   Linking GPS Data to GIS Databases

The applications of GIS have increased in a significant rate. These applications cover a number of fields, such as navigation, precision surveying and mapping. GPS has changed the way GIS collects and manages geographic data. GPS offers high accuracy and based on this accuracy, GIS can now support a double precision database while GIS users can develop new methods for the improvement of the spatial quality of the existing data of their systems (Esri 2009).

Naturalistic driving studies use electronic sensors and/or video recordings in order to check the behaviour of drivers under everyday conditions. The provision of a certain context in the analysis of naturalistic driving data is important. This contextualization can contribute in the clarification of the issue of the performance of drivers within specific driving environments and the frequency in which drivers are exposed to these environments. In order for this contextualization to be realised in an automated manner, the Global Positioning System (GPS) is merged with the GIS databases maintained by the Iowa Department of Transportation (Dawson et al. 2015).

19.12 Summary

This chapter was focused on Geographical Information Systems (GIS). Different types of GIS were analysed along with their characteristics. The chapter examined a number of GIS applications, such as landslide risk mapping, weather forecasting and urban planning.

19.13 Review Questions

The answers to these questions can be found in the text of this chapter.

- Describe the different types of GIS.
- Describe Fig. 2 of the chapter.
- Analyse the significance of GIS.

19.14 Group Work Research Activities

These activities require you to research beyond the contents of the book and can be tackled individually or as a discussion group.

Explore the issue of security of GIS based on the different applications they are applied to. Are there specific features of the security of GIS that are affected most based on the features of the application to which they are applied?

References

Cajot S, Peter M, Bahu JM, Guignet F, Koch A, Maréchal F (2017) Obstacles in energy planning at the urban scale. Sustain Cities Soc 30:223–236

Dawson JD, Yu L, Sewell K, Skibbe A, Aksan NS, Tippin J, Rizzo M (2015) Linking gps data to gis databases in naturalistic studies: examples from drivers with obstructive sleep apnea. In: Proceedings of the 8th international driving symposium on human factors in driver assessment, training, and vehicle design, Salt Lake City, United States, pp 148–154

Della Spina L, Lorè I, Scrivo R, Viglianisi A (2017) An integrated assessment approach as a decision support system for urban planning and urban regeneration policies. Buildings 7(4):85

Dou H, Zhao X (2011) Climate change and its human dimensions based on GIS and meteorological statistics in Pearl River Delta. Meteorol Appl 18:111–122

Dyras I, Serafin-Rek D (2005) The Application of GIS technology for precipitation mapping. Meteorol Appl 12:69–75

Eraydin A, Tasan-Kok T (eds) (2015) Resiliense thinking in urban planning. Springer, The Netherlands

Esri (2009) Using GIS with GPS. https://www.esri.com/library/bestpractices/using-gis-with-gps.pdf. Accessed 19 Oct 2019

Esri (2016) Geodatabase XML https://desktop.arcgis.com/en/arcmap/10.3/manage-data/gdb-architecture/geodatabase-xml.htm. Accessed 5 Dec 2020

Esri (2019) Types of geodatabases. https://desktop.arcgis.com/en/arcmap/latest/manage-data/geodatabases/types-of-geodatabases.htm. Accessed 11 May 2019

Etingoff K (2016) Sustainable cities: urban planning challenges and policy. Apple Academic Publishing

Fernandez C, Wu JQ, McCool DK, Stockle CO (2003) Estimating water erosion and sediment yield with GIs, RUSLE, and SEDD. J Soil Water Conserv 58(3):128–136

Ganasri BP, Ramesh H (2016) Assessment of soil erosion by RUSLE model using remote sensing and GIS - a case study of Nethravathi Basin. Geosci Front 7(6):953–961

Goodchild MF, Haining RP (2004) GIS and spatial data analysis: converging perspectives. In: Florax RJGM, Plane DA (eds) Fifty years of regional science. Advances in spatial science. Springer, Berlin

Goodchild MF (2007) Geographical Information Systems. http://www.geog.ucsb.edu/~good/papers/354.pdf. Accessed 10 May 2019

Grind GIS (2018) Importance of GIS in planning. https://grindgis.com/gis/importance-of-gis-in-planning. Accessed 11 May 2019

Huisman O, de By RA (eds) (2009) Principles of geographic information systems. The International Institute for Geo-Information Science and Earth Observation, Enschede, The Netherlands

Luna MY, Morata A, Almarza C, Martin ML (2006) The use of GISto evaluate and map extreme maximum and minimum temperatures in Spain. Meteorol Appl 13:385–392

National Geographic (2020) GIS (Geographic Information System). https://www.nationalgeographic.org/encyclopedia/geographic-information-system-gis/. Accessed 19 Nov 2019

Open Data Institute (2018) The UK's geospatial data infrastructure: challenges and opportunities. https://theodi.org/wp-content/uploads/2018/11/2018-11-ODI-Geospatial-data-infrastructure-paper.pdf. Accessed 12 Oct 2019

Open Data Team (2020) Geospatial data formats and file types. https://toolkit.data.wa.gov.au/hc/en-gb/articles/115001990033-Geospatial-data-formats-and-file-types. Accessed 1 Dec 2020

Pedro J, Silva C, Duarte Pinheiro M (2019) Integrating GIS spatial dimension into BREEAM communities sustainability assessment to support urban planning policies. Land Use Policy 83:424–434

Pellicani R, Argentiero I, Spilotro G (2017) GIS-based predictive models for regional-scale landslide susceptibility assessment and risk mapping along road corridors. Geomatics Nat Hazards Risk 8(2):1012–1033

Renschler CS, Mannaerts C, Diekkrüger B (1999) Evaluating spatial and temporal variability in soil erosion risk—rainfall erosivity and soil loss ratios in Andalusia, Spain. CATENA 34(3–4):209–225

Shareef MM (2012) Effective use of GIS for visualizing forecasted meteorological and marine data. Meteorol Appl 21:340–349

StackExchange (2020) Geographic Information Systems. https://gis.stackexchange.com/tags/vector-tiles/info. Accessed 18 Oct 2020

Swann D (2010) Military applications of GIS. In; Longley PA, Goodchild M, Maguire DJ, Rhind DW (eds) Geographical information systems. Wiley, pp 889–899

Ustrnul Z, Czekierda D (2005) Application of GIS for the development of climatology air temperature maps: an example from Poland. Meteorol Appl 12:43–50

Van Westen CJ (2000) The modelling of landslide hazard using GIS. Surv Geophys 21:241–255

Van Westen CJ, Van Asch TWJ, Soeters R (2006) Landslide hazard and risk zonation – why is it still so difficult? Bull Eng Geo Environ 65:167–184

Vardhan H (2017) Web Feature Service. Geospatial World. https://www.geospatialworld.net/entity/web-feature-service/. Accessed 15 Novr 2019

Varnes DJ (1984) Landslide hazard zonation: a review of principles and practice. United Nations International, Paris

Vysocina Region (2011) WMS – web map service. Undergraduate Topics in Computer Science. https://www.kr-vysocina.cz/en/vismo5/dokumenty2.asp?id_org=450028&id=1957610. Accessed 19 Oct 2020

Index

© Springer Nature Switzerland AG 2021
K. Domdouzis et al., *Concise Guide to Databases*, Undergraduate Topics
in Computer Science, https://doi.org/10.1007/978-3-030-42224-0

Printed in the United States
by Baker & Taylor Publisher Services